Boss Ladies, Watch Out! brings together in a convenient for-
mat Terry Castle's most scintillating recent essays on literary
criticism, women's writing and sexuality. Readers of Castle's
many books and reviews already know her as one of the
most incisive and witty critics writing today.

The articles collected in *Boss Ladies, Watch Out!* constitute
an extended meditation—both learned and personal—on
just what it means to be a Female Critic. In the book's opening essays Castle examines how women became critics in
the first place—scandalously at times—in the eighteenth
and nineteenth centuries. She explores in particular Jane
Austen's "talismanic" role in the establishment of a female
critical tradition. In the second part of the book, Castle
embraces, with gusto, the role of Female Critic herself.

In lively reconsiderations of Sappho, Brontë, Cather,
Colette, Gertrude Stein, and many other great women writers—"Boss Ladies" all—Castle pays a moving and civilized
tribute to female genius and intellectual daring.

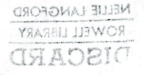

BOSS LADIES, WATCH'OUT!

essays on women, sex, and writing

TERRY CASTLE

Routledge
Taylor & Francis Group

NEW YORK AND LONDON

Published in 2002 by
Routledge,
29 West 35th Street
New York, NY 10001
www.routledge-ny.com

Published in Great Britain by
Routledge
11 New Fetter Lane
London EC4P 4EE
www.routledge.co.uk

Routledge is an imprint of the Taylor & Francis Group

Printed in the United States of America on acid-free paper.

10   9   8   7   6   5   4   3   2   1

Library of Congress Cataloging-in-Publication Data

Castle, Terry.
    Boss ladies watch out! : essays on women, sex, and writing / Terry Castle.
XXIII, 309 p. cm. ill
Includes bibliographical references and index.
    ISBN 0-415-93873-2 (alk. paper)—ISBN 0-415-93874-0 (alk. paper)
    1. English literature—Women authors—History and criticism—Theory, etc. 2. American literature—Women authors—History and criticism—Theory, etc. 3. Authorship—Sex differences. 4. Feminist literary criticism. 5. Feminism and literature. 6. Women and literature. 7. Women in literature. 8. Sex in literature. I. Title.
    PR111 .C38 2002
    820.9'9287—dc21
                                                                        2002002728

contents

To Blakey Vermeule, with love

acknowledgments

I am deeply grateful to Cambridge University Press, Oxford University Press, the *London Review of Books*, the *New Republic*, and the *Times Literary Supplement* for allowing me to reprint material originally published with them. I owe a tremendous debt of thanks to those generous, imaginative, and exacting editors—Leon Wieseltier, Alan Hollinghurst, Anna Vaux, Mary-Kay Wilmers, and Jean McNicol especially—who have made possible some of my less orthodox flights. The encouragement of Bill Germano and his wonderful staff at Routledge has made working on this collection a pleasure. Beverley Talbott, Diane Middlebrook, Nancy K. Miller, Nicholas Jenkins, Rob Polhemus, Stephen Orgel, Randy Nakayama, Tom and Joyce Moser, Eavan Boland, John L'Heureux, Toby Wolff, Mary Ann Tilotta, and my mother, Mavis K. Parker, have been cherished readers from day one. Tamara Bernstein has taught me about life as well as music and I am deeply grateful to her. I also owe thanks for many kindnesses to Dagmar Logie, Alyce Boster, and Margo Leahy. Over the past four or five years Susan Sontag has been an honored friend and inspiration. The love and intellectual companionship of Blakey Vermeule leave me a-stonied and flat-out glad.

introduction

It's a sad life one leads as a Female Literary Critic. All that pressure to live up to masculine expectations. "The sniffs I get from the ink of the women," Norman Mailer once wrote, "are always fey, old-hat, Quaintsy Goysy, tiny, too dykily psychotic, crippled, creepish, fashionable, frigid, outer-Baroque, *maquillé* in mannequin's whimsy, or else bright and stillborn."[1] Such words have haunted me all my life. How I have longed to be fey, Quaintsy, and old-hattish! To troll the regions of the dykily psychotic! To roam the cloudscapes of the outer-Baroque! Alas, Norman has set the bar very high. To my mother's undying dismay, I still refuse to don mannequin's whimsy—at the advanced age of forty-eight. And while Goysy, gaysy, and even frigid on occasion, I could hardly be described as tiny. Creepish fashionability, too, eludes me.

Some would say a Female Literary Critic is better off not being born. "I struggle to keep the writing as much as possible in Male hands," wrote T. S. Eliot in 1917, when he became the editor of the literary journal *The Egoist*, "as I distrust the Feminine in literature."[2] Me too! It's mortifying to find oneself adding to the problem. About the only thing that keeps me going these days is the helpful camouflage afforded by a butch-looking name—routinely assumed (by those who have never met me) to belong to a man. I admit that my literary-critical career—and my psyche—have often benefited from this sexual confusion. When my first article appeared in print in 1979—a psychoanalytic reading of Daniel Defoe's novel *Roxana*—a well-meaning male professor, eager to enter the lists as right-on feminist guy, took me to task for describing its "self-reliant and capable heroine" as a "simpering child." ("Castle . . . shows not the slightest concern for Defoe's actual intentions, instead admitting proudly that his reading is likely 'to debilitate utterly our conventional sense of the novel and its characters.'") Because I failed to appreciate Roxana's skill at making money—she finagles various gormless men into keeping her—the professor concluded that my view of the novel was reactionary and embodied "recent critics' worst nightmares about the nature of feminism." ("It is a sad testimony to the future of responsible literary research to consider that pronouncements such as this have come to be regarded as evidence of academic sophistication.") My heart swelled with pride. Piggish I might be—brazenly so—but at least I was One of the Boys.[3]

My greatest fake-bloke-triumph came in 1995, when the *London Review of Books* printed the essay that leads off the second part of this collection: "Was Jane Austen Gay?" I had speculated therein, to the displeasure of many readers, on what I felt to be a homoerotic dimension in the spinster Austen's deeply affectionate relationship with her elder sister, Cassandra. In the media hubbub that ensued—a tempest in a National Trust teapot if ever there was one—an outraged arts correspondent from the *Independent* wrote a letter to the *LRB* excoriating my "lurid" imagination and propensity for seeing things—again—"in a typically masculine fashion." "Has he never read a fashion magazine?" she asked. (I had suggested that Austen's descriptions of women's clothes were often oddly eroticized.) The official *LRB* response should have ended the matter ("we wonder what Ms. Macdonald would have written had she been alert to the fact that Terry Castle is a woman") but, mirabile dictu, did not. The correspondent then sent a second outraged letter, this time asserting that according to the *LRB*'s "own press release" publicizing my essay, I was indeed a man. This was wildly false, but I basked, even so, in my latest transsexual elevation. No more—ever again, it seemed—a mere Lady Scribbler! At least one person *refused* to regard me as female, even when faced with evidence of the fact. The editor of the *Spectator*, summarizing these exchanges a week or two later, lamented that my parents had not called me "Teri" instead of Terry.[4] I thanked my lucky stars they had not.

I will return to the curious paradox here—that when the Female Literary Critic (yours truly) is mistaken for a man, she is inevitably taken to be the most obnoxious sort of man possible: a monster of antifeminist sentiment. Some basic mental sorting mechanisms seem to go flailingly awry when people start trying to guess at the sex of unknown writers. (Virginia Woolf's famous hypothesis notwithstanding, there doesn't really appear to be anything one might identify as a "female sentence.") But for now I merely outline—not so innocently—a general situation: the Female Literary Critic remains an endangered species. She is not very popular. No one *really* likes her—even now, three hundred years after the birth of feminism. When Aphra Behn complained in the 1680s that women poets never got a fair shake ("What has poor Woman done that she must be/Debarred from . . . sacred Poetry?"), she might as well have been speaking of women critics, too: to be female and exercise one's intellectual authority in public—to express an opinion with firmness, vigor, and dispatch—is still to cause alarm in certain quarters.

The following collection of essays may be viewed, among other things, as a kind of brief on behalf of female authority. It's a bit of a gallimaufry, I confess—a devil's consort. No piece here was written with the others in mind; not every piece here deals with a female subject. The first and earliest essay in the volume, "Women and Literary Criticism," was written in 1989; the most recent, on

Gothic fiction and its discontents, in 2001. But every essay is in one way or another either a reflection upon—or dramatization of—the issue of Woman as
Critic. What happens when a woman proffers an opinion? When she sets up to
judge a book or painting, building or film, song or automobile? What distinctive
intellectual, ethical, and libidinal currents stand to be unleashed? Though I balk
(as above) at the notion of a female sentence, it seems undeniably the case that
something exists that we might call, very loosely, a female point of view—and
that from Behn to Susan Sontag, the critical writing of women has had its own
special flavor and *quidditas,* its own particular purchase on work and world.

Whether she is willing to acknowledge it or not, the primordial impulse mo-
tivating the woman critic is usually an urge to outfox anxiety—the anxiety that
comes of trying to say anything at all in a still often male-dominated intellectual
milieu. "When I read reviews," Virginia Woolf wrote in her diary in 1922, "I
crush the columns together to get at one or two sentences; is it a good book or a
bad? And then I discount those 2 sentences according to what I know of the
book & of the reviewer. But when I write a review I write every sentence as if it
were going to be tried before 3 Chief Justices: I can't believe that I am crushed
together & discounted."[5] As Woolf knew and was brave enough to admit (even
as such frailty disturbed her), the female "point of view" is almost always, in its
beginnings, an insecure one—a small, troubled, pathos-ridden thing. There are
so many internal blockages and inhibitions to be overcome: *that one might make
a lordly judgment in front of men.* It is difficult still for women to let themselves
be lordly, precisely because their opinions have been "crushed together & discounted" for so long. Yet in criticism, as in tennis, lordliness is requisite.
Tremors, blushes, insipid little grimaces: all useless in the arched-back unleash-
ing, stop-dead turns, and whistling volleys of intellectual debate.

I confess this has been my own struggle, and that much of my career as critic
and scholar has been devoted to trying to figure out *how it is done*: how one goes
about saying something strong and arresting and possibly even true—double-X
chromosomes and all—without excessive trepidation or self-hobbling. The study
of other women writers, past and present, has been bracing in this regard. As various essays in this volume will attest, there have been precursors enough to
demonstrate what *female lordliness* might look like: Jane Austen, Charlotte
Brontë, Willa Cather, Gertrude Stein, Sylvia Townsend Warner, Rebecca West,
Woolf, Simone de Beauvoir, Lillian Hellman, Hannah Arendt, Marguerite
Yourcenar, Colette.

The book is divided into two parts. The first part, composed of longer and
relatively formal pieces, is more scholarly and polite in nature; the second part,
made up of essays that began life as review-articles, somewhat less so. (I will
comment in a moment on the stylistic disparities obtaining between the two
parts.) The essays in the first section bear principally on what one might call the
historical question of women's criticism: how the Female Literary Critic came

into being. The key piece in this regard is the aforementioned "Women and Literary Criticism"—a short history of the Anglo-European female critical tradition from its earliest inception in the late seventeenth century to its first mature growth, around 1800. The eighteenth century was indeed the great birthing time of women's critical writing. Women had already begun setting up as professional authors, of course: Aphra Behn (1640–89) was the first Englishwoman to write for money; and over the next 120 years numerous female poets, playwrights, and novelists followed her example. As women struggled, sometimes stirringly, to assume a collective place in the larger Republic of Letters, a few also felt emboldened to comment more broadly on the history, techniques, and ideology of literary expression. They did so in the face of hostility. From Behn in the 1680s to Madame de Staël in the 1790s, the woman who dared to pronounce on aesthetic matters was typically regarded with contempt by male contemporaries. Particularly offensive, in the standard masculine view, was the "unsex'd" female brazen enough to pass judgment on the works of a celebrated man. It took a strong-minded individual—one as strong and choleric indeed as Mary Wollstonecraft, who in 1792 declared Rousseau's *Émile* a medley of "unintelligible paradoxes" designed to keep women "beautiful, innocent, and silly"— to barrel through such prejudice, if at painful psychological cost to herself.

Yet as will be seen, the remaining essays in the first part—two on Jane Austen novels (*Northanger Abbey* and *Emma*), two on Gothic fiction, and one on the existential affiliations I see between certain eighteenth-century and twentieth-century novels—are no less relevant to the issue at hand. It will not, I hope, seem odd or anachronistic to describe Austen as the first and greatest female critic we have ever had. We know her as a novelist, of course—not as a "critic" in the sense that Johnson or Coleridge or Hazlitt was a critic. But to the degree that her fiction represents the triumph of a supremely *critical* human intelligence—of precise, vivifying, often breathtaking powers of moral and aesthetic discrimination—she might be adjudged the prototypical Woman of Letters. Austen is the first woman to take the criticism of art and life as her inalienable task. The "divine Miss Jane" of sentimental caricature is irrelevant here—the dainty maiden aunt in bonnet and patterned chintz, working with yet "so fine a brush" on her "little bit (two inches wide) of ivory." In writing about life as she saw it—and in not caring what *this one* or *that one* might think of her—Austen is the first modern female embodiment of untrammeled intellectual daring. Reread any one of her novels: you cannot help but marvel how calmly and without preening she trusts to her own moral vantage point, her incomparable gifts of expression, her coruscating ability to make the shot, perfectly, every time.

I devote considerable time in these first essays to Austen's response to Gothic fiction. Gothic fiction was by far the most popular new literary genre of the later eighteenth century—largely, one suspects, because it was cheap, dumb, and undemanding, a primitive equivalent of the modern-day pulp shocker or low-budget horror film. In recent years the Gothic has gained a certain cachet among academic literary critics, who claim to find in it all manner of repressed "subversive" sexual and political content. But most of the stuff—from Horace Walpole's desiccated *Castle of Otranto* (1764) to the stupefying tripe issued by the Minerva Press in the first decades of the nineteenth century—remains as sleazy, badly written, and silly as ever. (Not to mention racist, sexist, anti-Catholic, anti-Semitic, and grossly homophobic.) Even the best of the Terror School—the famous Ann Radcliffe and the visionary Irishman Charles Maturin—tend, in the long run, to be rather good wasters of one's time. I have written a fair amount about the Gothic novel along the way and found some mental stimulation in doing so. But even so, I know that as I subside onto my deathbed, the sands of the hourglass ineluctably trickling downward, I shall no doubt regret the many lost evenings spent ploughing through *The Mysteries of Udolpho* and *Melmoth the Wanderer*. I could have been listening to Haydn, reading Proust or Musil, playing with my dog, or thinking about Le Corbusier.

If for no other reason, however, the late-eighteenth-century Gothic craze must be valued for its shaping role in the formation of Austen's critical intelligence. For any writer of the period interested in Truth and Beauty (as Austen was from the start), the Gothic was the Wrong Turn, the Big Goof—the Apotheosis of Naff. With its ludicrous plots, beetle-browed villains, and fainting heroines, it undid in a sickly flash all the work of the great midcentury masters—Richardson and Fielding—who had single-handedly transformed the once-despised genre of English popular fiction into a vehicle for grown-up human drama of the highest order. Particularly distressing for a woman of Austen's confidence and perspicuity, one suspects, was the Gothic's blighted rendering of female consciousness. The Gothic inevitably fixates on female panic disorder—how best and most salaciously to reduce a docile-genteel heroine into a gibbering nervous wreck. Fear and stupidity in fact *define* Gothic femininity; to be female and a character in a Gothic tale is to find oneself becoming mortally *dumb and afraid*. This is indeed the cherished Gothic game: turning grown women into idiots. Its cardboard heroines generally end up paralytic with fright: unable to think straight, unable to peek round corners, unable—like preemies in glass boxes—to breathe, laugh, or love unaided.

Yet the very insult that was Gothic gave Austen her head. Somebody had to say something—she knew it already in her teens—and she knew it might as well be she. *Northanger Abbey*, the first work of her brilliant maturity, and the subject of an essay here, is both a comic lampoon on the Gothic style and a passionate defense of female intelligence. Not for Austen Mrs. Radcliffe's relentless iterations of female dimness and dread. In the story of Catherine Morland, a young woman who gets smarter rather than dumber—calmer, sexier, and more joyous—even as she confronts, with growing moral sentience, the imperfect human world around her, Austen proves you don't have to be a moron to be a heroine.

In a single masterful stroke she gets back what's been lost: a world in which women *think*. *Northanger Abbey* is an extraordinarily personal book in this regard: both a profound youthful statement of artistic goals (Austen will *not* be yet another tawdry romancer) and the opening salvo in a lifelong battle against those who would deny women at large their cognitive powers and pleasures. Here and for eternity, Austen sets herself against the naysayers, troglodytes, and unreconstructed bimbo lovers. In turn, with a little help from their creator, her heroines unlearn their brainless ways and come, in timely fashion, to see the world around them for what it really is.

I take this affirmation of female *thoughtfulness* as Austen's revolutionary contribution to modern life. She suggested that one might be both female and critical in the deepest, most positive sense: someone, as Webster's puts it, who makes "an effort to see a thing clearly and truly in order to judge it fairly." Emotionally speaking, such a demonstration could not have been an easy task—and not only because certain male readers remained unsympathetic. There was a related problem facing her: *lots of women don't want to think*. It's much simpler, after all, being dumb—sliding along in a daze, cooking and shopping and having babies, fiddling with one's hair, letting the guys sort everything out, getting blurry and incurious, forgetting everything one used to know in college. (I can hardly exempt myself here. I once used to be able to recite all of the dynasties of China in chronological order. Ch'ing? Han? Tang? Um. Hand-me-that-IKEA-catalog-will-you-duckie.) A woman's assumption of critical authority often goes hand in hand—necessarily—with a certain jumpy misogyny: you have to differentiate yourself, at times harshly, from the babes in the bathing suits, the coquettes and puppets and body-only gals, the ones on the billboards, the ones who subside into being wives, the ones who can't (or won't) think for themselves, who don't even try.

Austen was well aware of the phenomenon: the smart-girl need to be hard on other women. After all, she suffered from it herself. In *Northanger Abbey* she's pretty rough on certain women—not only poor old Mrs. Radcliffe, her designated satiric butt, but also a number of incorrigibly stupid female characters (bovine Mrs. Morland, dithery Mrs. Allen, the coarse Isabella Thorpe). In *Emma*, the subject of another essay here, Austen would succeed in tempering the impulse somewhat, and even give it its own moral critique. The great lesson in the famous Box Hill episode—when Austen's smarty-pants heroine loses patience with dotty old Miss Bates and makes a joke at her expense, thus earning a reprimand from Mr. Knightley—would seem to be that, yes, some old ladies are appallingly out of it, but you damn well better not be cruel to them if you want to live with yourself afterward. Still, Austen could never rid herself of it entirely: the creeping exasperation—at times curiously mixed with envy—with women who played dumb. She couldn't really love a woman who *wasn't* a critic.

I mention the latter phenomenon—the "selective" misogyny of the female critic—because it bears directly on the essays in the second half of the book, most of which began as book reviews. The fact had never struck me until I began putting together this collection, but it is undeniable: how often in my own career as critic and reviewer I have ended up writing about books written by women—and especially books written by women about *other* women. There may be extraneous forces at work here: as I suggested earlier, speaking of "Women and Literary Criticism," there has always been a tendency among the editors of newspapers and journals and magazines *not* to give books by male authors to female critics to review. While I've never made a scientific study of the matter, it seems to me likely that many people remain uncomfortable at the thought of a woman freely "criticizing" a man. There seems to be something unnatural about it. The female reviewer somehow lacks the reach, the gravitas, the *scrotal prestige* perhaps, necessary for such a task. She is best equipped for dealing with her own kind. The same inhibition does not apply in reverse: there is no taboo against men criticizing women. They do it whenever the mood strikes.

At the same time, a woman criticizing another woman—especially when the criticism is hostile or carping—can produce a voyeuristic frisson. Men have always adored public feuding between females. This delight would seem to be allied to their love of female-on-female aggression generally. I recently conducted an Internet search on the topic of Female Mud Wrestling: the search yielded up more than 20,000 sites, including "Maniac Nurses," "Japanese Splosh Catfighting," and the home page of the official University of Idaho Women's Mud Wrestling Team. (There was no corresponding male team.) Still another link led to the home page of realcatfights.com, where one might view video footage gleaned by hidden security cameras of infuriated women hitting and clawing at one other in supermarket checkout lines and 7-11 stores.

Calumnies heaped by one woman on another—such as Mary McCarthy's celebrated dish on Lillian Hellman that "every word she writes is a lie, including 'and' and 'the'"—find a hallowed place in the critical archives. Perusing the *Oxford Dictionary of Literary Quotations* recently, I noticed that under the heading for Katherine Mansfield—the one living writer, Virginia Woolf confessed, whose prose style she envied—there was the following (single) quote from Woolf: "Her mind is a very thin soil, laid an inch or two upon very barren rock."[6] Bitchiness, rather than praise, one presumes, is what sells quotation dictionaries. The latter volume is in fact a veritable compendium of female-to-female trash talk—so much so that one sometimes finds the interlinked insults forming a surreal daisy chain in one's mind:

> Miss Austen, being, as you say, without sentiment, without *poetry*, maybe *is* sensible, real (more *real* than *true*), but she cannot be great.
>
> —Charlotte Brontë on Jane Austen

> Miss de Beauvoir has written an enormous book about women
> and it is soon clear that she does not like being a woman.
> —Stevie Smith on Simone de Beauvoir

> Enormous romping vitality and a love for the beauty of a lan-
> guage in which one would believe more thoroughly if she did
> not so frequently split her infinitives neatly down the middle.
> —Rebecca West on Marjorie Bowen

> A high altar on the move.
> —Elizabeth Bowen on Edith Sitwell

> I enjoyed talking to her, but thought *nothing* of her writing. I
> considered her "a beautiful little knitter."
> —Edith Sitwell on Virginia Woolf

> She was a bit malicious, you know—she'd say the most dread-
> ful things about people. Of course one does oneself. But one
> doesn't expect it of Virginia Woolf.
> —Ivy Compton-Burnett on Virginia Woolf[7]

Her late-twentieth-century elevation to the list of Sacred Feminist Worthies of All Time notwithstanding, Woolf in particular, one might note, still seems to come in for an awful lot of distaff abuse. Witness Brigid Brophy's comments on *To the Lighthouse* in *Fifty Works of English and American Literature We Could Do Without*:

> We are all conducting Virginia Woolf novels inside ourselves all day long,
> thinking how the sunset clouds look like crumbling cheese, wondering
> why the dinner party guests don't go, puzzling about children growing
> up, noticing for the first time the colour of a bus ticket. This famed sensi-
> tivity is everybody's birthright, and probably Virginia Woolf was ap-
> plauded first by those who were delighted to find literary expression of
> their own commonplace sensations. To have those put in a book and
> called a novel . . . only dots can do justice to their delight.[8]

I can't claim that my own critical endeavors have been unaffected by such factors. For better or for worse, I am often identified as "someone who mainly writes about women." When I do write about male subjects, as in the essays here on Casanova and Cole Porter ("Resisting Casanova," "Night and "Day"), the men in question have tended to be what one might call *effeminated* men: in the case of Casanova, a man so hypnotically attached to Woman that his whole life was a compulsive attempt to merge with Her; in the case of Porter, a man (homosexual) who always wrote best from an implicitly or explicitly female point of view ("Love for Sale," "Ace in the Hole," "I Get a Kick Out of You," "So in Love," "My Heart Belongs to Daddy"). From Ella Fitzgerald to Annie Lennox, women singers have owned Porter's songs—for obvious reasons.

And there is undoubtedly an element of "selective misogyny" in my work. It is a shame that recent feminist theorists—preferring to dwell on the male variant—have paid so little attention to this uncomfortable emotion. It undoubtedly plays a larger part in the genesis of female creativity than has been acknowledged. How many great women, indeed, have been inspired to accomplishment by an *annoyance with their mothers*? How many have been prompted to write or paint by a curious lurking envy of some female rival? How many, in the absence of viable female mentors, have chosen to model themselves on their fathers, brothers, teachers, or other suitably charismatic male acquaintances? Austen's rejection of "Mother Radcliffe" is paradigmatic; but so, too, is Charlotte Brontë's attack on Austen herself, or George Eliot's famous animadversions on Victorian "lady novelists." (See Eliot's 1856 essay "Silly Novels by Lady Novelists," published at the very outset of her magisterial career.) Women often find their own strength by attacking other women. Camille Paglia's recent assaults on contemporary feminists, inevitably reciprocated with unsisterly venom, would seem to be but the latest rage-filled round in a real-life catfight that has been going on for some time.

When it comes to my own writing, I prefer to think, naturally, that a deep-seated respect for female intelligence, rather than an unattractive mix of jealousy and self-aggrandizement, prompts the occasional railing against members of my own sex. I find myself getting impatient when it seems to me that a woman isn't working hard enough to stay sentient. In the shorter essays that make up the second half of this volume, this antipathetic sentiment comes to the fore in the (possibly) intemperate piece on Hélène Smith—a nineteenth-century spirit medium whose farcical, clotted self-interest, combined with her cynical exploitation of the age-old delusion that women were somehow more "spiritual" and "intuitive" than men, struck a particular nerve. (Smith not only claimed at séances to channel the spirit of Marie Antoinette but chatted away, across the ether, with various Martians.) It's also a not-so-hidden subtext in the piece on "Joe" Carstairs (1900–1993), a millionaire lesbian who raced speedboats, owned a private island in the Bahamas, caroused to excess, and conversed every day with a little articulated wooden male doll she named "Lord Tod Wadley." I have nothing against speedboat racing, the Bahamas, or indeed carousing to excess, but Carstairs's relationship with the diminutive Wadley, I'm afraid, pushed all the relevant buttons. Poor "Joe" had to come in for some slagging too.

Such tetchiness, combined with the androgynous monicker, perhaps explains why readers have occasionally mistaken me for a man. I can be sarcastic. (And I love sarcastic women: the late Brigid Brophy, mentioned a moment ago, is an

icon.) I find myself unable to endorse "feminism" when it involves the celebration of feminine inanity—just as I find myself unable to eulogize women merely
because they are women. Natalie Barney, the famous early-twentieth-century *salonnière* and self-described "Amazon" of the pen, once wrote that "a scholar's
mind is a deep well in which are buried aborted feelings that rise to the surface as
arguments." No doubt a psychotherapist could identify the root causes of my
occasional disaffection. (Clue: Mean Old Gal in Red Checked Lumberjack
Coat!) One expects so much *more* from women—unfairly perhaps. The want inevitably shows itself at times in arrogance and blindness: Emma-like petulance
without Emma's charm.

But criticism involves praise as well as blame, obviously, and I hope that my
reverence for female magnificence comes through here as well. As noted, many
of the shorter essays in this collection are reviews of books about women written
by *other* women. Over the past few years I have read with enormous pleasure a
number of studies of "great women"—Judith Thurman on Colette, Juliet Barker
on Charlotte and Emily Brontë, Yopie Prins on Sappho, Joan Acocella on Willa
Cather, Claire Harman on Sylvia Townsend Warner, Ulla Dydo on Gertrude
Stein, Rosemary Mahoney on Lillian Hellman. I am always curious how other
women writers deal with what might be called the "Boss Lady" problem. How to
cope with a larger-than-life female subject without gushing, groveling, or becoming abusive? How to reconcile one's own critical authority—always partial,
belated, contingent—with the overpowering intellectual force field exerted by
some acknowledged Female Genius or *monstre sacré*?

Emotional strategies vary. A modicum of anger is almost always present.
Rosemary Mahoney's pique-filled memoir about Hellman—for whom she
worked in her teens one summer as a grotesquely put-upon housemaid—has
given me my title for this volume, *Boss Ladies, Watch Out!* It's a fierce assault—
enough to make a Boss Lady wince—but not without its poignancy, and a final,
grudging respect for Hellman. And just so, most of the other critics I've reviewed
here eventually come to some instructive, fair-minded, even loving détente with
their subjects of study. Joan Acocella may lament what she sees as the narrow-
mindedness of some of Willa Cather's recent critics—especially her feminist
ones—but her insights into Cather's own artistic personality are stunningly
clear-sighted and judiciously expressed. And even the acerbic Judith Thurman,
keen to illuminate her subject Colette's colossal narcissism, and the defective
moral sense that led to various unsavory activities during World War II,
nonetheless provides the most emphatic account in English to date of that
writer's stupendous, life-loving genius. In such ambitious, intense, emblematic
forays one sees the female critical impulse at its best: confident, worldly, unafraid
to judge, yet also humane about the special pressures, internal and external,
bearing down upon the woman who aspires to intellectual or artistic mastery.

A word or two about style. Austen's great beacon notwithstanding, a strong personal style is—still—the most difficult thing for the female critic to achieve. Norman Mailer may not be entirely unfair when he complains of a certain "fey-ness" in some female literary productions—a certain dim, mannequin-like inau-thenticity. The alienated style is the sand trap in which good thoughts get lost. My own background is in the academic world—a place over which the gods (and goddesses) of alienation and inauthenticity preside. How best to stun one's reader into submission with jargon and pedantry? How best to make one's writ-ing sound as though it were translated (ineptly) out of some exceedingly foreign language? How best to disguise any emotional investment in the subject of one's research? Alas, the well-behaved academic, male or female, must ponder such questions endlessly. How can I make sure *not* to make myself clear?

With a few inspiring exceptions (and they are notable ones), female critics in the academy have been painfully willing of late to fall in with such obscuran-tism. It is surely one of the tragedies of contemporary feminist criticism—and I do consider myself an old-time roaring-girl feminist of the Mary Astell–Valerie Solanas school—that to sound sophisticated, academic women writers have em-braced some of the most deadening, soulless, and pseudointellectual modes of expression currently on offer. In the charmless new world of poststructuralist, postmodern, "post-human" scholarship, no one writes in a straight line any-more. Though perhaps well meaning, such sadly congealed semiprose makes lit-tle appeal to ordinary intelligent readers. Ordinary intelligent readers, in turn, have deserted the critical scene in droves. Who reads a tenth—even a hun-dredth—of the books of literary criticism published these days by British and American university presses? Whatever (academic) feminist criticism once was, it has lately been transmogrified into a lot of ideological posturing and dead air—sans teeth, sans readers, sans everything.

My own impulse has always been to write as clearly as possible, even when such efforts expose me to occasional attack. (In "Was Jane Austen Gay?" I was *too* clear, I guess, to judge by the spluttering tabloid mini-frenzy—fanned by the depraved rank-and-file of various local Jane Austen societies—that the piece elicited on both sides of the Atlantic.) In turn, my style has evolved over the years from one aiming at neutral, sober-sided academicism into something looser and more personal. Which isn't to say that the "formal" essays, even when written some years ago, lack a private dimension. Rereading "Women and Liter-ary Criticism" last month for the first time in a decade—I wrote it for the *Cam-bridge History of Literary Criticism* in 1990—I was struck by how closely, if cryptically, the piece bore upon my own earliest intellectual ambitions. Perusing once again Eliza Haywood's shining encomium in *The Female Spectator* on the value of female literacy ("What clods of earth should we have been but for read-ing! How ignorant of every thing but the spot we tread on!"), I had a comic vi-sion of myself at ten or twelve in the mid-1960s, with pixie cut and flip-flops, trundling every week out of the little local branch of the San Diego Public Library, a teetering pile of "grown-up" books in my arms. The haul always included things like *The Count of Monte Cristo* (yum), the louche historical romances of Norah Lofts (I especially admired *The Lute Player*, *Scent of Cloves*, and *Ann Boleyn*), and one or two big coffee-stained volumes of Will and Ariel Durant's *Story of Civilization*. Besides loving such tomes to distraction, I figured they would eventually help to airlift me out of the Buena Vista Apartments—the mortifying, pink-and-pale-green stucco "low-income" housing complex in which my divorced mother, younger sister, and I lived until I went away to college. In that I qualified for one of the decade's last remaining promising-poor-kid federal scholarships—a priceless little vestige (for me) of LBJ's almost defunct Great Society—I suppose in a way they did.

Back to the *Oxford Dictionary of Literary Quotations*. "Writing reviews can be fun," writes W. H. Auden, "but I don't think the practice is very good for the character." Fair enough. To write at all is an act of aggression, and writing about other people's writing is to compound aggression with hubris. But such aggression, too, makes the world go round. "From the moment I picked up your book until I laid it down, I was convulsed with laughter. Some day I intend reading it." The line is Groucho Marx's, not Jane Austen's. But she would have relished it, one suspects. It's the kind of thing a Boss Lady might say—slyly, and only if called upon—just to show that she's watching out for us.

notes

1. Norman Mailer, *Advertisements for Myself* (New York: Putnam, 1959), 435. "Since I've never been able to read Virginia Woolf, and am sometimes willing to believe it can conceivably be my fault," adds Mailer, "this verdict may be taken fairly as the twisted tongue of a soured taste, at least by those readers who do not share with me the ground of departure—that a good novelist can do without everything but the remnant of his balls."

2. T. S. Eliot, letter to his father, Henry Ware Eliot, October 31, 1917, in Eliot, *The Letters of T. S. Eliot*, ed. Valerie Eliot (San Diego: Harcourt Brace Jovanovich, 1988), vol. 1, 204. The sentence continues: "and also, once a woman has had anything printed in your paper, it is very difficult to make her see why you should not print everything she sends in."

3. See Bram Dijkstra, *Defoe and Economics: The Fortunes of "Roxana" in the History of Interpretation* (London: Macmillan, 1987), 203–4.

4. Dominic Lawson, "Hold On, the PC Lot May Be Right," *Daily Telegraph*, September 2, 1995, 15. Notices regarding my essay—all more or less scandalized—also appeared around this time in the *Guardian*, the *Independent*, *Time*, *Newsweek*, *Lingua Franca*, the *TLS*, the *New York Review of Books*, the *San Francisco Examiner*, and a slew of other British and American journals and newspapers. Thrillingly, a few months later, I received one of *Esquire* magazine's annual "Dubious Achievement Awards"—for arguing, according to the editors, that Jane Austen had committed lesbian incest with her sister. (See "Unfortunately, It's Too Late to Get On Howard Stern," *Esquire*, January 1996, 60.) Six years on, the controversy over the "les-

bian" Jane Austen still burbles along in academic circles: see comments in Deidre Lynch, ed., *Janeites: Austen's Disciples and Devotees* (Princeton, N.J.: Princeton University Press, 2000), and Peter Monaghan, "With Sex and Sensibility, Scholars Redefine Jane Austen," *Chronicle of Higher Education*, August 17, 2001.

5. Virginia Woolf, diary entry, February 18, 1922, in Woolf, *The Diary of Virginia Woolf,* ed. Anne Olivier Bell (San Diego and New York: Harcourt Brace, 1978), vol. 2, 169.

6. Peter Kemp, ed., *The Oxford Dictionary of Literary Quotations* (Oxford and New York: Oxford University Press, 1997), 315.

7. Kemp, *Dictionary of Literary Quotations*, 278, 280, 282, 328, 341.

8. Brigid Brophy, Michael Levey, and Charles Osborne, *Fifty Works of English and American Literature We Could Do Without* (New York: Stein and Day, 1968), 131.

part I

WOMEN AND LITERARY CRITICISM

Do women have the right to criticize? Throughout the eighteenth century it was commonly held that literary judgment was—or should be—a privilege reserved for men. A woman who set forth literary opinions in public exposed either her folly or her presumption. Women, according to Jonathan Swift, were the "ill-judging Sex," inclined, like Echo, to take more delight in repeating "offensive Noise" than in celebrating Philomela's song.[1] Henry Fielding, playing the role of "Censor" to the "great Empire of Letters" in the *Covent-Garden Journal*, debarred all "fine Ladies" from admission to the lofty "Realms of Criticism." Women, he averred, spoke only a debased critical language, a repetitious modern lingo composed of the phrases, "sad Stuff, low Stuff, mean Stuff, vile Stuff, dirty Stuff, and so-forth." They were "Gothic" marauders in the republic of letters, usurping authority "without knowing one Word of the ancient Laws, and original Constitution of that Body of which they have professed themselves to be Members."[2] In the 1750s, Oliver Goldsmith and Tobias Smollett took turns reviling Isabella Griffiths, the wife of Ralph Griffiths, who had dared to emend Goldsmith's works and publish reviews of her own in her husband's *Monthly Review*. Smollett boasted that his own journal, the *Critical Review*, was free of the depredations of "old women" like Griffiths, whom he dismissed, with palpable sexual disgust, as the "Antiquated Female Critic."[3] In 1769, when Elizabeth Montagu published her only critical work, *The Writings and Genius of Shakespear* [sic], James Boswell worried aloud about resentment which might be aroused by a woman "intruding herself into the chair of criticism" and was eager to defend his mentor Samuel Johnson against charges of prejudice against his bluestocking rival. But Johnson's distaste for modern-day "Amazons of the pen" was nonetheless apparent: "I am very fond of the company of ladies," he observed in one conversation. "I like their beauty, I like their delicacy, I like their vivacity, and I like their *silence*." Women were most pleasing, in Johnson's public view, "when they hold their tongues."[4]

In the face of such relentless contempt, it is not surprising that many eighteenth-century women writers—including some who published works of criticism—should have internalized painful doubts about their own powers of taste and discernment. Early in her married life Mary Wortley Montagu produced—at the request of her husband (who merely wished to distract her from the travails of pregnancy)—a detailed critique of the plot and diction of Addison's then-unproduced tragedy *Cato*. Addison was impressed enough by her criticisms, which were both piquant and precise, to revise the play extensively along the lines she had suggested. Despite such implicit approbation, however, Montagu felt obliged to apologize for taking on a task "so much above my skill" and, in a letter to her husband, begged him to remember that she had done so only by his "Command." The essay itself (which at Addison's request was never circulated) bears Montagu's self-deprecating heading, "Wrote at the desire of Mr. Wortley; suppressed at the desire of Mr. Addison."[5]

In an even more paradoxical case of self-disparagement later in the century, the educational writer Hannah More (who also wrote a treatise on the theater) judged women intrinsically incapable of critical thought. Because women were "naturally more affectionate than fastidious," she wrote in *Strictures on the Modern System of Female Education* (1799), they were likely "both to read and to hear with a less critical spirit than men, they will not be on the watch to detect errors, so much as to gather improvement; they have seldom that hardness which is acquired by dealing deeply in the books of controversy; but are more inclined to the perusal of works which quicken the devotional feelings, than to such as awaken a spirit of doubt or scepticism." It was true, she allowed, that a female reader might display "delicacy and quickness of perception," as well as an "intuitive penetration" into character, but these were mere reactive powers, "like the sensitive and tender organs of some timid animals," bestowed by Providence "as a kind of natural guard, to warn of the approach of danger." Women lacked "the *wholeness* of mind" that critical judgment required and were defective in the crucial faculty of "comparing, combining, analysing, and separating" ideas.[6]

It would require a separate study to explain adequately why the prospect of women critics provoked so much anxiety in eighteenth-century commentators. Traditional misogynistic fears of female insubordination were at least partly responsible: a woman who assumed authority in the great "Republic of Letters" (to adopt Fielding's political terminology) might be encouraged to train her critical faculties on the world at large. The persistent taboo against women criticizing *male* authors in particular—a prejudice which continues to influence reviewing practice in our own day—may have been motivated by deeper masculine anxieties about the "Amazonian" sentiments a liberated women's criticism might be expected to unleash.

At the same time, women writers (of any sort) represented a new and destabilizing force in the eighteenth-century literary marketplace. Traditionally, of course, women had been granted a symbolic role in literary production: in the time-honored formulations of classical rhetoric, masculine poetic genius owed its flights to the enabling inspiration of the Muses. But real women, in the prevailing archaic conception, were not supposed to take up the pen themselves. A few seventeenth-century feminists had complained of the exclusion. Bathsua Makin (?1612–?74) argued that the very cult of the Muses itself proved that women had once been—and could become again—creators in their own right. The arts were represented "in Womens Shapes," she wrote in 1673, because women had in fact been their "Inventors" and chief "Promoters" in antiquity. "Minerva and the nine Muses were women famous for learning whilst they lived, and therefore thus adored when dead."[7] Other women, equally celebrated in their day, had invented the poetic genres: "The Sybils could never have invented the heroic, nor Sappho the sapphic verses, had they been illiterate."[8] It was time, wrote Makin, for women to make themselves preeminent once again in the "Arts and Tongues" of civilization.

By the end of the seventeenth century, with a slow but perceptible rise in female literacy, the weakening of court patronage, and the growing commercialization of literary activity throughout Western Europe, Makin's wish had begun to come partly true: more women than ever before were indeed becoming writers and getting paid for it. In early-eighteenth-century London (somewhat later in Paris, Amsterdam, and Berlin), the presence of a female literary subculture—a new class of "scribbling females," composed of novelists, editors, hack journalists, booksellers, and the like—was increasingly visible. Forced to compete with their new distaff rivals, the male literary establishment responded with alarm and resentment. The complaint against women critics drew much of its particular animus, one suspects, from larger impinging professional jealousies; in the eyes of traditionalists, the female critic was simply the most blatant example of woman's new and overweening literary ambition. She could easily be made to stand for any sort of illegitimate hankering after authority. It is symptomatic of the deeper sexual tensions in eighteenth-century intellectual culture that Swift, in his diatribe against the corruption of learning in *The Battle of the Books* (1704), should blame the collapse of traditional aesthetic values on the feminization of contemporary taste. In the nightmare emblem-world of the satirist, the "malignant deity" Criticism takes shape as a rampant, monstrous female, chaotically ruling over her offspring the Moderns, who suckle on her nastiness and squalor:

> She dwelt on the Top of a snowy Mountain in *Nova Zembla*; there *Momus* found her extended in her Den, upon the Spoils of numberless Volumes half devoured. At her right Hand sat *Ignorance*, her Father and Husband, blind with Age; at her left, *Pride* her Mother, dressing her up in the Scraps of Paper herself had torn. There was *Opinion* her Sister, light of Foot, hoodwinkt, and headstrong, yet giddy and perpetually turning.

About her play'd her Children, *Noise* and *Impudence, Dullness* and *Vanity, Positiveness, Pedantry,* and *Ill-Manners.* The Goddess herself had Claws like a Cat; Her Head, and Ears, and Voice resembled those of an *Ass;* Her Teeth fallen out before; Her Eyes turned inward; as if she lookt only upon herself; Her Diet was the overflowing of her own *Gall;* Her *Spleen* was so large, as to stand prominent like a Dug of the first Rate, nor wanted Excrescencies in form of Teats, at which a Crew of ugly Monsters were greedily sucking; and, what is wonderful to conceive, the bulk of Spleen encreased faster than the Sucking could diminish it.[9]

One could hardly ask for a more flagrant image of a threatening gynocriticism.

Such vivid antipathy undoubtedly discouraged many women authors from ever attempting the business of criticism at all. But even in the case of women who did produce critical writing, particularly in the years between 1720 and 1780, one cannot avoid noticing in their works the often distorting effects of cultural prejudice. Exaggerated self-consciousness—a stylized display of authorial timidity or self-effacement—frequently mars eighteenth-century feminine critical rhetoric. Frances Brooke, introducing her theater reviews and critical essays in *The Old Maid* in 1755, observed apologetically that such writing could only seem "an odd attempt in a woman." In the preface to her study of Shakespeare from 1769, Elizabeth Montagu deferred to the "superiority of talents and learning" of Shakespeare's male editors and abjured "the vain presumption of attempting to correct any passages of this celebrated Author" herself. Even the usually forthright Marie-Jeanne Riccoboni, embarking in 1782 on what would become a celebrated epistolary debate with Choderlos de Laclos over his novel *Les Liaisons dangereuses,* disclaimed any right to criticize Laclos as a fellow *author*: her own novels, she said, were mere "bagatelles." She could only judge his work—and that diffidently—as a *woman ("en qualité de femme").* Likewise, the recurrence of certain themes and issues in women's criticism—the obsession, for example, with the moralizing aspects of literary works—also signaled underlying self-doubt: female critics compensated for their profound sense of professional insecurity by paying exaggerated attention to the piety (or lack thereof) in the works they scrutinized. From Eliza Haywood on, eighteenth-century women critics made a cult of their moral respectability. Only near the end of the century, with the debut of charismatic literary figures like Germaine de Staël and Stephanie de Genlis in France, or Mary Wollstonecraft and Elizabeth Inchbald in England, did a less hidebound image of the female critic begin to emerge— the image of the woman confident enough in her intellectual abilities to pass judgment, without excessive scruple, on the great works of past and present.

Given such inhibitions, what sort of criticism did women write? Women critics employed a variety of rhetorical formats, reflecting the assortment of contexts in which the practice of criticism itself—which had yet to be defined in strictly professional or academic terms—was pursued in the period. Eighteenth-century critics worked in general in a hodgepodge of styles and genres; the formal critical essay, typified by Samuel Johnson's *Rambler* 4 "On Fiction" or Edward Young's *Conjectures on Original Composition*, was only one form among many. Prefaces, dedications, epilogues, linguistic treatises, translations, reviews, anthologies, biographical memoirs, private correspondence, and literary works themselves (one thinks of Austen's remarks on the novel in *Northanger Abbey*) all provided contexts in which a distinctly "critical" discourse might flourish.

Certain styles and genres, of course, were more accessible than others. Generally speaking, the more formal critical subgenres—the philological treatise, the learned dialogue, the refined verse epistle—were less popular with women than ad hoc forms, for obvious reasons. Owing to the defects of female education in the period, women seldom had the background in classical languages and literature necessary to engage in the erudite skirmishing of philological debate, though even here, it is important to note, a handful of exceptional women succeeded in making a mark. The seventeenth-century Dutch learned lady Anna Maria van Schurman (1607–78), known to her contemporaries as the "Star of Utrecht," was famous throughout Europe for her extraordinary linguistic accomplishments—besides learning all the modern languages, she had taught herself Hebrew, Greek, Latin, Arabic, Chaldee, Syriac, and Ethiopian and written grammars for several languages—and her feats proved an inspiration to a number of eighteenth-century female scholars. The celebrated classicist Anne Lefèvre Dacier (1654–1720), for example, translated the *Iliad* and the *Odyssey* into French in 1711 and took a vigorous part in the *querelle des Anciens et des Modernes*, publishing *Homère défendu contre l'Apologie du R. P. Hardouin; ou Suite des causes de la corruption du goust* in 1716. (So renowned were her Greek translations that even Fielding, some thirty years after her death, paid homage to the great "Madam *Daciere*" in *Tom Jones*.[10]) Dacier's English contemporary Elizabeth Elstob (1683–1756), sometimes called the "Saxon Muse," was another brilliant female scholar: after translating Aelfric's *English-Saxon Homily on the Birth-day of St Gregory* in 1709, she produced the first English Anglo-Saxon grammar, *Rudiments of Grammar for the English-Saxon Tongue . . . with an Apology for the Study of Northern Antiquities*, in 1715. Besides revealing Elstob's wide knowledge of English poetry, the *Rudiments* was noteworthy for its defense of Anglo-Saxon studies against the criticisms of Swift, who had complained that such knowledge was uselessly pedantic. Other gifted women followed in the footsteps of Dacier and Elstob: Constantia Grierson (1706–33), though born into a poor and illiterate family, mastered Greek and Latin and edited Virgil, Terence, and Tacitus in the 1720s; Elizabeth Carter (1717–1806), the friend of Samuel Johnson, produced a scholarly edition of Epictetus in 1758. In 1781, Ann Francis (1738–1800) published a poetic translation of the Song of Solomon, complete with historical and critical notes on the ancient Hebrew.

Several women in the second half of the century, likewise, produced learned books on the writings of Shakespeare. The novelist Charlotte Lennox (?1729–1804) published a source study of the plays, *Shakespear Illustrated*, in 1753. Samuel Johnson particularly admired this work, and drew upon it (without acknowledgment) in his own *Preface to Shakespeare*. Montagu's *The Writings and Genius of Shakespear* (1769) was primarily an attack on Voltaire, who had judged Shakespeare inferior to the French neoclassical dramatists and mistranslated (in Montagu's view) certain important passages in the plays. Elizabeth Griffith (?1720–93) published her own lengthy vindication of the poet, *The Morality of Shakespeare's Drama Illustrated*, in 1775.

Yet the fact remains that such extended treatises were rare. As for verse epistles, critical dialogues, and the formal essay itself (as opposed to reviews or prefaces)—these too were primarily masculine forms in the period. Judith Madan (1702–81) published "The Progress of Poetry" in 1731—a 264-line verse essay on the development of poetry from Homer to Addison, which antedated Gray's similarly-titled poem on the same subject by twenty years. But her example seems not to have been followed by other women writers. Elizabeth Montagu's short work *Three Dialogues of the Dead* from 1769 (which includes a fanciful dialogue between Plutarch and a modern bookseller on the vagaries of taste) and Clara Reeve's *The Progress of Romance* (1785) were among the only literary-historical works written by women in the period in dialogue form.

Women occasionally published isolated critical essays and polemical pieces, though again rarely, and usually anonymously. Elizabeth Harrison (fl. 1756) published a pamphlet defense of Gay, *A Letter to Mr. John Gay, on His Tragedy Call'd "The Captives,"* in 1724, using the pretense of the private letter to expound her views. The novelist Sarah Fielding (1710–68) printed her influential *Remarks on "Clarissa"* anonymously in 1749. Before her marriage, the editor-critic Anna Laetitia Barbauld (1743–1825) collaborated with her brother John Aikin on a collection of essays entitled *Miscellaneous Pieces in Prose* (1773), which included short articles on comedy and romance, a longer piece on Davenant's *Gondibert*, a vaguely Burkean meditation "On the Pleasure derived from Objects of Terror," and commentaries on the *Arabian Nights, The Castle of Otranto* and other icons of contemporary taste. Barbauld did not distinguish her contributions from her brother's, however, and her name appears on the title page only as "A. L. Aikin." Only near the end of the century would a woman unhesitatingly embrace the independent essay format and produce a work of outstanding significance. Germaine de Staël's *Essai sur les fictions* (1795)—devoted to the novel's power of providing "intimate understanding of the human heart"—remains one of the century's most thoughtful and impressive pieces of genre criticism.

The bulk of women's critical writing, however, was more impromptu—even haphazard—in style and scope; a great deal of it has undoubtedly been lost. Women tended to work in the ephemeral branches of criticism: the short review or squib (often unsigned) was a typically feminine genre throughout the century. Eliza Haywood published occasional pieces on Shakespeare and other poets in *The Female Spectator* in the 1740s; Frances Brooke reviewed theatrical productions in *The Old Maid* in the 1750s. (Reviewing the heavily doctored Garrick-Tate version of *King Lear* in 1756, Brooke was one of the first critics to call for a return to authentic Shakespearean texts.) Charlotte Lennox wrote book reviews for the *Lady's Museum* in 1760–61, as did Mary Wollstonecraft (1759–97) and Mary Hays (1760–1843) for the *Analytical Review* and the *Monthly Review* at the end of the century. On the continent, Luise Adelgunde Victoria Gottsched (1713–62), the wife of Germany's best-known neoclassical critic, Johann Christoph Gottsched, almost certainly collaborated with her husband on his literary journal *Die vernünftigen Tadlerinnen* (modeled on *The Spectator*) in the 1720s, though the precise extent of her contributions cannot be determined. In the 1780s and 1790s, again in Germany, Sophie von La Roche (1731–1807) and Sophie Mereau (1770–1806) also produced occasional critical remarks for their influential publications *Pomona für Teutschlands Töchter* (1783–84) and *Kalathiskos* (1801–2).

Prefaces, usually written for popular anthologies or translations, were another female speciality. As a secondary or "satellite" form, the preface, like the unsigned review, seems to have allowed women writers room for the kind of aggressive critical intervention they did not feel free to make elsewhere. Prefaces to works of drama were especially popular—perhaps because so many professional literary women had begun their careers as actresses or playwrights. Aphra Behn (1640–89) provided several memorable prefaces for the published editions of her own plays in the 1670s; her introduction to *The Dutch Lover* (1673) contains an important early comparison of Jonson and Shakespeare. The actress-playwright Susannah Centlivre (d. 1723) followed in Behn's path, producing a number of lively prefaces and dedications during her career, including one for her translation of Molière, *Love's Contrivance* (1703), in which she analyzed the differences between French and English taste. The same theme was taken up later on the opposite side of the Channel by Riccoboni, in the introduction to the *Nouveau théâtre anglais*, the anthology of contemporary English comedies she edited in 1768.

Prefaces to works of poetry and fiction were fewer, but several important examples may be cited. In 1737 Elizabeth Cooper (fl. 1735–40) provided a lengthy scholarly introduction to *The Muses' Library*, an anthology of English poetry, in which she traced the history of English versification from its early "Gothique Rudeness" in Langland and Chaucer up to the refinements of Spenser and Daniel. (Chatterton, it is thought, knew Cooper's work and drew on it during the fabrication of the notorious Rowley manuscripts.[11]) The industrious Anna Barbauld produced a number of prefatory pieces at the end of the century: she edited the poetry of Akenside and Collins in the 1790s, wrote a critical and biographical introduction to Richardson's *Correspondence* in 1804, and composed the introductions for the fifty-volume series *British Novelists* in 1810. The latter, together with the Richardson essay, make up a kind of embryonic genre history: Sir Walter Scott relied upon both heavily in his own *Lives of the Novelists* (1821–24). Occasionally, it should be noted, women novelists wrote prefaces for their own works: Françoise de Graffigny's impassioned "Avertissement" to *Lettres d'une péruvienne* (1747), highlighting the anticolonialist theme of her fiction, and Frances Burney's preface to *Evelina* (1778), condemning slavish imitation in authors, stand out as valuable critical statements in their own right.

In 1798, the Scottish dramatist Joanna Baillie (1762–1851) produced an unusually lengthy and ambitious critical introduction for her *Plays on the Passions*, in which she analyzed the different "passions" evoked by tragedy and comedy and outlined a psychological defense of dramatic spectacle. Tragedy, she wrote, aroused the "sympathetic curiosity" of the viewer and offered "an enlarged view of human nature." Comedy, meanwhile, with its focus on love, revealed "the human heart" in all its intricacy. Theater itself was a school in which moral wisdom might be learned. Baillie's dour contemporary Hannah More (1745–1833) shared none of these views. More's fiercely moralistic "Observations on the Effect of Theatrical Representations with respect to Religion and Morals," advocating a ban on all theatrical performances, first appeared, paradoxically enough, as a preface to a collection of More's own dramatic works in 1804. Yet despite the oddity of the context, the essay remains a perversely appealing tour de force of antitheatrical writing. Of particular note are More's comments on the differences between reading plays and seeing them performed on stage. The power of acting, she acknowledged sadly, was to heighten "the semblance of real action" into "a kind of enchantment." The effect was to induce in spectators a state of "unnerving pleasure."[12]

The most incisive editorial prefaces of the period, however, were undoubtedly those of Elizabeth Inchbald (1753–1821), who wrote over a hundred introductory essays for Longman's twenty-five–volume series *The British Theatre* between 1806 and 1809. These biographical and critical notes are little known today, but as examples of practical criticism, bear comparison—in wit, style, and intellectual scope—with the prefaces of Johnson. Inchbald was as opinionated as her mighty predecessor: *Henry IV*, she wrote, "is a play which all men admire; and which most women dislike"; Addison's *Cato,* while undoubtedly patriotic, suffered badly from its "insipid" love scenes. And she could be as moralistic: *The Beggar's Opera*, she thought, though superbly comic, had "the fatal tendency to make vice alluring." But Inchbald's own experience as a player led her to some interestingly unorthodox judgements. Centlivre's plays, she argued, were more successful on the stage than Congreve's; Colley Cibber's work had been persistently undervalued. While "many a judicious critic," she wrote,

> boasted of knowing what kind of drama the public ought to like; Cibber was the lucky dramatist generally to know what they *would* like, whether they ought or not. If he secured their interest, he defied their understanding; and here, in the following scenes, so far he engages the heart in every event, that the head does not once reflect upon the improbabilities, with which the senses are delighted.[13]

Sampled at random, Inchbald's essays seldom fail to interest; taken in chronological sequence, they represent an outstanding intellectual achievement—the first truly critical history, in essence, of the English drama from the Renaissance to the late eighteenth century.

So far we have been dealing, of course, with "official" kinds of critical activity—printed books, essays, reviews, prefaces, and so on—yet many of the most interesting critical contributions by women during the century were made, it should be noted, in rather more spontaneous and informal contexts. Numerous miscellaneous reflections on books and poetry are to be found, for example, scattered through women's personal letters, journals, and private papers. This kind of impromptu, "behind-the-scenes" commentary, despite its seemingly evanescent nature, occasionally had surprisingly immediate impact. Correspondence could itself become a form of critical intervention. Women readers, for example, sometimes wrote directly to authors—with provocative results. In 1749, soon after the publication of the first volumes of *Clarissa*, Lady Bradshaigh (Dorothy Bellingham) wrote to Samuel Richardson complaining about the plausibility of the novel and exhorting him to alter its projected ending: she wished for the heroine to marry her seducer instead of dying. Richardson rejected this drastic proposal but made several changes in subsequent editions of the novel to forestall some of the other criticisms Bradshaigh had raised. Riccoboni provoked an even more celebrated contretemps with Laclos, author of *Les Liaisons dangereuses*, when she wrote to him in 1782 condemning his character Madame de Merteuil on moral and feminist grounds. He replied at length, and without her permission published the resulting correspondence in the 1787 edition of his novel. (Riccoboni protested but may have secretly enjoyed the fray: she carried on similar epistolary disputes with Diderot and Garrick.) The "letter to the author" format seems to have unleashed in a number of women writers a subversive fantasy of rewriting received (male) texts. This fantasy was itself at times realized. Lady Bradshaigh's sister, Elizabeth, Lady Echlin (?1704–82), produced a revised version of *Clarissa* (unpublished until 1982) in which the heroine indeed avoided being raped and succeeded in converting her persecutor. Later in the century the novelist Anne Eden (fl. 1790) rewrote Goethe's *The Sorrows of*

Young Werther from the perspective of the husband, Albert, stressing his sympathetic qualities, while Ann Francis published *A Poetical Epistle from Charlotte to Werther* (1788), focusing on Goethe's heroine's point of view.

We should not forget, finally, that some of the most important female criticism in the period was never written down at all. Eighteenth-century women *talked* about literature, even when they did not always feel free to write about it. Literary salons and bluestocking clubs became increasingly popular and influential over the course of the century. In England, Elizabeth Montagu, known to contemporaries as "the Queen of the Blues," presided over a fashionable literary coterie in the 1760s and 1770s; Elizabeth Carter, Mary Delany (1700–88), Hester Mulso Chapone (1727–1801), Catherine Macaulay (1731–91), and Hannah More were also active bluestocking leaders. Important French *salonnières* included Claudine-Alexandre Guérin de Tencin (1682–1726), Marie-Thérèse Geoffrin (1697–1777), Emilie du Châtelet (1706–1749), Julie de Lespinasse (1732–1776), Suzanne Necker (1739–1794), and later Necker's daughter, Germaine de Staël. Salons developed somewhat later in Germany; nonetheless, as the letters and diaries of Sophie von La Roche, Dorothea Schlegel (1763–1839), Caroline (Schlegel) Schelling (1763–1809), and Rahel Varnhagen (1777–1833) indicate, women had begun to make a similar place for themselves in German literary society by the end of the century.

While not criticism in any conventional sense, the unofficial advocacy of the salon women was often instrumental in shaping contemporary literary taste. Richardson's circle of female admirers (including Hester Chapone and Mary Delany) did much, for example, to promote his literary reputation in the 1740s and 1750s; Suzanne Necker was a leading supporter of Rousseau. In Germany, the charismatic Rahel Varnhagen, leader of the most important salon in Berlin at the end of the century, almost single-handedly established Goethe's reputation as the reigning genius of European literature after the publication of *Wilhelm Meister's Apprenticeship* in 1796. Indeed, precisely when women's access to the official "Republic of Letters" was so limited, the conversation of the salons provided them with a needed psychological outlet—a way of discharging aggressive intellectual energies. As Samuel Johnson grudgingly acknowledged of Elizabeth Montagu, his adversary in a number of verbal battles, "[she] is an extraordinary woman; she has a constant stream of conversation, and it is always impregnated; it has always meaning."[14]

In order to give a full account of eighteenth-century female criticism, it is not enough, however, merely to enumerate the *kinds* of criticism women produced. What we might call the theoretical problem of women's criticism demands comment. How did women's new and somewhat vulnerable position in the "Republic of Letters" shape their critical views? In what ways did women's literary values differ from those of men? And what impact did this minority criticism have on larger developments in contemporary critical thought? Let us begin by examining some of the characteristic themes of eighteenth-century women's criticism, paying particular attention to features that distinguished it from mainstream (male-authored) criticism. Then we can attempt, by way of conclusion, to address the larger question of historical influence.

The celebration of original or "untutored" genius—coupled with a rejection of learning and decorum—was a favorite topic for women from the late seventeenth century on. That this should have been the case is hardly surprising, given that so many female critics were themselves untutored in the rules and prescriptions of classical rhetoric. Women writers turned their lack of erudition into a virtue. "I do not repent that I spent not my time in learning," wrote Margaret Cavendish, the Duchess of Newcastle (1623–73), of her early years, "for I consider it is better to write wittily than learnedly."[15] True poetic genius, according to most female observers, did not inhere in erudition, or in the slavish concern with correctness, but in a spontaneous overflow of native wit and imagination.

Thus Aphra Behn argued that "the immortal Shakespeare's plays" had "better pleased the world than Jonson's works" precisely because Shakespeare (unlike Jonson) did not have much Greek or Latin—indeed "was not guilty of much more of this than often falls to women's share." The "musty rules of unity" derived from classical literature were useless, according to Behn: "methinks," she wrote sardonically, "that they that disturb their heads with any other rule of plays besides the making them pleasant, and avoiding of scurrility, might much better be employed in studying how to improve men's too imperfect knowledge of that ancient English game which hight Long Laurence."[16] Susannah Centlivre concurred: neoclassical critics might "cavil most about Decorums, and crie up *Aristotle's* Rules as the most essential part of the Play," yet "they'll never persuade the Town to be of their Opinion, which relishes nothing so well as Humour lightly tost up with Wit, and drest with Modesty and Air."[17]

The unconscious identification with Shakespeare—the great example of "unlettered" genius—runs like a golden thread through eighteenth-century women's critical writing. Shakespeare's plays were so filled with moments of genius, wrote Elizabeth Montagu, that "it avails little to prove, that the means by which he effects them are not those prescribed in any Art of Poetry." By deviating from the rules, the poet "[rose] *to faults true critics dare not mend*."[18] Montagu's disciple Elizabeth Griffith went even further. Shakespeare, she argued, took the wreath from "the whole collective Host of Greek or Roman writers, whether ethic, epic, dramatic, didactic or historic." "Though the dead languages are confessed to be superior to ours," Griffith observed, "yet even here, in the very article of diction, our Author shall measure his pen with any of the ancient *styles* in their most admired compound and decompound epithets, descriptive phrases, or figurative epithets." The "living scene" of Shakespeare's plays exceeded "the dead letter, as action is preferable to didacticism, or representation to declamation."[19] Griffith was particularly attuned to the polymorphous, even feminist aspects of the poet's genius: fifty years ahead of Keats, she observed that "our Author" could "not only assume all characters, but even their sexes too."[20]

Other untutored geniuses, however, inspired similar encomiums. The persistent preference of women critics later in the century for Richardson over Fielding, for example, was at least partly due to the fact that Richardson was perceived as less educated—and hence more like a woman—than his rival. Richardson, wrote Anna Barbauld in her introduction to his *Correspondence*, exemplified "natural talents making their way to eminence, under the pressure of narrow circumstances, the disadvantages of obscure birth, and the want of a liberal education." He spoke no language besides English, she marveled—"not even French." Later female critics would praise Robert Burns and other "rustic" bards for similar reasons.

Not surprisingly, women had little sympathy for writers who cultivated an ostentatiously learned style. Samuel Johnson's prose, Elizabeth Montagu confided in a series of private letters to Elizabeth Carter, was *"trop recherché."* He wrote like a "parnassian beau," cramming his essays with so many "ornaments of study" that his writing was more properly called "writation." This attack on Latinate diction, it should be noted, often took on an explicitly chauvinistic edge. Women, Maria Edgeworth (1768–1849) asserted in her *Letters for Literary Ladies* (1795), wrote far more elegantly than men did, the female style being happily free of "the melancholy apparatus of learning."

Among the genres, women tended to prefer fiction, drama, and the popular essay to poetry—again, one suspects, because the received poetic styles were so imbued with masculine and elitist associations. Women critics seem to have had little interest in the epic or other exalted classical genres. Nor, despite their attachment to genius, did they share their male contemporaries' fascination with the poetical sublime. (Eighteenth-century women wrote relatively little, for example, about Milton.) On the whole, women preferred "native wit" and accessibility—what could be called a domesticated poetic vision—to rhapsodic or visionary flights. They were suspicious of claims of mystical or vatic inspiration. This rejection of the hieratic mode would have interesting consequences at the end of the century: women often found themselves at odds with the more highflown and visionary strains of Romanticism. There was a certain sexual logic in this resistance: besides disliking the solipsism and masculine conceit in high Romantic discourse—in the cult, for example, of the Wordsworthian "egotistical sublime"—women could hardly afford to endorse its anti-intellectualism. Precisely because they had so often been accused of irrational flights themselves, they wanted little part of a poetic manner that seemed to value such things above all else.

By contrast, the more demotic and inclusive genres—plays, essays, and prose fiction—won universal feminine approval. The drama, wrote Joanna Baillie, spoke more directly to the "lower orders of society" than any other genre except the folk ballad, hence its value as a tool of moral instruction. Baillie saw no use in writing closet drama for an elite; had her own plays been more widely performed, she said, "the spontaneous, untutored plaudits of the rude and uncultivated would have come to my heart as offerings of no mean value."[21] Women cherished the popular essay for similar reasons; throughout the century female writers were especially attracted to the informal, ingratiating essay style perfected by Addison and Steele in the *Tatler* and the *Spectator*.[22]

Women's most heartfelt advocacy, however, as one might expect, was reserved for the novel—the literary form most powerfully grounded in everyday experience. Female critics were among the first to valorize the putative "truthfulness to life" of the new genre. In a well-known passage in *The Progress of Romance*, Clara Reeve judged the novel superior to the older form of the romance precisely on account of its greater verisimilitude. While the romance, she wrote, was a "heroic fable," treating of "fabulous persons and things," the novel was "a picture of real life and manners, and of the times in which it is written." Its "perfection" lay in representing scenes "in so easy and natural a manner, and [making] them appear so probable, as to deceive us into a persuasion (at least while we are reading) that all is real, until we are affected by the joys or distresses of the persons in the story, as if they were our own."[23] Barbauld agreed: the novel had evolved, she argued in her essay on Richardson, out of a desire for "a closer imitation of nature." Though it preserved the "high passion, and delicacy of sentiment of the old romance," it was superior to the older form precisely because it depicted "characters moving in the same sphere of life with ourselves, and brought into action by incidents of daily occurrence." Unlike its precursor form, the novel was not concerned with "giants and fairies," or even "princes and princesses," but with "people of our acquaintance."[24]

Female critics were also the first to explore the technical aspects of the new genre. Barbauld again, anticipating the concerns of twentieth-century narratology, identified three types of fictional narration: the kind in which an author related the whole adventure (as in Cervantes and Fielding), the memoir, or first-person account (found in Marivaux and Smollett), and the epistolary mode, in which characters addressed one another in letters. Each narrative technique, she felt, had its drawbacks. The authorial mode could seldom become "dramatic" without the introduction of dialogue; the memoir-novel made the reader wonder how an "imaginary narrator" could remember so precisely; the epistolary novel had problems of exposition. In the end, however, she preferred epistolary narration to the other two modes. Private letters, describing the emotions of characters as they felt them "*at* the moment," had the power, she thought, to make "the whole work dramatic."[25]

Women labored to free the novel of its popular associations with scandal and triviality. The great power of the novel, wrote Germaine de Staël, was its capacity to "move the heart." Because it engaged the reader's feelings directly, prose

fiction could exert, Staël felt, an uplifting moral and social force far greater than
that of any abstract philosophy. Virtue, she observed,

> must be animated to struggle effectively against the passions, to create an
> exalted feeling so that we may be attracted to sacrifice—in brief, to beau-
> tify misfortune so that it will be preferred to sinful pleasures. Fiction that
> really moves us to noble emotions makes them habitual to us. It leads us
> unwittingly to make a pledge to ourselves that we would be ashamed to
> go back on.[26]

For Barbauld, the novel was likewise a kind of moral therapy: from the perusal
of a serious work of fiction, she wrote, "we rise better prepared to meet the ills of
life with firmness, or to perform our respective parts in the great theatre of life."[27]

Such claims were not merely rhetorical. A concern for the moral and social
effects of literature was another standard feature in women's criticism throughout the century. Perhaps paradoxically (given their otherwise iconoclastic intellectual attitudes), female critics tended to moralize about works of literature far
more often, and with greater fervor, than male critics did. This was due in part,
as we saw earlier, to lingering professional insecurities: the best way to avoid re-
proach for trespassing in the masculine "Republic of Letters," it seemed, was to
pretend that one did so solely, as Clara Reeve put it, "to promote the cause of religion and virtue." And precisely because their literary tastes *were* somewhat unconventional, women may have felt obliged to emphasize their moral
conservatism as a counterbalance. But female critics had also internalized the
same sexual stereotypes that affected all women in the period: as members of the
(supposedly) more delicate and refined sex, it was their duty, they believed, to
uphold cultural standards of modesty and piety.

In particular, despite their professed regard for verisimilitude, women opposed the explicit depiction of the sexual passions. Female critics were quick to
condemn works containing any hint of immorality or coarseness. Even "with its
worst pages curtailed," wrote Elizabeth Inchbald of Vanbrugh's *The Provok'd
Wife*, "too much that is bad still lingers behind."[28] Clara Reeve found Fielding's
novels full of "objectionable scenes"; Rousseau's *La Nouvelle Héloïse* was "dangerous and improper."[29] Even Shakespeare came under fire: the character of Doll
Tearsheet, according to Elizabeth Montagu, was an "obscenity"—"not only inde-
fensible but inexcusable."[30] "Who can deny," wrote Hannah More, "that all the
excellencies we have attributed to [Shakespeare] are debased by passages of offensive grossness?" His plays, she felt, were certainly too voluptuous to be performed; only "the discriminated, the guarded, the qualified perusal of such an
author"—i.e., reading a bowdlerized text in private—could be permitted.[31] Nor
were such puritanical comments confined to British critics: Stephanie de Genlis
(1746–1830), in her 1811 history of French women writers, *De l'Influence des*

femmes sur la littérature française, condemned Madame de Lafayette's *La Princesse de Clèves* for depicting "une passion criminelle." Far from being moral, it was too dangerous a book to be put into the hands of "les jeunes personnes."[32]

Such views are easy enough to satirize; they seem to anticipate the worse excesses of Victorian prudery. Yet it is also possible to interpret some of this feminine resistance to the "improper" in a more complex light. Very often women's real objection seems to have been not so much to the depiction of sexuality per se but to the misogyny that frequently accompanied the explicit representation of sexual themes. Riccoboni's criticism of *Les Liaisons dangereuses* is a good case in point. In attacking Laclos's novel for what she saw as its "revolting" picture of French morals, Riccoboni took particular exception to the portrait of the female villain, the wicked Madame de Merteuil. Merteuil's character was not only implausible, she told Laclos, but insulting to women readers: he had drawn a caricature of female iniquity. Laclos, with barely concealed condescension, responded that he had simply presented nature with "exactitude et fidélité" and that it was hypocritical to pretend that depraved creatures such as Merteuil did not exist.[33]

Laclos's defense has often been seen as a heroic vindication of realist principles. Yet if we take Riccoboni's point of view seriously—and indeed rehabilitate it as a *feminist* point of view—a number of interesting theoretical and historical questions arise. To what extent is "realism" itself a gender-bound concept? How much so-called true-to-life or naturalistic writing has actually been grounded in the misogynistic biases of Western culture? Without a doubt many of the most famous exponents of the uncensored mode—Swift in his scatological poems, Flaubert in *Madame Bovary*, Zola in *Nana*, Ernest Hemingway, D. H. Lawrence, or Henry Miller in any of their various novels—have shown themselves to be peculiarly obsessed with representing women as devious and manipulative, physically or morally corrupt. For a woman to reject the "truth" of such writing, therefore, may not necessarily be a sign of false modesty. In the case of Riccoboni, she seems to have been motivated less by prudishness than by a desire for a new kind of literary representation—a more exacting realism, unmarred by sexual prejudice, and faithful to the experience of all its readers.

Which brings us, by a somewhat paradoxical route, to the most subversive aspect of women's critical writing in the period: its implicitly adversarial content. Female critics, as we have seen, were acutely conscious of being interlopers in the "Republic of Letters"—at times debilitatingly so. Yet on occasion they were able to transform this sense of marginality into a kind of covert intellectual resistance. While not feminists in the modern sense—few wished for a complete overhaul of male and female social roles—many eighteenth-century women critics resented the masculine bias of traditional literary discourse, and said so. A strain of incipient sexual protest informed their writing, becoming particularly pronounced as the century drew to a close.

This nascent feminism took a number of forms. Sometimes it surfaced only in a coded or oblique fashion—as in Eliza Haywood's praise of reading in *The Female Spectator*. Haywood describes a conversation between herself and two book-loving female friends. "What clods of earth should we have been but for reading!" she is moved to exclaim, "how ignorant of every thing but the spot we tread upon!" Mira and Euphrosyne agree: to reading—with its power of "informing the mind, correcting the manners, and enlarging the understanding"—"we owe all that distinguishes us from savages."[34] The praise is couched in conventional terms, yet also has a curiously "gendered" feeling to it: one cannot help sensing that Haywood's real subject is *female* literacy—still a relatively new and uncommon phenomenon in the 1740s. It was the idea of *women* reading, specifically, that excited her imagination. The passage can thus be read as an unconscious vindication of female mastery: for a woman to read books is to enter, at last, a world of knowledge and self-understanding.

At other times, feminist sentiments surfaced more directly—in complaints, for example, about the patronizing attitudes of male writers. At the end of her otherwise laudatory essay on Richardson, Barbauld could not help remarking, with ill-disguised irritation, that the author of *Clarissa* did not properly value intellectual women. Though she was willing to allow that "the prejudice against any appearance of extraordinary cultivation in women, was, at that period, very strong," her hero's disdain clearly rankled. "What can be more humiliating," she asked, "than the necessity of affecting ignorance?" The only good result of such prejudice, she concluded, was that it gave "female genius" something to overcome—"so much, as to render it probable, before a woman steps out of the common walks of life, that her acquirements are solid, and her love for literature decided and irresistible."[35]

Female critics were particularly affronted by what they perceived as the double standard informing masculine literary judgment: male writers were celebrated, whatever their talent, while women writers were almost always ignored. Because men alone assigned the ranks in literature, complained Stephanie de Genlis, female genius went unrecognized; praise was reserved for other men, including very mediocre talents. D'Alembert, she thought, was a blatant example of overrated mediocrity: he was considered important only because he had the support of the male-run Academy. If an academy of women existed, it would conduct itself better and judge more sanely.[36]

In an attempt to redress such injustice, women critics regularly commended the accomplishments of their fellow women writers. Susannah Centlivre, wrote Inchbald, "ranks in the first class of our comic dramatists." Hannah Cowley's *The Belle's Stratagem* was an "extremely attractive" play, replete with "forcible and pleasing occurrences."[37] The novels of Sarah Fielding, wrote Clara Reeve, were eminently worthy of comparison with her brother Henry's: if they did not equal them in "wit and learning," they excelled "in some other material merits, that are more beneficial to their readers."[38] Reeve also praised the fiction of Charlotte

Lennox, Frances Brooke, Elizabeth Griffith, Frances Sheridan, Marie-Jeanne Riccoboni and Stephanie de Genlis. Barbauld's *British Novelists* series was in itself an act of feminist advocacy: out of the twenty-eight novels Barbauld included in the series, twelve were written by women.

Women critics conferred on certain "female geniuses" an almost cult status. The acclaim bestowed on the seventeenth-century letter writer, Madame de Sévigné, for example, bordered on hero worship. There was only one work in the French language no one had ever thought to criticize, declared Genlis, "and that work was written by a woman." Sévigné's letters were a "perfect model" of style—superior in "spirit, imagination and sensibility" to anything else in the epistolary genre.[39] Elizabeth Montagu agreed: the noble pen of Sévigné, she declared, had inscribed its wielder's character "on every mind capable of receiving impressions of virtue, and of wit." "She was surely the most amiable of Women," she told Elizabeth Carter. "I am interested in every circumstance that relates to her."[40] Similar encomiums appeared in the works of contemporary German women writers—notably in the letters of Sophie von La Roche, herself a fluent and stylish correspondent.

Yet for some female critics the eulogizing of individual women writers, however enthusiastic, did not go far enough. At the end of the century two writers sought to reclaim for women a central role in literary history itself. In *De l'Influence des femmes sur la littérature française*, Genlis argued that women, not men, had been responsible for the development of French literature. Genlis was not deterred by the fact that few women had written before the seventeenth century: the role of "protectrice," or literary patroness, was just as important, in her view, as actual authorship. Women exerted a civilizing force in culture; when women held power and social authority, genius and taste flourished. Among the great makers of French literature, therefore, she counted most of the early queens and princesses of France, as well as modern "protectrices" such as Madame de Maintenon and the marquise de Rambouillet. All of these women, she maintained, had used their status and prestige to cultivate "les gens de lettres" and promote the arts: without them, French literature would not have come into existence.

A similar argument was put forth by the greatest female critic of the age, Germaine de Staël (1766–1817). Women, she believed, were the natural arbiters of taste. Thus advances in the arts took place in societies in which women were held in highest esteem. In her early masterpiece of literary sociology, *De la Littérature considérée dans ses rapports avec les institutions sociales* (1800), Staël made a direct connection between the status of women and the evolution of genres. The novel had developed in England, she said, because England was that country "where women are most truly loved": "Tyrannical laws, coarse desires, or cynical ideas have settled the fate of women, whether in the ancient republics or in Asia or in France. Nowhere so much as in England have women enjoyed the happiness brought about by domestic affections."[41]

In France, by contrast, despite the upheavals of the Revolution, women were still treated with contempt. "Men have thought it politically and morally useful to reduce women to the most absurd mediocrity," Staël complained. "Women have had no incentive to develop their minds; manners have thus not improved."[42] French literature had stagnated as a result. Rousseau's *La Nouvelle Héloïse*, she allowed, "was an eloquent and impassioned piece of writing," but "all the other French novels we like are imitations of the English."[43]

Both Genlis and Staël defended women's writing and predicted that female authors, and especially female critics, would play an increasingly prominent role in the literature of the future. Women were not only capable of producing great works of their own, wrote Genlis; their natural "finesse d'observation" and elegance of style made them excellent judges of the works of others. According to Staël, as society moved closer toward moral and social enlightenment and more and more women took part in literary life, literature itself would evolve in a feminist direction. While the comedy of the ancien régime had focused, for example, on "the immoral behavior of men toward women" precisely in order "to ridicule the deceived women," in the perfected drama of the future, male deception itself would become the satiric target. Corrupt "purveyors of vice"—men who imposed on women—would themselves be "exposed as wretched beings, and abandoned to children's jeers."[44] Female critics, Staël implied, would play a crucial part in these uplifting developments. As she would argue later in *De l'Allemagne* (1813), "nature and society have given women a great capacity for endurance, and it seems to me that it cannot be denied that in our day they are in general more meritorious than men."[45]

Such heady sentiments, as one might expect, found little immediate echo in mainstream criticism. Nor must it be said—in the decades to come—did female critics find the acceptance that Staël and Genlis so optimistically predicted. Indeed, as the study of literature became more and more professionalized and institutionalized after 1800, the opposite often seemed to be the case. For most of the nineteenth century, literary criticism remained a predominantly male-identified activity: the early contributions of women to critical thought were soon forgotten. Dryden, Pope, Boileau, Johnson, Diderot, Wordsworth, Coleridge, and other male writers were canonized as the great originators of the modern literary-critical tradition; the works of Behn, Montagu, Riccoboni, Inchbald, Barbauld, Genlis, and even Staël herself (not to mention those of lesser figures) were consigned to oblivion.

Does this mean, therefore, that eighteenth-century women had relatively little impact on the early development of modern literary criticism? Here one must take issue with the masculinist biases of traditional literary history. The fact that individual women critics were so quickly forgotten does not mean that their influence on contemporary taste was itself negligible. Indeed, one might make a powerful revisionist claim on their behalf: that they represented the critical vanguard of their epoch. As we have seen, female critics regularly gravitated to the more iconoclastic topics of the day—the power of original genius, the rejection of classical models, the superiority of fiction and drama over poetry. They were impatient, by and large, with received styles and genres and turned instead to newer forms, such as the novel, which seemed to articulate in a powerful yet accessible way the moral and intellectual concerns of a growing middle-class (increasingly female) reading public. To borrow the language of the eighteenth century itself, women critics were almost always on the side of the "Moderns"— in favor of novelty and experimentation, vernacular styles, and the democratization of reading and writing.

Over the next two centuries, of course, these literary values would gradually triumph. The history of modern criticism, one could argue, is a history of the feminization of taste. In the nineteenth century, with the continuing rise of female literacy, literature itself underwent a feminization: with the emergence of celebrated women writers—Jane Austen, George Eliot, George Sand, the Brontës, Emily Dickinson (and somewhat later, Edith Wharton, Virginia Woolf, Willa Cather, Colette, and Gertrude Stein)—the "Republic of Letters" seemed to evolve, if not into a women's domain, into a community in which women could at least claim an authority equal to that of men. In turn, what we might call "female" literary values—informality, inventiveness, accessibility—gained a new prestige and importance. The canonization of the novel as the preeminent genre of "modern life" was itself a testimony to women's growing critical influence.

Eighteenth-century women critics—who of course represented a much larger body of women readers—can be said to have anticipated this feminization of taste. Though unable to win legitimation for their own writing, they articulated for the first time an alternative to traditional male-oriented literary values. Fittingly, the process they initiated would culminate, in the twentieth century, in the vindication of women's role in the history of literary criticism itself—to which the existence of this essay may bear witness.

notes

1. Jonathan Swift, *"A Tale of a Tub," "The Battle of the Books" and "The Mechanical Operation of the Spirit,"* ed. A. C. Guthkelch and D. Nichol Smith, 2d ed. (Oxford: Clarendon Press, 1958), 257.

2. See Henry Fielding, *"The Covent-Garden Journal" and "A Plan of the Universal Register-Office,"* ed. Bertrand A. Goldgar (Middletown, Conn.: Wesleyan University Press, 1988), 18, 96.

3. Janet Todd, ed., *Dictionary of British and American Women Writers 1660–1800* (Totowa, N.J.: Rowman and Littlefield, 1985), 143.

4. The phrase "Amazons of the pen" is from *The Adventurer*, 115 (December 11, 1754). Johnson, it is true, often generously supported individual women writers (notably Charlotte Lennox and Anna Williams), but this did not keep him from making less charitable observations in public. For the context of the antifemale remarks cited, see Reginald Blunt, ed., *Mrs. Montagu, "Queen of the Blues"—Her Letters and Friendships from 1762 to 1800* (London: Constable, 1923), vol. 2, 140–41.

5. See Robert Halsband, "Addison's *Cato* and Lady Mary Wortley Montagu," *PMLA* 65 (1950): 1123–24.

6. Hannah More, *Strictures on the Modern System of Female Education*, in *The Works of Hannah More* (London, 1803), vol. 4, 196–97, 200–201.

7. Bathsua Pell Makin, *An Essay to Revive the Antient Education of Gentlewomen, in Religion, Manners, Arts & Tongues*, ed. Paula L. Barbour (Los Angeles: William Andrews Clark Memorial Library, 1980), 9.

8. Ibid.

9. Swift, *"Battle of the Books,"* in *"A Tale of a Tub,"* 240. Exceptions to the general antifeminist sentiment of the period should be noted: George Ballard (1706–55) and John Duncombe (1729–86) both wrote encomiastic works celebrating women's contributions to the world of arts and letters. Ballard's *Memoirs of Several Ladies of Great Britain, who have been Celebrated for their Writings or Skill in the Learned Languages, Arts and Sciences* appeared in 1752; Duncombe's *The Feminiad* in 1754. Thomas Seward (1708–90), father of the poet and letter writer Anna Seward (1747–1809), published a poem provocatively entitled "The Female Right to Literature" in the second volume of Dodsley's *Miscellany* in 1748.

10. Henry Fielding, *Tom Jones*, ed. John Bender and Simon Stern (Oxford and New York: Oxford University Press, 1996), 372.

11. Todd, *Dictionary of Women Writers*, 93.

12. More, "Preface to the Tragedies," in *Works*, vol. 2, 23.

13. Elizabeth Inchbald, preface to Colley Cibber's *Love Makes a Man*, in *The British Theatre; or, A Collection of Plays, which are acted at the Theatres Royal, Drury Lane, Covent Garden and Haymarket* (London, 1808), vol. 14, 4.

14. Blunt, *Mrs. Montagu*, vol. 2, 166.

15. Cited in Mary R. Mahl and Helene Koon, eds., *The Female Spectator: English Women Writers Before 1800* (Old Westbury, N.Y.: Feminist Press, 1977), 136–37.

16. Aphra Behn, preface to *The Dutch Lover* (1673). To "play at Long Laurence," according to Wright's *English Dialect Dictionary*, means to do nothing, to laze. St. Laurence is the patron saint of idleness.

17. Susanna Centlivre, preface to *Love's Contrivance* (1703).

18. Elizabeth Montagu, *An Essay on the Writings and Genius of Shakespear* (London, 1769), xxii–xxiii.

19. Elizabeth Griffith, *The Morality of Shakespeare's Drama Illustrated* (London, 1775), 525–26.

20. Ibid., 481.

21. Joanna Baillie, preface to *A Series of Plays: in which it is attempted to delineate the Stronger Passions of the Mind, Each Passion being the Subject of a Tragedy and a Comedy* (London, 1798).

22. On the influence of Steele in particular, see Alison Adburgham, *Women in Print: Writing Women and Women's Magazines from the Restoration to the Accession of Victoria* (London: Allen and Unwin, 1972), 53–66.

23. Clara Reeve, *The Progress of Romance and the History of Charoba, Queen of Egypt* (New York: Facsimile Text Society, 1930), vol. 1, 111.

24. Anna Laetitia Barbauld, ed., *The Correspondence of Samuel Richardson* (London, 1804), vol. 1, xvi.

25. Ibid., xxvi.

26. "Il faut animer la vertu pour qu'elle combatte avec avantage contre les passions; il faut faire naître une sorte d'exaltation pour trouver du charme dans les sacrifices; il faut enfin parer le malheur pour qu'on le préfère à toutes les passions généreuses, lui en donnent l'habitude, et lui font prendre à son insu un engagement avec elle-même, qu'elle honte de rétracter, si une situation semblable lui devenoit personelle" (Staël, *Essai sur les fictions* [1795] in *Oeuvres complètes de Mme. la baronne de Staël* [Paris, 1820–21], vol. 2, 207. Here, as in subsequent citations from Staël's works, I have relied on the translation by Morroe Berger in *Madame de Staël on Politics, Literature, and National Character* [Garden City, N.Y.: Doubleday, 1964]).

27. Barbauld, *Correspondence of Richardson*, vol. 1, xxi–xxii.

28. Inchbald, preface to Vanbrugh's *The Provok'd Wife*, in *British Theatre*, vol. 9, 9.

29. Reeve, *Progress of Romance*, vol. 1, 140, and vol. 2, 14.

30. Montagu, *Writings and Genius of Shakespear*, 105.

31. More, "Preface to the Tragedies," in *Works*, vol. 2, 24.

32. Stephanie de Genlis, *De l'Influence des femmes sur la littérature française, comme protectrices des lettres et comme auteurs* (Paris, 1811), 114.

33. "Correspondance de Laclos et de Madame Riccoboni au sujet de *Liaisons dangereuses*," in Marie-Jeanne Riccoboni, *Oeuvres complètes de Choderlos des Laclos*, ed. Maurice Allem (Paris: Gallimard, 1951), 759.

34. Eliza Haywood, *The Female Spectator* (London, 1750), vol. 2, 39.

35. Barbauld, *Correspondence of Richardson*, clxiv.

36. Genlis, *De l'Influence des femmes*, 134.

37. See Inchbald, preface to Centlivre's *The Wonder: A Woman Keeps a Secret*, in *British Theatre*, vol. 11, 3; and preface to Cowley's *The Belle's Stratagem*, in *British Theatre*, vol. 19, 2.

38. Reeve, *Progress of Romance*, vol. 1, 142.

39. Genlis, *De l'Influence des femmes*, 134.

40. Cited in Blunt, *Mrs. Montagu*, vol. 2, 98.

41. "Des lois tyranniques, des désirs grossiers, ou des principes corrompus, ont disposé du sort des femmes, soit dans les républiques anciennes, soit en Asie, soit en France. Les femmes n'ont joui nulle part, comme en Angleterre, du bonheur causé par les affections domestiques" (Staël, *De la Littérature*, vol. 2, 228).

42. "Néanmoins, depuis la révolution, les hommes ont pensé qu'il étoit politiquement et moralement utile de réduire les femmes à la plus absurde médiocrité...elles n'ont plus eu de motifs pour développer leur raison: les moeurs n'en sont pas devenues meilleures" (Ibid., 335).

43. "La Nouvelle Héloïse est un écrit éloquent et passionné, qui caracterise le génie d'un homme, et non les moeurs de la nation. Tous les autres romans françaises que nous aimons, nous les devons à l'imitation des Anglais" (Ibid., 230).

44. "...des hommes puissans, ces charlatans de vices, ces frondeurs de principes élévés, ces moqueurs des âmes sensibles, c'est eux qu'il faut vouer au ridicule qu'ils préparent, les dépouiller comme des êtres misérables, et les abandonner à la risée des enfans" (Ibid., 350).

45. "La nature et la société donnent aux femmes une grande habitude de souffrir, et l'on ne saurait nier, ce me semble, que de nos jours elles ne vaillent, en général, mieux que les hommes" (Staël, *De l'Allemagne*, vol. 1, 64).

2

ON NORTHANGER ABBEY

Northanger Abbey, the earliest of Jane Austen's great comedies of female enlightenment, begins with a resounding NO. "No one," announces the narrator, "who had ever seen Catherine Morland in her infancy, would have supposed her born to be an heroine." For Catherine, we learn, is not a forlorn orphan or put-upon maiden: her robust mother did *not* expire giving birth to her; nor was her indulgent father ever "addicted to locking up his daughters." At seventeen, though "*almost* pretty," Catherine is not spectacularly beautiful, nor a prodigy of wit. "Not less unpropitious for heroism," Austen slyly observes, "seemed her mind." Granted, she exhibits "neither a bad heart nor a bad temper," but she has "no taste for a garden"; her French is "not remarkable"; her skill at drawing "not superior"; and she has "no chance" of throwing a party into raptures by a "prelude on the pianoforte." Books she has learned to like, but only when they are "all story and no reflection."[1]

If Catherine, Austen's antiheroine, is defined by a series of "no's," "not's," "neither's," and "nor's," the story Austen tells about her is also fraught with negatives. Henry Tilney, the engaging lover-to-be whom Catherine first meets at the Lower Rooms at Bath, where she has gone with old family friends, Mr. and Mrs. Allen, is "not quite handsome" (though very near it); naïvely, Catherine does "not know" whether to laugh or look serious at the odd yet delightful things he says to her. When he asks her what she is thinking about after their first dance together ("not of your partner, I hope, for, by that shake of the head, your meditations are not satisfactory"), she can only respond inanely: "I was not thinking of any thing." Smiling, he says he would "rather be told at once that you will not tell me." "Well then, I will not," she somewhat wildly replies. Whether the bewildered Catherine dreams of Henry that night, Austen tells us, "cannot be ascertained" (p. 15).

Still more "no's," "not's," and "cannots" proliferate as the central business of the novel gets under way. While gratifying, Catherine's new friendship with Henry and his appealing sister Eleanor (whom she meets a few days later) is not as unruffled as it might be. Two other Bath acquaintances—the gaily impervious Isabella Thorpe, who has "no notion of loving people by halves," and her fortune-hunting brother John, with whose crudities Catherine often finds herself "not pleased"—embroil her in a constant train of embarrassments. On the worst occasion, after she has explained to the Thorpes that she cannot go out driving with them owing to a prior engagement with the Tilneys, John Thorpe brazenly informs her that he has already told Miss Tilney that Catherine "will not have the pleasure of walking with her till Tuesday" (p. 77). Mortified, Catherine is forced to run after Miss Tilney to tell her none of it is true: she "never promised" to go with the Thorpes at all. This awkward explanation ("defective only in being—from her irritation of nerves and shortness of breath—no explanation at all") is kindly accepted (p. 78); but Catherine is nonetheless relieved when "no new difficulty" prevents her from walking with Henry and Eleanor round Beechen Cliff the next day. Nor is she unhappy, soon after, to receive an invitation from Eleanor and her widowed father, General Tilney, to visit the three of them at their country home of Northanger Abbey. "No endeavours shall be wanting on our side," Miss Tilney politely assures her, "to make Northanger Abbey not wholly disagreeable" (p. 109).

Yet Northanger, as the "no" lurking in the very name suggests, is itself a site of negation. Hearing about the abbey for the first time, the impressionable Catherine—who has read Mrs. Radcliffe's sensational *The Mysteries of Udolpho* and a host of other romantic novels foisted on her by Isabella Thorpe in Bath— longs for, and half-expects to see, a stupendous Gothic pile, complete with haunted passageways and the relics of murdered maidens. Sorely is she disappointed. "So low did the building stand, that she found herself passing through the great gates of the lodge into the very grounds of Northanger, without having discerned even an antique chimney" (p. 127). Her room, she is astounded to find, is "by no means unreasonably large," nor does it contain any ancient tapestries, crumbling parchments, or secret doorways. Nothing more mysterious than "a white cotton counterpane" lies hidden in an old chest in one corner of the room, nor are the contents of a curious "high, old fashioned black cabinet" any more exciting: "Could it be possible, or did not her senses play her false?—An inventory of linen, in coarse and modern characters, seemed all that was before her!" (p. 137).

Still more disconcerting, however, is the behavior of her host at Northanger, the insinuating, inscrutable General Tilney. He is not, to be sure, what she first imagines him to be—an outright Gothic monster, with the "air and attitude of a Montoni" and the blood of a dead wife on his hands. Henry, who loves her, tactfully dismisses Catherine's lurid fantasy regarding the General and the late Mrs. Tilney: "you have erred in supposing him not attached to her" (p. 158). Nonetheless, General Tilney is hardly a man of simple goodwill. When—in the critical penultimate episode of the novel—Eleanor, in visible anguish, tells

Catherine the desolating news that her father has ordered Catherine to leave Northanger Abbey at once ("Not even the hour is left to your choice . . . and no servant will be offered you"), the only explanation offered—again a negative one—is that Catherine has given General Tilney "no just cause of offence" (p. 182). Not until the final pages of the novel, when Henry, disobeying his father's command to think of Catherine "no more," comes to her parents' house in order to propose to her, does she grasp what she has not previously understood: that people, regrettably, are often not what they seem.

Why so many "no's" in *Northanger Abbey*? In part, one suspects, because the young Jane Austen herself felt a need to say no. *Northanger Abbey* was the first of Austen's six major novels to be offered for publication—to Crosby & Co. in 1803—and might be described, in a number of senses, as an experiment in negation.[2] In telling a story of "no's" and "not's," Austen was making a statement about her own art—about what it would *not* be, what it would *not* describe, what it would *not* endorse. Yet at the same time, through this very act of symbolic negation, she also succeeded, paradoxically, in liberating that spirit of comic affirmation—of delight in the ongoing drama of human life and in the power of her own observing intelligence—which informs, and indeed so brilliantly animates, all of her subsequent fiction.

What was Austen saying "no" to? First, and perhaps most explicitly, to a certain type of contemporary popular fiction. *Northanger Abbey* is famous for its burlesque of the eighteenth-century Gothic novel, and, in particular, of the works of Ann Radcliffe, whose most elaborate production in the Gothic style, *The Mysteries of Udolpho*, had appeared to huge acclaim in 1794. One should not, by any means, underestimate the temerity of Austen's satirical assault on the Radcliffean school. In 1798, when Austen (at the age of twenty-three) began composing *Northanger Abbey*, *The Mysteries of Udolpho* was probably the most widely read novel in Europe. Set in sixteenth-century France and Italy in a fantastical world of impenetrable castles, gloomy convents, and bloodthirsty banditti, Radcliffe's sensational account of the innocent Emily St. Aubert's suffering at the hands of the diabolical Montoni, brigand chieftain of the castle of Udolpho, made few concessions to historical or emotional plausibility. Its characters were romantic stereotypes; its psychological range limited. Nevertheless, thanks to a stupefying combination of dramatic plot twists, exotic scenery, and carefully manipulated hints of supernatural horror, *Udolpho* was an unparalleled publishing success. Like its follow-up volume, *The Italian: or, the Confessional of the Black Penitents* (1797), about a homicidal friar who runs amok in the time of the Inquisition, Radcliffe's novel went through numerous editions and spawned a host of imitations at home and abroad. To debunk such a work—however insouciantly—was to debunk one of the cherished icons of late-eighteenth-century popular taste.

By daring to parody the most famous female novelist of the age (the same writer Keats would later refer to, with ill-disguised trepidation, as "Mother Radcliffe"), Austen performed an essential act of artistic self-individuation. Parody, one might argue, achieves its typically ridiculous effect by recalling the work to be parodied (either stylistically or thematically) while at the same time differing from it in some subtle yet critical way. A superficial resemblance is established only to be negated on another level. In *Northanger Abbey*, Austen repeatedly sets up a superficial resemblance between her own fiction and Radcliffe's only to revoke it with a simple yet devastating shift in context. *Udolpho*'s romantic situations are reconstituted—but in the comically *un*romantic (and quintessentially Austenian) milieu of "the midland counties of England." By this method of ironic dislocation, Austen both acknowledged her powerful precursor and signaled her separation from her: to parody Radcliffe was also to escape her.

Examples of this recall-and-displace technique occur throughout *Northanger Abbey*. Whereas *Udolpho* opens with Emily St. Aubert accompanying her mysteriously ailing father, the aristocratic St. Aubert, to the sublime and supposedly healing climes of Languedoc and Provence, *Northanger Abbey*—in immediate and deflating contrast—opens with Catherine Morland accompanying the neighbours Mr. and Mrs. Allen to the mundane environs of Bath, where Mr. Allen has been ordered for the benefit of his "gouty constitution." Whereas Radcliffe's heroine, carried off to the exotic cities of "Tholouse" and Venice, is threatened with torture and rape by the wicked Madame Cheron and Count Morano, Catherine's persecutions at Bath include being made to go out driving with the bothersome John and Isabella Thorpe. And most ridiculously, though Catherine's unsettling visit to Northanger Abbey at first seems to parallel Emily St. Aubert's dreadful sojourn with Montoni at the "Chateau of Udolpho," it turns out to be nothing like: linens and laundry lists are not exactly Gothic horrors, and General Tilney (though an authentic bourgeois villain) is no brooding Radcliffean uxoricide. In each of these instances, through the critical incongruities of burlesque, Austen made clear the sort of novelist she was *not* going to be. The events of ordinary life, with their special admixture of joy and fiasco, were to be the subject of her fiction—not the sensational doings of romance.

Yet Austen's novel is more than just a send-up of Radcliffe. Indeed, in a purely technical sense, the element of explicit anti-Radcliffean parody in *Northanger Abbey* is perhaps the weakest feature of an otherwise elegantly wrought and emotionally complex novel. The slapstick scene of Catherine's goofy rummaging through the guest rooms of Northanger Abbey in search of Gothic artifacts is *so* absurd as to seem unbelievable: if only for a moment, we feel Austen's satirical impulse undermining any illusion of psychological verisimilitude. More masterful, one might argue, are those moments in which Austen uses her heroine's absorption in romantic fiction, and the distressing consequences it produces, to broach certain larger moral, philosophical, and social issues: the folly of letting literature get in the way of life, the inexcusability of not thinking for oneself, the painful difficulties involved—especially for women—in growing up.

The "no" in *Northanger Abbey* is not merely to a kind of literature—the so-called Gothic or sentimental mode—but to a certain conception of the relationship between literature and experience, and, beyond that, to a certain conception of what it means to be a heroine. Catherine Morland is foolish (and Austen makes no bones about her foolishness) in part because she lets what she has read, rather than the evidence of her own eyes, shape her vision of life. Consider, for example, this early exchange between Catherine and Henry Tilney as they walk around Beechen Cliff near Bath:

> "I never look at it," said Catherine, as they walked along the side of the river, "without thinking of the south of France."
>
> "You have been abroad then?" said Henry, a little surprized.
>
> "Oh! no, I only mean what I have read about. It always puts me in mind of the country that Emily and her father travelled through, in the 'Mysteries of Udolpho.' But you never read novels, I dare say?"
>
> "Why not?"
>
> "Because they are not clever enough for you—gentlemen read better books."
>
> "The person, be it gentleman or lady, who has not pleasure in a good novel, must be intolerably stupid. I have read all Mrs. Radcliffe's works, and most of them with great pleasure. The Mysteries of Udolpho, when I had once begun it, I could not lay down again;—I remember finishing it in two days—my hair standing on end the whole time." (p. 82)

The satire here, we note, appears to be not so much upon *Udolpho* (though Henry's tongue-in-cheek reference to his hair "standing on end" suggests a certain irreverence) as upon Catherine, who cannot see what is before her—a real landscape—without comparing it with one in a book. She has never been to the south of France, has no notion of what it looks like, yet because she has read about it in *Udolpho*, she assumes that the scene around Beechen Cliff must resemble it. Accepting Radcliffe's visionary scenery—as she will later—as a kind of substitute-reality, she lets it come between her and the world, like a mirage. (The fact that Radcliffe herself had never been to the south of France and composed her own often fanciful descriptions of its terrain only after consulting guidebooks significantly compounds the irony.) Like a child, Catherine has both read too much and observed too little: she cannot see the living forest, so to speak, for the fictional trees.

Austen was not the first writer, of course, to expose the folly of valuing literature over life, nor would she be the last. Cervantes, in *Don Quixote* (1605), had dramatized the fatuousness of putting art before lived experience: the hapless

Quixote, whose reading of chivalric romances sends him off tilting at windmills in the mistaken belief that they are giants, is one obvious prototype for the book-befuddled Catherine Morland. But other writers had also addressed the theme. John Locke, whose philosophical and educational writings (as Jocelyn Harris has pointed out) Austen knew well, warned in *An Essay Concerning Human Understanding* (1690) of the danger of letting the "false ideas" of poetry and fancy come between one and one's direct apprehension of the world. Men feared ghosts, Locke argued, because, instead of trusting to the evidence of their own senses, they let tales of fancy and superstition, imbibed in infancy, confuse their imaginings.[3]

Yet the writer to influence Austen most intimately on this point, one suspects, was Charlotte Lennox, whose popular comic novel, *The Female Quixote*, appeared in 1752. The protagonist of Lennox's novel, the "female Quixote" Arabella, is so crazed by reading seventeenth-century French romances that she begins to imagine herself a heroine in one of "Scudéry's" tales, surrounded by love-struck suitors and would-be ravishers. She is rescued from this childish delusion only after a series of disasters—and the catechistical ministrations of a kindly clergyman—persuade her that her "romantick Expectations" are a form of self-injurious, if not suicidal, folly. Austen clearly seems to have had Arabella in mind when she wrote up the first of the two great disillusionment scenes in *Northanger Abbey*. Following her embarrassing colloquy with the clergyman, Lennox's heroine retires to her room in a state of "inconceivable Confusion" and is "for near two Hours afterwards wholly absorb'd in the most disagreeable Reflections on the Absurdity of her past Behavior, and the Contempt and Ridicule to which she now saw plainly she had exposed herself."[4] In turn, in Austen's novel, after Henry (who is also a clergyman) rebukes Catherine at Northanger Abbey for imagining his father a Radcliffean brute—imploring her instead to "consult your own understanding, your own sense of the probable"—she too retires to her room in sorrowful humiliation:

> The visions of romance were over. Catherine was completely awakened. Henry's address, short as it had been, had more thoroughly opened her eyes to the extravagance of her late fancies than all their several disappointments had done. Most grievously was she humbled. Most bitterly did she cry. (p. 159)

Painful though it is, this first "awakening," like that of the besotted Arabella before her, snaps Catherine out of the silliest of her literary daydreams: she is closer now than ever before to confronting the world on its own authentic, if disenchanting, terms. No such fortunate fall, one might note in passing, will be granted the most pathetic of book-ensnared heroines. Forty years after the publication of *Northanger Abbey*, Flaubert depicted a heroine too incorrigibly romantic (and too incorrigibly stupid) to escape the hallucinatory coils of the literary—except in death. Emma Bovary, rhapsodizing with the lover Léon over a seascape she has read about but never seen, might be considered a Catherine Morland without brains and *Madame Bovary* a *Northanger Abbey* without hope.

But this is not, even so, the whole story. For, though Catherine Morland believes her eyes fully "opened" after her conversation with Henry, she has yet, of course, to undergo a second and far more decisive kind of enlightenment. One might almost view the first disillusionment scene in *Northanger Abbey* as a sort of decoy or smoke screen—a moment of seeming resolution that temporarily forestalls, or blocks from view, the novel's real moment of crisis and unveiling. The true climax of *Northanger Abbey* comes about not when Catherine realizes she has been mistaken about General Tilney, but at the moment at which (to put it as paradoxically as Austen does) she realizes that she has not: when she is at last compelled to notice, after being so rudely expelled from his home, that the general, though not perforce a Montoni, is still a man capable of behaving "neither honourably nor feelingly." At this moment of utmost disorder and dismay (none of it of her own making), Catherine finally grasps, traumatically, what she has in fact half-known all along—"that in suspecting General Tilney of either murdering or shutting up his wife, she had scarcely sinned against his character or magnified his cruelty" (p. 201). No murderer he—but in his own banal way, a cruel man nonetheless.

What to make of this second, more paradoxical illumination? With this additional "blow against sentiment"—the novel's most excruciating moment of demystification—Austen utters, it seems to me, her most powerful "no" of all. But it is a more complex kind of negative than any we have encountered so far. For to appreciate it fully we need to take into account not only the immediate literary context of *Northanger Abbey*, but something of its social and philosophical context as well. In particular, as Margaret Kirkham has suggested, we need to relate Austen's novel to late-eighteenth-century feminism and the issue of female education.

It would be easy enough (though also a mistake) to conclude that, by humiliating her heroine a second time, Austen wished, in some sense, to punish her—to say "no" to Catherine herself, as it were—for being so obtuse. For Catherine *is* obtuse, and not only when she so clownishly tries, and fails, to read the world as though it were a book. Her problem with novels is that she believes in them too much. But she has exactly the same problem with people. She relies on others, often with an almost reckless gullibility, to explain the world for her. Thus her slavish relationship to the blatantly self-interested Isabella Thorpe, whom she adopts at Bath as her oracle on literature, fashion, and the enigmatic ways of the opposite sex. Isabella, it is true, is a magnificent comic creation, given to uttering the novel's most absurdly quotable lines ("But, my dearest Catherine, have you settled what to wear on your head to-night?"), yet her domination of the younger woman also has its sinister side. The slow-witted Catherine seems incapable of recognizing, for example, when Isabella is simply using her to get at her marriageable brother James.

Catherine is even less critical of the men around her. When John Thorpe boasts idiotically about the virility of his horse ("look at his loins; only see how he moves; that horse *cannot* go less than ten miles an hour") she is willing enough to believe him, even while the beast in question stands shyly and placidly by (p. 29). When the devious General Tilney compliments her on the "elasticity" of her walk, Catherine proceeds gaily down Pulteney Street, "walking, as she concluded, with great elasticity, though she had never thought of it before" (pp. 79–80). She is most powerfully struck, of course, by the seemingly inexhaustible brilliance of Henry Tilney. Though Henry will repeatedly resist the role of moral and intellectual tutor, Catherine is eager to be instructed by him on any topic—from landscape drawing and perspective to the puzzling behavior of friends and acquaintances. Indeed "it was no effort to Catherine to believe that Henry Tilney could never be wrong. His manner might sometimes surprize, but his meaning must always be just: —and what she did not understand, she was almost as ready to admire, as what she did" (p. 89).

Austen takes a good deal of comic delight, to be sure, in highlighting this aspect of her heroine's character. For much of *Northanger Abbey* Catherine behaves like someone drugged or half-asleep. (No previous heroine in English literature, one might add, is so often *literally* asleep. It is hardly coincidental that so many chapters in the novel end with Catherine going to bed and falling into a child-like slumber—her somnolence is an essential clue to her nature.) Though warned by Henry that "to be guided by second-hand conjecture is pitiful" (p. 119), she seldom questions the opinions of others; she simply accepts what she is told. A moral shock of the sort she is made to undergo at the hands of General Tilney might be considered a fitting penalty for such mental laziness and inattention.

But Austen is careful in the end not to make Catherine alone to blame for her somewhat moronic behavior. Austen goes out of her way to place her heroine's problem in a larger satiric context. We have no direct evidence that Austen had read Mary Wollstonecraft's *Vindication of the Rights of Woman*—no references in surviving letters, no explicit comments in any of her novels. Yet to judge by Austen's powerful meditation on the problem of female enlightenment in *Northanger Abbey*, it is almost impossible to believe that Wollstonecraft's impassioned feminist treatise, first published (to scandalized outcry) in 1792, was unknown to her.[5] Wollstonecraft's argument, in brief, was that society kept women—as a sex—in a state of intellectual childishness from which few were able to escape. Because they were brought up only to please men, who in turn tyrannized over them, women failed to develop their own innate powers of judgment and understanding. "Told from their infancy, and taught by the example of their mothers, that a little knowledge of human weakness, justly termed cunning, softness of temper, *outward* obedience, and a scrupulous attention to a puerile kind of propriety, will obtain for them the protection of a man," wrote Wollstonecraft, most women grew up as mere "creatures of sensation."[6] Novels, poetry, conduct books, and "gallantry"—men's patronizing contempt for female intelligence—all conspired to keep women in a condition of mental and emotional dependence. As a result, most women were "either foolish or vicious." "The slave of her own feelings," Wollstonecraft argued, woman "is easily subjugated by those of others. Thus degraded, her reason, her misty reason! is employed rather to burnish than to snap her chains."[7] She called for "a REVOLUTION in female manners" to restore women to the status of rational beings, equal in "power of understanding" to men and capable, by "reforming themselves," of reforming the world.[8]

As if to dramatize Wollstonecraft's thesis, Austen repeatedly connects Catherine Morland's failure to think with the fact that she has never been *taught* to think. The problem is not individual incapacity but lack of education: Catherine has been made stupid—by a society that fails to honor the intelligence of its female members. "In justice to men," the narrator observes, "though to the larger and more trifling part of the sex, imbecility in females is a great enhancement of their personal charms, there is a portion of them too reasonable and too well informed themselves to desire any thing more in woman than ignorance" (p. 86). The bitter, booby-trapping irony here is as obvious a clue as any to Austen's larger satiric intentions.

For Wollstonecraft, the conditioned "imbecility" of women was self-perpetuating: since most girls were educated solely by their mothers or other women, the pattern of female folly reproduced itself over generations. Few women had the ability to train their daughters in the ways of logical reasoning:

> To do everything in an orderly manner is a most important precept, which women, who, generally speaking, receive only a disorderly kind of education, seldom attend to with that degree of exactness that men, who from their infancy are broken into method, observe. This negligent kind of guesswork—for what other epithet can be used to point out the random exertions of a sort of instinctive common sense never brought to the test of reason?—prevents their generalizing matters of fact; so they do today what they did yesterday, merely because they did it yesterday.[9]

Yet this is Catherine's situation exactly. No one—until she meets Henry Tilney—has ever shown her that she might be anything other than a "sad little shatterbrained creature." Her mother, to whom we learn her education has been solely entrusted, is no intellectual model: like Mrs. Bennet in *Pride and Prejudice*, Mrs. Morland is one of the more oblivious parents to be found in Austen's fiction. Preoccupied with the physical burdens of motherhood, she is herself too distracted to instill in her daughter any sense of the value of hard-won knowledge. Thus Catherine's failure to learn to play the spinet at an early age: Mrs. Morland, we are told, "did not insist on her daughters being accomplished in spite of incapacity or distaste" and simply "allowed her to leave off" (p. 2). She is incapable of giving even the most rudimentary advice: when Catherine departs for Bath, Mrs. Morland hardly seems to notice that her daughter has gone. And after Catherine returns from Northanger Abbey, stunned with misery and unable to cope with the task (maternally imposed) of mending her father's cravats, all her bewildered parent can do is commend to her, somewhat fatuously, "a very clever Essay in one of the books up stairs" about "young girls that have been spoilt for home by great acquaintance" (p. 196).

Nor do any of the other older women in Catherine's life offer any better support. Mrs. Allen, Catherine's Bath guardian, is even less comprehending than Mrs. Morland. The one topic on which she can converse with any accuracy is muslins; her usual talk, delivered in a manner of frightening, almost psychotic vacancy, consists of mindlessly repeating the sentiments of others—as when she attempts to discuss the weather (p. 61). As for Mrs. Thorpe, Isabella's mother, *her* conversation is entirely devoted to her children, whose interest she seeks to advance in the crassest and most self-interested ways possible. The one older woman who, one suspects, might have been able to nurture Catherine's youthful understanding—Mrs. Tilney—is dead: her absence from the novel is a telling sign of a generalized failure of maternal guidance in *Northanger Abbey*. Under the circumstances it is perhaps not surprising that Catherine turns to "Mother Radcliffe" for advice about the world.

Yet Austen, like Wollstonecraft before her, also affirms that escape is possible. The most profound "no" in *Northanger Abbey*, finally, is addressed to the notion that the seemingly pervasive "imbecility" of women is either natural or inevitable. "I wish to see women neither heroines nor brutes," Wollstonecraft had written, "but reasonable creatures."[10] Recognizing the familiar negative-to-positive syntax, we might take this sentiment as Austen's motto also. For by instilling in her heroine—along with her flaws—a capacity for enlightenment, Austen gives life and form to what Margaret Kirkham calls the "central tenet" of late-eighteenth-century feminism—"that individual women have those powers of mind which enable them to acquire moral principle through rational reflection on experience."[11]

For Catherine, enlightenment comes about in part through the tactful ministrations of Henry Tilney. Henry's role in *Northanger Abbey* has frequently been misunderstood. Because he teases Catherine—baits her, challenges her, forces her to attend to what is going on around her—some readers have found him patronizing or pedantic, even misogynistic.[12] It is true that he can be rude: "No one," he laughingly assures his sister and Catherine, "can think more highly of the understanding of women than I do. In my opinion, nature has given them so much, that they never find it necessary to use more than half" (p. 89). But his comments are almost always interestingly double-edged. For he *is* an admirer of female understanding; what he regrets (though he never says so directly) is that women do not take their own intelligence seriously enough. Hidden in his mock-insult is a poignant awareness of what individual members of the opposite sex might achieve should they ever recognize—and exert on their own behalf—all the innate "powers of mind" that they possess.

Henry does not so much tell Catherine *what* to think as show her that she *can* think. His teasing, his irony, his enchanting negativity, is his way of fixing her attention on her own powers of judgment and understanding. By his very contrariness he challenges her to pay attention, to start figuring things out for herself. When Catherine demands to know, for example, why his brother Frederick flirts with Isabella Thorpe after Isabella has already announced her engagement to James Morland, Henry forces her—by playfully refusing to answer her questions—to make sense of the situation on her own:

> "But what can your brother mean? If he knows her engagement, what can he mean by his behaviour?"
> "You are a very close questioner."
> "Am I?—I only ask what I want to be told."
> "But do you only ask what I can be expected to tell?"
> "Yes, I think so; for you must know your brother's heart."
> "My brother's heart, as you term it, on the present occasion, I assure you I can only guess at."
> "Well?"
> "Well!"

"The premises are before you," he will remind her; "If it is to be guess-work, let us all guess for ourselves" (p. 119). Austen's hero, one suspects, has read his Wollstonecraft too.

Henry possesses a sense of intellectual mastery—a happy confidence in his own judgment—that Catherine sadly lacks. He is wise enough, however, to realize that his sense of mastery is merely the by-product of a superior education. (When Catherine laments the "torment" that little boys and girls go through when they learn to read, Henry teases her for not being "particularly friendly" to the "very severe, very intense application" that such tasks require [p. 85]. He is right: owing to her own haphazard upbringing Catherine has never learned the value of mental discipline.) Yet he also knows that Catherine's problem can only be rectified by letting her muddle through on her own. Only by *not* explaining—by refusing to treat her as anything other than an intellectual equal—can he help her to develop, belatedly, an equivalent sense of autonomy.

The paradoxical strategy pays off. For, when Catherine faces her greatest moral and intellectual challenge—how to judge the behavior of Henry's own father—she faces it utterly on her own. In the scene of Catherine's lonely homecoming after the expulsion from Northanger Abbey, Austen allegorizes the coming of a woman into a sense of her own cognitive and ethical powers. Neither parent nor lover nor friend can guide her now: she has to decide for herself the meaning of the general's behavior. Yet she meets the challenge triumphantly. In trusting, through all of the pain she feels, to her own deepest understanding of the general's character—that despite his authority he is a vain and misguided man—she lays claim to her own "powers of mind" and achieves for the first time an exhilarating and (for her) revolutionary inner freedom.

Catherine Morland (whose name may be intended to echo that of one of the late-eighteenth-century pioneers of feminist thought[13]) is a new kind of heroine in English literature: a thinking woman's heroine. With Henry's encouragement, she makes her way out of mental slavishness toward a kind of liberation. The marriage of Henry and Catherine at the end of *Northanger Abbey* delights us, because both parties have shown themselves to advantage. Henry, by choosing Catherine, dissociates himself from the self-serving patriarchism so repellently embodied by his father. Catherine, by choosing Henry, retains her newly discovered intellectual freedom. By loving the one person who refuses to condescend to her, she demonstrates—joyfully—that condescension is no longer necessary.

Does this mean that Austen thought that women could escape their folly only by joining themselves to understanding men? Hardly—the existence of *Northanger Abbey* itself suggests otherwise. In perhaps the most famous authorial aside in all of Austen's fiction—the exalted defense of the novel at the end of the fifth chapter—Austen celebrates prose fiction as that "species of composition" in which "the greatest powers of the mind are displayed, in which the most thorough knowledge of human nature, the happiest delineation of its varieties, the liveliest effusions of wit and humour are conveyed to the world in the best chosen language" (p. 22). The implication here, at the very least, is that a certain strengthening awareness can be passed—from woman to woman—through the genre of the novel itself. A novelist with the ability to express her own "powers of mind" in a richly symbolic form (a novelist, in other words, like Austen herself) acts as a beacon to her female readers: an inspiriting reminder that women as well as men can achieve—and bear witness to—the "most thorough knowledge of human nature."

Even at this early stage in her career, Austen realized that the novel itself could serve as an instrument of enlightenment. To read *Northanger Abbey* for the first time is to undergo an intellectual process somewhat akin to Catherine Morland's. For Austen, like Henry Tilney, seldom explains things directly. Irony is her treasured mode; obliquity her delight. We have to pay attention, work things out for ourselves, catch when she is joking and when she is not. The ideal reader for *Northanger Abbey* would be one (to borrow a phrase from Henry James) on whom nothing is lost: the narrator's sly outrageousness, the scene-stealing absurdity of Isabella Thorpe ("Oh, these odious gigs!"), the sexual panic of her brother John, the fallibility of various Morlands and Allens, the pathos and complexity of the bonds that Catherine forms with the three Tilneys. Yet precisely by inviting us to exert our own "powers of mind" as we read, Austen affirms her faith in us—that we might indeed become, male and female alike, that ideal reader for whom she writes.

notes

1. Jane Austen, *"Northanger Abbey"; "Lady Susan"; "The Watsons"; and "Sanditon,"* ed. John Davie (Oxford and New York: Oxford University Press, 1990), 1–3. All subsequent references are to this edition. Page numbers are noted parenthetically.

2. Despite holding on to the manuscript of *Susan* (as *Northanger Abbey* was then called) for several years, Richard Crosby never published Austen's novel. Why he did not (he paid Austen £10 for the manuscript) remains unclear.

3. John Locke, *An Essay Concerning Human Understanding* (London, 1690), bk. 2, ch. 33. On the influence of Locke on Austen, see Jocelyn Harris's discussion of *Northanger Abbey* in *Jane Austen's Art of Memory* (Cambridge: Cambridge University Press, 1989).

4. Charlotte Lennox, *The Female Quixote*, ed. Margaret Dalziel (Oxford: Oxford University Press, 1989), 383.

5. For a discussion of Wollstonecraft's influence on Austen, see Margaret Kirkham, *Jane Austen: Feminism and Fiction* (Brighton: Harvester Press, 1983).

6. Mary Wollstonecraft, *Vindication of the Rights of Woman*, ed. Miriam Kramnick (Middlesex, Eng.: Penguin Books, 1975), 100.

7. Ibid., 202.

8. Ibid., 317.

9. Ibid., 104.

10. Ibid., 147.

11. Kirkham, *Jane Austen*, 36.

12. Not among them, however, is the British novelist Sylvia Townsend Warner. In a letter to George Plank in 1961, Townsend Warner complimented him on his resemblance to Henry Tilney, whom she considered the most delightful of Austen heroes:

> You have the nicest hand with a parcel. I can't think of anyone to match you in parcelling except perhaps Henry Tilney, to whom I attribute *all* the graces. Mr. Knightley's parcels would never come undone, true; but think of all the paper and string involved. Elinor had to do up all Edward's: Edward required a good deal of buttoning and unbuttoning, though she enjoyed his dependence on her: the butler did all Marianne's & Colonel Brandon's. Mr. Darcy did exactly three parcels a year, for Lizzy's birthday, for New Year's day, & for their wedding anniversary. The product was excellent, but he took *hours* to achieve it. And locked the library door.

(Sylvia Townsend Warner, *The Letters of Sylvia Townsend Warner*, ed. William Maxwell [New York: Viking, 1982], 191–92.)

13. The works of the late-eighteenth-century historian and feminist thinker Catherine Macaulay (1731–91), author of *Letters on Education: with Observations on Religious and Metaphysical Subjects* (1790)—a defense of female learning—were almost, if not quite, as well known as those of Wollstonecraft in the 1790s. (In the fifth chapter of the *Vindication*, Wollstonecraft eulogized her illustrious predecessor as "the woman of the greatest abilities . . . that this country has ever produced.") Had Austen herself read Catherine Macaulay? It is intriguing to speculate that by changing the name of her heroine from Susan to "Catherine Morland" (as she did between the original and the revised versions of *Northanger Abbey*), Austen too may have intended a subtle tribute to the decade's most famous advocate of female education.

3
AUSTEN'S Emma

It might be said of Jane Austen's comic masterpiece *Emma* that no other novel has a greater power of making its detractors look foolish. For detractors it has had—precisely, one suspects, because it is so patently a work of genius. The unpretentious yet perfectly calibrated style, the deeply intransigent female wit, the self-confident moral sense—the sheer unencumbered fearlessness of it all—inevitably infuriate he-men of both sexes. Witness Charlotte Brontë, in a famous letter to a friend from 1850, jealously assailing the spinster Austen for a supposed dearth of passionate feeling:

> [What] the blood rushes through, what is the unseen seat of Life and the sentient target of death—*this* Miss Austen ignores; she no more, with her mind's eye, beholds the heart of her race than each man, with bodily vision sees the heart in his heaving breast.[1]

John Henry Newman blustered against Austen's lack of piety (the author of *Emma*, he complained to a friend, had "not a dream of the high Catholic *nous*"), while Mark Twain, in a fit of manly aversion, spoke of feeling an "animal repugnance" for her novel and its characters. For a pixilated D. H. Lawrence, writing in 1930, the sublimely funny woman who wrote *Emma* was nothing but a pathetic "old maid"—"thoroughly unpleasant, English in the bad, mean, snobbish sense of the word."[2]

And yet such criticisms seem inevitably to backfire upon their utterers—comically and smartingly and forever. Attacking this most humane and joyful of novels, Brontë and Twain come off sounding vulgar and hysterical, Cardinal Newman like a fatuous Firbankian fool. (Lawrence, one might say, is simply Lawrence: wrong on all the salient points.) Austen's art may be a delicate thing—subtle at times to the point of heartbreak—but it is also infinitely expansive and curiously indestructible. Reading her critics, one has the sense of watching a judo exhibition: the big guys all seem to be throwing themselves.

Has anything changed of late? One might expect *Emma* to forfeit some of its charmed effect as the pattern of human life that it describes becomes increasingly antique and strange to us. Virginia Woolf wrote of Austen's fiction "that it is where the power of the man has to be conveyed that her novels are always at their weakest."[3] And recently certain feminist critics—finding Austen's unabashed delight in the traditional courtship plot something of an ideological embarrassment—have echoed this judgment. How aggravating that Austen felt compelled to supply husbands for her brilliant and attractive heroines! How much more subversive had she dispensed with some of the euphoric final matchmaking! *Emma's* tender Mr. Knightley has come in for especially harsh attack, and not only on account of his suspiciously heroic-sounding name. By taking Emma to task for her thoughtlessness in the crucial Box Hill episode of the novel—when she flirts with Frank Churchill then is rude to the elderly Miss Bates—he epitomizes what one critic calls the "odious Big Brotherism" of classic Austenian narrative: heroine behaves foolishly, hero chastises her, heroine is contrite, hero marries her.

The problem with such arguments is how deeply they betray the experience of reading. Useful though they can sometimes be, what is ignored in such readings is the sheer pleasure-effect that *Emma* generates: the suffusing, exhilarating, almost physical sensation of joy and well-being that Austen's image of human life provides. No one, in the moment of reading, can regret either the fierce moralizing of Knightley after the Box Hill episode or Emma's appropriately chastened response. Knightley must argue with Emma here because he loves her; his untrammeled exasperation, the reader realizes with deepening delight, is the very sign of his love. In turn, when he proposes to Emma not long after, one cannot help but rejoice, for we know him—have known him all along—to be the only worthy and desirable mate for the heroine. (He is the only person who dares speak to her with the freedom and loving candor of an equal.) The euphoria is real. Woolf may have been partly right—the diffident heroes of *Mansfield Park* and *Persuasion* do not always inspire utmost confidence—but in the case of *Emma*, Austen's greatest and most characteristic work, Woolf's generalization seems more grudging than accurate. Perhaps the first and most important thing to do in approaching *Emma* is to let go of the desire to carp, to take Austen down—anachronistically—for some presumed ideological failing. We need to acknowledge freely the book's tremendous emotional power. Only then, with luck, can we begin to understand the true nature of Austen's artistic achievement.

How exactly does *Emma* produce its vivid pleasure-effect? The answer, psychologically speaking, is multifaceted. First of all—and it would be silly to deny it—the book ineluctably appeals to what might be called one's intellectual narcissism. By this I do not mean anything so banal as that it satisfies a certain snobbish readerly vanity in us ("I am a person who has read and enjoyed *Emma*"), though it is undoubtedly the case that for over a hundred years "reading and enjoying *Emma*"—and then talking about it—has been a standard way for members of the Anglo-American educated classes to show off their possession of what the Marxist sociologist Pierre Bourdieu calls "intellectual capital." Especially for upwardly mobile young females, declaring one's enthusiasm for Austen (whose heroines almost always move up in social and economic status as a result of the sterling marital alliances they form) has been a classic means of indicating one's purported good taste, good breeding, and good sense: I am an especially adorable member of the ruling class. It is a tribute to Austen's novel that it not only survives but transcends this somewhat degrading sociocultural inscription. Were its author alive today, one suspects, she would probably be aiming some of her comic darts at people who wear Jane Austen T-shirts and put "I'd rather be reading Jane Austen" stickers on their cars—much as she lets fly, in the novel itself, at the florid and fatuous, divinely self-congratulatory Augusta Elton.

By intellectual narcissism I mean something at once less pejorative and more fundamental: the satisfaction that comes of finding the world intelligible. Intelligibility is an issue, obviously, *within* the novel: how one goes about making sense of the world—especially the world of other people—might indeed be said to be one of *Emma*'s central themes. Austen's heroine, the delightful yet fallible Emma Woodhouse, is convinced she understands the world, of course; witty, charming, and utterly self-confident in her role as youthful mistress of Hartfield, she rules over her invalid widowed father and their little circle of friends and relations in the village of Highbury like a kind of self-appointed Minerva. Yet as Austen tell us, "The real evils indeed of Emma's situation were the power of having rather too much her own way, and a disposition to think a little too well of herself; these were the disadvantages which threatened alloy to her many enjoyments."[4] The central comedy of the book will result from seeing how often this would-be oracle is mistaken. In love matters especially—for she is an obsessional yet inept matchmaker—Emma's failures of understanding will be numerous and spectacular. The first and most obvious victim of her incomprehension is "little" Harriet Smith, her all-too-malleable protégée from Miss Goddard's school for girls. (The overbearing Emma will delude poor Harriet into believing that three different men in succession are in love with her: the clergyman Elton, the handsome Frank Churchill, and even—by accident—gruff Mr. Knightley.) But Emma is also her own victim, comically estranged from her own heart. As she comes, over the course of the novel, to recognize her own desires, her own intellectual narcissism will suffer a shock—but end up the better for it.

Not surprisingly, the word *intelligible* crops up often in the novel, like a talisman. Early on, for example, when Emma browbeats Harriet into rejecting a marriage proposal from an honest young farmer, Robert Martin—mistakenly believing that Harriet is about to receive a better offer from Highbury's obsequious new clergyman, Mr. Elton (who is actually in pursuit of Emma herself)—she demands that the dim-witted Harriet be as "intelligible" as possible in her letter of refusal (p. 45). In the crucial middle chapters of the novel, when everyone is mystified by the erratic comings and goings of the secretly engaged Frank Churchill, Emma alone finds his behavior "intelligible"—to the point of exchanging what she imagines (wrongly) are "smiles of intelligence" with him (p. 198). And near the end of the novel, after she has thoroughly embarrassed herself at Box Hill—in part because she has so utterly misjudged her relation to Frank and everyone else—Emma longs for some sign from Mr. Knightley, whom she meets in the garden at Hartfield, that her conduct, while mistaken, has at least been "intelligible" (p. 387). He will respond in turn—as the one who loves her "in spite of her faults"—by quietly proposing marriage, "in a tone of such sincere, decided, intelligible tenderness as was tolerably convincing" (p. 390).

But Austen spotlights the issue of intelligibility in other ways too. *Emma* is— quite literally—a book of puzzles and enigmas. Conundrums, riddles, and word games figure prominently in the plot of *Emma*—as when Emma demands that Mr. Elton supply a charade for Harriet Smith's riddle book (p. 63), or Emma, Frank Churchill, and Jane Fairfax play a children's alphabet game on the table at Hartfield (p. 313). Typically characters distinguish themselves by the perspicacity—or comic lack of it—that they display at these moments of explicit intellectual challenge. (Thus the hapless Harriet will dither over Mr. Elton's rhyming charade in "all the confusion of hope and dulness," while Emma sits comfortably by, already "quite mistress of the lines.") But another important function of such scenes is to focus our attention on reading itself—the complicated cognitive act by which words themselves come to seem "intelligible." For the reader, too, gets caught up in the game. It is difficult to resist trying to work out the novel's embedded conundrums oneself—though Mr. Woodhouse's fragmentary "Kitty, a fair but frozen maid" is apt to mystify most modern readers, at least until the accompanying footnote (p. 442) is consulted.

Yet this unraveling of riddles and mysteries could also be considered a metaphor for the reader's role in *Emma*. Austen's novel appeals so strongly, among other reasons, because it gives us the constant illusion of successfully working out a puzzle. The illusion operates at several levels. At the most basic level Austen reminds us that we know how to read—that we know how to work out the meaning of written words. This is not as simpleminded as it sounds. One of the great pleasures of discovering Austen in the early twenty-first century is the delight of experiencing a genuinely intellectual prose style: individual sentences so cleverly and elaborately wrought that one's skills as a reader are constantly being challenged, yet that also satisfy—immediately and deeply—one's primitive longing for intelligibility. Nowadays, in an age of sound bites and advertising slogans, we are not much used to such marvelous sentences, though as Virginia Woolf once observed in connection with Austen's contemporary, the Gothic novelist Ann Radcliffe, virtually every woman who took up the pen in the later eighteenth and early nineteenth centuries seems to have been able to write them without blinking. Austen is in this respect one of the greatest of masters. Witness the following—describing Emma's preening self-delight at convincing Harriet that Harriet is admired by Mr. Elton:

> Emma could not feel a doubt of having given Harriet's fancy a proper direction and raised the gratitude of her young vanity to a very good purpose, for she found her decidedly more sensible than before of Mr. Elton's being a remarkably handsome man, with most agreeable manners; and as she had no hesitation in following up the assurance of his admiration, by agreeable hints, she was soon pretty confident of creating as much liking on Harriet's side, as there could be any occasion for. (pp. 36–37)

Or this, describing Elton's own satisfaction when after having been refused by Emma (and disdaining the unfortunate Harriet) he succeeds in finding a bride at Bath:

> The charming Augusta Hawkins, in addition to all the usual advantages of perfect beauty and merit, was in possession of an independent fortune, of so many thousands as would always be called ten; a point of some dignity, as well as some convenience: the story told well; he had not thrown himself away—he had gained a woman of 10,000*l.* or thereabouts; and he had gained her with such delightful rapidity—the first hour of introduction had been so very soon followed by distinguishing notice; the history which he had to give Mrs. Cole of the rise and progress of the affair was so glorious—the steps so quick, from the accidental rencontre, to the dinner at Mr. Green's, and the party at Mrs. Brown's—smiles and blushes rising in importance—with consciousness and agitation richly scattered—the lady had been so easily impressed—so sweetly disposed—had in short, to use a most intelligible phrase, been so very ready to have him, that vanity and prudence were equally contented. (pp. 162–63)

To get to the end of one of these beautiful and ingenious sentences—the punctuation alone would repay a study—is to relive, one might argue, the primal satisfaction of learning to read itself. If the sign of the great stylist is that she makes it all look easy, in mastering Austen's intricate syntax, we re-create that moment when it first became easy for us: when the marks on the page first began to "make sense," the words began to form, and we found our way into the magic of the book.

Yet on another level *Emma* is itself a puzzle that the reader, with Austen's help, successfully "works out." Much has been made of the novel's supposed resemblance to a detective story, and there are indeed certain superficial similarities. Like the writer of a good mystery, Austen is careful to withhold important facts from us when it suits her purposes: she is adept at controlling the flow of information both inside the novel and out. Because we see things almost entirely from Emma's point of view, we are restricted in one sense to knowing only what *she* knows. As events unfold, we are forced—as she is—to read between the lines for "clues" about other characters' motives and desires. Most strikingly, when it comes to the central enigma of the plot—the precise nature of the relationship between Frank Churchill and the elusive Jane Fairfax—we know as little about it as Emma herself does, until quite late in the novel.

Or do we? The detective story may to some degree be a false analogy, for, insofar as the reader is concerned, no "mystery" ever stays a mystery in the novel for very long. There is very little real suspense in *Emma*: from the start we know—or intuit—far more than we ever would in any ordinary mystery. We certainly know more than the self-blinded Emma does. It must be a colossally incompetent reader who misses, for example, that Mr. Elton does not in any way pine for Harriet Smith; or that Frank Churchill and Jane Fairfax are in some manner romantically involved; or indeed that Emma herself—for all of her speeches on the joys of a single life—is in love with Mr. Knightley. (Is there anyone who does not instantly guess that it is Frank who sends Jane the anonymous gift of the Broadwood fortepiano?) We cannot predict exactly how matters will fall out, but the sensation of understanding-in-advance is so strong that even as the narrative yields up its "secrets," we have a sense of having known them all along.

Austen here again, one might say, flatters our readerly vanity. She does so through the use of irony, which is always flattering to the person at whom it is directed. (Irony in prose is invariably a compliment paid to the reader's intelligence.) We are in on the joke, of course, from the start: Emma, the brilliant one, the genius of Hartfield, does not understand. But the joke is conveyed obliquely, through sophisticated authorial signals—like those glances of communion that pass between two people in a crowded room who understand each other perfectly. Emma's first great mistake—persuading Harriet to refuse Robert Martin and hold out for Mr. Elton—is crucial here: Austen uses the episode to establish what quickly becomes a kind of complicity with the reader. For without ever criticizing her directly, Austen nonetheless makes us acutely aware of the frailty of Emma's judgments. There is Harriet's timid yet palpable regret; there is Knightley's rather more abrupt disapproval—which he makes known to Emma in one of those queer, awkward scenes between them that fairly buzz with sexual tension; there is Elton's own somewhat suspect behavior. (When Elton picks up a little sketch by Emma of Harriet so he can take it to be framed in London— mooning delicately over the "precious deposit" (p. 43)—one already fears the worst.) When the narrator blandly observes after Emma and Mr. Knightley quarrel over Harriet that "[Emma] was sorry, but could not repent" and that "on the contrary, her plans and proceedings were more and more justified, and endeared to her by the general appearances of the next few days," one cannot help but read in the brimming irony: O foolish one!

Our vanity is engaged because we can almost hear Austen addressing us sotto voce: you and I know just how *wrong* Emma is. Intensifying the feeling of pleasure is in turn the fact of Emma's own intelligence and undeniable (if erratic) moral charm. Austen's novel would not be half so delightful were it retitled *Harriet* and told from Harriet Smith's somewhat befuddled point of view. Gaffes committed by the unintelligent do not, on the whole, amuse us for very long: the spectacle of human error, unenlivened by mental energy, quickly becomes merely tedious or depressing. What truly entertains, on the contrary, is the folly of the superior individual—and the more exorbitant the folly the better. We enjoy Emma because she is smart and she is good; but we positively dote on her mistakes, because they allow *us* to feel superior. At moments of maximum comic absurdity—Emma's farcical coach ride with Mr. Elton, for example, or the scene in which the besotted Harriet shares with Emma her precious "relicks" of Frank Churchill (a grubby sticking plaster and a piece of an old pencil "without any lead")—we seem to gaze down at Austen's heroine from some lofty and pleasant comic Olympus.

And yet the pleasures of *Emma* are not just of a puzzle-solving or interpretative nature. Great masterpieces do not become so merely by catering to readerly self-regard. Indeed, longtime admirers of Austen may object to my characterization of the novel here as already too cynical by far—the sort of analysis that Emma herself, in one of her more sprightly and irritating moods, might lay out before a harrumphing Knightley. Can it indeed be fair to say that Austen's sole intention in *Emma* is to flatter us? Or that her celebrated artistic method can be reduced to a kind of subliminal conniving with the reader? Certainly, within the novel, characters who form "secret understandings" of this sort seem to evoke Austen's contempt, Frank Churchill and Jane Fairfax being only the most glaring case in point. In all of her novels, though perhaps most conspicuously in *Emma* and *Mansfield Park*, Austen shows herself deeply suspicious of couples who shut out the rest of the world or pretend to a kind of superior knowledge. She is hostile toward antisocial human pairings—couples who relate only to one another and contribute nothing to a common good. (Marriages in her novels are deemed good to the extent that they *integrate* the couple involved into the larger social community in which the marriage takes place.) To the degree that Frank and Jane set themselves apart as what one might call a "privileged couple"—as The Two Who Know Better, a pair with a secret—they are unlikable; and it is questionable whether they are ever really rehabilitated, even at the end of the novel, after they have revealed their clandestine alliance and apologized for it. (Austen, we notice, carefully removes them from Highbury before staging her happy closing scenes.) If in aligning ourselves imaginatively with Austen, we end up no better than Frank and Jane, or worse yet, the vainglorious Mr. and Mrs. Elton—another of *Emma*'s "knowing" twosomes—we may rightly feel some confusion about Austen's intentions.

A distinction might be made here between knowingness and what used (in simpler days) to be called wisdom. *Emma* has its knowing couples, but it also has its wise couples—or at least its couples on the way to becoming wise. Emma and Knightley are the most important among the potentially "wise couples," of course, though Austen also presents the recently married Mr. and Mrs. Weston (Frank's father and Emma's beloved former governess, Miss Taylor) in a similarly favorable light. Characterizing each of these "wise" pairings is a kind of positive dynamism: not only do the partners ultimately bring out the best in each other—Emma and Knightley will both be improved by their relationship—their bond in some fashion proves beneficial to the fictional world as a whole. They bring happiness to others as well as to themselves. The most striking proof of this moral synergy occurs at the end of the novel when Emma and her new husband—at some expense to their own privacy and comfort—decide not to move to Mr. Knightley's house, Donwell, but to stay at Hartfield so as not to discompose Emma's father, the invalid Mr. Woodhouse. But Austen hints at it earlier too, as in the scene in which Emma and Mr. Knightley end their argument over Harriet Smith by playing together with the infant daughter of John and Isabella Knightley (p. 89). Throughout *Emma* infants and children will figure as living emblems of a world beyond the self. Those who care for them are honored. Thus when we see Emma and Knightley here together, taking turns at delighting a happy little eight-month-old girl—he will at one point take the baby from Emma's arms "with all the unceremoniousness of perfect amity"—we have an intimation indeed of the larger good their union portends.

The author/reader relationship Austen aims to establish in *Emma* might be depicted as one of these fruitful, outward-looking couplings. Like most writers of the late eighteenth and early nineteenth centuries, Austen believed in the moral efficacy of art—that the best prose fiction might improve its readers and be a force for social good. One need only recollect the famous passage from *Northanger Abbey* (1797–98) in which she defends the novel of her age as that "species of composition" in which "the greatest powers of mind are displayed, in which the most thorough knowledge of human nature, the happiest delineation of its varieties, the liveliest effusions of wit and humour are conveyed to the world in the best chosen language" to recognize her faith in the ultimate seriousness of literary endeavor. Art, for Austen, has an important role to play in civilization; it is precisely through art that a civilization represents to itself—and reflects upon—its most cherished values and ideals. At the heart of her conception of the novel, thus, is a notion of sociability: to read a novel is to take part—not in some segregating, secret society of two—but in a larger cultural conversation.

What this comes down to for the reader of *Emma* is the illusion of being included in a palpably human world. For all that we share in Austen's own comic viewpoint and relish our moments of ironic connection with her, we also feel ourselves profoundly involved in Emma's destiny and that of the little community in which she lives and moves. The ironic distance set up between reader and character is never so great as to become estranging; on the contrary, we may often feel strangely, even passionately, absorbed into the heroine's mental and physical life. For all of its verbal sophistication, *Emma* has to be one of the least alienating fictions ever written. Reading it, we are constantly getting lassooed by feeling. Perhaps the greatest triumph of Austen's method is that without ever compromising her satiric spirit, or sacrificing any of those "lively effusions of wit and humour" that so distinguish her style, she is able to produce such consistently powerful emotional effects.

The celebrated Box Hill episode might be taken as a case in point. It is often thought to be the height of critical naïveté to say one "identifies" with a character, or that a scene in a novel overpowers one with its air of reality. Yet how else to describe this episode—unquestionably one of the most renowned in the history of English fiction? From the weather (hot, dulling, and uncomfortable) to the curious disaffection of the characters, who wander about here in a state of stale, almost Beckett-like boredom and disconnection, Austen captures the very essence of a social occasion gone wrong:

> Nothing was wanting but to be happy when they got there. Seven miles were travelled in expectation of enjoyment, and every body had a burst of admiration on first arriving; but in the general amount of the day there was deficiency. There was a languor, a want of spirits, a want of union, which could not be got over. They separated too much into parties. The Eltons walked together; Mr. Knightley took charge of Miss Bates and Jane; and Emma and Harriet belonged to Frank Churchill. And Mr. Weston tried, in vain, to make them harmonize better. It seemed at first an accidental division, but it never materially varied. Mr. and Mrs. Elton, indeed, showed no unwillingness to mix, and be as agreeable as they could: but during the two whole hours that were spent on the hill, there seemed a principle of separation, between the other parties, too strong for any fine prospects, or any cold collation, or any cheerful Mr. Weston, to remove. (p. 332)

One's uneasiness grows as the strange spirit of malice in the air seems to lodge itself in Emma, who becomes callous and hysterical, flirting unpleasantly with Frank: "She laughed because she was disappointed; and though she liked him for his attentions, and thought them all, whether in friendship, admiration, or playfulness, extremely judicious, they were not winning back her heart" (p. 333). When she flares out against Miss Bates with the famous, saddening insult, one is acutely embarrassed for her; for who has not, at some time or other, behaved so appallingly? Finally, after Mr. Knightley reproaches her and she climbs into the carriage with Harriet to go home—after this botched, interminable day—we recognize all too well her ache of self-disgust and the hot pressure of tears about to fall:

> Time did not compose her. As she reflected more, she seemed but to feel it more. She never had been so depressed. Happily it was not necessary to speak. There was only Harriet, who seemed not in spirits herself, fagged, and very willing to be silent; and Emma felt the tears running down her cheeks almost all the way home, without being at any trouble to check them, extraordinary as they were. (pp. 340–41)

Tears are a staple in eighteenth-century sentimental fiction; the novels of Austen's precursors, Samuel Richardson, Frances Burney, Charlotte Smith, and Ann Radcliffe, are full of weeping, labile heroines. Yet there is something in these particular searing droplets—something so expressive of pain, exhaustion, and sheer wretchedness—one is tempted to call them the first real female tears shed in English literature.

What is disturbing about the Box Hill episode is that it intimates, momentarily, a world in disorder, and a "principle of separation" at work in human affairs. For an instant civility itself seems to break down and the novel verges on nightmare. (Emma's baiting of Miss Bates, witnessed by a group of unwilling yet fascinated onlookers, bears more than a passing resemblance to the scapegoating rituals of primitive societies, in which the weakest member of the group is selected for sacrifice.) Nor does Emma's own embarrassment and remorse do much—at least at first—to alter the mood. As Emma is taken off in the carriage, more miserable than "at any circumstance in her life," we sense Austen tapping into certain primal human fears—of abandonment, of violent expulsion from the group, of being sent away to die.

Yet the anxiety here is temporary, of course: Emma will make it up to Miss Bates; Mr. Knightley will forgive her; the reader's spirits will be solaced and refreshed. Indeed, in the few remaining chapters of the novel, other sources of narrative tension quickly dissipate: Frank and Jane's union is discovered and accepted; Emma establishes a proper friendship with Jane; Harriet is reconciled with Robert Martin and agrees to marry him after all; Mr. Knightley proposes to Emma. The weather itself will participate in the general renovation, turning—in classic Austen fashion—from dismal to delightful on the very afternoon that Knightley comes to propose:

> The weather [had] continued much the same all the following morning; and the same loneliness, and the same melancholy, seemed to reign at

Hartfield—but in the afternoon it cleared; the wind changed to a softer quarter; the clouds were carried off; the sun appeared; it was summer again. (p. 384)

Which brings us to the deepest source of pleasure in *Emma*: its profoundly therapeutic emotional rhythm. Fears are raised in the novel—dangers threatened—only to be assuaged through a process of cathartic recovery and regeneration. The fictional world exhibits a constant predisposition to right itself—to restabilize quickly, after moments of shock or disequilibrium. "There does seem to be a something in the air of Hartfield," Emma says at one point, "which gives love exactly the right direction, and sends it into the very channel where it ought to flow" (p. 68). This is a world that reassures us with its underlying stability, that refuses to abandon us to our own worst imaginings. Like Emma herself, we are never left alone for long.

There is nothing abstract or sentimental about this cathartic process. And here one's disagreement with Charlotte Brontë must be total. In charging in her famous attack on *Emma* that Austen ignored "the unseen seat of Life and the sentient target of death"—the body and its passions—Brontë's goal was unmistakably self-serving: to boost her own art at the expense of Austen's. Austen, she suggested, knew nothing of the world of physical sensation or what "the blood rushes through." Yet one cannot help but feel an element of denial here, as if Brontë did not wish to recognize how closely Austen's fiction in fact *resembled* her own, precisely in its underlying existential concerns. For in her own tactful, untheatrical way, Austen is as preoccupied with the body as Brontë is. (As Rebecca West put it: "There are those who are deluded by the decorousness of [Austen's] manner, by the fact that her virgins are so virginal that they are unaware of their virginity, into thinking she is ignorant of passion. But look through the lattice-work of her neat sentences, joined together with the bright nails of craftmanship, painted with the gay varnish of wit, and you will see women haggard with desire or triumphant with love."[5]) Quite as much as *Jane Eyre* or *Villette, Emma* might be described as a "book of the body" and its deepest satisfactions, paradoxically, as kinesthetic ones.

I have mentioned the strange physical immediacy of the Box Hill scene— how we seem here to be penetrated by Emma's own emotions, by her own poignant fantasies of abandonment and loss. Losing or being abandoned by a person one loves is one of the recurrent *physical* anxieties operating under the surface in *Emma*; a fear of being cast off or ignored unites, in one way or another, virtually all of its characters. This is a world, after all, full of motherless or unmothered children. Neither Emma, Frank, Jane, nor Harriet has a living female parent (or one who can be acknowledged); all four are half-orphans at the very least. Nor are the various maternal surrogates in the novel entirely dependable. In the very opening pages, we recall, Emma herself is suffering from the loss of her dear Miss Taylor, who has married Mr. Weston and gone to live with him at Randalls:

> It was Miss Taylor's loss which first brought grief. It was on the wedding-day of this beloved friend that Emma first sat in mournful thought of any continuance. The wedding over and the bride-people gone, her father and herself were left to dine together, with no prospect of a third to cheer a long evening. Her father composed himself to sleep after dinner, as usual, and she had then only to sit and think of what she had lost. (p. 4)

Certainly, much of Emma's hectic behavior in the early part of the novel—including the silly, unequal crush on Harriet Smith—can be read as a kind of obsessive-compulsive effort to fill the maternal space left by Miss Taylor. Emma's lonely predicament is in turn mirrored in Harriet's and Jane's. Harriet, though a "parlour-boarder" still at Mrs. Goddard's school, faces the inevitable day when she will have to leave; her threatened kidnapping by Gypsies (pp. 300–301) simply underscores her motherless status. And Jane Fairfax, though a welcome guest at her impoverished aunt Bates's, has no better prospect—or so it would seem for much of the novel—than of spending her life as an underpaid governess in some isolated country house, caring for someone else's neglected children. (Austen was at least as hard-nosed as Brontë about the social and economic difficulties faced by women without husbands.)

And yet this is a world in which no deprivation is permanent, and comfort not long in arriving. There is mothering, even in the absence of actual mothers. It is as if the well-being of Highbury's inhabitants were regulated by some benevolent unseen power, a kind of nurturing Providence, balancing longing with possibility. Knightley calls Frank Churchill a "favourite of fortune" (p. 388), but all of *Emma*'s characters seem favored in this way, even the more squalid ones. Even the outrageous Mrs. Elton lands on her feet at the end of the novel: she has the match she deserves in the form of Mr. Elton, and can also look forward to much happy social skirmishing with the future Mrs. Knightley. (The developing relationship between Emma and Mrs. Elton is surely the model for that between Lucia and Miss Mapp, the dueling doyennes of Tilling, in the twentieth-century comic novelist E. F. Benson's ineffable *Mapp and Lucia* series.) There is something profoundly touching in this: Austen's tender embrace of all her characters, no matter how wayward.

One wants to call such magnanimity Shakespearean, and a connection between Austen's novel and Shakespearean comedy has often been drawn—most recently by Jocelyn Harris, who in a brilliant analysis of *Emma* finds in it a subtle reworking of elements from *A Midsummer Night's Dream*.[6] Austen organizes her chronology so as to follow Shakespearean precedent: the Box Hill episode, the novel's central moment of comic chaos and bewilderment, falls exactly on Midsummer's Day. And Austen's characters bear a shifting, sometimes phantasmagorical resemblance to Shakespeare's. Emma is at times like a new Titania, ruling over Highbury with queenly aplomb (with Knightley as her argumentative Oberon); and at other times like Bottom, comically mistaking every object for something it isn't. Frank Churchill is a mischief maker like Puck, but so too again is Emma: when she at last realizes how much she loves Mr. Knightley ("It darted through her, with the speed of an arrow, that Mr. Knightley must marry no one but herself!" [p. 370]), she is like a female Puck-Cupid, shot in the heart by one of her own darts. But what secures the connection most thoroughly is perhaps the almost visceral feeling of *safety*—of freedom from anxiety—that each work instills. As long as we remain within *Emma*'s magic circle, we may feel, no lasting evil can befall us, for like Bottom and Titania we inhabit, metaphorically speaking, a kind of enchanted ground.

This feeling of being protected even as one reads has everything to do, it seems to me, with a particular pattern of imagery at work throughout the novel. I mentioned earlier the importance of infants and children in *Emma*. Emma's little nieces and nephews—the five children of her sister Isabella and Knightley's brother John—appear in the background in numerous scenes; at the end of the novel, Emma's friend Mrs. Weston has just given birth to a little girl. A way of characterizing the benevolent world of the novel might be to say that this is a world in which children are never dropped. They may be playfully flung in the air—Mr. Knightley, as the horrified Mr. Woodhouse observes, likes to greet his little nephews and nieces by "[tossing] them up to the ceiling in a very frightful way"—but they are always caught (p. 74). Indeed—as Emma says, comforting her father—"there is nothing they like so much."[7] In turn, when it is time to sleep, *Emma*'s infants slumber peacefully, with the adults who care for them close by. One of the sketches Emma shows Mr. Elton early in the novel, as she prepares to draw Harriet, is of her baby nephew George, "sleeping on the sofa" with his head "nestled down . . . most conveniently" (p. 40).

The fictional world constantly adjusts itself so as to keep its babies comfortable. Hunger will be unknown to them, and no cold—not even a draught—will ever disturb their profound relaxation. We see this adjusting mechanism at work most comically, of course, in the scenes involving the novel's most demanding baby—Emma's own father, Mr. Woodhouse. I have said little about Mr. Woodhouse up to this point, but he is in some ways *Emma*'s emblematic character: the Child who is also (perhaps) the Reader. Is he a human being? At times—with his tiny shut eyes, burrowing behavior, and mewling, open mouth—he seems more like a little animal, something out of children's fiction, a kind of infantile Squirrel Nutkin, craving gruel and succour. As in the story of the Three Bears, everything around him has to be "just right"—the temperature of the beloved gruel, the precise amount of fresh air coming into the room, his daughter's erotic life. He is a bit of a monster—selfish as well as feebleminded—and one feels sorry for everyone who has to put up with him.

But even this most fretful of babies will be pacified. His daughters coddle him—the gruel will always be prepared exactly to his liking, "thin, but not too thin" (p. 95); he has a doctor, Perry, ready to attend him at any moment. In an age without thermostats, his friends and relations improvise a kind of climate control around him—constantly checking on his proximity to fireplaces and the possibility of draughts. With his shawls carefully disposed about him, Mr. Woodhouse inhabits his own artificial weather system. Most important, even if he fails to grow up, and one suspects he won't, he will never be left—ever. If Emma's real goodness is known to us (even in the difficult days of her folly) because she is unfailingly kind to her father, her decision to stay with him at the end of the novel confirms it. Her lover too knows what has to be done with a problematic child-father. Like the perfect fantasy-parents that they are, the new Mr. and Mrs. Knightley simply refuse to drop him.

The reader in turn feels caught and safely held. It is hardly a coincidence that E. M. Forster, an ardent Austen admirer, once compared the experience of reading *Emma* to a kind of wordless, infantile gratification.

> I am a Jane Austenite, and therefore slightly imbecile about Jane Austen. My fatuous expression and airs of personal immunity—how ill they set on the face, say, of a Stevensonian! But Jane Austen is so different. She is my favourite author! I read and re-read, the mouth open and the mind closed. Shut up in measureless content, I greet her by the name of most kind hostess, while criticism slumbers.[8]

For we too sense *Emma's* physical world adjusting itself around us. Objects end up in their rightful places; rooms arrange themselves—seem magically to shrink or expand—to fit our needs. The proportions, in the end, are always "just right." Thus at the Coles' dinner party, where Emma gossips with Frank about Jane Fairfax, "every corner dish was placed exactly right" (p. 196). For Frank Churchill's dancing party, the Westons' house Randalls seems too small; the Crown Inn, however, with its slightly larger rooms, is just the "perfect" size (p. 228). Once the flow of cooling air through the window sashes is stabilized, balancing the pleasant warmth of the fire, everything is indeed "as it should be" (p. 287).

Human beings too seem to be perfectly in scale: Mr. Elton, neither too tall nor too short, "is just the happy medium" (p. 156), and Jane Fairfax likewise "a most becoming medium, between fat and thin" (p. 149). The differing reactions evoked by certain individuals will be regularized. Says Emma to Mr. Knightley, before Frank Churchill comes on the scene, "We are both prejudiced; you against,

I for him; and we have no chance of agreeing till he is really here" (p. 136)—which is of course what happens. Cognitive dissonances will be resolved, disparities smoothed out. Emma herself resolves differences. Arriving at the Westons' with her friends and relatives for a dinner party, she is herself a happy medium, neither obsequious nor sullen, with features expressing exactly who she is:

> Some change of countenance was necessary for each gentleman as they walked into Mrs. Weston's drawing-room;—Mr. Elton must compose his joyous looks, and Mr. John Knightley disperse his ill-humour. Mr. Elton must smile less, and Mr. Knightley more, to fit them for the place.—Emma only might be as nature prompted, and shew herself just as happy as she was. (p. 105)

Most important, here and elsewhere, we have a sense of looking into the right face, and of being looked at in turn. The glances of love and recognition that pass between Emma and Knightley (surely among the most erotically satisfying in all of English fiction) seem mysteriously to take us in as well. "Emma had no opportunity of speaking to Mr. Knightley till after supper; but, when they were all in the ball-room again, her eyes invited him irresistibly to come to her and be thanked" (p. 297). Nothing can destroy this circuit of communication: angry with Emma over Miss Bates, Mr. Knightley looks briefly "unlike himself," yet on hearing of Emma's visit to her, "It seemed as if there were an instantaneous impression in her favour, as if his eyes received the truth from her's, and all that had passed of good in her feelings were at once caught and honoured" (p. 349). For in such looking lies a deep mutual pleasure: "He stopped in his earnestness to look the question, and the expression of his eyes overpowered her" (p. 390).

Austen, as Forster notes, is indeed a "most kind hostess," concerned in all things with our delight and gratification. Like a good parent, she does not mind replaying things with us, going back a bit in time and space, helping us sense again, often in the most literal way, what it meant to be seen and held. As Mr. Knightley says to Emma at one point: "we all feel the influence of a something beyond common civility in our personal intercourse with each other—a something more early implanted" (pp. 257–58). Yet for all its atavisms, Austen's world is not like Freud's, tragically weighted with the possibility of permanent neurosis. On the contrary, it is more like the world imagined by the British psychoanalyst D. W. Winnicott—a therapeutic world, a world in which cures are possible, a "good enough" world. *Emma* is an allegory about physical and psychic renewal. It reassures and relieves. It is easy enough to disdain works of literature that console in this way: pleasure of such a fundamental kind is too much for many people to handle. For others, however, Austen's "good enough" world is likely to remain—for some time—a world yet worth living in.

notes

1. Letter to W. S. Williams, Apr. 12, 1850. Reprinted in Brian C. Southam, ed., *Jane Austen: The Critical Heritage* (London and New York: Routledge and Kegan Paul, 1968), vol. 1, 127–28.

2. Quoted in J. David Grey, A. Walton Litz, and Brian Southam, eds., *The Jane Austen Companion* (New York: Macmillan, 1986), 96, 240.

3. "Jane Austen," in Virginia Woolf, *The Essays of Virginia Woolf,* ed. Andrew McNeillie (London: Hogarth Press, 1987), vol. 2, 12.

4. Jane Austen, *Emma*, ed. James Kinsley (Oxford and New York: Oxford University Press, 1995), 4. All subsequent references are to this edition. Page numbers are noted parenthetically.

5. From *The Strange Necessity* (London, 1928), 263–64; reprinted in Southam, *Austen: The Critical Heritage*, vol. 1, 290–91.

6. Jocelyn Harris, *Jane Austen's Art of Memory* (Cambridge: Cambridge University Press, 1989), 169–87.

7. Babies and children are not the only ones in Jane Austen's novels to enjoy the sensation of being caught and held. Jane Fairfax, or so Emma learns from Frank Churchill, once started to fall overboard at a "water-party" at Weymouth, but was happily caught in time by Mr. Dixon (195). And one recollects Louisa Musgrove's curious, almost sexual pleasure, in *Persuasion*, in being "jumped down" stiles and steps by Captain Wentworth: "the sensation was delightful to her."

8. Quoted in Grey et al., eds., *Jane Austen Companion*, 241.

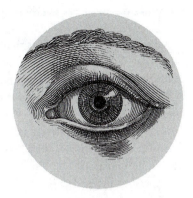

4
ANN RADCLIFFE'S
THE MYSTERIES OF UDOLPHO

Perhaps no work in the history of English fiction has been more often caricatured—trivialized, misread, remade as hearsay—than Ann Radcliffe's late-eighteenth-century Gothic classic *The Mysteries of Udolpho*. Some readers, indeed, will know Radcliffe's novel *only* as hearsay: as that delightfully "horrid" book—full of castles and crypts and murdered wives—pressed upon Catherine Morland, the gullible young heroine of Jane Austen's *Northanger Abbey* (1817), by her Bath friend Isabella Thorpe. After consuming the book in a great voluptuous binge, the impressionable Catherine begins to see the everyday world around her as a kind of Gothic stage set against which friends and acquaintances metamorphose—absurdly—into outsized Radcliffean villains and victims. The results are amusing: *Northanger Abbey* remains one of the great spoofs on reading-as-hallucination. But *Udolpho* itself is mere pretext—the intertextual cliché, or *thing already known*, upon which Austen builds her chic comedy of misapprehension.

How well do we really know *The Mysteries of Udolpho*? We may be able to recite the familiar commonplaces: that it is the greatest (or at least most famous) of Gothic romances; that it's got an archetypal "Gothic villain" (the nasty Montoni); that it's loaded with exotic scenery; that its heroine, a victim of "sensibility," faints a lot. We may even venture the opinion that it's a bit of a silly book too—or at least so everyone says. Yet even while reciting, the conscientious reader—anyone who reads what Radcliffe really wrote—must feel a twinge of bad faith. For none of the clichés quite seems to get at it: the sheer capacious strangeness of the work before us. *Udolpho* has a way of escaping critical formulas: it's always bigger and baggier and more uncanny than one thought it was. No trite summing-up can capture the novel's dreamy, surreal flow of incident, the odd, mediumistic shifts through space and time, the often bewildering vagaries in Radcliffe's handling of plot, character, and scene. To say what *Udolpho* "is" is inevitably to reduce it.

Consider the very notion that it is a "Gothic" fiction. If by "Gothic" we mean that *The Mysteries of Udolpho* caters in parts to a decadent late-eighteenth-century taste for things gloomy, macabre, and medieval, then Gothic it certainly is. Horace Walpole had ushered the Gothic craze into England thirty years earlier with *The Castle of Otranto* (1764), a short and often campy tale of usurpation, incest, and accidental child murder in twelfth-century Sicily. While thin-seeming to most modern readers, Walpole's dire little Italian romance undoubtedly impressed Radcliffe greatly. In the second volume of *Udolpho,* when the rapacious brigand-chieftain Montoni threatens Emily St. Aubert, his beautiful orphaned niece, with "remorseless vengeance" for refusing to sign over to him the Gascon estates she has inherited from her father, the exorbitantly melodramatic situation is straight out of *Otranto's* overheated pages. Likewise, the grim castle in the Apennines in which Emily is held captive—full of dungeons and crypts, blood-spattered walls, and dank, labyrinthine passageways—is a crumbling medieval fortress in the Walpolean mode.

In the crucial matter of architecture Radcliffe might even be said to improve upon the prototype. While fearsome to its inhabitants, *Otranto's* eponymous castle is a curiously indistinct and unmemorable edifice, a mere cardboard surround for the novel's frenetic, artificial chain of action. The Castle of Udolpho, however, is a full-blown Gothic pile, glowering, savage, and immense—as the heroine discovers on glimpsing it first from afar:

> Emily gazed with melancholy awe upon the castle, which she understood to be Montoni's; for, though it was now lighted up by the setting sun, the gothic greatness of its features, and its mouldering walls of dark grey stone, rendered it a gloomy and sublime object. As she gazed, the light died away on its walls, leaving a melancholy purple tint, which spread deeper and deeper, as thin vapour crept up the mountain, while the battlements above were still tipped with splendour. From those too, the rays soon faded, and the whole edifice was invested with the solemn duskiness of evening. Silent, lonely and sublime, it seemed to stand the sovereign of the scene, and to frown defiance on all, who dared to invade its solitary reign.[1]

With so glorious and horrible a structure as part of the fictional landscape, it is no wonder that so many of *Udolpho's* readers have seen the various events taking place in and around the castle—the terrorizing of Emily by assorted ruffians, the cruel torment of her aunt, who is tricked into marriage with Montoni and ends up as his starving victim, or the celebrated episode of the black veil, in which Emily, exploring a mysterious abandoned chamber, discovers under a veil something too "ghastly" to be described (pp. 248–49)—as the defining events of the novel itself.

And yet to label *The Mysteries of Udolpho* "Gothic" and leave it at that would be a mistake. Great swatches of the text—too much of it to ignore—have little to do with Montoni or his villainies. As the first-time reader will discover, the heroine doesn't even hear about Udolpho, let alone pass through its hoary precincts, for almost two hundred pages, a good third of the way into the novel. Instead Radcliffe devotes her entire first volume to a bizarre quasi travelogue: the fantastically elaborated account of a "tour" that Emily and her father, the noble but ailing St. Aubert, take through Languedoc and the Pyrenees. While important events in the plot transpire in the course of their wanderings—Emily meets the handsome huntsman, Valancourt, with whom she will fall in love, St. Aubert eventually dies and is buried at the convent of St. Clair—the narrative repeatedly dissolves into extended, diffuse, often phantasmagoric descriptions of landscape:

> It was evening when they descended the lower alps, that bind Roussillon, and form a majestic barrier round that charming country, leaving it only on the east to the Mediterranean. The gay tints of cultivation once more beautified the landscape; for the lowlands were covered with the richest hues, which a luxuriant climate, and an industrious people can awaken into life. Groves of lemon and orange perfumed the air, their ripe fruit glowing among the foliage; while, sloping to the plains, extensive vineyards spread their treasures. Beyond these, woods and pastures, and mingled towns and hamlets stretched towards the sea, on whose bright surface gleamed many a distant sail; while, over the whole scene, was diffused the purple glow of the evening. (p. 55)

At moments like this (and there are many) the novel seems hypnotized by the possibility of *not* becoming a Gothic novel—of remaining instead in a world of beautiful, unfolding description. Transported by the hallucinatory "charms" of nature, Emily and her friends may in turn remind us of moon walkers, traveling in endless slow motion through a mauve-tinted dusk.

When Montoni appears on the scene near the end of volume 1 and takes Emily and her aunt (whom he has just married) to Venice, this sense of psychic digression—of the novel refusing to become itself—persists. Radcliffe's images of the city, to which Byron would pay homage in *Childe Harold's Pilgrimage*, shimmer, it is true, in visionary light:

> Nothing could exceed Emily's admiration of her first view of Venice with islets, palaces, and towers rising out of the sea, whose clear surface reflected the tremulous picture in all its colours. The sun, sinking in the west, tinted the waves and the lofty mountains of Friuli, which skirt the northern shores of the Adriatic, with a saffron glow, while on the marble porticos and colonnades of St. Mark were thrown the rich lights and shades of evening. As they glided on, the grander features of this city ap-

peared more distinctly: its terraces, crowned with airy yet majestic fabrics, touched, as they now were, with the splendour of the setting sun, appeared as if they been called up from the ocean by the wand of an enchanter, rather than reared by mortal hands. (p. 175)

Yet as we float with Emily and her party down the Grand Canal, past gleaming Palladian villas and gay masqueraders disporting on balconies, we are far from any realm of medieval horrors. Though *Udolpho* is set in 1584, blatant anachronisms abound here—from the laughing revelers "drinking coffee" at open-air cafés to the glittering "casinos" to which Montoni and his henchmen retire during their sojourn in the city. These anachronisms can be explained: having never visited Venice (or any other of the exotic places depicted in her novel), Radcliffe was forced to rely for local color on contemporary travel books such as Hester Thrale Piozzi's *Observations and Reflections Made in the Course of a Journey through France, Italy and Germany* (1789). What she ends up giving us is the elegant Venice of Canaletto and Goldoni. But the explanation cannot alter one's sense of a generic violation. When Emily is shown delicately imbibing "collations of fruits and ice" and hearkening with pleasure to the *canzonetti* of passing gondoliers, the novel seems perversely anti-Gothic in mode: luminous, neoclassical, even oddly comic, as in the scenes between her and an Italian would-be suitor, the lute-plucking Count Morano.

And perhaps most odd, even in the Udolpho section itself, the novel is not always as "Gothic" as it might be. The castle, it is true, is a place of bloodshed and mayhem—Montoni is waging a war against rival robber bands and faces a constant threat of rebellion among his own forces—but Emily's own physical safety, paradoxically, is never really in question. Although she fears sexual violation (or worse) at his hands, Montoni's interest in her is more economic than libidinal: he simply wants her money. Even then, he seems too preoccupied with his own affairs to give her much thought. (She is left alone in her room in the castle for pages and pages.) When he does fix his attention on her, he functions more as protector than ravisher. Twice he rescues her from potential kidnappers, the spurned Count Morano (pp. 266–67) and the "ruffianly" porter Barnardine (pp. 348–49). And toward the end of the Udolpho sojourn, he actually sends her *out* of the castle for her own safety. While he and his troops clash with rampaging condottieri Emily is happily ensconced, as if on a Club Med vacation, in a pleasant Tuscan cottage near the Mediterranean coast, surrounded by woods and vineyards and purling streams (p. 413). So amusingly incongruous is this interlude (Radcliffe spends two whole chapters on it) that it is no wonder that critics have never known what to do with it.

A similar point might be made about the long concluding section of the novel. If in its first two thirds, *Udolpho* seems not always to know it is a Gothic novel, in its last third—after Emily escapes (rather easily and anticlimactically) from Montoni and his minions and finds safety at Château-le-Blanc, the estate of the benevolent Count De Villefort—it seems to forget it ever was one. "Gothic" passages can of course be found here, the most famous being when Emily and Dorothée, the count's ancient housekeeper, venture into an unused bedchamber in which the chateau's former mistress, the Marchioness of Villeroi, died some years before. Seeing a pall on the bed appear to move by itself and "the apparition of a human countenance" rising above it, the two women flee in terror, thinking the room haunted (pp. 535–36). Only later will it be revealed—after the servant Ludovico mysteriously disappears from the same room, only to appear again unharmed a week or two later—that pirates have been using the room (which has a secret tunnel to the outside) as a storage place for smuggled goods. In a classic instance of the Radcliffean "explained supernatural," Emily learns that it was these same pirates, pretending to be ghosts, who moved the pall to frighten her and Dorothée away (p. 633).

Yet here too Radcliffe unhinges stereotypes: by shifting toward outright satire. At times it is almost as if she were trying to write in advance of Austen her own version of *Northanger Abbey*. Despite its "haunted" chamber, Château-le-Blanc turns out to be more English-Neoclassical than Gothic-Hideous in style; though it has an ancient turret and a Gothic wing, the greater part of it is "light and airy" like a Georgian country house (p. 472). And Henri and Blanche de Villefort, the count's grown-up children, curiously prefigure Henry and Eleanor Tilney, the witty brother and sister who befriend the credulous Catherine Morland in Austen's novel. Like his Tilney namesake, Henri de Villefort has the teasing manner we associate with Austen heroes; and Blanche, who has just left a convent, is firmly opposed to "monkish" gloom and doom. When Mademoiselle Bearn, a fashionable visitor from Paris, jokingly says to her, after Blanche absents herself a while from company, that she had begun to wonder if "the giant of this enchanted castle, or the ghost, which, no doubt, haunts it, had conveyed you through a trap-door into some subterranean vault, whence you was never to return," Blanche banters in reply, and Henri caps their dialogue with a typically Tilneyish gallantry:

> "No," replied Blanche, laughingly, "you seem to love adventures so well, that I leave them for you to achieve."
>
> "Well, I am willing to achieve them, provided I am allowed to describe them."
>
> "My dear Mademoiselle Bearn," said Henri, as he met her at the door of the parlour, "no ghost of these days would be so savage as to impose silence on you. Our ghosts are more civilized than to condemn a lady to a purgatory severer even, than their own, be it what it may." (p. 473)

One might object that Henri and Blanche remain undeveloped as characters and disappear altogether when Radcliffe turns to sorting out (and happily resolving) Emily's tangled love affair with the long-lost Valancourt in *Udolpho*'s final chapters. But their chaffing presence is symptomatic of larger incoherencies of style and tone. In moments such as the foregoing—or indeed when the somewhat ridiculous truth emerges about the not-very-frightening pirates in the "haunted room"—Radcliffe seems not only to repudiate the label "Gothic novelist" but to anticipate, peculiarly, her most famous lampooner.

Other *Udolpho* "clichés" are equally problematic. Virtually anything one might say about the work—down to its most basic textual features—can be countered. The book is its own antithesis; the clichés fail to hold. Witness its curious formal oscillations between prose and poetry. We typically classify *The Mysteries of Udolpho* as a novel, of course, because it is long and in prose. Or is it? A more poetry-ridden kind of "prose" can scarcely be imagined. Radcliffe regularly begins each chapter with a formal poetic epigraph—usually a chunk from Shakespeare or Milton or a mid-eighteenth-century poet such as Thomson, Beattie, or Blair. In turn, her characters write poems, which are then inserted more or less gratuitously into the narrative. (The twenty-five-stanza poem "The Sea-Nymph," supposedly composed by Emily while floating in a gondola down the Grand Canal [pp. 179–81], is a typical specimen.) And perhaps most interestingly, the third-person narrator sometimes uses poetic epithets to lend fervor to her own omniscient utterances:

> The solitary life, which Emily had led of late, and the melancholy subjects on which she had suffered her thoughts to dwell, had rendered her at times sensible to the "thick-coming fancies" of a mind greatly enervated. (p. 102)

> Yet, why remove her from the castle, where deeds of darkness had, she feared, been often executed with secrecy?—from chambers, perhaps

> With many a foul, and midnight murder stain'd. (p. 407)

This "sampling" of the poetic is unquestionably of literary-historical significance. Radcliffe is the first important English novelist to use poetic epigraphs, interpolated poems, and poetic fragments decoratively, as it were, for their suggestive or mood-enhancing effects. (Matthew Lewis, Sir Walter Scott, Edward Bulwer-Lytton, and countless minor novelists of the nineteenth century would follow in her stead.) The phenomenon says a great deal about the new preeminence of the novel genre at the end of the eighteenth century. Mikhail Bakhtin has suggested that since its beginnings the novel's great power as a literary form has been its uncanny ability to "incorporate"—and thus render obsolete or superfluous—other kinds of writing through citation. The Radcliffean use of epigraphs illustrates the process perfectly. By compulsively excerpting from Shakespeare, Milton, and the rest, Radcliffe invests her narrative with a kind of supplemental "poetic" authority—often to the point of thematic overkill. (By volume 2, chapter 3, we already know that Montoni is wicked and devious: the prefatory epigraph here from *Julius Caesar*—describing a similarly scheming Cassius—simply reinforces the point.) But the obsessional work of cutting and pasting also enacts, in the most literal way possible, the generic cooptation of the poetic by the novelistic. When Shakespeare, Gray, or *Il Penseroso* is reduced to a sound bite, a tiny mood-setting fragment within a great wash of prose narrative, the impinging obsolescence of the poetic—its loss of cultural relevance—is palpably if paradoxically confirmed.

For the reader, however, the effect of such sampling is to turn the fiction into a discombobulating textual hybrid. We are constantly forced to switch gears as we read; to adjust our concentration; to decide—indeed—how much of the work before us we will try to absorb. Do we read or skip Radcliffe's poetical interpolations? Some readers, eager for the illusion of a continuously unfolding story, will bypass them altogether—more or less guiltily. But even with rampant skipping, the sense of interrupted flow, of having to respond subliminally to constant changes in textual format, persists. The experience of cognitive dissonance may be frequent enough—and severe enough—to make us question at times whether we are reading a "novel" at all. When Radcliffe cuts away from the intensifying psychic conflict between Emily and Montoni in volume 2, for example, to inflict upon us Emily's seemingly irrelevant verses on "Ilion's plains, where once the warrior bled" ("Stanzas," pp. 206–8), the sense of formal instability is overpowering.

When it comes to technique—Radcliffe's handling of point of view, narrative tempo, and so on—the standard formulas fail yet again. *Udolpho* is often described as a psychological fiction, with Emily's "sensibility"—her "maturing" response to the world—a central and compelling focus. We see things from her vantage point, supposedly, and feel along with her as she comes to understand events and the motivations of others. This might be true, were she more consistently the novel's presiding consciousness. But she is not. She is absent from long stretches of narrative—most disconcertingly in some of the Château-le-Blanc scenes. And even when she is there, she is not always "there." Radcliffe often switches away from her viewpoint abruptly—as when we jump between paragraphs from Emily's thoughts to Valancourt's or Montoni's (pp. 116, 189). The craziest of these jumps is when Radcliffe moves from Emily's point of view to *nobody's* point of view in the celebrated incident of the black veil:

> Emily passed on with faltering steps, and having paused a moment at the
> door, before she attempted to open it, she then hastily entered the cham-

ber, and went towards the picture, which appeared to be enclosed in a
frame of uncommon size, that hung in a dark part of the room. She
paused again, and then, with a timid hand, lifted the veil; but instantly let
it fall—perceiving that what it had concealed was no picture, and, before
she could leave the chamber, she dropped senseless on the floor.
(pp. 248–49)

Apart from leaving the reader with the sense of being cheated—what Emily
sees here won't be revealed for four hundred more pages—the episode epitomizes
her lack of epistemological authority. *We* may learn what is under the veil (a
waxwork figure), but Emily remains permanently under the delusion that she
has seen a corpse. With so much information withheld from her—she will also
remain in the dark about many of Montoni's crimes and the exact nature of
Valancourt's doings in Paris—it is difficult to see how she "develops" as a character at all. Psychically speaking, she remains a cipher.

The fictional tempo is likewise far less consistent than it is often said to be.
Udolpho is typically characterized as slow-going—no doubt because Radcliffe so
often "stops" the action, as we have seen, to indulge in extravagant pictorialism:

The solitary grandeur of the objects that immediately surrounded
[Emily], the mountain-region towering above, the deep precipices that
fell beneath, the waving blackness of the forests of pine and oak, which
skirted their feet, or hung within their recesses, the headlong torrents
that, dashing among their cliffs, sometimes appeared like a cloud of mist,
at others like a sheet of ice—these were features which received a higher
character of sublimity from the reposing beauty of the Italian landscape
below, stretching to the wide horizon, where the same melting blue tint
seemed to unite earth and sky. (pp. 165–66)

She undoubtedly sought by such passages to achieve in prose the same visionary
effects she admired in the works of the seventeenth-century landscape painters
Salvator Rosa, Claude Lorrain, and Nicholas Poussin. As Sir Walter Scott wrote
in his commentary on Radcliffe in *Lives of Eminent Novelists and Dramatists*
(1824), her landscapes resemble "splendid and beautiful fancy-picture[s]."[2]

But even when not depicting nature—as in the scene below of Madame Montoni's creepy nocturnal burial in the crypt at Udolpho—she is inclined to bring
the plot to a standstill whenever a chance for a striking tableau presents itself:

At the moment, in which they let down the body into the earth, the scene
was such as only the dark pencil of a Domenichino, perhaps, could have
done justice to. The fierce features and wild dress of the condottieri,
bending with their torches over the grave, into which the corpse was de-

scending, were contrasted by the venerable figure of the monk, wrapt in long black garments, thrown back from his pale face, on which the light gleaming strongly shewed the lines of affliction softened by piety, and the few grey locks, had spared on his temples: while, beside him, stood the softer form of Emily, who leaned for support upon Annette; her face half averted, and shaded by a thin veil, that fell over her figure; and her mild and beautiful countenance fixed in grief so solemn as admitted not of tears, while she thus saw committed untimely to the earth her last relative and friend. (pp. 377–78)

The effect is one of suspended animation—of bodies frozen in painterly attitudes.

Elsewhere Radcliffe's characters seem to get stuck in a sort of narrative Möbius strip, inside which they can only perform the same repetitive gestures over and over. The analogy here may be with the obsessional "standing in place" found in opera. When Emily and Valancourt have to separate at the end of volume 1, for example, but can't bring themselves to make the move, they resemble lovers in Italian grand opera, planted in position, unable to do anything but repeat their stylized addios for close to three pages (pp. 158–60). As in operatic representation, the effect of stasis can only be broken, it seems, by a sudden exaggerated movement: after one last embrace, Valancourt abruptly "hastens" away, stage left, while Emily runs off in the opposite direction. One can almost see the end-of-act curtain coming down.

And yet precisely at those times when one would most expect a setpiece—some grand painterly tableau or operatic showstopper—Radcliffe unaccountably hurries on by. Then her narrative rushes forward, helter-skelter, as if to make up for its previous moments of dawdling. Emily's daring escape from Udolpho for example (pp. 450–51), the sort of episode a Hugo or Dumas would have lingered over for pages, building up excitement through a series of increasingly suspense-laden vignettes, is over almost before one realizes it has begun (pp. 450–51). Similarly, when Emily and her rescuers, having made it in the space of a few sentences to the coast of France, seem about to perish in a shipwreck (Blanche, at Château-le-Blanc, watches their vessel "labouring" helplessly in a terrible storm) . . . nothing happens. A couple of flares are sent up, the ship anchors safely, and Emily is soon conversing happily with the Count de Villefort (p. 487). (No doubt recognizing the missed opportunity here, the Irish novelist Charles Maturin would open his own Gothic masterwork of 1820, *Melmoth the Wanderer*, with a stupendous Caspar David Friedrich-like shipwreck scene.) Perhaps most surprising of all, given the highly theatrical deathbed scenes staged elsewhere in her fiction, the death of Montoni by poison happens offstage and only warrants a sentence or two, as if Radcliffe had become bored with her own villain (p. 569).

When it comes to *Udolpho*'s themes—the novel's underlying structure of meaning—similar paradoxes prevail. Since the nineteenth century critics have labeled Radcliffe's fiction a romance—that is, a work with little or no connection to "real life." Not for Radcliffe, wrote Scott, the stark moral and psychological realism of Samuel Richardson's *Clarissa*. Her characters "belong rather to romance than to real life."[3] Comparing *Udolpho* disparagingly with Wilkie Collins's *The Woman in White* (1860), Henry James found Radcliffe's far-flung settings and exotic situations painfully irrelevant to modern experience:

> To Mr. Collins belongs the credit of having introduced into fiction those most mysterious of mysteries, the mysteries which are at our own doors. This innovation gave a new impetus to the literature of horrors. It was fatal to the authority of Mrs. Radcliffe and her everlasting castle in the Apennines. What are the Apennines to us, or we to the Apeninnes? Instead of the terrors of "Udolpho," we were treated to the terrors of the cheerful country-house and the busy London lodgings. And there is no doubt that these were infinitely the more terrible. Mrs. Radcliffe's mysteries were romances pure and simple; while those of Mr. Wilkie Collins were stern reality.[4]

James too invoked the genius of Richardson: *The Woman in White* "is a kind of nineteenth-century version of 'Clarissa Harlowe.'"[5] The Apennines couldn't compete.

Yet even such eminently forceful pronouncements might be countered. For all of its romantic ambiance, *The Mysteries of Udolpho* also has moments of surprising naturalism. Some of these have only a fugitive or tangential relationship to the plot, as when Emily, St. Aubert, and Valancourt, searching for a night's lodging during their travels through Languedoc, enter some miserable peasant cottages and are appalled by what they find:

> In several, which they entered, ignorance, poverty, and mirth seemed equally to prevail; and the owners eyed St. Aubert with a mixture of curiosity and timidity. Nothing like a bed could be found, and [Valancourt] had ceased to enquire for one, when Emily joined him, who observed the languor of her father's countenance, and lamented, that he had taken a road so ill provided with the comforts necessary for an invalid. Other cottages, which they examined, seemed somewhat less savage than the former, consisting of two rooms, if such they could be called; the first of these occupied by mules and pigs, the second by the family, which generally consisted of six or eight children, with their parents, who slept on beds of skins and dried beech leaves, spread upon a mud floor. Here, light was admitted, and smoke discharged, through an aperture in the roof; and here the scent of spirits (for the travelling smugglers, who haunted

the Pyrenées, had made this rude people familiar with the use of liquors)
was generally perceptible enough. (p. 33)

This glimpse of peasant squalor contrasts sharply with the images of happy rus-
tics dancing "picturesquely" found elsewhere in the fiction (cf. pp. 3–4, 65, and
97). One has the sense of Radcliffe describing something she has actually seen.
And for a sentence or two she veers toward the bleak social vision we associate
with Mrs. Gaskell or Hardy. Yet the description remains unintegrated—a fleeting disquiet in an otherwise Arcadian scene.

Later in the novel Radcliffe incorporates realistic elements with greater success—notably in the rendering of the fraught economic relationship between
Emily and her jailer-guardians, the Montonis. Interestingly, especially given
Scott's and James's suggestions to the contrary, Emily St. Aubert's situation in the
middle part of *Udolpho* in some ways exactly mirrors the harsh scenario at the
heart of Richardson's *Clarissa*. Just as Richardson's heroine is abused—
grotesquely—for refusing to marry the rich yet odious suitor her avaricious parents have picked out for her, so Emily too is tormented by "parents" who seek to
sell her off to the highest bidder. When Montoni tries to bully Emily into marriage with one of his allies and Madame Montoni assails her with cruel insults
(pp. 204, 218), they behave exactly like Richardson's depraved Harlowes. (The
scenes with Madame Montoni are particularly disturbing in this regard, since
the older woman is after all Emily's closest blood relation. One of Radcliffe's
darkest and most Richardsonian insights is that kinship doesn't guarantee loving
feeling: the same family may breed both saints and monsters. Madame Montoni,
nightmarishly, is the benevolent St. Aubert's sister, yet she is also Emily's most
sadistic tormentor.) *Udolpho* may be far from social realism, yet as recent feminist critiques of the novel have shown, it is not pure romance either.[6] In the unsentimental handling of Emily's powerlessness within the "family" unit in which
she finds herself, Radcliffe shows a paradoxical affinity with more engaged female novelists of the later eighteenth century—Frances Burney, Maria Edgeworth, even the fiercely unromantic Mary Wollstonecraft.

On the question, finally, of Radcliffe's overall artistic achievement—a curate's
egg if ever there was one—the clichés are once again misleading. The general
consensus among twentieth-century critics, of course, is that *Udolpho* is "bad"
and fully deserving of Austen's satire. At times one may feel this is so. The book
is undoubtedly too long, feeble in characterization, and often lacking in moral
or intellectual gravitas. It is full of absurdities and logical solecisms—as when
Radcliffe seems to forget momentarily that all of her characters (apart from
Montoni) are meant to be French and not English. (When Emily and her father
happen to meet some unusually "polite" French peasants while traveling through
Languedoc, she feels obliged to remind us that "St. Aubert was himself a Frenchman; he therefore was not surprised at French courtesy" [p. 66].) Occasionally

Radcliffe makes bloopers of Gong-Show exquisiteness. Finding some "letters en-graved on the stone postern" while walking near Château-le-Blanc, Emily recog-nizes in them the familiar "hand-writing" of Valancourt, who has inscribed a melancholy poem (p. 538). In some surrealist film—one of Cocteau's perhaps—one can imagine finding letters carved in stone that resemble someone's hand-writing, but here we must laugh out loud, or else commiserate with Valancourt over what must have been an agonizing case of writer's cramp.

But Radcliffe is hardly the laughingstock her harshest critics make her seem. The distinction is there and it is real. She is a meticulous stylist; even Austen may have learned how to write a sentence (or two) from her.

> When [Madame Clairval] gave her approbation to Valancourt's marriage, it was in the belief, that Emily would be the heiress of Madame Mon-toni's fortune; and, though, upon the nuptials of the latter, when she per-ceived the fallacy of this expectation, her conscience had withheld her from adopting any measure to prevent the union, her benevolence was not sufficiently active to impel her towards any step, that might now pro-mote it. She was, on the contrary, secretly pleased, that Valancourt was re-leased from an engagement, which she considered to be as inferior, in point of fortune, to his merit, as his alliance was thought by Montoni to be humiliating to the beauty of Emily; and though her pride was wounded by this rejection of a member of her family, she disdained to shew resentment otherwise, than by silence. (p. 148)

She can create moments of considerable drama—particularly between female characters. The scenes between Emily and Madame Montoni are brilliantly han-dled; likewise the episode near the end of the novel in which Emily encounters the raving "Sister Agnes," one-time mistress of Udolpho and lover of Montoni (pp. 643–49). In the protracted sequence at Château-le-Blanc in which Emily and Dorothée enter the apartments of the deceased marchioness of Villeroi—the overwrought Dorothée stopping at one point to throw the dead woman's veil over Emily's head ("'I thought,' added she, 'how like you would look to my dear mistress in that veil;—may your life, ma'mselle, be a happier one than hers!'")—Radcliffe achieves an atmosphere of oppressive, almost Hitchcockian horror (pp. 532–36).

And her descriptive fluency can still amaze, as in the following mountain prospect—

> Emily, often as she travelled among the clouds, watched in silent awe their billowy surges rolling below; sometimes, wholly closing upon the scene, they appeared like chaos, and, at others, spreading thinly, they opened and admitted partial catches of the landscape—the torrent,

whose astounding roar had never failed, tumbling down the rocky chasms, huge cliffs white with snow, or the dark summits of the pine forests, that stretched mid-way down the mountains. (p. 165)

As Emily makes her descent through a swirling "sea of vapour," Radcliffe seems to anticipate—vertiginously—the (Olympian or phobic) view of the modern-day airplane passenger.

Yet if *Udolpho* resists encapsulation in so many ways, then what *can* we say of it? I have characterized it as an unstable, erratic work, resistant to critical labels, but does that mean that we can say nothing about its overall effect or emotional power? Few late-eighteenth- and early-nineteenth-century readers would have thought so. Along with Rousseau's *La Nouvelle Héloïse* (1761) and Goethe's *Sorrows of Young Werther* (1774), Radcliffe's book was one of the most celebrated and influential European fictions of its epoch. The novel brought its author £500 (an unheard-of sum at the time) and went through countless editions well into the later nineteenth century. Naysayers like Austen notwithstanding, the majority of contemporary readers found *The Mysteries of Udolpho* an absorbing, even mind-altering experience, and its author an "enchantress" of the highest order. In *Literary Hours* (1800) Nathan Drake described Radcliffe as "the Shakespeare of Romance writers." Sir Walter Scott concurred: she was a "mighty magician"—"the first poetess of romantic fiction." For Keats she was simply "Mother Radcliffe."[7]

What accounted for *Udolpho's* extraordinary appeal? A clue may lie in the key word of its title: mysteries. Radcliffe, one might argue, was a purveyor of mysteries—but of a new kind, adapted for a secular age. Her book itself is a kind of mystery machine, of course, full of local puzzles and conundrums. Who has stolen the miniature of Emily in the book's opening chapters? What is in her dead father's secret papers? Who walks the ramparts at night under her window at Udolpho? What is under the black veil? What has happened to Montoni's one-time lover, the mysterious Signora Laurentini? And so on and so on. For much of the novel, as the uncertainties pile up, we are indeed Mother Radcliffe's children: lost in a cloud of unknowing.

But the "mysteries" permeating *Udolpho* are not simply the mysteries of plot. In foregrounding the mysterious—inevitably associated for her with the uncanny powers of the human mind—Radcliffe sought to do more than merely excite readerly curiosity. She wished to reawaken in her readers a sense of the numinous—of invisible forces at work in the world. The Enlightenment, arguably, had done much to eradicate such feeling. By rationalizing human experience to an unprecedented degree, science and the skeptical philosophy together had rendered certain old-style "mysteries" nearly obsolete. The history of English usage suggests as much. Before the eighteenth century, the word *mystery* had an almost exclusively religious, indeed Christian, meaning. In the Middle Ages, for example, one spoke of "the mysteries of faith," referring to those elements of Christian doctrine—such as the Trinity, Original Sin, and the Incarnation—beyond the power of human reason to comprehend. Similarly, a "mystery play" was a work dealing with crucial events in the life of Christ, typically his miracles and the Resurrection. By the beginning of the eighteenth century, however, not only was orthodox religious belief under threat from many sources, the traditional focus on divine mysteries was itself weakening. It is surely significant that one of the most influential English theological works of the early eighteenth century was John Toland's pointedly titled *Christianity Not Mysterious* (1696), a paradoxical effort to reconcile Christianity with scientific and other strands of skeptical thought by explaining away various miraculous episodes recounted in the Scriptures.

Though nostalgic about traditional religious belief—at times to the point of kitsch—Radcliffe was aware of its decaying emotional relevance in an increasingly secularized world. Throughout *Udolpho*, even as she relentlessly draws upon Christian (and especially Catholic) symbolism, one has the sense of its having been "emptied out"—divested of its uniquely numinous aura. Christian icons serve a largely decorative or aesthetic function in the novel. Thus when Emily and her father encounter "a monumental cross" atop a cliff while traveling through Languedoc, they regard it merely as one "terrific sight" among many— part of the general sublimity of the landscape. It inspires no spiritual reflections: indeed the susceptible Emily immediately imagines it "the very haunt of banditti," and almost expects "to see them stealing out from some hollow cave to look for their prey" (p. 54). Similarly, the numerous monks and nuns who pop up in the novel function more as picturesque adjuncts to the action than as emblems of religious authority. Their main purpose seems to be to supply the eerie unseen chanting that so often accompanies Emily's sentimental or erotic reveries.

For Radcliffe, as for her contemporaries Wordsworth and Blake, the new mysteries are those of the imagination. "Thought" itself is that sublime power, which like a "Great First Cause," allows us to ascend to "those unnumbered worlds, that lie scattered in the depths of aether, thousands of them hid from human eyes, and almost beyond the flight of human fancy" (p. 114). The phantasmagoric reveries of *Udolpho*'s heroine are exemplary in this regard: we are constantly seeing Emily lost in "pensive visions," haunted by "charming recollections," or given over to "melancholy imaginings." Consciousness itself, endlessly making and unmaking the world, is the uncanny thing—the source of all joy, terror, and wonderment.

This may seem paradoxical, given that Radcliffe is known as a rationalist of a sort. It is true that she is unfailingly condescending toward what she refers to in *Udolpho* as "vulgar superstition"—the bugaboo of lesser minds. There are no actual supernatural forces at work in her fiction; indeed, she goes to great lengths to show that characters who believe that there are (like the servant Annette, for example, who thinks that when her lover Ludovico vanishes from the "haunted" room at Château-le-Blanc he has been carried off by evil spirits) are foolishly mistaken. For each apparently marvelous event in the novel—every moving shroud, weird knocking, or spectral emanation glimpsed from afar—some non-supernatural explanation is ultimately forthcoming.

These explanations have often been seen as anticlimactic. "A principal characteristic of Mrs. Radcliffe's romances," wrote Scott, "is the rule that [. . .] all the circumstances of her narrative, however mysterious, and apparently superhuman, were to be accounted for on natural principles, at the winding up of the story. It must be allowed, that this has not been done with uniform success, and that the author has been occasionally more successful in exciting interest and apprehensions, than in giving either interest or dignity of explanation to the means she has made use of." Most readers experienced "disappointment and displeasure," he wagered, when they read for the first time "the unsatisfactory solution of the mysteries of the black pall and the wax figure, which has been adjourned from chapter to chapter, like something suppressed, because too horrible for the ear."[8] As charismatic an imaginist as Radcliffe was, he thought she might have done better to avow "boldly" the use of supernatural machinery, like her predecessor Walpole.

Such criticisms are just. Radcliffe's supposedly "rational" explanations are at times almost more implausible than the supernatural explanations they are meant to displace. In the episode of Ludovico and the supposedly haunted room, for example, a kind of gothicized rewrite of the story of Christ's disappearance from the tomb after the Crucifixion, we may feel Ludovico's fantastic tale of pirates and secret passageways to be as "miraculous" as any spirit-raising. Tellingly, when he reappears before Emily and Annette after his rescue, like Christ before Mary and Mary Magdalene after the Resurrection (Luke 16:1–13), Annette's joy at seeing him, writes Radcliffe, "could not have been more extravagant, had he arisen from the grave" (p. 630).

But to dwell overmuch on the clumsy device of the "explained supernatural" is to miss a more fundamental point: that Radcliffe represents the human mind itself as a kind of supernatural entity. If ghosts and specters are resolutely excluded from the plane of action, they reappear—metaphorically at least—in the visionary fancies of the novel's exemplary characters. Indeed, to be a Radcliffean hero or heroine in one sense means just this: to be "haunted" by the spectral mental images of those one loves. One sees in the mind's eye those who are absent; one is befriended and consoled by "phantoms" of the beloved. Radcliffe makes it clear how such phantasmata arise: they are the products of refined sentiment, the characteristic projections of a feeling heart. To be haunted, according to the novel's romantic myth, is to display one's powers of sympathetic imagination. The cruel and the dull (such as Montoni or his ruffians) have no such hallucinations; but those who love, like Emily, Valancourt, or St. Aubert, are possessed—quite literally—by the spirit of the other.

Examples of this supernaturalization of mental space are everywhere in

Udolpho; and give the book much of its surreal character. Thanks to the imagination's uncanny alchemy, the "familiar objects of former times" have the power to make dead or departed loved ones seem "present" again in thought. Thus St. Aubert, early in the novel, is reluctant to leave his home at La Vallée because "every surrounding scene" prompts phantasmatic visions of his dead wife (p. 22). Retracing a page in one of Valancourt's books and "dwelling on the passages, which he had admired," Emily is able to summon her lost lover "to her presence" again (p. 58). Pieces of furniture in the study of the dead St. Aubert at La Vallée bring his "image" into his daughter's mind, almost as if he were standing there (pp. 94–98). And Valancourt, having been reunited with Emily at the end of the novel, then temporarily banished once again from her presence, finds that "her image, her look, the tones of her voice, all dwelt on his fancy, as powerfully as they had late appeared to his senses" (p. 628).

Above all, befitting a work in which landscape plays so large a role, the scenes of nature are supremely affecting in this regard. Separated from Valancourt by the Montonis, Emily meets him again "in thought" by watching the sun set over mountain crags at an agreed-upon time of day (pp. 163–64). The vast "chain of the Pyrenées" stretching toward Gascony transports her with visions of her lost parents: "O my father,—my mother!" (p. 580). And at the end of the novel she is convinced that they "live again" in the gardens and woodlands around La Vallée. "[As] she walked beneath the groves, which her father had planted, and where she had so often sauntered in affectionate conversation with him, his countenance, his smile, even the accents of his voice, returned with exactness to her fancy, and her heart melted to the tender recollections" (p. 592). One is put in mind of that patient of Freud's, mentioned in the case history of Dr. Schreber, who having "lost his father at a very early age, was always seeking to rediscover him in what was grand and sublime in nature."[9]

In part if not wholly, *Udolpho*'s exorbitant popularity among eighteenth- and nineteenth-century readers seems to have derived from this profoundly magical rendering of human consciousness. By giving themselves up to the nostalgic reveries of its characters, Radcliffe's readers also gave themselves up to a fantasy about mind itself: that by its godlike powers of spiritual transformation, the imagination itself might assuage longing, provide consolation, and reinfuse everyday life with mysterious and fantastic beauty. In the increasingly unromantic world of post-Enlightenment culture, such dreams, as even Scott was forced to acknowledge, could be cathartic indeed:

> When a family was numerous, the volumes always flew, and were sometimes torn, from hand to hand, and the complaints of those whose studies were thus interrupted, were a general tribute to the genius of the author. Another might be found of a different and higher description, in the dwelling of the lonely invalid, or unregarded votary of celibacy, who

was bewitched away from a sense of solitude, of indisposition, of the neglect of the world, or of secret sorrow, by the potent charm of this mighty
enchantress.[10]

The effect of a work like *Udolpho*, he ventured, might be fittingly compared
with the use of opiates—"baneful, when habitually and constantly resorted to,
but of the most blessed power in those moments of pain and languor, when the
whole head is sore, and the whole heart sick."

Few readers today, perhaps, will find *The Mysteries of Udolpho* as therapeutic
as Scott and his contemporaries did. We have other opiates nowadays, even for
the unregarded votaries of celibacy. Some readers—put off outright by *Udolpho*'s
artificial conventions, local incoherencies, and languorous challenge to recuperation—will undoubtedly prefer Prozac to this most intransigent of eighteenth-
century best-sellers. Art is long and life is short and *Udolpho* is long indeed. Even
taking into account Radcliffe's historic displacement of supernatural "mysteries"
into human psychology, a lot of the book's original emotional force has dissipated. Thanks to Freud (who knew his Gothic fiction), most of us are accus-
tomed to the idea of the mind as spectropia, full of importuning, uncanny
presences. Radcliffe's revolutionary representation of human consciousness has
lost its power to entrance, in part because it is now so familiar: we have all become believers in the "haunted" contents of the human psyche.

Must we then go back to our caricatures? Perhaps not, if we refuse to be over-
set, like Emily St. Aubert in one of her swoons, by the moment-to-moment odd-
ities of the fictional world. For the reader willing to enter into Radcliffe's novel
with an open, relaxed, even labile attitude—with some of that curious "pensive-
ness" of approach Radcliffe elsewhere praises in her heroine—something of the
work's original effect must still come across. There is simply too much in
Udolpho that is interesting, even hypnotic, for this not to be so. Like a long and
complex dream—the kind in which pleasure and apprehension are so closely in-
termingled as to become indistinguishable—the book repays imaginative intro-
spection. Read in such a mood, as a strange survival out of that reverie we call
the past, *The Mysteries of Udolpho* reveals itself in turn as permanently and deeply
avant-garde.

notes

1. Ann Radcliffe, *The Mysteries of Udolpho*, ed. Bonamy Dobrée (Oxford and New York:
Oxford University Press, 1998), 226–27. All subsequent references are to this edition. Page
numbers are noted parenthetically.

2. Sir Walter Scott, *Lives of Eminent Novelists and Dramatists*, rev. ed. (London and New
York: Frederick Warne, 1887), 573.

3. Ibid., 564.

4. Henry James, "Mary Elizabeth Braddon," in *Literary Criticism: American Writers, English Writers,* ed. Leon Edel (New York: Library of America, 1984), 742.

5. Ibid.

6. See, for example, Claudia Johnson's insightful reading of *Udolpho* in Johnson, *Equivocal Beings: Politics, Gender, and Sentimentality in the 1790s—Wollstonecraft, Radcliffe, Burney, Austen* (Chicago: University of Chicago Press, 1995).

7. See Nathan Drake, *Literary Hours, or Sketches Critical and Narrative,* 2d ed. (1800; rpt. New York: Garland, 1970), vol. 1, 273; Scott, *Lives,* 553, 565; and Keats, *The Letters of John Keats,* ed. Hyder Edward Rollins (Cambridge: Harvard University Press, 1958), vol. 2, 62.

8. Scott, *Lives,* 568–69.

9. Sigmund Freud, "Psychoanalytic Notes upon an Autobiographical Account of Paranoia" (1911), in *Three Case Histories,* ed. Philip Rieff (New York: Macmillan, 1963), 155.

10. Scott, *Lives,* 555.

5
THE GOTHIC NOVEL

L ike literature itself, literary criticism has its fashions—its fads and caprices and strange gleamings—all of which can shed an instructive light on intellectual history and indeed life itself. Surely no literary-historical phenomenon has undergone a more sweeping critical reevaluation over the past one hundred years than the late-eighteenth-century vogue for the "Gothic"—that exorbitant hankering after horror, gloom, and supernatural grotesquerie so palpable in Britain in the literature and art of the 1790s especially. Long disparaged as one of the more regrettable, even absurd episodes in English literary history, the so-called Gothic Revival of the later eighteenth century has in recent decades come to be seen as one of the signal aesthetic manifestations of the age—as a phenomenon both fascinating in its own right and crucial to a proper understanding of eighteenth-century art and culture more generally. Whether this renewed enthusiasm for the Gothic—and for Gothic fiction in particular—will result in some new consensus regarding the value of Gothic as a creative mode seems doubtful, given the extraordinarily polarizing effect the style has always exerted upon readers and critics alike. Yet one feels it nonetheless to be the case: that modern-day literary history has been "gothicized" more starkly and deeply than ever before.

Literary critics of the early decades of the twentieth century, contriving to establish the moral and intellectual gravity of their enterprise, had little patience with Gothic whimsy and extravagance. The Gothic craze has always been easy to satirize of course: Jane Austen's delightfully irreverent *Northanger Abbey*, composed in the mid-1790s, when the vogue for the emotionally supercharged "tale of terror" was at its height, provided the pattern for a host of later comic spoofs and burlesques. Most early-twentieth-century scholars, eager to enter the lists against vulgarity (past and present) and the excesses of popular taste, took the great novelist's cue more or less reflexively. If Gothic fiction was to be discussed at all, it was hardly something to be taken very seriously. Thus Sir Leslie Stephen's animadversions in *English Literature and Society in the Eighteenth Century* (1907) on Horace Walpole's *The Castle of Otranto*, the first English novel to advertise itself (on its title page) as "a Gothic Story." Even as Sir Leslie confirmed, somewhat unwillingly, *Otranto*'s convulsive effect on contemporary readers—thanks to a sensational plot, exotic fake-medieval setting, and welter of supernatural devices the book had undoubtedly helped to establish an influential "literary school"—it was nonetheless a mere "squib" or "plaything," and Walpole himself an "indifferent dilettante, caring little for any principles and mainly desirous of amusement."[1] On the Walpolean "school" itself Sir Leslie wasted no time at all: the names of Ann Radcliffe, Matthew Lewis, Clara Reeve, Sophia Lee, William Beckford, James Hogg, William Godwin, Regina Maria Roche, Charlotte Dacre, W. H. Ireland, Charles Maturin, and other exponents of the post-*Otranto* Gothic mode are strikingly absent from his pages.

The pattern of disparagement continued into the teens and twenties. In *The Peace of the Augustans: A Survey of Eighteenth-Century Literature as Place of Rest and Refreshment*, the otherwise exhaustive history of eighteenth-century prose and poetry he published in 1916, the great Edwardian critic George Saintsbury devoted only a few (characteristically risible) sentences to the Gothic and its admirers. Regarding Walpole's self-congratulatory claim in the preface to the second edition of *Otranto* to have reintroduced "imagination" and "romance" into the desiccated purlieus of English fiction ("invention has not been wanting; but the great resources of fancy have been dammed up, by a strict adherence to common life"), Saintsbury was both arch and dismissive. "Certainly no stranger Moses ever led children of Israel or Jacobel back to a land flowing with the old milk and honey; and few more rotten craft have ever carried any discoverer to his goal."[2] "We put [*The Castle of Otranto*] beside a book of the *Morte d'Arthur* or one of the *Faerie Queene*"—next to a real fifteenth- or sixteenth-century romance in other words—"and we find it ludicrously and disgustingly wanting—a complete failure in what we wish it to be."[3] Yet the same "Sham Castle" effect was palpable everywhere in the Walpolean mode. As Saintsbury drolly noted, not only was little "Horace" a literary innovator, the self-appointed resuscitator of "ancient romance," but a book collector, antiquarian, and architectural tastemaker too. Besides producing the eighteenth century's first Gothic novel, he also created its first neo-Gothic private house: the elaborately turreted, much-imitated, pseudomedieval fantasia known as Strawberry Hill. Using part of a vast fortune inherited from his father, the former Whig prime minister Sir Robert Walpole, Walpole had erected this fanciful "little Gothic castle" in the countryside near Twickenham in gradual stages between 1752 and the mid-1770s. He subsequently commemorated its design and lavish accoutrements in a privately published folio volume, *A Description of the Villa Of Horace Walpole, Youngest Son of Sir Robert Walpole, Earl of Orford, at Strawberry-Hill near Twickenham. With an Inventory of the Furniture, Pictures, Curiosities, etc.* (1784). Yet despite these pretensions to connoisseurship, concluded Saintsbury, Walpole was nothing more than a frivolous *pasticheur.*

[He] had no real love for things mediaeval in general, and no real understanding of romance in particular. His fad *was* a fad pure and simple and
might have dated and directed itself in any other way and time where he
could attain the credit of singularity and originality. There is hardly a single genuine and unguarded expression of taste, throughout his immense
body of writing, which is sincerely Romantic when he is not "speaking in
character"—"talking Strawberry."[4]

No surprise, perhaps, that the bizarre episode he initiated in popular taste—a
sort of mass devolution into "talking Strawberry"—should have been "irremedi-
ably ridiculed in Miss Austen's *Northanger Abbey*."[5]

In *The Architecture of Humanism: A Study in the History of Taste* (1914) the
poet, art historian, and (later) Boswell editor Geoffrey Scott was yet more
scathing—if not outright apocalyptic. Scott's focus, as his title suggests, was
architectural: his book is primarily a vindication of the Renaissance style of
building—tempered, classical, and reposeful—over the romantic would-be-me-
dievalism perpetrated first by eighteenth-century Gothic revivalists such as Walpole, Batty Langley, James Wyatt, and William Beckford, and later, by Victorian
enthusiasts such as Ruskin, Pugin, and Morris. Yet Scott's excoriation of what he
called the "Romantic Fallacy" of the past two centuries was as much an attack on
a certain kind of literary sensibility as on neo-Gothic building itself. The late-
eighteenth-century "catastrophe for style," he argued—by which he meant the
supplanting of the abstract, classically derived, and "purely sensuous" forms of
Renaissance art and architecture by the stagily emblematic devices of Gothic—
had likewise been a "catastrophe for thought."

> Romanticism may be said to consist in a high development of poetic sen-
> sibility towards the remote, as such. It idealises the distant, both of time
> and place; it identifies beauty with strangeness. In the curious and the ex-
> treme, which are disdained by a classical taste, and in the obscure detail
> which that taste is too abstract to include, it finds fresh sources of inspira-
> tion. It is most often retrospective, turning away from the present, how-
> ever valuable, as being familiar. It is always idealistic, casting on the screen
> of an imaginary past the projection of its unfulfilled desires. Its most typ-
> ical form is the cult of the extinct. In its essence, romanticism is not
> favourable to plastic form. It is too much concerned with the vague and
> the remembered to find its natural expression in the wholly concrete. Ro-
> manticism is not plastic; neither is it practical, nor philosophical, nor sci-
> entific. Romanticism is poetical.[6]

To be "poetical"—or in love with the "extinct"—was for Scott the worst kind
of regressive fantasy and incompatible with the creation of a viable human

world. The Gothic forms might be a "romantic material, rich with the charm of history," but they could never be reconciled, he insisted, with a "living style," or result in anything other than "a wholly false aesthetic."[7] William Beckford's absurdly grandiose Fonthill Abbey (1796–1812)—a huge mock-monastery featuring a soaring three-hundred-foot Gothic spire that subsequently collapsed in 1825, taking most of the surrounding buildings with it—was for Scott the perfect symbol of the fatal spuriousness of the Gothic mode. Beckford, like Walpole, was the author of a lurid supernatural tale—the notorious "Oriental" fable *Vathek* (1786). Among various *diableries*, the hero-villain of the work, a depraved Arabian caliph named Vathek, erects a monstrous tower—subsequently destroyed by fire—in which he imprisons and torments various luckless members of his court. At Fonthill, wrote Scott, "impressive galleries of flimsy Gothic delighted their master with vague suggestions of the Hall of Eblis, and a tower, three hundred feet in height, rose above them to recall the orgies of the wicked Caliph." But as on a stage set, all was composed of veneer and hollow timber and the shoddiest of plasterwork:

> Five hundred workmen laboured here incessantly by day, and with torches in the night. But the wind blew upon it, and the wretched structure fell incontinently to the ground. The ideal of a monastic palace "partly ruined" [Beckford's original conception for his creation] was ironically achieved. And the author of *Vathek*, contemplating in the torchlight his now crumpled, but once cloud-capped pinnacles, may stand for the romantic failure of his time—for the failure of the poetic fancy, unassisted, to achieve material style.[8]

One might multiply indefinitely, perhaps, examples of anti-Gothic sentiment from the early part of the twentieth century. True, a few writers, if not exactly sympathetic, were somewhat less judgmental—including, interestingly enough, a number of women critics of the day. Virginia Woolf—or so some of her reviews from the 1920s would suggest—took both a historical and a technical interest in Gothic experimentation, and even acknowledged finding "considerable power" in the novels of Ann Radcliffe (1764–1823), the leading English proponent of the "terror fiction" school of the 1790s.[9] At least two female critics of the period aimed at a more ambitious kind of rehabilitation. Both Edith Birkhead in *The Tale of Terror* (1921) and J. M. S. Tompkins in *The Popular Novel in England, 1770–1800* (1932) sought to explain the late-eighteenth-century vogue for the supernatural tale in light of certain complex changes—social, psychic, and philosophical—in eighteenth-century British culture itself.[10] Yet even these rather more dispassionate commentators could not always keep from indulging in the self-protective facetiousness that the Gothic mode so often seemed to provoke. Confronting Joseph Fox's ludicrous advertisement to the

reader in the preface to his *Santa-Maria; or the Mysterious Pregnancy* (1797)—
"Things MAY come out to chill—to make the sensitive soul thrill with horror—
to make the very hair stand perched on its native habitual roost, where so long it
had lain recumbent"—even the donnish Joyce Tompkins could not resist the
comic opening: "And [thus] the sensitive reader, tired of recumbent hair, bought
the book, and indulged in 'the strange luxury of artificial fear.'"[11]

Since the twenties and thirties, the aims and methods of literary study have
altered, of course, as critics in England and America have moved away from the
primarily aesthetic and evaluative type of commentary favored by writers like
Saintsbury and Scott toward an intellectual approach at once (supposedly) more
objective, historically inflected, and sociological in emphasis. Over the last half
century literary scholars have come to concern themselves less with traditional
matters of judgment and taste—with determining whether, say, *The Castle of
Otranto* is a good or bad or foolish work of art—and more with the intellectual,
social, and political contexts in which literary works (good *and* bad) have been
produced. Our understanding of the Gothic has undoubtedly benefited from
this "postmodern" turn in critical method. Seen in retrospect, the anti-Gothicism of the first decades of the twentieth century was clearly powerfully aligned
with other important intellectual tendencies of the time—notably literary modernism itself. Geoffrey Scott's brisk dismissal of the Gothic style of building—
that it was excessively concerned with picturesque "detail," too caught up in the
"poetical" evocation of distant times and places, and not expressive enough of
"those more general values of Mass, Space, Line, and Coherence with which architecture properly deals"—echoed the anti-Romantic principles of modernist
writer-aestheticians from T. E. Hulme to T. S. Eliot, Ezra Pound, and Wyndham
Lewis.[12] Indeed, Scott's cool preference for form over content ("a combination of
plastic forms has a sensuous value apart from anything we may *know* about
them") seems from one angle but another version of modernism's own predilec-
tion for abstraction over symbolism, reason over sentiment, and classical (or
"universal") forms over Romantic and particularizing ones.[13]

The anti-Romantic point of view held sway for a long time—approaching a
kind of zenith with the New Criticism of the 1940s and 1950s. (It is safe to say
that there has never been a "New Critical" examination of a Gothic novel.) The
pendulum has swung back again, of course, with a vengeance. We are now in
love with historical detail, with the palpable *strangeness* of the past, and with recovering and rehabilitating once-derided, supposedly suspect, or merely "popular" literary modes. The classical interest in *form*, in how well a literary work is
put together, has been superseded by an interest in *mentalité*—in what a work
tells us (or what we presume it to be telling us) about the lost human world from
which it emanates. The change, paradoxically, has been at once extraordinarily
informative and in its own way curiously limiting. I shall return to the evaluative
question—what good is Gothic?—toward the end of this chapter. It is not en-

tirely clear that in seeking to overturn the anti-Gothic prejudices of early modernism through an appeal to history (to the notion that the Gothic can instruct us about late-eighteenth-century social, political, and cultural "realities"), recent critics have taken full account of—let alone neutralized—some of the more disturbing moral and psychological aspects of the Gothic mode. Yet for now it is enough to make a simpler point. The Gothic was itself in a manner of speaking the first "postmodern" experiment in English literary history: the first full-blown effort to reanimate, artificially, an extinct historical style for the purposes of mass entertainment. It sought in the anachronistic resurrection of "romance" an uncanny intensification of everyday emotional life. It should not surprise us that in our own age—in which demonic images from the past haunt us sleeping and waking—we should find in the Gothic resurgence of the late eighteenth century such a powerful reflection of our own aspirations and fears.

What have we learned about the Gothic of late? One might begin with the derivation of the word itself, and in particular its architectural application. (It is difficult—one quickly realizes—to keep the architectural and the literary aspects of the Gothic phenomenon apart, even for the purposes of semantic clarification. As in Gothic fiction, where physical space and psychological space are routinely confounded, the one kind of Gothic "infestation" was intellectually implicated in the other from the outset.) The words *Goth* and *Gothic* were originally ethnographic terms—used in England since the Middle Ages to refer to those warlike Germanic tribesmen, traditionally thought to have emanated from the Baltic island of Gotland, who between the third and fifth centuries A.D. invaded western and central Europe from the north and east, drove out the occupying Roman legions, and helped precipitate the collapse of the Roman Empire in the West in A.D. 476 (The Goths overran the British Isles earlier in the fifth century, forcing the withdrawal of Roman troops there in 426 or 427.) The marauding Gothic tribes were described in two well-known Latin texts of late antiquity: Julius Caesar's *De Bello Gallico*, or *Commentaries on the Gallic War* (c. 52 B.C.) and Tacitus's *Germania* (c. A.D. 98), an influential translation of which, entitled *A Treatise on the Situation, Manners, and Inhabitants of Germany*, was published in England in 1777.

Not surprisingly, during the Italian Renaissance, with a rebirth of interest in classical antiquity, the term *Gothic* became a byword for savagery and destructiveness. Humanist poets and philosophers regularly deprecated the Goths as crude barbarians who by obliterating the brilliant legacy of Greco-Roman culture had plunged Europe into centuries of moral and intellectual darkness. The spread of Christianity had alleviated the gloom somewhat, but much in the way of "civilization" had been lost. True, once established and diversified into the modern nations, the various fair-haired peoples descended from the Goths (the English, French, German, Dutch, and Scandinavians) had developed their own artistic and architectural traditions: the great medieval cathedrals of northern

Europe—so different in style from the ancient light-filled temples of the Mediterranean—were their most obvious and lasting monument. Yet *Gothic* retained its negative associations, even as it developed new aesthetic meanings. It was in Italy, during the High Renaissance, that the term first took on its now-standard architectural sense—coming to signify any northern, nonclassical, or "Germanic" style of building. The highly rationalized architecture of Greece and Rome had been founded on the so-called system of orders, codified by Vitruvius in his *De Architectura* in the first century B.C. (In classical architecture, an "order" is a column with base, shaft, capital, and entablature, decorated and proportioned according to one of five accepted modes, the Doric, Tuscan, Ionic, Corinthian, or Composite.) Balance, symmetry, and a strict mathematical adherence to decorum were the defining features of the classical style. Yet the "rude" Gothic builders of the Middle Ages had wilfully ignored the orders and evolved instead their own "free" and "irregular" motifs: the pointed arch, the rib vault, the flying buttress, long galleries, clerestory windows, and a type of arcaded wall-passage (still seen in surviving medieval English churches) known as a triforium.[14] In its various phases this "Gothic" style had persisted in parts of Europe through the late fifteenth century. Today we revere the astounding visual intelligence and uncanny engineering skills exemplified in magnificent Gothic cathedrals, say, at Chartres, Salisbury, or Winchester. By the time the Renaissance architect Alberti came to publish his *De Re aedificatoria* in 1482, however, a polemical brief on behalf of the ancient Vitruvian system of orders, Gothic building had come to seem grotesque and bizarre, evocative indeed of the uncouth hordes among whom it had supposedly originated.

In England, the anti-Gothicism of the Renaissance survived in certain quarters well into the late seventeenth and early eighteenth century. For many classically educated men and women the terms *Goth* and *Gothic* would remain for some time loose catchwords for any kind of primitivism or offence to reason. Ancient Rome—or so wrote the poet John Dryden in his "To Sir Godfrey Kneller" (1694)—had preserved the great artistic legacy of Greece, "Till *Goths* and *Vandals*, a rude *Northern* Race, / Did all the matchless Monuments deface."[15] Assailing an intellectual opponent in his *Characteristics* of 1733, the Earl of Shaftesbury complained that "hardly a Tartar or a Goth would . . . reason so absurdly."[16] "O more than *Gothic* Ignorance!" exclaims Mrs. Western of her loutish brother, Squire Western, in Henry Fielding's famous comic novel *Tom Jones* (1749).[17] And in *The Dunciad* (1743), his apocalyptic satire on the decay of wit and culture in the modern "Age of Lead," Alexander Pope lamented the gloomy depredations of "bold Ostrogoths" and "fierce Visigoths"—whose mindless assaults on ancient learning foreshadowed the "Hyperborean" ignorance of the present day.[18]

Yet as early as the 1720s strong intellectual counterforces began to make themselves felt—first in architecture, then in the world of letters. In the wake of

the Protestant revolution of 1688 and the (relatively) peaceful Hanoverian succession of 1714, Britain had entered on a period of both general political stability and enormous economic growth. Its commercial empire was expanding; its
navy dominated the seas; and thanks to the institution of a national credit-based
economy and accelerating developments in technology and manufacturing, it
was modernizing faster than any other country in Europe. National pride demanded new patriotic myths to underwrite Britain's growing power and prominence around the globe.[19] One of the first intellectual by-products of this new
cultural self-consciousness was a renewed interest in "ancient" British history
and the Goths in particular—who gradually came to be seen, through a complex
process of ideological transvaluation, not as the illiterate marauders of old, but as
primordial embodiments of a distinctively "British" genius and cultural energy.[20]
Tacitus's fleeting description in *Germania* of the old tribal councils of the Goths
was both salient and exciting here: early-eighteenth-century jurists and political
commentators claimed to find in them not only the noble origins of the celebrated Anglo-Saxon *Witangemot,* or parliament, but the genesis of those age-old
"liberties" (the rights of assembly, habeas corpus, freedom of speech) guaranteed
by the British constitution itself. Thus the poet James Thomson's paean in *Liberty* (1734–36) to those inspired "northern nations . . . fierce with freedom"
who had thrown off the tyrannical Roman yoke in the person of Julius Caesar
himself:

> Witness, Rome,
> Who saw'st thy Caesar from the naked land,
> Whose only fort was British hearts, repelled,
> To seek Pharsalian wreaths.[21]

Other writers eulogized the Goths' valor and magnanimity in battle, their innate
love of fairness—they were thought to have devised the jury system—and their
supposedly chivalrous treatment of women.[22]

One of the signal accomplishments of late-twentieth-century scholarship has
been to call attention to precisely this ideological and "myth-making" aspect of
the Gothic revival—especially in its early, mainly architectural, phase. The first
half of the eighteenth century saw a veritable flurry of neo-Gothic construction
in Britain, as various powerful Whig landowners, in league with nostalgically-in-
clined architects and antiquarians, sought ways to celebrate in stone and plasterwork the growth and consolidation of the ancient "British" constitution and the
recently-secured Protestant dispensation. It was a paradoxical process indeed: via
the enabling myth of the ancient Goths, the architectural styles of the Middle
Ages—in actuality a legacy of Britain's Catholic and feudal past—came to symbolize instead a new self-consciously Protestant (and specifically Whiggish) conception of evolving British political freedoms. The career of James Tyrrell,

builder of the first *faux*-medieval folly in England—the "Gothic Temple" at Shotover Park near Oxford (1716–17)—encapsulates the paradox. As author of the influential constitutional treatise *Bibliotheca Politica* (1692–1702), he had been one of the first writers after the Glorious Revolution to make an ideological connection between the ancient Goths and the rise of parliamentary government. With the accession of George I in 1714 and the defeat of the Jacobite rebels in Scotland the following year, it was just the moment—as a recent historian of Gothic has put it—"for Tyrrell, one of the architects of gothic's ideological triumph, actually to build in gothic."[23] To do so meant "wresting" medieval forms away from their traditional association with "feudal and Catholic authority." But this Tyrrell managed—thus "[liberating] medieval style from the contexts prescribed by medieval buildings."[24] Detached—at least in theory—from any lingering ecclesiastical meanings, Gothic became "a repertoire of formal elements—pinnacles, tracery, pointed arches—that could be endlessly recontextualized, never wholly losing their evocative reference to the past, but capable of semantic adventure" and "of assuming a new range of identities for the present."[25]

Over the century hundreds of neo-Gothic structures were erected around the British Isles, typically on the grounds of the great aristocratic country seats. As the fashion for Gothic spread, every important landowner, it seemed, demanded a little mock-medieval tower or picturesque monastic "ruin" somewhere on his property. Some of these whimsical creations were inspired pieces of architectural fantasia: Roger Morris's "Gothic Tower" at Whitton Park (1734–35); William Kent's "Merlin's Cave" at Richmond (1733); James Gibbs's "Temple of Liberty" in the garden at Stowe (1741); Daniel Garrett's "Culloden Tower" in Yorkshire (erected in 1746 to celebrate the Protestant rout of Bonny Prince Charlie and his supporters at Culloden the previous year); Robert Adam's Brizlee Tower at Alnwick Castle (1781); Michael "Angelo" Rooker's Gatehouse at Battle Abbey, Sussex (1792). Others, like Beckford's Fonthill, verged, rather more unpleasantly, on monstrosity and kitsch. Yet informing every new "Gothic" elevation was the nostalgic urge to connect—however oddly and artificially—with an imagined (romantic and heroic) national past. "The result," writes the architectural historian Chris Brooks, "was a new class of landscape structure which as the poet and landscape gardener William Shenstone remarked, could "turn every bank and hillock . . . into historical ground."[26] Individual connoisseurs might experiment with different components of the style: Walpole at Strawberry Hill—infatuated with the decorative caprices of late medieval church interiors—contrived a method for imitating fan-vaulting and filigreed tracery in papier-mâché. But by the second half of the century most "Persons of Refinement" were agreed—to build in Gothic was not only a way "to say something about being British," but a potent means of asserting a deeper (if sometimes wishful) link between past and present.[27]

Over the decades the same kind of transvaluation took place in the realm of letters—and, from one angle at least, for similarly chauvinistic reasons. As early as 1712, in a meditation on the "Fairy Way of Writing" in *Spectator* No. 419, the critic Joseph Addison had playfully lamented that while admirable in other respects, the cherished literary productions of classical antiquity lacked a certain "Poetry": the sort that came of introducing into one's writing "Persons who are not to be found in Being"—notably "Fairies, Witches, Magicians, Demons, and departed Spirits."

> The Ancients have not much of this Poetry among them, for, indeed, almost the whole Substance of it owes its Original to the Darkness and Superstition of later Ages, when pious Frauds were made use of to amuse Mankind, and frighten them into a Sense of their Duty. Our Forefathers looked upon Nature with more Reverence and Horrour, before the World was enlightened by Learning and Philosophy, and loved to astonish themselves with the Apprehensions of Witchcraft, Prodigies, Charms and Enchantments. There was not a Village in *England* that had not a Ghost in it, the Churchyards were all haunted, every large Common had a Circle of Fairies belonging to it, and there was scarce a Shepherd to be met with who had not seen a Spirit.[28]

The dearth of "Spirits" in ancient literature was to be regretted, the essayist averred, because tales of the supernatural inevitably "raise a pleasing kind of Horrour in the Mind of the Reader, and amuse his Imagination with the Strangeness and Novelty of the Persons who are represented in them."[29] Luckily, however, such pleasing horror was yet to be found—and close to home indeed. Precisely because of their dark and ghost-ridden past—not to mention a distinctly morbid national temperament—"the *English*" had always excelled in the creation of baleful fancies. "Among all the Poets of this Kind our *English* are much the best, by what I have yet seen, whether it be that we abound with more Stories of this Nature, or that the Genius of our Country is fitter for this sort of Poetry. For the *English* are naturally Fanciful, and very often disposed by that Gloominess and Melancholly of Temper, which is so frequent in our Nation, to many wild Notions and Visions, to which others are not so liable."[30] The greatest example of this "wild" native genius was indisputably the poet Shakespeare. Even when flouting the laws of nature outright, Shakespeare had an unmatched ability to make the reader believe in the vivacity of his visionary creations:

> That noble Extravagance of Fancy, which he had in so great Perfection, thoroughly qualified him to touch this weak superstitious Part of his Reader's Imagination; and made him capable of succeeding, where he had nothing to support him besides the Strength of his own Genius. There is something so wild and yet so solemn in the Speeches of his Ghosts,

Fairies, Witches, and the like Imaginary Persons, that we cannot forbear thinking them natural, tho' we have no Rule by which to judge of them, and must confess, if there are such Beings in the World, it looks highly probable they should talk and act as he has represented them.[31]

Still other English masters had a similar "Talent in Representations of this Kind": Milton when he depicted the frightful apparitions of Sin and Death in *Paradise Lost*, Spenser when he evoked "a whole Creation of . . . shadowy Persons"—weird and arabesque—in his romance of *The Faerie Queene*.[32]

It was not long before critics were correlating the English poetic genius—and kindred fondness for the supernatural—with both the Goths and the Middle Ages. As in architecture, a pronounced taste for nonclassical aesthetic models had begun to infiltrate the world of British letters by midcentury. As poets, playwrights, and novelists—like their counterparts in the visual and plastic arts—came increasingly to derogate classical tradition, they turned once again to an imaginary English past to underwrite new and dizzyingly romantic creative imperatives. The Goths—now imagined as *ur*-poets, intoning "sacred fables" in Britain's primordial forests—became the human symbols of a supposedly indigenous "bardic" tradition: one untrammeled by the rules of decorum and the oppressive regularities of Greek and Latin aesthetics. English authors were at their strongest and most sublime—or so patriotically minded commentators came to insist—when they returned to their native "Gothic" roots. Thus Spenser, Bishop Hurd asserted in his *Letters on Chivalry and Romance* (1762), was one of the noblest of English poets precisely because he revitalized those "Gothic fictions and manners" first allegorized in the works of Chaucer and Malory.[33] Living in the "dark shades of Gothic barbarism," wrote Elizabeth Montagu, "before philosophy had . . . mitigated the austerity of ignorant devotion, or tamed the fierce spirit of enthusiasm," the "wondrous" Shakespeare "had no resources but in the very phantoms that walked the night of ignorance and superstition." Yet the very credulity of his "Gothic" age was a priceless boon—for all these "ghosts, fairies, goblins, elves, were as assistant to Shakespear, and gave as much of the sublime, and of the marvellous, to his fictions, as nymphs, satyrs, fawns, and even the triple Geryon, to the works of ancient bards."[34] Contemporary poets and fabulists soon came to identify powerfully with the bardic model of old. Greek poetry was all very well—Coleridge would declaim a few decades later—"but if I wish my feelings to be affected, if I wish my heart to be touched, if I wish to melt into sentiment and tenderness, I must turn to the heroic songs of the Goths, to the poetry of the middle ages."[35]

The wave of recent critical interest in the "Britishness" of Gothic—in its not-so-secret role in animating certain useful collective fantasies about the English political and cultural past—has been illuminating indeed. More acutely than ever we now apprehend the intellectual consanguinity between the Gothic phenomenon and the increasingly nationalistic preoccupations of eighteenth-century criticism: the effort to define a specifically "English" literary canon, the rise of the cult of original genius, the celebration of Shakespeare as national poet, the revival of interest in local folk culture, "popular antiquities," and vernacular literary genres such as the ballad and oral epic. We have likewise been helped—if at times a bit doggedly—to understand the often comical xenophobia of Gothic fiction itself. Even while reveling in murky exotic locales and romantic ages past—Walpole's *Castle of Otranto* is set in thirteenth-century Italy, Ann Radcliffe's *Mysteries of Udolpho* (1794) in sixteenth-century France and Italy during the wars of religion, and Matthew Lewis's *The Monk* (1796) in Madrid during the Inquisition—English Gothic novelists regularly expatiated on the vice and superstition to be found in Catholic countries and on the natural predisposition of certain non–Anglo-Saxon (usually Mediterranean) racial types toward credulity, hypocrisy, physical cruelty, and sexual depravity. Thus Radcliffe's sinister references to "Italian revenge" and "the delirium of Italian love" in *Udolpho*, or Matthew Lewis's ultralurid depiction of secret convent excesses in *The Monk*. In one of the numerous anti-Catholic vignettes in the Anglo-Irish writer Charles Maturin's *Melmoth the Wanderer* (1820), a character is held against his will in a "convent of Ex-Jesuits" in Madrid, where he witnesses an especially grisly episode of monkish abuse:

> A naked human being, covered with blood, and uttering screams of rage and torture, flashed by me; four monks pursued him—they had lights. I had shut the door at the end of the gallery—I felt they must return and pass me—I was still on my knees, and trembling from head to foot. The victim reached the door, found it shut, and rallied. I turned, and saw a groupe [*sic*] worthy of Murillo. A more perfect human form never existed than that of this unfortunate youth. He stood in an atmosphere of despair—he was streaming with blood. The monks, with their lights, their scourges, and their dark habits, seemed like a groupe of demons who had made prey of a wandering angel,—the groupe resembled the infernal furies pursuing a mad Orestes. And, indeed, no ancient sculptor ever designed a figure more exquisite and perfect than that they had so barbarously mangled. Debilitated as my mind was by the long slumber of its powers, this spectacle of horror and cruelty woke them in a moment. I rushed forward in his defence—I struggled with the monks—I uttered some expressions which, though I was hardly conscious of, they remembered and exaggerated with all the accuracy of malice.[36]

The sado-homoerotic element here—at once voyeuristic and repellent—is typical of both Maturin's fiction and the Gothic genre in general. Like eighteenth-century pornographers (with whom they had more than a little in common),

Gothic novelists almost reflexively associated the monastic or conventual setting with the purportedly foreign "abomination" of same-sex desire. It is peculiar, once again, that British fantasists should seek to restore a lost "romance" to English literature by demonizing the imagined erotic habits of Catholic monks and nuns, but there it is: the medievalized settings of the Gothic mode, conjoining with nationalistic imperatives, combined to produce—as if by sociochemical reaction—precisely such dire yet titillating references to the "pollutions" to be found in benighted nations across the Channel.

Yet at the same time it might be argued that despite their many virtues recent "ideological" treatments of the Gothic have not entirely reversed the early-twentieth-century prejudice against Gothic writing—nor gone very far toward assessing the deeper cultural and psychological significance of characteristic Gothic themes and motifs. To the basic generic problem—why tales of horror and the supernatural should have proliferated so wildly in the British Isles during the second half of the eighteenth century—the responses typically proffered by modern-day scholars remain partial, muted, even oddly dissociated. To affirm, with Addison, that there is something distinctively "British" about the Gothic mode is undoubtedly true, but it is hardly the whole story. Such bland generalization does not begin to explain why the tale-of-terror craze spread so quickly to other countries and climes (notably Germany and the United States) or how we should understand the genre's strange kinetic shifts in mood and manner—from the epicene, campy, highly theatrical medievalism of Horace Walpole, through the dreamy, feminized, vision-weaving of Radcliffe, to the febrile sensation-mongering of Lewis, Hogg, Maturin, Bram Stoker, and Poe. The emotional "common denominator" linking such ill-assorted phenomena remains, it must be said, somewhat elusive.

In seeking a broader explanation for the popularity of Gothic, one could do worse than begin with a view much promulgated in the eighteenth century itself: that the appetite for Gothic story arose out of an encroaching sense of boredom and loss. Certainly by the 1760s, when Walpole galvanized the literary world with *The Castle of Otranto*, certain kinds of imaginative writing once popular in Britain had come to seem stale and over-familiar. "The books that formed part of the ordinary library in the year 1764," Virginia Woolf reminds us in her review of Edith Birkhead's *Tale of Terror* from 1921,

> were, presumably, Johnson's *Vanity of Human Wishes*, Gray's Poems, Richardson's *Clarissa*, Addison's *Cato*, Pope's *Essay on Man*. No one could wish for a more distinguished company. At the same time, as literary critics are too little aware, a love of literature is often roused and for the first years nourished not by the good books, but by the bad. . . . In the eighteenth century there must have been a very large public which found no delight in the peculiar literary merits of the age; and if we reflect how

long the days were and how empty of distraction, we need not be surprised to find a school of writers grown up in flat defiance of the prevailing masters. Horace Walpole, Clara Reeve, and Mrs. Radcliffe all turned their backs on their time and plunged into the delightful obscurity of the Middle Ages, which were so much richer than the eighteenth century in castles, barons, moats, and murders.[37]

Woolf's characteristic diffidence notwithstanding—elsewhere she will refer to Gothic romance as "a parasite, an artificial commodity, produced half in joke"—the novelist touches here on a midcentury mood still insufficiently anatomized by historians of eighteenth-century taste. What seems to have taken hold in the world of English letters by the 1760s was in fact a kind of collective readerly malaise—a growing sense of vacuity, disappointment, and anomie. Something mysterious and exciting had *gone*, both from literature and the world, and human emotional life was impoverished by its absence. In identifying the lost thing as "poetry" and connecting it with the "Reverence and Horrour" of the supernatural, Addison—to judge by the approbation of his contemporaries—moved on just the right track. A deep sense of imaginative deprivation pervades the works of midcentury commentators. Thus the wistful, almost erotic languor in Bishop Hurd's *Letters on Chivalry and Romance*. Exquisite "Tales of Faery" had once predominated in English literature, he opined, until cruel "Reason . . . drove them off the scene, and would endure these *lying wonders*, neither in their own proper shape, nor as masked in figures." After "[wantoning] it so long in the world of fiction," lovely "Fancy" had been "constrained, against her will, to ally herself with strict truth, if she would gain admittance into reasonable company." Hurd grieved at her fettering. "What we have gotten by this revolution, you will say, is a great deal of sense. What we have lost, is a world of fine fabling; the illusion of which is so grateful to the *charmed Spirit*."[38]

In his *History of English Poetry* (1778) the poet and critic Thomas Warton was similarly disconsolate. He blamed the cold, "scientific," and rationalizing spirit of the sixteenth and seventeenth centuries for suppressing those wondrous "incredibilities" more precious to the soul of man than truth itself.

The study of the classics, together with a colder magic and a tamer mythology, introduced method into composition: and the universal ambition of rivalling those new patterns of excellence, the faultless models of Greece and Rome, produced that bane of invention, IMITATION. Erudition was made to act upon genius. Fancy was weakened by reflection and philosophy. The fashion of treating every thing scientifically, applied speculation and theory to the arts of writing. Judgment was advanced above imagination, and rules of criticism were established. The brave eccentricities of original genius, and the daring hardiness of native thought,

were intimidated by metaphysical sentiments of perfection and refinement. . . . [The] lover of true poetry will ask what have we gained by this
revolution? It may be answered, much good sense, good taste, and good
criticism. But, in the mean time, we have lost a set of manners, and system of machinery, more suitable to the purposes of poetry than those
which have been adopted in their place.[39]

Without its "romantic legends," Nathan Drake lamented, "our national poetry"
had already begun to sink into "mere morality, criticism, and satire."[40]

What seemed, above all, to have vanished was the experience of *belief* itself.
Try as one might to regain it, the state of credulous "awe" produced by the ancient tales of miracles and witchcraft, ghosts and enchantments, seemed impossible to recover: humanity itself had been cruelly awakened from some long,
dream-ridden, yet deeply enthralling slumber. Like the "chimeras" of chivalry,
the metaphysical visions of the past had evaporated "as snow melts before the
sun." Contemplating this process of spiritual disillusionment, writers like Hurd
and Warton found a sad, strange kinship with Cervantes's Don Quixote. He was
both soul mate and culture hero, a mournful companion in loss. Just as the
would-be knight had been jarred out of his fantasies by his crass friends, shaken
from his chivalric daydreams and brought back to a world without magic—the
dreariness of the merely *real*—so they felt themselves exiled in the ordinary, cut
off from passionate feeling, estranged from some deeper and more intense mode
of being. They deplored the heartlessness of his creator. In that Cervantes had
willfully embraced the role of skeptic and comic debunker, wrote John Pinkerton in his *Dissertation on the Origin and Progress of the Scythians or Goths* (1787),
he was surely to be "execrated." Had Cervantes written three centuries sooner—
depriving later ages of even more in the way of beautiful fable making—"we
must have branded him as the greatest enemy of society that ever wrote."[41]

For those less demoralized by Quixotean pathos, the question was how to restore—or at least approximate through art—a lost world of numinous sensation.
The ruined architectural spaces of the medieval past once again provided a crucial hint. Something about the looming, claustral grandeur of the Gothic cathedrals had a power, it seemed, of reawakening exactly that "sacred awe"—a sense
of vast, encompassing, and imponderable spiritual forces—elsewhere absent
from the world. "The contemplation of the works of antique art," Coleridge
would subsequently argue, "excites a feeling of elevated beauty, and exalted notions of the human self; but the Gothic architecture impresses the beholder with
a sense of self-annihilation; he becomes, as it were, a part of the work contemplated."[42] Might it not be possible to devise a kind of literature with the same
soul-shaking effect? In the 1797 novel *Family Secrets*, the orator and bookseller
Courtney Melmoth (Samuel Jackson Pratt) called explicitly for a mode of imaginative writing that would reproduce the primitive *étonnement* experienced in

Gothic cathedrals.[43] It should hardly surprise us that the dank yet magnificent spaces of real-world Gothic—castles, crypts, cloisters, and the like—figure so prominently *within* Gothic fiction. The late eighteenth century ineluctably regarded the Gothic edifice as a kind of *sensation-machine*: a sort of fantastic psychic compression chamber in which one might re-create, atavistically, the thrilling sense of being overwhelmed by something bigger and more potent than oneself. In the absence of a real building, a literary fabrication might serve just as well. In Gothic fiction's relentlessly "architectural" obsessions—witnessed in titles such as *The Castle of Otranto, The Mysteries of Udolpho, The Castles of Athlyn and Dunbane, The Recess, The Old English Manor House, The Abbey of Clugny, The Priory of St. Clair, Emmeline: or, The Orphan of the Castle, The Midnight Groan: or, The Spectre of the Chapel, The Children of the Abbey, The Church of St. Siffrid, The Castle of Wolfenbach, The Castle of Hardayne,* or *The Castle of St. Vallery* (not to mention "The Fall of the House of Usher," *The Tenant of Wildfell Hall,* or *Wuthering Heights*)—we not only see the inevitable (punning) Gothic linkage between *buildings* and *stories* but the genre's presiding fantasies of self-enclaustration, physical debilitation, and psychic surrender writ large.[44]

In order to replicate the "sense of self-annihilation" associated with Gothic buildings, a novel—it was argued—had to arouse in its readers nothing less than metaphysical dread: some version—however fleeting or artificial—of that "universal apprehension of superior agency" commonly associated with the supernatural. Here Gothic aestheticians drew fruitfully on contemporary psychological theory—notably John Locke's famous notion that feelings and emotions derived from the association of ideas. (Men were afraid of the dark, Locke argued in his *Essay Concerning Human Understanding,* because as children they been taught by "nursemaids" or old women to connect "the ideas of ghosts and goblins with that of darkness." The association once made, "night ever after becomes painful and horrible to the imagination."[45]) Of all the human passions, wrote the critic John Dennis in 1704, none was "more capable of giving a great spirit to poetry" than "terror." Terror was precisely that "disturbance of mind proceeding from an apprehension of an approaching evil, threatening destruction or very great trouble to us or ours." It made sense, therefore, that the greatest "enthusiastic terror" should derive from "religious ideas." For what he concluded, "can produce a greater terror than the idea of an angry god?"[46]

In calling for this spiritually fraught "literature of terror," promoters of the Gothic usually invoked, in turn, the concept of the sublime—that rampant, radiant, yet also problematic master trope of eighteenth-century psychology and aesthetics. The theory of the sublime seemed to authorize precisely those extreme themes and techniques necessary for the reengagement of jaded readers. The concept itself had its origins in late antiquity. In *Peri Hupsous* (or *On the Sublime*) the first- or second-century Greco-Christian rhetorician Longinus had defined the sublime as any phenomenon that provoked "astonishment" in a

viewer and prompted him to contemplate the infinite majesty of God. Magnificent or threatening objects in nature (mighty torrents of water, erupting volca-
noes, dizzying precipices) were sublime, but so too was any sort of poetry
characterized by "greatness" or "grandeur" of expression. Confronting the dazzling verbal flights of Homer, Pindar, Sappho, or the anonymous author of
Scripture, Longinus suggested, the reader was drawn out of himself, lifted up,
and "transported" into a state of religious ecstasy.[47]

In his 1757 *Philosophical Enquiry into the Origin of Our Ideas of the Sublime
and the Beautiful*, Edmund Burke updated Longinus's concept of sublimity by
relating it, once again, to the Lockean theory of mind. A sublime object, according to Burke, was anything that evoked an "idea" of pain and terror, yet did not
pose any real danger to the observer. When contemplated from a safe distance,
objects ordinarily frightening in the extreme (typically anything dark, vast, powerful, obscure, gloomy, towering, or "irregular" in shape) became sources of
deep, if perverse, excitement and pleasure. They stimulated the instinct of "self-
preservation," resulting in "certain violent emotions of the nerves," but since
they did no actual harm, the viewer was left with a paradoxical feeling of "delight" and self-expansion.[48] Burke agreed with Longinus that poetry could induce the same sublime emotions inspired by real-world phenomena. Thanks to
his magnificent yet sometimes "obscure" trains of imagery—as in the description
in *Paradise Lost* of "the travels of the fallen angels through their dismal habita-
tion" in Hell:

> O'er many a dark and dreary vale
> They pass'd, and many a region dolorous;
> O'er many a frozen, many a fiery Alp;
> Rocks, caves, lakes, fens, bogs, dens and shades of death,
> A universe of death.

—Milton, for example, was able to produce in his readers the same gratifying
state of "fearful delight" associated with sublime objects in nature.[49] "The sublime is an idea belonging to self-preservation," wrote Burke; "it is therefore one
of the most affecting we have."[50]

This is not the place for a thoroughgoing analysis—let alone a philosophical
critique—of the sublimity cult, but its exorbitant influence on Gothic fiction
must be noted. Like antiquarianism and the craze for things medieval, the cult
of the sublime provided Gothic novelists with a certain (dubious) intellectual respectability—not to mention a handy quasi-ethical justification for the somewhat distasteful psychic shock tactics they now began to unleash on more or less
eager readers. Granted, certain aspects of the cult were benign enough. In the
novels of Ann Radcliffe the new taste for sublimity expressed itself mainly in la-
dylike passages of nature description—albeit of an unusually protracted, en-

gorged, and stupendous sort. Radcliffe inevitably emphasized the sublime's up-lifting effect on the mind and soul of the observer. Confronted by gleaming mountain crag, crashing torrent, or bottomless chasm, even her most abused and downtrodden heroines find themselves exhilarated by such "fearsome" evi-dences of God's omnipotence. Thus the somewhat incongruous fit of spiritual transport felt by Emily St. Aubert, heroine of *Udolpho*, when she is dragged through the Alps by her villainous brigand-kidnapper, Count Montoni—

> Emily, often as she travelled among the clouds, watched in silent awe their billowy surges rolling below; sometimes, wholly closing upon the scene, they appeared like a world of chaos, and, at others, spreading thinly, they opened and admitted partial catches of the landscape—the torrent, whose astounding roar had never failed, tumbling down the rocky chasm, huge cliffs white with snow, or the dark summits of the pine forests, that stretched mid-way down the mountains. But who may de-scribe her rapture, when, having passed through a sea of vapour, she caught a first view of Italy; when, from the ridge of one of those tremen-dous precipices that hang upon Mount Cenis and guard the entrance of that enchanting country, she looked down through the lower clouds, and, as they floated away, saw the grassy vales of Piedmont at her feet, and, be-yond, the plains of Lombardy extending to the farthest distance, at which appeared, on the faint horizon, the doubtful towers of Turin? [51]

It's as if Janet Leigh, assailed by Tony Perkins in the shower scene in Hitchcock's *Psycho*, were suddenly to enthuse over the view from the Bates Hotel bathroom window.

Often enough, however, objects and scenes once deemed far too macabre, horrific, or sexually perverse for polite literature came now to be valued for ex-actly those qualities: for their kinky-delightful effect on readers' nerves. Classical aesthetics held that some subjects were simply too shocking for a poet to repre-sent directly: "you will not let Medea slay her boys before the audience, or Atreus cook his horrid banquet of human flesh," wrote Horace in his *Ars Poetica*; "any-thing that you thus thrust upon my sight I discredit and revolt at."[52] Yet under the sway of the sublime, nothing—no matter how ghastly or repugnant—seemed too outré to enlist as a subject, so long as it provoked in readers some thrilled or "affrighted" response. Thus Lewis in *The Monk* could depict the evis-ceration of an evil nun—she is mauled by a mob of "Rioters" until "no more than a mass of flesh, unsightly, shapeless, and disgusting"—without regard for decorum or good taste: the "strong" sensations elicited by such a description—of fright, nausea, repulsion, Schadenfreude, relief—merely set the seal on the sub-limity of the work and its devices.[53] The decaying corpse, the carious skeleton, the blood-soaked apparition: such were the Boschean dramatis personae of the new "Satanic School" of British fiction. Literary *fashionistas* reveled in the gore. Even in "the present polished period of society," Nathan Drake asserted, "there are thousands who are yet alive to all the horrors of witchcraft, to all the solemn and terrible graces of the appalling spectre."[54] Artfully conducted, even the most grisly spectacle might result in the "grateful astonishment" of readers and a "welcome" (if regressive) sensation of fear.

We do well to take seriously the extraordinary malaise—physical and metaphysical—that prompted this hunger for stimulation. The Gothic obsession with things dire and obscene sheds light not only on the evolution of taste but on certain troubled (and troubling) aspects of modernity itself. The reiterated complaint about the withdrawal of the numinous—the abrupt departure of "wonder" from the world—should first of all be deeply heeded; for seen in broadest terms, the collective craving after Gothic was a kind of *symptom*—of the emotional void left by that complex and momentous historical transformation known as secularization. It is no accident that the Gothic craze arose precisely at a time when age-old folk beliefs regarding apparitions, witchcraft, demonic possession, miracles, omens, and the like had been largely supplanted—at least superficially—by new skeptical attitudes. Thanks to accelerating developments in science and technology, the waning of religious controversy, and the subsequent rationalization of countless aspects of everyday life, educated English men and women were now far less inclined than in past centuries to resort to supernatural explanations for bizarre or unsettling events. Official culture registered the change: Parliament made witchcraft accusations illegal in Britain in 1736; and by midcentury necromancy, astrology, and other forms of occult belief had been similarly discredited.[55] A raft of phenomena once held to be supernatural in origin were reinterpreted in new and strictly materialistic terms. Ghosts and specters, for example, traditionally seen as marvelous emissaries from an invisible spirit world, came increasingly to be regarded as *mental* entities: hallucinatory figments arising from the diseased brain or "sensorium" of the person who claimed to see them. By the 1790s—the breakout decade of Gothic experimentation—this "scientific" theory of apparitions was widely accepted, as popular medical treatises such as Alexander Crichton's *Nature and Origin of Mental Derangement* (1798) and Christoph Friedrich Nicolai's *Memoir on the Appearance of Spectres or Phantoms Occasioned by Disease* (1799) attested.[56]

Some Gothic novelists, paradoxically, sought to present themselves as propagandists for the new enlightened dispensation. Ann Radcliffe always played a famous double game. Her novels are crammed full of *apparently* supernatural events—strange knockings, unearthly music, subtly moving shrouds under which corpses seem to stir—all meant to keep the reader (like the heroine) in a state of "terrific" mental unease. Yet by the end of the Radcliffean narrative, some all-too mundane explanation is inevitably forthcoming for every disturbing incident— usually accompanied by pedantic editorial asides on the follies of credulity and superstition.[57] Radcliffe was much criticized for this banalizing technique, and most of the terror writers who followed in her stead wholeheartedly rejected the clumsy "explained supernatural" device. The gloomy fiends of Lewis and Maturin prowl the human world at will, unmolested by authorial temporizing.

Yet even Radcliffe's ambiguous commitments do not undermine the larger point: that by the end of the eighteenth century, "ghosts," as J. M. S. Tompkins puts it, "were a felt want." For all of its self-conscious archaism the Gothic is painfully modern in this aspect: its ineluctably god-deprived outlook. To be "Gothic" in tendency is to hanker nostagically for some—*any*—spiritual manifestation, whether of deity, devil, or something in between. (Figures such as Maturin's immortal Melmoth, living painfully on through the centuries, seem to inhabit an eerie realm between the human and the demonic.) But the missing *pneumaton* never materializes. The pathos—or bathos—of the Gothic mode lies precisely in the fact that no matter how dotingly invoked, the "Invisible World" of old cannot be artificially reanimated. Reciting some gloomy passage from *The Monk* or *Udolpho* will never bring grim-faced Mephisto—or even a reeking minion—to one's darkened chamber at midnight. Critics often complain about the artistic ineptitude of Gothic fiction: that the things meant to boggle make us laugh. Yet at the deepest level such complaints register ontological as well as aesthetic disappointment. Even while celebrating the new imperatives of the Enlightenment, the eighteenth century also mourned—as we do—a lost world of supernatural beings. In the pale, magic-lantern-like illusionism of Gothic it learned to make do with cheap simulacra. Today, despite all the "spectralising" marvels of photography, film, computer animation, and virtual reality, we have no doubt learned to do the same.

Granted, even as the Gothic failed at the larger task—the reintegration of human and spirit worlds—it indubitably succeeded at a lesser: the intense arousal of readers. By eighteenth-century standards the novels of Walpole, Radcliffe, and Lewis were extravagantly popular, spawning hundreds of imitations and knockoffs over the decades. (As Byron's touching tribute to her in *Childe Harold* attests, Radcliffe's vogue was particularly enduring, lasting well into the nineteenth century.) If Gothic necromancers inevitably failed to raise up real ghosts, their literary "phantomising" exerted, over a generation, a kind of convulsive, contagious mass appeal. "When a family was numerous," wrote Sir Walter Scott of *Udolpho*, "the volumes always flew, and were sometimes torn, from hand to hand, and the complaints of those whose studies were thus interrupted, were a general tribute to the genius of the author. Another might be found of a different and higher description, in the dwelling of the lonely invalid, or unregarded votary of celibacy, who was bewitched away from a sense of solitude, of indisposition, of the neglect of the world, or of secret sorrow, by the potent charm of this mighty enchantress."[58] *Something* about the form managed to gratify—the bathos of its spiritual ambitions notwithstanding.

This appeal was not at bottom, one suspects, primarily an intellectual one. Which isn't to say that Gothic fiction lacked a cognitive or epistemological dimension. At least since the 1960s critics have argued, if sometimes inchoately, for a certain "heuristic" efficacy in the tale of terror: that it allowed for the expression of ideas and themes too difficult, taboo, or transgressive to articulate in any other form. In a now-classic study, *The Fantastic: A Structural Approach to a Literary Genre* (1970), Tzvetan Todorov suggested, for example, that supernatural tales flourished when they did because, in an age of repressive decorums, they provided an imaginative format in which forbidden psychosexual themes—"incest, homosexuality, love for several persons at once, necrophilia [and] excessive sensuality"—might be broached with relative impunity. According to Todorov the supernatural itself licensed this exploration of "unspeakable" topics. "The penalization of certain acts by society," he writes, "provokes a penalization invoked in and by the individual himself, forbidding him to approach certain themes. More than a simple pretext, the fantastic is a means of combat against this kind of censorship as well as the other: *sexual excesses will be more readily accepted by any censor if they are attributed to the devil.*"[59] A good example of the "blame it on the devil" phenomenon occurs in the opening sequence of Lewis's *The Monk*, when the proud yet susceptible cleric of the title, Ambrosio, appears to fall in love—scandalously enough—with a pretty boy-novice in his convent. Quasi-catamitical caresses ensue, but just as Ambrosio seems intent on consummating his unlawful passion, the "boy" is revealed as a she-devil in disguise. Lewis is thus able to have it both ways: the taboo subject is foregrounded—homosexuality—only to be quickly neutralized by the supernatural (yet erotically normalizing) explanation. Such teasing play with conceptual categories, Todorov argues, played a historic role in the creation of modern consciousness. By bringing subjects such as homosexuality at least partly into view, the Gothic fantasists of the late eighteenth century in fact prepared the intellectual ground, Todorov concludes, for pioneering new cognitive regimens—such as psychoanalysis—in which such themes might be confronted with greater directness, clarity, and intellectual dispassion.[60]

Other critics find other kinds of "ideas" in Gothic fiction. Feminist critics argue that by virtue of its melodramatic plots and exotic settings, the genre allowed for the covert expression of unorthodox opinions on gender and the moral, social, and political status of women in late-eighteenth-century British society. This "subversive" articulation, the feminist argument usually goes, was allegorical in nature—a matter of hidden metaphors and symbolic topographies. Thus the grim Gothic castle might stand for the oppressive rulings of masculine law; the terrorization of the heroine by the Gothic villain for the abusive nature of male-female relations under patriarchy; the penetration of cryptlike spaces for the threat (real or imagined) of female sexuality. An ideological contrast is sometimes drawn between Gothic novels written by men and those written by women—the former usually being seen, in the feminist view, as more complacent, if not reactionary, in their handling of sexual politics than the latter. A number of recent scholars have gone so far as to find in the fiction of Radcliffe, Reeve, Lee, and the other female Gothicists a major critique of contemporary gender relations—one hauntingly akin, despite the fantastic displacement, to that put forward in Mary Wollstonecraft's *Vindication of the Rights of Woman* (1792) and other polemical feminist works of the period.[61]

Yet for all of its interest and value, such theorizing still seems to miss out on something: the essentially crude, even somatic exigencies of the genre. (Feminist critics in particular tend to overintellectualize the form—with sometimes pedantic and repetitive results.) For a clue to the "deep" pleasure of Gothic, we might ponder for a moment the intensely corporeal, even *kinesiological* language of its admirers. Enthusiasts like Sir Walter Scott and Nathan Drake wrote vividly of the physical responses a truly "thrilling" Gothic tale could induce: gasping and breathlessness, chills, prickling hair on the neck, a sensation of immobilization and panic, the convulsive tensing of "nervous fibers," followed (usually) by exquisite feelings of relaxation and relief. Such responses were inevitably modeled *within* Gothic texts; Gothic heroines, for example, experience such kinetic arousal constantly—indeed, often appear incapable of experiencing anything *but* such arousal. (The primary function of the Gothic protagonist, one is tempted to suggest, may be to serve on the reader's behalf as a kind of primitive "sensing device" within the fictional world—as a sort of surrogate "stimulus-receptor," whose reported reactions are meant to "cue up" the same reactions in the reader. Self-analysis, moral problem solving, the intellectual examination of one's surroundings—all of the other quasi-cognitive activities traditionally attributed to literary characters—seem here subordinated, if not overridden completely, by this single Pavlovian, even robotic, textual function.) Thus in *Udolpho*, when Emily St. Aubert comes abruptly upon a mangled body being borne through a tunnel in Montoni's castle, her "strength" immediately fails her and she has to grasp at a wall for support: "A damp chillness came over her; her sight became confused; she knew not what had passed, or where she was, yet the groans of the wounded person still vibrated on her heart." As always, Radcliffe notates the process of kinesiological normalization too, for "in a few moments," once the cortège has passed, "the tide of life seemed again to flow; [Emily] began to breathe more freely, and her senses revived."[62] If the emotional self-reporting of Radcliffe's contemporaries is to be believed, such a passage might serve as a trigger point for similar responses in a susceptible reader.

Why should readers have *enjoyed* the vicarious activation of such responses? Perhaps, to put it baldly, because physical life itself had come to seem too safe, predictable, and banal. Consider for a moment the nature of that "present polished state of society" described by commentators like Nathan Drake. Though undoubtedly harsh by modern standards, late-eighteenth-century bourgeois

British culture represented, in phenomenological terms, the most comfortable, sedating, existentially "buffered" society the Western world had yet seen. Scientific improvements, social and political reforms, the gradual "refinement" of manners, the rise of new, cultivated pleasures—all had brought about, in the privileged classes especially, a growing faith in the perfectibility of human life. "It is an age so full of light," wrote Sterne in *A Sentimental Journey* (1768), "that there is scarce a country or corner of Europe whose beams are not crossed and interchanged with others."[63] Once-dire threats to human security had been lessened or even abrogated—in some cases fairly recently. (Not least among these was the age-old menace posed by animal predators.) To be a prosperous denizen of a late-eighteenth-century English city or town was to experience, increasingly, a generalized sense, above all, of being *safe from attack*: a kind of psychosomatic well-being—and concomitant moral optimism—unimaginable to previous generations.[64]

But such complacency had its negative side too: sensual life had come to seem diminished, even deadened. A good deal of the psychic malaise of the mid-to-late eighteenth century may have been due, simply enough, to what might be called *kinesiological ennui*. Spontaneous responses seemed to have been dulled, the instinctive life of the body routinized and overregulated. Polite society was no doubt tranquil—"barbaric customs" had been banished—but it was also increasingly tedious. In the absence of strong sensation, more and more individuals seemed prone to psychosomatic disorders—such as that "languor, listlessness, or want of resolution" described so painfully by James Boswell (a lifelong sufferer) as "Hypochondria" or the spleen.[65] Some artificial shock or stimulus was required: something to reopen, as it were, the blocked channels of feeling. The Gothic novel worked like caffeine in this respect, being first and foremost a stimulant, a kind of auto-intensifier, a way of feeling one's own body.

Yet we might take the hypothesis further. One is struck by a resemblance between the symptoms of "Gothic arousal" and that atavistic physiological reflex— present in all living creatures including human beings—colloquially known as the "fight or flight response." Chills, involuntary tensing, a racing heart, shortness of breath: such indeed are the stereotypical symptoms of the mammalian "stress response"—that dramatic biochemical and hormonal reaction set in motion by the sympathetic nervous system whenever an organism confronts a threat to its survival. Such changes—in the view of evolutionary biology—serve a crucial adaptive function. By reallocating physiological resources in the most efficient way, the "fight or flight" mechanism allows an organism to respond quickly to a perceived danger, either by attacking it or running away.[66]

According to Elias Canetti, the deepest, most ancient human fear is that of becoming *prey*. It expresses itself, even in the midst of civilized life, in lingering anxieties about being touched, grasped, or seized, especially from behind.

There is nothing that man fears more than the touch of the unknown. He wants to *see* what is reaching towards him, and to be able to recognise or at least classify it. Man always tends to avoid physical contact with anything strange. In the dark, the fear of an unexpected touch can mount to panic. Even clothes give insufficient security: it is easy to tear them and pierce through to the naked, smooth, defenceless flesh of the victim.

All the distances which men create round themselves are dictated by this fear. They shut themselves in houses which no-one may enter, and only there feel some measure of security. The fear of burglars is not only the fear of being robbed, but also the fear of a sudden and unexpected clutch out of the darkness.

The repugnance to being touched remains with us when we go about among people; the way we move in a busy street, in restaurants, trains or buses, is governed by it. . . . The promptness with which apology is offered for an unintentional contact, the tension with which it is awaited, our violent and sometimes even physical reaction when it is not forthcoming, the antipathy and hatred we feel for the offender, even when we cannot be certain who it is—the whole knot of shifting and intensely sensitive reactions to an alien touch—proves that we are dealing here with a human propensity as deep-seated as it is alert and insidious; something which never leaves a man when he has once established the boundaries of his personality. Even in sleep, when he is far more unguarded, he can all too easily be disturbed by a touch.[67]

With such observations in mind, one might float a theory: that through its charged symbolic play with the imagery of predation in particular—*of being seized and incorporated by something larger and more powerful than oneself*—the Gothic novel stimulated certain primitive affective mechanisms that had begun to atrophy as a result of the extraordinarily rapid civilization—and banalization—of contemporary life. The point was precisely to feel afraid, like a trapped or cornered animal. Such a theory would accord neatly with the ethnographic and symbolic meanings of *Gothic* noted earlier in this chapter. Though not, as we have seen, without their romantic admirers, the ancient Goths inevitably held sway in the eighteenth-century popular imagination as being among the great *predators* of human history—fabled marauders who had brought down Rome with the grim rapacity of wild beasts. It makes powerful metaphoric sense that a literary genre designed to arouse in the reader the visceral sensation of *becoming prey* should take on a name evoking the reputedly most fearsome and aggressive men and women of Western antiquity.

No reader of Gothic fiction can fail to notice how relentlessly it foregrounds the fight-or-flight scenario—sometimes again and again in the same work. Gothic fabulists delight in creating worlds in which assault is repeatedly threatened and escape nightmarishly difficult. The labyrinthine spaces of Gothic architecture, so emblematic of the form, seem designed precisely to intensify the vicarious sensation *that one is about to be seized*. With its bewildering irrationalization of space—the mysterious portals and stairways, tunnels that seem to go nowhere, clanging trapdoors, blacked-out dungeons and crypts—the Gothic castle or convent, we realize, provides an exquisitely sinister mise-en-scène for fantasies of entrapment and immobilization. One can't move in a straight line in Gothic space: everywhere one turns, it seems, there is something to impede one's movement or obscure the way, even as one senses a predator coming closer and closer.[68] The panic-filled "trap and release" scenes so endlessly played out in classic Gothic narrative—Isabella's hysterical flight from Manfred through the maze-like basements of Otranto, Emily St. Aubert's grim nocturnal escape from the fortress of Udolpho, Raymond's squirming, scrambling, frantic efforts to evade homicidal bandits in the "German" section of *The Monk*—all evoke the syndrome in different ways: one *must get away*, but the way is potentially blocked or barred. The door is padlocked, the passageway sealed, one's screams muffled or smothered. One is literally on the verge of becoming *prey*—ensnared and consumed—as the churning, bestial imagery of Gothic pursuers and victims incessantly emphasizes.

Such moments of threatened seizure, one may speculate, function as kinesiological arousal points. When carried off artfully, they can exact from a reader, quite literally, a kind of mediated "fight or flight" response: an artificial nervous excitement, or psychosomatic *consternation*, profoundly linked—however distantly—to what Burke called the "instincts of self-preservation." We cannot help but identify with the potential victim. Nor, perhaps, can we help sharing in the relief when the Gothic protagonist (inevitably) makes his or her way to safety. (All three of the breathless flights mentioned above turn out to be successful.) If it is intoxicating to imagine oneself a prey animal, it is even more delightful to imagine oneself eluding capture: the fox disappearing into the undergrowth.

It is my suspicion that such identification ultimately overrode gender roles: the I-am-being-menaced fantasy gratified male and female readers alike. It is true that most Gothic victims are female; most Gothic predators male. Yet it is not the case, I think, that male readers necessarily identified with the predator figure. (The passing comments of contemporary enthusiasts such as Scott and Drake would suggest the opposite.) No one would wish to discount the appalling sociological truth regularly encrypted in Gothic fiction: that in real life, women are more frequently victims of male violence than vice versa. And though I referred earlier to the increasingly "buffered" nature of late-eighteenth-century bourgeois culture—and even postulated that a new sense of *being safe from attack* had begun to insinuate itself among the privileged classes—I am aware how much such speculation would need to be qualified along sexual lines. Even among women of the highest class, the sense of increasing physical security was surely never as great as it was for their male contemporaries.

But fantasies of being chased, assailed, broken in upon—cruelly seized—seem to have carried a powerful cross-sex appeal. Aspects of narrative technique were no doubt partly responsible: just as makers of horror and suspense films do today, Gothic novelists typically presented their predation scenes from the victim's point of view—i.e., the "prey" position—thus intensifying the reader's own sense of vulnerability and isolation. A passage like the following, from *Otranto*, shows just how much the grippingly subjective camera work of a filmmaker like Hitchcock owes to Gothic narrative devices:

> Words cannot paint the horror of the princess's situation. Alone in so dismal a place [an underground passageway], her mind imprinted with all the terrible events of the day, hopeless of escaping, expecting every moment the arrival of Manfred, and far from tranquil on knowing she was within reach of somebody, she knew not whom, who for some cause seem concealed thereabouts, all these thoughts crowded on her distracted mind, and she was ready to sink under her apprehensions.[69]

Yet at the same time we should not underestimate the universal potency of certain reflexive impulses. In a recent study of contemporary Hollywood slasher films, a prominent feminist film scholar discovered that, contrary to her expectations, a majority of teenage boys who habitually attended such films reported identifying not with the films' ravening stalkers and serial killers but with their set-upon female victims.[70] Just so, one suspects—eighteenth-century men too became invested in the Gothic's masochistic psychic structures. Men as well as women have anxiety dreams, after all—and the same surfeiting relief when such dreams come to an end.

Were space permitting one might take such conjectures further—into the still-mysterious realms of evolutionary psychology and neural biochemistry. If it is indeed the case that the "civilizing" tendencies in late-eighteenth-century culture had somehow deadened age-old affective responses—might not Gothic fiction have had a useful adaptive function? To keep in train, so to speak, the physiological "alert systems," once so necessary to the survival of the human organism? And what of the "exquisite delight" associated with the Gothic's trap-and-release narrative rhythms? The prey animal possesses yet another adaptive reflex: when it is attacked, its sympathetic nervous system releases a massive stream of pain-killing endorphins—presumably, zoologists speculate, to block the agony of being torn apart and consumed. Might it not be bruited that the raising and calming of fictional terrors prompted a similar, if fleeting, sensation of chemically induced euphoria?

Such questions will no doubt strike some as deeply fanciful.[71] We have no scientific mechanisms for measuring the biochemical aspects of literary response—nor despite startling developments in neuroscience are we likely to have one any time soon. We have no way of knowing whether reading Gothic fiction delivers, say, an intoxicating rush of l-dopamine to the central nervous system, or a pleasing series of jolts to the readerly hypothalamus. Nonetheless, the notion that the Gothic tale, like the modern-day horror film, functioned primarily as a *sensation-trigger* is an extraordinarily clarifying one. It helps to explain, among other things, why eighteenth-century readers were so ready to tolerate the palpable absurdities of the genre. Gothic novels are notoriously full of solecisms: dropped plot lines, disappearing characters, historical anachronisms, strange authorial non sequiturs. (Often one has the unsettling feeling reading Radcliffe, for example, that one knows more about the fictional world than she does.) But few contemporary readers seemed to mind the sloppiness. If a story produced the obligatory "chills" it had accomplished its task. In this brazen instrumentality the Gothic might again be compared to pornography—the other eighteenth-century "master-genre" preeminently devoted to the physical arousal of readers. In fact, if one's hypothesis regarding the somatic ennui of the late eighteenth century is correct, it is no surprise that both sorts of "arousal-writing" should have proliferated so spectacularly in the period. In neither mode— Gothic or pornographic—was authorial success necessarily dependent on intellectual content, felicity of style, or philosophical consistency. Even in Sade, the most cerebral of pornographers and a great admirer of Gothic, the "shudder" was still the first thing, whether the blissful convulsion of orgasm or the involuntary spasm of mortal terror.

Yet to mention Sade and pornography is to circle back, by a somewhat scandalous roundabout, to the larger question of value raised in the opening pages of this essay. One still wants to ask: What *good* is Gothic? The critics of the early twentieth century no doubt disparaged the Gothic mode as vehemently as they did partly because of its flagrant instrumentality. As with pornography, the Gothic's crassly "kinesthetic" designs on the reader were glaring, monotonous, and ultimately degrading. Could a literary genre really be valuable, after all, whose principal goal seemed merely to induce a kind of reflexive nervous agitation in its readers? What of art's grander imperatives—to speak the truth? to register beauty? to clarify human consciousness? to help us live our lives?

I suggested at the outset, no doubt rather too grandiosely, that modern-day Gothic scholars had yet to take account of some of the "more disturbing moral and psychological aspects of the Gothic mode." But some version of the point stands: despite recent critical attempts to amplify the sociocultural importance of Gothic fiction, it is still possible to feel a fairly profound dissatisfaction with it— and on exactly such old-fashioned grounds. Mere chills are not enough, one often feels, to compensate for deeper emotional vacancies. Indeed, for all its advertised "horrors," Gothic fiction may still strike an honest reader as inherently escapist and trivializing—and as a kind of "wrong turn" in English literary history— despite the army of ideological claims now sometimes made for it. While the tendency of recent criticism to upgrade the form is understandable—the jocose dismissals of Gothic in the first half of the century, it is true, were often blithely reductive and ahistorical—contemporary scholars have nonetheless been too quick to accept, perhaps, the wishful self-justifications offered by Gothic authors themselves. A more skeptical and expansive reconsideration of the place of Gothic fiction in the history of the novel would seem now to be especially desirable.

With such possibilities in mind, I shall conclude by throwing down the polemical gauntlet. Horace Walpole, we recall, published *The Castle of Otranto* in 1764, a mere decade and a half after the appearance of what is surely the eighteenth century's greatest novel in any language: Samuel Richardson's *Clarissa* (1748–49). In the preface to *Otranto*'s second edition (1765), Walpole complained that too strict an adherence to "common life" on the part of his fellow novelists had "cramped" imagination and dammed up "the great resources of fancy." In launching this squib he undoubtedly had Richardsonian realism in mind. By "leaving the powers of fancy at liberty to expatiate through the boundless realms of invention," he hinted, his own novelistic procedures had allowed for "more interesting situations" and the reanimation of "romance."[72]

Yet place *Otranto* next to *Clarissa*. Which is in fact the more "interesting" work? The more unflinching? The more majestic? The more terrifying? *Otranto*'s most recent editor argues—in defense of Walpole—that his "Gothic story" is really an important "social allegory" in disguise: in the tale of Manfred, the usurper prince of Otranto, who seeks to marry off his hapless daughter Matilda to a kinsman of the man he has dethroned in order to secure his unlawful hold on power, we have a paradigm of civic and paternal authority monstrously abused. That Manfred should end up murdering Matilda—ostensibly by accident, in a farcically melodramatic scene in the novel's final pages—merely sets the seal on his exemplarity. He is the brutal embodiment of patriarchal greed and psychopolitical violence. "Although at one level," she writes, "*Otranto* could be read as an attempt to exorcize political demons by reworking and containing them within an amusing and fantastical story, there is another level at which the representation of power remains troublingly open and unresolved. Once we get beyond spotting Gothic conventions, the central logic of the story becomes apparent: the control of property over people. . . . Far from being a problem restricted to the feudal past, or to the pages of romance, this was a live issue, bearing on the conflict between aristocratic and bourgeois ideals of social being."[73]

But can we really "get beyond" Gothic conventions? The conventions are the *Ding an sich*. From one angle *Otranto* is simply a rewrite of *Clarissa*—without the emotional insight, wealth of psychological detail, or intransigent artistic force. *Clarissa* too, of course, features a heroine cruelly persecuted by a father bent on enriching the family patrimony by marrying her off to the suitor of his choice. Yet in no way does Walpole imbue his puny version of the Richardsonian "family romance" with the dire psychic potency of the earlier novel. On the contrary: the very displacements that define Walpolean Gothic—the shift back to the medieval past, the leap across space to an exotic Italian "clime," the often ludicrous evocation of supernatural forces—drain away any real psychic energy (not to mention authentic dread) from the supposed allegory. They work, at times perniciously, to distract us from the real emotional issue. Thus in *Otranto*'s opening paragraph, when the narrator tells us that Manfred "never showed any symptoms of affection to Matilda," we confront, as in *Clarissa*, the tragic gist of the situation: a father holds an inexplicable, dehumanizing contempt for his daughter. But this passing, primal observation—surely the novel's only truly frightening sentence—is never allowed to sink in. Instead, Walpole immediately sets in motion a clamorous welter of Gothic "business": colossal falling helmets, ancient prophecies, dour troops of knights who materialize out of nowhere, clacking skeletons, gesticulating servants, and all the rest of it.

An argument could be made that, far from liberating the novelistic imagination, the Gothic craze of the later eighteenth century was a *repressive* cultural phenomenon—an ornate, often puerile attempt to defend against the truly devastating moral information brought by the eighteenth-century *realist* novel: that ordinary human beings were capable of behaving satanically; that men could drive women to despair (and vice versa); that parents could be so wicked as to hound their own children to death. For sheer moral horror, there is nothing in Walpole, Radcliffe, Lewis, or the other major Gothic writers to match certain passages in Defoe, Richardson, Fielding, Marivaux, Diderot, Laclos, Burney, Rousseau, Godwin, Inchbald, or even Wollstonecraft. (Lest the presence of his name here surprise, it should be remembered that Fielding's view of familial relationships is often hardly less bleak than Defoe's or Richardson's.) Yet what do Gothic writers do when confronted with the prospect of such local and inalienable horror? As if to erect an emotional screen, they hurry us along elsewhere—to a place of convents, potions, trapdoors, specters, and other flimsy decorative fakery—all designed to keep us from thinking too hard about what is really wrong with our lives.

In the skeptical reading I outline here, the spatio-temporal displacements of Gothic are precisely the problem: they invite us *not* to connect the abuses of the Gothic world with those of our own.[74] Infernal wickedness embodied in a literary character who supposedly "lived" long ago, in a strange and faraway place, is undoubtedly easier to deal with than infernal wickedness embodied, say, in one's own father, mother, lover, or child. Exotic evils can serve, ably enough, to draw attention away from the evil that lives at home. It would take the English novel some time, one might argue, to recover from the Gothic's Big Lie. Only when writers began setting their novels once again in "real" time and space—in "our" world, or some reasonable approximation of it—would contemporary fiction start to get its nerve back. Austen was crucial here, of course, but so too were figures like Mary Shelley and the Brontës. With them, horror came home again, to take up residence again with us—in the uncanny purlieus of the everyday.

notes

1. Sir Leslie Stephen, *English Literature and Society in the Eighteenth Century* (New York and London: G.P. Putnam's Sons, 1907), 160.

2. George Saintsbury, *The Peace of the Augustans: A Survey of Eighteenth-Century Literature as a Place of Rest and Refreshment* (1916; rpt. London: Oxford University Press, 1946), 168.

3. Ibid., 169.

4. Ibid.

5. Ibid., 170–71. For a more sympathetic view of Walpole's literary and architectural achievements, see Stephen Calloway, Michael Snodin, and Clive Wainwright, *Horace Walpole and Strawberry Hill* (London: London Borough of Richmond-on-Thames, 1980); Hugh Honour, *Horace Walpole* (London: Longman, Green, 1957); W. S. Lewis, *Horace Walpole* (New York: Pantheon Books, 1961); David D. McKinney, "The Castle of My Ancestors: Walpole and Strawberry Hill," *British Journal of Eighteenth-Century Studies* 13 (1990): 199–214; Timothy Mowl, *Horace Walpole: The Great Outsider* (London: John Murray, 1996); and Peter Sabor, ed., *Horace Walpole: The Critical Heritage* (London: Routledge and Kegan Paul, 1987).

6. Geoffrey Scott, *The Architecture of Humanism: A Study in the History of Taste* (1914; rpt. New York: Norton, 1974), 41.

7. Ibid., 43.

8. Ibid., 41. On the construction (and dilapidation) of Fonthill, see Brian Fothergill, *Beckford of Fonthill* (London: Faber and Faber, 1979), and Peter Hewat-Jaboor, "Fonthill House: 'One of the Most Princely Edifices in The Kingdom'" and Megan Aldrich, "William Beckford's Abbey at Fonthill: From the Picturesque to the Sublime," both in Derek E. Ostergard, ed., *William Beckford, 1760–1844: An Eye for the Magnificent* (New Haven and London: Yale University Press, 2001), 51–72, 117–35.

9. Virginia Woolf, "Gothic Romance," in *The Essays of Virginia Woolf,* ed. Andrew McNeillie (London: Hogarth Press, 1988), vol. 3, 305.

10. See Edith Birkhead, *The Tale of Terror: A Study of the Gothic Romance* (London: Constable, 1921) and J. M. S. Tompkins, *The Popular Novel in England 1770–1800* (Lincoln: University of Nebraska Press, 1961).

11. Tompkins, *Popular Novel,* 222.

12. See Scott, *Architecture of Humanism,* 53.

13. Ibid., 51.

14. For a general survey of the development of Gothic architecture in Europe, see Paul Frankl, *Gothic Architecture,* trans. Dieter Pevsner (Baltimore: Penguin Books, 1962). On the English Gothic style, see Francis Bond, *Gothic Architecture in England: An Analysis of the Origin and Development of English Church Architecture from the Norman Conquest to the Dissolution of the Monasteries* (London: B. T. Batsford, 1905); Jean Bony, *The English Decorated Style: Gothic Architecture Transformed, 1250–1350* (Ithaca, N.Y.: Cornell University Press, 1979); Peter Hampson Ditchfield, *English Gothic Architecture* (London: J. M. Dent, 1920); Samuel

Gardner, *A Guide to English Gothic Architecture* (Cambridge: Cambridge University Press, 1922); and Nikolaus Pevsner, *The Englishness of English Art* (London: Architectural Press, 1956).

15. John Dryden, "To Sir Godfrey Kneller," lines 47–48; in James Kinsley, ed., *The Poems and Fables of John Dryden* (London and Oxford: Oxford University Press), 497.

16. Anthony Ashley Cooper, Earl of Shaftesbury, *Characteristics of Men, Manners, Opinions, and Times* (1711; rpt. London, 1733), 1, 2, 86.

17. Henry Fielding, *Tom Jones* (1749), bk. 7, ch. 3.

18. Alexander Pope, *The Dunciad* (1743), bk. 3, lines 83–94. On Pope's satiric depiction of the ancient Goths, see Richard Braverman, "'Dunce the Second Reigns Like Dunce the First': The Gothic Bequest in *The Dunciad*," *ELH: A Journal of English Literary History* 62 (Winter 1995): 863–82.

19. For a capacious overview of these and other historical developments in eighteenth-century British culture and society, see John Brewer, *The Pleasures of the Imagination: English Culture in the Eighteenth Century* (New York: Farrar, Straus and Giroux, 1997) and Linda Colley, *Britons: Forging the Nation 1707–1837* (New Haven and London: Yale University Press, 1992), especially ch. 2.

20. On eighteenth-century views of the ancient Goths and their contribution to British cultural and poetic tradition, see E. J. Clery and Robert Miles, eds., *Gothic Documents: A Sourcebook 1700–1820* (Manchester and New York: Manchester University Press, 2000), 48–98; Paul Frankl, *The Gothic: Literary Sources and Interpretations through Eight Centuries* (Princeton, N.J.: Princeton University Press, 1960); Samuel Kliger, *The Goths in England: A Study in Seventeenth- and Eighteenth-Century Thought* (Cambridge, Mass.: Harvard University Press, 1952); Mark Madoff, "The Useful Myth of Gothic Ancestry," *Studies in Eighteenth-Century Culture* 8 (1979): 337–50; R. J. Smith, *The Gothic Bequest: Medieval Institutions in British Thought, 1688–1863* (Cambridge: Cambridge University Press, 1987); Katie Trumpener, *Bardic Nationalism: The Romantic Novel and the British Empire* (Princeton N.J.: Princeton University Press, 1997); and Howard D. Weinbrot, *Britannia's Issue: The Rise of British Literature from Dryden to Ossian* (Cambridge and New York: Cambridge University Press, 1993).

21. James Thomson, *Liberty* (1734–36), in J. Logie Robertson, ed., *Poetical Works of James Thomson* (London: Oxford University Press, 1908), pt. 4, ii, 640–43.

22. A discussion of the Goths' "refined gallantry" with regard to women is to be found, for example, in Letter III of Richard Hurd's *Letters on Chivalry and Romance* (1762). See also Clery and Miles, *Gothic Documents*, 67–77.

23. Chris Brooks, *The Gothic Revival* (London: Phaidon Press, 1999), 51. Here and elsewhere, I am extraordinarily indebted to Brooks's lucid overview of the evolving ideological meanings of Gothic architecture in Britain over the course of the eighteenth century. See also Megan Aldrich, *Gothic Revival* (London: Phaidon Press, 1994); Sir Kenneth Clark, *The Gothic Revival: An Essay in the History of Taste* (Middlesex, Eng.: Penguin Books, 1964); Charles L. Eastlake, *A History of the Gothic Revival* (London: Longman, Green, 1872); Anne F. Janowitz, *England's Ruins: Poetic Purpose and the National Landscape* (Oxford: Blackwell, 1990); James Macaulay, *The Gothic Revival 1745–1845* (Glasgow: Blackie, 1975); Michael J. McCarthy, *The Origins of the Gothic Revival* (New Haven and London: Yale University Press, 1987); and Stuart Piggott, *Ruins in a Landscape: Essays in Antiquarianism* (Edinburgh: Edinburgh University Press, 1976).

24. Brooks, *Gothic Revival*, 52.

25. Ibid.

26. Ibid., 62.

27. Ibid., 56.

28. Joseph Addison, *The Spectator*, no. 419 (1712), in *The Spectator*, ed. Donald F. Bond (Oxford: Oxford University Press, 1965), vol. 3, 572.

29. Ibid., 571.

30. Ibid., 572.

31. Ibid., 572–73.

32. Ibid., 573. On some of the literary-historical ramifications of Addison's comments—especially regarding Spenser—see chapter 4 in Jonathan Brody Kramnick, *Making the English Canon: Print-Capitalism and the Cultural Past, 1700–1770* (Cambridge: Cambridge University Press, 1998): "The Cultural Logic of Late Feudalism: or, Spenser and the Romance of Scholarship, 1754–1762."

33. See Hurd, *Letters on Chivalry and Romance*, Letter VII. For a superb analysis of Hurd's feudal-nostalgic aesthetic and the evolution of Gothic style, see Kramnick, *Making the English Canon*, 176–89.

34. Elizabeth Montagu, *An Essay on the Writings and Genius of Shakespear, Compared with the Greek and French Dramatic Poets, with Some Remarks upon the Misrepresentations of Mons. de Voltaire* (London, 1769), 119.

35. Samuel Taylor Coleridge, "General Character of the Gothic Literature and Art" (1818), in Coleridge, *Coleridge's Miscellaneous Criticism*, ed. Thomas Middleton Raysor (London: Constable, 1936), 12.

36. Charles Robert Maturin, *Melmoth the Wanderer*, ed. Victor Sage (London: Penguin Books, 2000), 120.

37. Woolf, "Gothic Romance," 305.

38. Hurd, *Works*, vol. 4, 350.

39. Thomas Warton, *The History of English Poetry from the Close of the Eleventh to the Commencement of the Eighteenth Century* (London: J. Dodsley, 1778), vol. 2, 463.

40. Nathan Drake, "On Gothic Superstition," in *Literary Hours, or Sketches Critical and Narrative* (New York: Garland, 1970), vol. 2, 137–38.

41. John Pinkerton, *A Dissertation on the Origin and Progress of the Scythians or Goths, Being an Introduction to the Ancient and Modern History of Europe* (London: John Nichols, 1787), 138.

42. Coleridge, "General Character," in *Miscellaneous Criticism*, 7.

43. See Tompkins, *Popular Novel*, 221.

44. There is a large and diverse critical literature on the symbolic function of architecture in eighteenth-century Gothic fiction. For a broad sampling of views, see Manuel Aguirre, *The Closed Space: Horror Literature and Western Symbolism* (Manchester: Manchester University Press, 1990); Kate Ferguson Ellis, *The Contested Castle: Gothic Novels and the Subversion of Domestic Ideology* (Urbana: University of Illinois Press, 1989); Richard Davenport-Hines, *Gothic: Four Hundred Years of Excess, Horror, Evil and Ruin* (New York: North Point Press, 1998); Robin Lyndenberg, "Gothic Architecture and Fiction: A Survey of Critical Responses," *Centennial Review* 22 (1978): 95–109; Lee Morrissey, *From the Temple to the Castle: An Architectural History of British Literature, 1660–1760* (Charlottesville: University Press of Virginia,

1999); and Anthony Vidler, *The Architectural Uncanny: Essays in the Modern Unhomely* (Cambridge, Mass.: MIT Press, 1992).

45. See John Locke, *An Essay Concerning Human Understanding* (London, 1690), bk. 2, ch. 3.

46. John Dennis, "The Grounds of Criticism in Poetry" (1704), in *Eighteenth-Century Critical Essays,* ed. Scott Elledge (Ithaca, N.Y.: Cornell University Press, 1961), vol. 2, 121–22.

47. On the Longinian sublime and its place in eighteenth-century literature and aesthetics, see Andrew Ashfield and Peter De Bolla, eds., *The Sublime: A Reader in British Eighteenth-Century Aesthetic Theory* (Cambridge: Cambridge University Press, 1996); Peter De Bolla, *The Discourse of the Sublime: Readings in History, Aesthetics and the Subject* (Oxford and New York: Oxford University Press, 1989); Frances Ferguson, *Solitude and the Sublime* (London and New York: Routledge, 1992); T. R. Henn, *Longinus and English Criticism* (Cambridge: Cambridge University Press, 1934); Samuel Holt Monk, *The Sublime: A Study of Critical Theories in XVIII-Century England* (Ann Arbor: University of Michigan Press, 1960); and Marjorie Hope Nicolson, *Mountain Gloom and Mountain Glory: The Development of the Aesthetics of the Infinite* (Ithaca, N.Y.: Cornell University Press, 1959).

48. Edmund Burke, *A Philosophical Enquiry into the Origin of Our Ideas of the Sublime and Beautiful* (1757), ed. J. T. Boulton (London: Routledge and Kegan Paul, 1958), 38–40.

49. Ibid., 174–75.

50. Ibid., 86.

51. Ann Radcliffe, *The Mysteries of Udolpho,* ed. Bonamy Dobrée (Oxford and New York: Oxford University Press, 1998), 165.

52. Horace, *The Art of Poetry,* in E. C. Wickham, *Horace for English Readers: Being a Translation of the Poems of Quintus Horatius Flaccus into English Prose* (Oxford: Clarendon Press, 1903), 350.

53. Matthew Lewis, *The Monk,* ed. Howard Anderson (Oxford and New York: Oxford University Press, 1973), 356.

54. Drake, "On Gothic Superstition," 137.

55. On the waning of supernatural belief in England, see W. E. H. Lecky's magisterial nineteenth-century study, *The History of the Rise and Influence of the Spirit of Rationalism in Europe* (1865; rpt. New York: D. Appleton, 1919). For a brilliant and authoritative modern treatment of the phenomenon, see Keith Thomas, *Religion and the Decline of Magic* (New York: Charles Scribner's Sons, 1971).

56. See Terry Castle, "Spectral Politics: Apparition Belief and the Romantic Imagination," in *The Female Thermometer: Eighteenth-Century Culture and the Invention of the Uncanny* (Oxford and New York: Oxford University Press, 1995), 168–89.

57. On Radcliffe's ambiguous handling of the supernatural, see Castle, "The Spectralization of the Other in *The Mysteries of Udolpho,*" in *The Female Thermometer,* 120–39.

58. Sir Walter Scott, *Lives of Eminent Novelists and Dramatists,* rev. ed. (London and New York: Frederick Warne, 1887), 555.

59. Tzvetan Todorov, *The Fantastic: A Structural Approach to a Literary Genre,* trans. Richard Howard (Ithaca, N.Y.: Cornell University Press, 1975), 159.

60. See ibid., 160–62.

61. Feminist readings of Gothic fiction have proliferated—with learned and invigorating

results—since the 1970s. See, for example, Margaret Anne Doody, "Deserts, Ruins and Troubled Waters: Female Dreams in Fiction and the Development of the Gothic Novel," *Genre* 10
(1977): 529–72; Ellis, *The Contested Castle*; Claudia L. Johnson, *Equivocal Beings: Politics,
Gender, and Sentimentality in the 1790s—Wollstonecraft, Radcliffe, Burney, Austen* (Chicago:
University of Chicago Press, 1995); Ellen Moers, *Literary Women* (Garden City, N.Y.: Anchor
Press, 1977); Juliann E. Fleenor, ed., *The Female Gothic* (Montreal and London: Eden Press,
1983); Elizabeth Napier, *The Failure of Gothic: Problems of Disjunction in an Eighteenth-Century Literary Form* (Oxford: Clarendon Press, 1987); Mary Poovey, "Ideology in *The Mysteries
of Udolpho*," *Criticism* 21 (1979): 307–30. A related critical development has been the recent
growth of interest in Gothic representations of male sexuality—particularly in its unorthodox
(usually homoerotic) manifestations. See, for example, Eve Kosofsky Sedgwick on James
Hogg in *Between Men: Male Homosocial Desire in English Literature* (New York: Columbia
University Press, 1985); Richard Davenport-Hines on Walpole in *Gothic: Four Hundred Years*;
and George Haggerty, "Literature and Homosexuality in the Later Eighteenth Century: Walpole, Beckford and Lewis," *Studies in the Novel* 18 (1986): 341–52, and Haggerty, *Men in
Love: Masculinity and Sexuality in the Eighteenth Century* (New York: Columbia University
Press, 1999).

62. Radcliffe, *Mysteries of Udolpho*, 318.

63. Laurence Sterne, *A Sentimental Journey Through France and Italy*, ed. Graham Petrie
(Middlesex, Eng.: Penguin Books, 1968), 36.

64. It has been suggested that one hallmark of bourgeois consciousness in the modern era
is a deep-seated presumption that one is not likely to die by violence. Austen's novels—as
compared, say, with those of Defoe—might be said to illustrate the late-eighteenth-century
triumph of such existential (and actuarial) complacency. In Austen's middle-class universe
most of the physical dangers posed by the natural world have been mitigated, and once-lethal
forms of social aggression abolished. Yet this "civilization" of everyday life also results in the
loss—or at least muting—of a certain phenomenological immediacy. Defoe's Robinson Cru-
soe fears the assaults of wild beasts and cannibals; Catherine Morland (in *Northanger Abbey*)
the cancellation of a pleasant social outing by rainy weather. For a broader account of the "civilizing process" in Western culture—and its inhibiting effects on the sensual and emotional
life—see the work of Norbert Elias, especially *The Civilizing Process: Sociogenetic and Psychogenetic Investigations*, rev. ed., trans. Edmund Jephcott, ed. Eric Dunning, Johan Goudsblom,
and Stephen Mennell (Oxford: Blackwell, 2000), and Elias and Eric Dunning, "The Quest
for Excitement in Leisure," in *Quest for Excitement: Sport and Leisure in the Civilizing Process*
(Oxford and New York: Basil Blackwell, 1986), 63–99. In the latter essay, Elias describes in
brilliant detail how a range of artificially "exciting" phenomena—"from sports to music and
drama, from murder films to Westerns, from hunting and fishing to racing and painting, from
gambling and chess to swinging and rocking"—have evolved in advanced industrial societies
since the eighteenth century precisely as compensation for the gradual eradication of primal
"situations" in which the life of the individual is directly threatened.

65. See Peter Martin, *A Life of James Boswell* (New Haven and London: Yale University
Press, 1999), 16. On eighteenth-century attitudes toward melancholia, the spleen, and other
"hypochondriacal" maladies now usually categorized as psychogenetic in origin, see G. J.
Barker-Benfield, *The Culture of Sensibility: Sex and Society in Eighteenth-Century Britain*
(Chicago: University of Chicago Press, 1992); John Mullan, *Sentiment and Sociability: The*

Language of Feeling in the Eighteenth Century (Oxford and New York: Oxford University Press, 1988); and Roy Porter, *Mind-Forg'd Manacles: A History of Madness in England from the Restoration to the Regency* (London: Athlone Press, 1987).

66. The term *fight or flight response* was coined by the pioneering Harvard physiologist Walter B. Cannon in 1929. See Cannon, *Bodily Changes in Pain, Hunger, Fear and Rage*, 2d ed. (New York: Appleton, 1929). For a basic neurophysiological account of the phenomenon, see C. Barr Taylor and Bruce Arnow, *The Nature and Treatment of Anxiety Disorders* (New York: Free Press, 1988), and Debra A. Hope, ed., *Perspectives on Anxiety, Panic, and Fear* (Lincoln: University of Nebraska Press, 1996).

67. Elias Canetti, *Crowds and Power*, trans. Carol Stewart (1962; rpt. New York: Continuum Press, 1978), 15.

68. Compare Geoffrey Scott on the feeling of psychokinetic freedom—a sense that one can move about in swift and unimpeded ways—intimated by the regular forms of classical architecture. Renaissance buildings please us over those of the Gothic, he maintains, because with their open interior spaces and long, "readable" perspectives, they represent "the translation into architectural language of our pleasure in rapid, joyous, and even humorous physical movements." Scott, *Architecture of Humanism*, 44.

69. Horace Walpole, *The Castle of Otranto*, ed. E. J. Clery (Oxford and New York: Oxford University Press, 1996), 28–29.

70. For a persuasive psychoanalytic account of the "male viewer's stake in horror spectatorship," see Carol J. Clover, *Men, Women, and Chainsaws: Gender in the Modern Horror Film* (Princeton, N.J.: Princeton University Press, 1992).

71. This said, it should be noted that at time of writing (2001) neurologists have already succeeded in locating some of the chemical changes taking place in the brain during unusual emotional states—as, for example, when individuals have "near-death" experiences or describe feelings of overwhelming spiritual ecstasy. See Sharon Begley, "Religion and the Brain," *Newsweek*, May 7, 2001, 50–55. A growing body of scientific evidence suggests that not only is there "a neural basis for religious experience" but that strong biochemical reactions in the brain may be at work in other powerful subjective states as well, including those associated with aesthetic experience.

72. Walpole, *Castle of Otranto*, 9.

73. See E. J. Clery's introduction to ibid., xxv, xxx–xxxi.

74. The point cannot be stressed enough—that classic Gothic fiction is defined not only by its supernaturalist leanings but by the spatio-temporal displacement of its main action. Though often described as Gothic in inspiration, a work such as Mary Shelley's *Frankenstein* (1818) would not be a "true" Gothic novel according to this definition, precisely because it is set in the near-present and in "realistic" geographical spaces easily discoverable on a map (the Arctic Circle, Geneva, London, Scotland). Shelley, of course, makes no reference to supernatural forces—preferring to present the main events of her novel as the tragic repercussions of a scientific experiment gone awry.

6

TO THE FRIENDS WHO DID NOT SAVE MY LIFE

Friend (*frend*) 1. One joined to another in mutual benevolence and intimacy. 2. Used *loosely* in various ways: e.g. applied to a mere acquaintance, or to a stranger, as a mark of goodwill or kindly condescension on the part of the speaker; by members of the "Society of Friends" adopted as the ordinary mode of address. 3. A kinsman or near relation. Now only in *pl.* (one's) relatives, kinfolk, "people." 4. A lover or paramour, of either sex. 5. One who wishes (another, a cause, etc.) well; a sympathiser, favourer, helper, patron, or supporter. 6. As opposed to *enemy* in various senses: One who is on good terms with another, not hostile or at variance; one who is on the same side in warfare, politics, etc.

From the *Oxford English Dictionary*

What might be the relation—historical, formal, critical, ideological—between the eighteenth-century novel and the late-twentieth-century novel? I recently attended a conference of eighteenth-century scholars at which precisely this momentous question was addressed. If the novel had "risen" in the eighteenth century—I and my fellow guest speakers were asked to consider—was it now "falling" or declining? Were the narrative conventions so admirably set in place by Aphra Behn, Daniel Defoe, Samuel Richardson, Henry Fielding, and Laurence Sterne still functioning reliably in the complex world of "postmodern" fiction making, or had they been superseded by newer, more up-to-date modes of representation? What, then, of contemporary novels—such as J. M. Coetzee's *Foe*, Catherine Schine's *Rameau's Niece*, Milan Kundera's *Slowness*, or Beryl Bainbridge's *According to Queeney*—that openly pastiched eighteenth-century novels? Were they simply ironic throwbacks? And what did we think would be the effects of new modes of communication on the future evolution of the novel genre? Did the invention of e-mail mean that people would start writing eighteenth-century–style epistolary novels again? Et cetera, et cetera.

As I somewhat nervously confessed to my audience, I am coming to find such questions curiously beside the point these days—even tedious—so much so that I fear that I fall into a kind of irritable, Man (or Woman) of the Hill–type misanthropy when confronted by them. When you get right down to it, I am not particularly concerned, moment to moment, with whether "the novel" is rising or falling: all I know is that there are currently so many novels in the world (even without any more being written) that I will have no difficulty finding works of fiction to occupy me in my leisure moments until my death, which is really all I care about. My private taste for longish prose fiction printed in book form may be one that is rapidly declining worldwide—with the global supervention of visual modes of communication, with the creation of virtual reality and cyberspace, with the fearsome return among the young and less privileged members of the American polity of a kind of Dark Ages illiteracy—but that doesn't really bother me: as long as no one is stopping *me* from reading novels—as long as my habit is tolerated as a kind of harmless antiquarian hobby, like coin collecting or folk dancing or reenacting Civil War battles—I am not particularly bothered.

Some of my disaffection no doubt stems from a certain "theory overload" I have come to associate with my own longtime scholarly speciality. For some while I've felt peculiarly surfeited by academic studies of eighteenth-century fiction—especially those bearing on the history and nature of the genre *qua* genre. While vast intellectual gains have been made in recent decades—I think the astonishing store of new historical, genealogical, and bibliographic information about the early English novel accumulated over the past thirty years represents one of the great triumphs of twentieth-century literary scholarship—I also think we have reached a kind of intellectual dead end in the matter, and like exhausted little Lovelaces-with-word-processors can go no farther. The soaring critical trajectory extending from Ian Watt's *The Rise of the Novel* (1957) through the work of Michael McKeon, J. Paul Hunter, John Richetti, Lennard Davis, Nancy Armstrong, John Bender, Margaret Doody, William Warner, Clifford Siskin, and Catherine Gallagher—eminent, perspicuous Watt disciples all—may have reached its natural terminus point, at least for a while. *Ars longa, vita brevis,* and especially lately, while wearily perusing new-book advertisements from university presses, I have come to feel we hardly need yet more critical tomes on the Eighteenth-Century Novel and Romance, the Eighteenth-Century Novel and Criminal Biography, the Eighteenth-Century Novel and Travel Narrative, the Eighteenth-Century Novel and Print Capitalism, the Eighteenth-Century Novel and the Rise of Bourgeois Subjectivity, the Eighteenth-Century Novel and Empire, the Eighteenth-Century Novel and Domesticity, the Eighteenth-Century Novel and Sensibility, the Eighteenth-Century Novel and the English Literary

Canon, the Eighteenth-Century Novel and All Those Other Things People Like to Talk about These Days. We have gained all the yardage we are going to get on these points for a while: indeed, I happen to think that with Catherine Gallagher's brilliantly argued *Nobody's Story: The Vanishing Acts of Women Writers in the Marketplace, 1670–1820* (1994)—the finest and most challenging recent response to Watt of all—the battered pigskin of eighteenth-century fiction studies has been definitively kicked through the goal posts.

What then to say about the topic proposed? As I ponder the matter again now—what *are* some meaningful connections between eighteenth- and twentieth-century fiction?—I find myself contemplating, returning heart and soul to, over those elements that drew me to the early English novel in the first place, and continue to inform my reading of prose fiction generally, including the admittedly selective strands of contemporary writing to which I am most drawn. I throw the word *soul* in here in part to be provocative, but also because it seems important to gesture toward the metaphysics, or "soul," of the novel. I take a cue not only from Lukacs's famous description of the novel as the "transcendentally homeless genre," but also from its dark correlative: that characters in novels are (as we are) *homeless* beings, and *homeless* in all of the contemporary permutations of the term: lost, abused, desperate, spiritually bereft, monstrously dehumanized by others, inwardly and outwardly estranged, hungry, needy, sad. At least since Cervantes, the novel has been the preeminent genre of human sadness—our principal literary register of the inescapable facts of abandonment, loss, physical disintegration, and death. In modern life—and here I play on the title of both the well-known Haydn orchestral piece and Edmund White's recent autobiographical fiction about life and death as a gay man in late-twentieth-century America and Europe—the novel has served as our Farewell Symphony: the point of which has been to confirm (as if it needed confirming) that human truth at once agonizing and irresistible—that in the end, whatever the gaiety and warmth of life's individual moments, whatever illusions of harmony, pleasure, and joyful conjunction may for a time seem to prevail, everyone, whether by accident, weakness, treachery, or some existentially determined failure of love and imagination, is left alone in the end. One by one all the players exit the scene—and one is alone on an empty stage, alone in an empty room, alone on a crumbling piece of rock hurtling silently through dark, cold space.

Thinking back over the eighteenth-century novels that have had the most profound impact on me, I find they are those that assert most drastically the sensation of abandonment, the murder of souls. It is of course profoundly unfashionable (at least in academic circles) to talk about the spiritual or metaphysical dimensions of fiction—a fact that perhaps explains the otherwise mystifying scholarly obsession lately with such heartless and mediocre eighteenth-century texts as Sarah Fielding's *David Simple* (1744) or Charlotte Lennox's *The Female Quixote* (1752), a work that, 250 years after its publication seems more a kind of deracinated postmodern exercise in generic self-denomination than any sort of living, breathing human artifact. I suspect it will sound eccentric to say so, but what brings me back again and again to certain overwhelming eighteenth-century novels—to Daniel Defoe's *Roxana*, Samuel Richardson's *Clarissa*, Choderlos de Laclos's *Les Liaisons dangereuses*, Elizabeth Inchbald's *A Simple Story*—is how exactingly and excruciatingly they dramatize certain primordial themes: how they grasp and disorient and *frighten* me. These are all novels I first encountered in my early twenties: books I have thought about and written about and taught many times, yet that continue to haunt me—especially as I become older, more panicky about the lapse of time, and sunk deeper and deeper in the ever-present coils of an unasked-for and saddening mortality.

How to put a finer point on what by now must be sounding impossibly grandiose and narcissistic? The fictional theme that preoccupies me most these days is what I have come to think of as *the ironic perversion of kinship*: the inexplicable transformation of once-cherishable bonds of flesh and spirit into hatred, spite, brutality, even outright murderousness. There is a reason why so many characters in eighteenth-century novels are literally or metaphorically homeless: because home itself—the domain of the Family, the ancestral site (presumably) of comfort, safety, and human connection—is a fucking nightmare. Home is ghastly, a kind of obscene joke—the place you have to get away from. True, to exploit a common eighteenth-century usage, home is typically inhabited by "friends": blood relatives, kinsmen and kinswomen, people who might be expected by cultural convention to link their happiness to yours. (The usage is everywhere in Richardson's *Clarissa*.) Yet by some dire metamorphosis, these "friends" become enemies. They do not wish you well. In fact they want to kill you, or at least kill your soul—either by throwing you away at the start, or more perversely, by holding up false promises of felicity, exploiting you for their own ends as long as possible, then dumping you.

I had occasion to think about kinship bonds and their deformation recently while editing Radcliffe's *The Mysteries of Udolpho*. I was struck again by what may seem on the face of it a minor detail: namely, that the heroine is persecuted not only by the Gothic villain Montoni, but also by her closest living relation, an evil and avaricious aunt named Madame Cheron, who later marries Montoni. The strangeness of the detail inheres in the fact that Madame Cheron/Montoni is the *only sibling* of Emily's dead father, St. Aubert, one of the novel's impossibly "good" characters. (St. Aubert dies early on in the fiction, so that Emily, whose mother is also dead, becomes first the ward of her aunt, and then, after her aunt's marriage to Montoni, of Montoni himself.) Commenting on a passage in the novel in which Madame Montoni showers the defenseless Emily with insults and abuse, I wrote the following: "One of Radcliffe's darkest and most Richardsonian insights is that kinship does not guarantee loving feeling: the same family may breed both protectors and persecutors, saints and monsters. Madame Montoni, nightmarishly, is the benevolent St. Aubert's sister, yet she is also Emily's most sadistic tormentor."

Like the Gothic generally, *Udolpho* shows us that blood relationships can be cruel—at times even lethal. Improbable as it may seem, someone from the most intimate realm of life (usually a parent or stepparent, but not always) has *turned against you*. Granted, there is typically some superficial reason why "friend" has become enemy—there is some legacy under dispute, or controversial choice of marriage partner to be made—yet there is ultimately no *real* explanation for the deranging, disproportionate, dehumanizing hatred one has come to evoke. At the deepest level it remains underdetermined.

This indeterminate, inexplicable hatred is, to my mind, the most shocking thing about the Gothic. All the loathsome scenic apparatus we associate with eighteenth-century Gothic fiction—dungeons, castles, catafalques, corpses rotting under bloody shrouds—is from one angle, one can argue, a mere screen work thrown over something far more primal and horrifying: namely, the realization that someone close to you, the one by all rights who should be protecting you, has not only withdrawn any goodwill, but actively seeks your physical or moral obliteration. In Horace Walpole's *The Castle of Otranto* (1764), a novel full of classic Gothic "business," the most chilling element by far, in my view, is the second sentence, in which it is asserted (in a brief throwaway clause) that Manfred, the novel's villain, "never showed any symptoms of affection to Matilda"—his entirely inoffensive daughter.

> Manfred, prince of Otranto, had one son and one daughter: the latter, a most beautiful virgin, aged eighteen, was called Matilda. Conrad, the son, was three years younger, a homely youth, sickly, and of no promising disposition; yet he was the darling of his father, who never showed any symptoms of affection to Matilda. Manfred had contracted a marriage for his son with the marquis of Vicenza's daughter. . . .[1]

The narrator presents the death-dealing clause without explanation—hurries right past it as it were—yet here indeed is a true Gothic horror: the unprovoked antipathy of father for daughter. It will lead, catastrophically, to Matilda's murder at her father's hands, in the novel's final pages:

> Manfred, whose spirits were inflamed, and whom Isabella had driven from her on his urging his passion with too little reserve, did not doubt but the inquietude she had expressed had been occasioned by her impatience to meet Theodore. Provoked by this conjecture, and enraged at her father, he hastened secretly to the great church. Gliding softly between the aisles, and guided by an imperfect gleam of moonshine that shone faintly through the illuminated windows, he stole towards the tomb of Alfonso,

to which he was directed by indistinct whispers of the persons he sought. The first sounds he could distinguish were—Does it, alas, depend on me? Manfred will never permit our union.—No, this shall prevent it! cried the tyrant, drawing his dagger, and plunging it over her shoulder into the bosom of the person that spoke—Ah me, I am slain! cried Matilda sinking: Good heaven, receive my soul!—Savage, inhuman monster! what hast thou done? cried Theodore, rushing on him, and wrenching his dagger from him.—Stop, stop thy impious hand, cried Matilda; it is my father![2]

In accordance with the Gothic's usual sickly-sentimental bad faith, Manfred's stabbing of Matilda is presented as horrific paternal error, part of a grotesque series of missteps and misapprehensions. (And how pathetic her attempts to save *him* from the vengeful Theodore!) Yet it is entirely consistent with the covert animosity—the lurking infanticidal wish—shaping Walpole's narrative from the beginning.

Two early-eighteenth-century novels have always epitomized the "perverted kinship" syndrome for me in an especially visceral way. The first is Defoe's *Roxana: or, The Fortunate Mistress* (1724)—a book I find utterly appalling—all the more so because the perversion of kinship is seen from the perverter's point of view. I speak here of Roxana herself, the courtesan-narrator: a mother who kills her children. Scattered throughout the novel one can find dissociated, blandly horrific passages, like the two following, in which she expresses her distaste for progeny born and unborn:

> I was with-Child again in this Journey, and Lay-in at *Venice*, but was not so happy as before; I brought him another Son, and a very fine Boy it was, but it liv'd not above two Months; nor, after the first Touches of Affection (which are usual, I believe, to all Mothers) were over, was I sorry the Child did not live, the necessary Difficulties attending it in our travelling, being consider'd.

> I would willingly have given ten Thousand Pounds of my Money, to have been rid of the Burthen I had in my Belly, as above; but it cou'd not be; so I was oblig'd to bear with that part, and get rid of it by the ordinary Method of Patience, and hard Travel. . . .[3]

In the novel's grim finale—just after she succeeds in making a marriage to a wealthy man (who knows nothing of her past as a prostitute)—Roxana is rediscovered by Susan, a grown-up daughter, long ago abandoned, who now wishes to be acknowledged as her child. The familiar wish—to *have the girl die*—immediately surfaces when Roxana confers with her wicked servant, Amy, about what to do:

This put *Amy* into such a Hurry, that she cry'd; she rav'd; she swore and curs'd like a Mad-thing; then she upbraided me, that I wou'd not let her kill the Girl when she wou'd have done it; and that it was all my own doing, *and the like.* Well however, I was not for killing the Girl yet, I cou'd not bear the Thoughts of that neither.

It is true, I wanted as much to be deliver'd from her, as ever a Sick-Man did from a Third-Day Ague; and had she dropp'd into the Grave by any fair Way, *as I may call it*; I mean had she died by any ordinary Distemper, I shou'd have shed but very few Tears for her. . . .[4]

The fatal hope would seem to be fulfilled: after further murky confabs between Roxana and her accomplice, Susan disappears and is never seen again. The reader is left mystified and anxious—even as Roxana succumbs to her own morbid "Frights" and the narrative abruptly breaks off. After "some few Years of flourishing, and outwardly happy Circumstances"—she writes, in the novel's final sentence—"I fell into a dreadful Course of Calamities, and *Amy* also; the very Reverse of our former Good Days; the Blast of Heaven seem'd to follow the Injury done the poor Girl, by us both; and I was brought so low again, that my Repentance seem'd to be only the Consequence of my Misery, as my Misery was of my Crime."[5] *Mater dolorosa. Finis horribilis.*

Similar infanticidal energies loom up in *Clarissa*—surely the most painful and oppressive novel about family life ever written. The most harrowing part of the novel (for me) has never been Clarissa's protracted torment at the hands of the rapist Lovelace. To the contrary, what rends most deeply is everything that precedes it: her corrosive, surreal, dehumanizing sufferings "at home" with the Harlowes—her own "flesh and blood." Their corporate cruelty will continue to afflict her long after she makes her escape from Harlowe Place. Indeed, compared with this inaugural monstrosity—*once they all loved her, but now suddenly they don't*—the abuse she undergoes later, if no less degrading, seems somehow less psychically devastating. Clarissa will recover, morally and emotionally, from almost all of Lovelace's outrages, but the primal dereliction of her "Friends"— her father's curse, her mother's rejection, her siblings' uncanny spite—is fatal to her well-being. In Richardson's tragic vision it all happens right at the start: the Harlowes wound Clarissa, deep in her soul, and months later, after scarifying anguish, she will collapse from the wound. *Friends become enemies. They are trying to kill you for no good reason. You're starting to die already.* I won't belabor the point but will merely itemize instead a few of the novel's most desolating utterances on this theme:

(**Lovelace** to **Belford**)—But here's her mistake; nor will she be cured of it—she takes the man she calls her father (her mother had been faultless, had she not been her father's wife); she takes the men she calls her uncles; the fellow she calls her brother; and the poor contemptible she calls her sister; to *be* her father, to *be* her uncles, her brother, her sister; and that as such, she owes to some of them reverence, to others respect; let them treat her ever so cruelly!—sordid ties! mere cradle-prejudices!— For had they not been imposed upon her by nature, when she was in a perverse humour, or could she have chosen her relations, would any of these have been among them?

(**Clarissa** to **Solmes**)—When you first came acquainted with my father's family, you found the writer of this one of the happiest creatures in the world, beloved by the best and most indulgent of parents, and rejoicing in the kind favour of two affectionate uncles, and in the esteem of every one.
But how is this happy scene now changed!

(**Anna** to **Clarissa**)—What *can* I advise you, my noble creature? Your merit is your crime. You can no more change *your* nature, than your persecutors can *theirs*. Your distress is owing to the vast disparity between you and them. What would you have of them? Do they not act in character?—and to whom? To an alien. You are not one of them.

(**Uncle John Harlowe** to **Clarissa**)—Everybody loves you; and you know they do. The very ground you walk upon is dear to most of us. But how can we resolve to see you? There is no standing against your looks and language. It is the strength of our love makes us decline to see you.[6]

What does this all have to do with later fiction, and especially contemporary writing? From its beginning the novel documents, we've been told, the rise of modern individualism, and we are all more or less existentially invested in *that*. But this development can also be seen, reverse-wise, more balefully, as a specimen of cultural loss. What is fading from the human scene, even as the realistic novel is struggling into being, is a collective spiritual faith in the value of kinship ties. The startlingly rapid modernization of eighteenth-century British society is at least partly to blame. With the fragmentation of age-old "face-to-face" communities, increasing personal mobility, and the explosive growth of towns and cities—those dank, roiling concatenations of total strangers—traditional family networks are shaken, deformed, or broken up altogether. Individuals begin to move farther and farther away from the "Friends" they grew up with. The human world becomes more sinister and bewildering. (Novel plots involving accidental or threatened incest—one thinks of *Moll Flanders* or *Tom Jones*—no doubt became as popular as they did in the eighteenth century because they captured so pointedly this frightening new cultural anxiety: in the welter of strange new social aggregates, no one *really* knows to whom he or she is related anymore.) As critics, we have been inclined—following Watt—to give a heroic and entrepreneurial cast to the rise of radical individualism. Yet as so many early novels show, the new world of *individuals* is also a world of escalating horrors—a potential labyrinth of lost, isolated, "friendless" souls. In the existentially damaged fictional landscapes of Behn, Defoe, Richardson, Fielding, and Smollett, life is reduced, more often than not, to little more than a morbid competition for resources, marked by recurrent, sometimes homicidal, scapegoating manias. Just about everyone—in the end—is an emotional orphan. To borrow the title of Beryl Bainbridge's recent fiction about the *Titanic*, the prevailing axiom of the early English novel might well be "every man for himself." The children have to look after themselves.

I find similar insights in some of the contemporary novels I have been reading lately. Two of the most memorable have been Hervé Guibert's *To the Friend Who Did Not Save My Life* and Edmund White's *The Farewell Symphony*. Both are "AIDS novels," from 1990 and 1997, respectively; both document appalling personal and cultural loss. And both, curiously enough, have their eighteenth-century aspects. White's allusion in his title to the famous Haydn symphony—in which the members of the orchestra playing the piece leave the stage one by one as the music draws to a close—is at once a kind of witty rococo joke and an almost intolerably poignant symbol of his opulent, ruinous narrative—in which just about every major character apart from the narrator dies of AIDS. In one somber, curt, oddly Johnsonian passage—just after the death of his friend Marston—the narrator reflects on the senseless devastation he has witnessed and the vanity of human wishes:

> After he died I remembered I'd told him that I was sure he was going to beat this disease. My reputation as a writer, even my age, now lent my words a weight they hadn't had in the past. I realized that reluctantly, hopefully, Marston had believed me.
>
> He shouldn't have. I was wrong. He did die, as did the writers from my literary club, the guys in advertising I knew, the lawyers, the fellows at the gym, the men I'd shared houses with on Fire Island—they were all dying, even though they'd all been told they wouldn't. I heard stories of a friend leaving his loft to his surviving lover, who was then ousted by the dead man's parents. I heard of a group of friends who decided to help their buddy die. He was blind and incontinent, weighed just seventy pounds and had nothing to look forward to except dementia. But at the last moment one of the angels of mercy cracked, called an ambulance. The dying man was resuscitated, only to die a month later in howling pain.[7]

Yet Guibert's novel has a no less powerful "eighteenth-century" aspect. Guibert died in 1991 of AIDS-related wasting disease at the age of thirty-six, having written five novels in the last five years of his life. (*To the Friend Who Did Not Save My Life* is the first of these; the others are *The Compassion Protocol, The Man in the Red Hat, Blindsight,* and *Paradise.*) All are autobiographical and all document in minute detail the treacherous course of his illness. Coincidentally, White, who knew him, mentions the frantic productivity of Guibert's last days in *The Farewell Symphony.* Late in the fiction, White's narrator, a writer, is describing his own HIV diagnosis:

> I went to bed for a month. I just pulled the covers over my head and prepared myself for dying. Other writers I knew who'd been diagnosed flung themselves into feverish activity, determined to write in the two or three years that remained to them all the books they would have written had they been allowed to live to eighty ("Even if I have to write them badly," said the dying Hervé Guibert). But my ambition had been not only to express myself and create ingenious artefacts but also to pay my admission into a club that, now I was ill, had caught fire and dissolved into ashes.[8]

Guibert's freneticism—presented here ironically, as yet another mode of human futility—inevitably makes me think of eighteenth-century characters such as Valmont or Clarissa. In a famous commentary on Laclos and *Les Liaisons dangereuses,* Tzvetan Todorov describes the "death-haunted" epistemology of the classic eighteenth-century novel in letters: a character in an epistolary fiction remains "alive" only to the degree that he or she *writes.* To be present on the page is to "live": not to write is a kind of textual death. (Indeed: in epistolary fiction, as in AIDS-ridden America, *Silence = Death.*) Characters like Valmont and Clarissa must constantly pour out letters—not only to stay "alive" as fictional characters, but also to keep the epistolary narrative itself alive. Without them, the novel they inhabit dies.

Guibert lived out this write-or-die phenomenon in the most literal, appalling way. Gathered together and read in sequence, *To the Friend Who Did Not Save My Life* and its successor volumes—each one shorter than the last—could be said to make up a kind of *mortifying* picaresque. True, Guibert is often a wildly comic novelist—almost Sternean or Fieldingesque in manner at times—and no less so than when he describes himself rambling from one grim outpatient clinic to another, or finding on his increasingly dilapidated person yet another loathsome physical symptom. As with Sterne—the death-on-the-brain Sterne of *A Sentimental Journey* or the *Journal to Eliza*—Guibert's impinging demise inspired him to grave yet witty flights of articulation and artistry. Yet we sense in him too, literally burning him up, the feverish desperation and encroaching despair of the epistolary character. He is writing for us, we realize, precisely because it is the only way he can stay alive.

Yet interesting as such parallels may be, they do not constitute for me, still, the most important link between White's and Guibert's fiction and the death-dealing novels of the eighteenth century. Once again, what I see most powerfully binding together the fiction of past and present is the theme of perverted kinship—the iniquity of "Friends" who seem to owe us something, but end up failing or betraying us. Granted, in both *The Farewell Symphony* and *To the Friend Who Did Not Save My Life,* traditional family ties ("friends" in the eighteenth-century sense) are mostly absent or irrelevant. In White's novel, the narrator ("Ed") seems not to have any parents or close relations; the only pair of parents he mentions are the greedy mother and father who, after their son dies of AIDS, "oust" his devastated lover from the son's New York loft. In Guibert's novel, parents are mentioned only fleetingly—in connection with the pain of a childhood the narrator ("Hervé") has relentlessly sought to escape through art and sex and bohemianism. This is perhaps what the gay world, in particular, has always been: a world of lost children, attempting to find in one another—in the friends of the moment, in the vicissitudes of unorthodox sexual love—a substitute for a certain kind of parental love that has gone missing.

Friends—*friends* in the contemporary sense—might be presumed to compensate for one's absent or hostile kinfolk. Except they don't. Both of these novels deal with the egregious failure of friends, even one's *new* friends—one's "replacement friends"—to save one from oneself and one's fate. The new friends turn out to be just as miserably useless as the old friends. In White's novel, quite baldly, all the "friends" go away and die—instead of doing what they were supposed to do: namely, *keep one from dying oneself.* Guibert's novel literalizes the problem in its title, which refers to at least two different people. The first "friend" is Musil, a character based very closely on Michel Foucault, the narrator's intellectual mentor and charismatic father figure, whose own death from AIDS in fact precedes the narrator's. Musil is an excruciating mixture of mental power and physical powerlessness, who topples over in the course of the novel, like a decayed giant redwood. The second "friend" is a character named Bill, a wealthy gay American businessman who has promised to bring the ailing narrator, the Guibert character, an underground experimental drug. He never shows up, of course, and in the final pages of the novel the narrator sinks into a kind of macabre comic exasperation with him, which we know will have fatal consequences. I am going to conclude simply by quoting the last two sections of the novel. (The narrative is divided into 100 small fragments.) The first, a squalid and disturbing anecdote involving Bill, the businessman, thematizes the issues of kinship, lost kinfolk, attempts at symbolic compensation, and the disastrous failure of such attempts. The second short passage will put a Richardsonian seal, I hope, on my comments, even as it shows us, in little, how we will all fade away.

99

Driving home from Miami Airport one night, in the glare of his head-lights Bill sees a barefoot, unkempt young man in shorts running by the side of the highway. He makes him get into his American Jaguar, takes him home, and cleans him up in the bathtub, except for his genitals, which this guy won't let him touch, even in bed in the dark. The next day, Bill takes him shopping, outfits him from head to toe, and the boy's call-ing him his uncle. The day after that, the boy's calling him his father, which starts to worry Bill, and besides, he's got to go away on a business trip, so he takes the kid to a youth hostel and pays his lodging there for ten nights or so, as well as giving him fifty dollars in cash. When Bill re-turns from his trip, he finds all his security systems going nuts: the alarms are on in his garage, his elevator, his apartment. The security guards in-form Bill that the young man, wearing his new suit, has been trying day and night to force his way past them, claiming that he's Bill's son and has been abandoned by a worthless father. Bill finds his answering machine full of messages from the boy, so he gets a new, unlisted number. In no time the kid has wangled it out of some inexperienced employee and calls up his supposed father. Bill can't deal with this, gets a different unlisted number, and returning home one night from another trip, sees the guy, all filthy again, barefoot and in shorts, come bursting out from behind a bush and crash into the Jaguar, which goes into a skid. Bill threatens to call the police on him, while the guards look on. He goes home, unplugs his alarm system up on the thirty-fifth floor of the high rise, turns off the microphones that connect him with the security guards' office; the phone rings, he answers it, and hears a man's smooth and implacable voice say, "Hello, this is Plumm, the monkey handler. I see you have a weakness for little monkeys. I've just received a new shipment, which I've started to train. If you're interested, please don't hesitate to let me know . . . I'll leave you my phone number."

100

My book is closing in on me. I'm in deep shit. Just how deep do you want me to sink? Fuck you, Bill! My muscles have melted away. At last my arms and legs are once again as slender as they were when I was a child.[9]

notes

1. Horace Walpole, *The Castle of Otranto*, ed. E. J. Cleary (Oxford and New York: Oxford University Press, 1996), 17.

2. Ibid., 108–9.

3. Daniel Defoe, *Roxana: or, The Fortunate Mistress,* ed. Jane Jack (Oxford and New York: Oxford University Press, 1981), 104, 163.

4. Ibid., 298, 302.

5. Ibid., 329–30.

6. Samuel Richardson, *Clarissa: or, The History of a Young Lady*, ed. Angus Ross (Middlesex, Eng.: Penguin Books, 1985), 145, 159, 237, 253.

7. Edmund White, *The Farewell Symphony* (New York: Random House, 1997), 387–88.

8. Ibid., 385–86.

9. Hervé Guibert, *To the Friend Who Did Not Save My Life*, trans. Linda Coverdale (London: Quartet Books, 1991), 244–46.

part II

WAS JANE AUSTEN GAY?

It is impossible for the lover of Jane Austen—and lover is the operative word here—to have anything but mixed feelings about Austen's older sister, Cassandra. On one hand, we owe to Cassandra the only surviving (if bad) portraits of Austen other than silhouettes: the famous, somewhat lopsided sketch of 1801, in which the novelist's mouth is awkwardly pursed and her eyes, gazing in different directions, look like small, astigmatic raisins; and an equally inept watercolor back view from 1804, in which nothing of Austen can be seen—Cassandra giving her all to the rendering of the complicated dress and bonnet—except the nape of a neck, the exposed back of one hand, and a tentative, slipper-clad foot. Crude they may be, yet without these sisterly gleanings we would know next to nothing of Austen's face or figure or how she held herself in space: dead at forty-two in 1817, she is part of that last, infinitely poignant generation of human beings who lived and died before photography.

On the other hand, one can only deplore Cassandra's high-handed actions after Austen's death; these included burning great quantities of her sister's letters and censoring others by snipping pieces out of them. The vast majority of these letters were written to Cassandra herself. Though Austen wrote from time to time to other members of the large Austen clan—her three brothers and their wives, various favorite nieces and nephews—Cassandra was the person around whom her life revolved, and she wrote regularly to her whenever they were separated. (Spinsters both, the two Austen sisters lived together all their adult lives—first at Steventon and Bath with their parents, then after their father's death in 1805, with their mother and a female friend at Chawton in Hampshire.) At her own death in 1845, Cassandra bequeathed the scant batch of letters she had saved from the flames to her grand-niece, Lady Knatchbull, whose son, Lord Brabourne, had them published—like precious relics—in 1884. A number of other letters have surfaced since then; the great Austen scholar, R. W. Chapman, issued the first modern edition of the correspondence in 1932. Still, only 161 Austen letters are known to exist today, and many only in Cassandra-mangled form.

Deirdre Le Faye, editor of the excellent new revised Oxford edition of the letters,[1] defends Cassandra somewhat backhandedly, suggesting that her weeding-out and censorship "shows itself more in the complete destruction of letters rather than in the excision of individual sentences; the 'portions cut out' usually only amount to a very few words, and from the context it would seem that the subject concerned was physical ailment." Le Faye speculates that Cassandra, not wishing to cause embarrassment or ill-feeling, destroyed letters in which Austen wrote too freely or satirically about other family members. But for the reader of Austen's fiction, hungry for a sense of the author's inner life, Cassandra's depredations can only seem like older-sister arrogance of the most mortifying sort: a jealous winnowing down of her brilliant younger sister's personality in the name of a dubious decorum.

What was their relationship like? In a telling family memoir from 1867, James Edward Austen-Leigh, Austen's nephew, described it thus:

> Their sisterly affection for each other could scarcely be exceeded. Perhaps it began on Jane's side with a feeling of deference natural to a loving child towards a kind elder sister. Something of this feeling always remained; and even in the maturity of her powers, and in the enjoyment of increasing success, she would still speak of Cassandra as of one wiser and better than herself. In childhood, when the elder was sent to the school of a Mrs. Latournelle in the Forbury at Reading, the younger went with her, not because she was thought old enough to profit much by the instruction there imparted, but because she would have been miserable without her sister; her mother observing that "if Cassandra were going to have her head cut off, Jane would insist on sharing her fate." This attachment was never interrupted or weakened. They lived in the same home, and shared the same bedroom, till separated by death.

Cassandra was "colder and calmer," wrote Austen-Leigh; the family said that "Cassandra had the *merit* of having her temper always under her command, but that Jane had the *happiness* of a temper that never required to be commanded." When *Sense and Sensibility* was published in 1811, some readers thought Austen had modeled the characters of the Dashwood sisters—the sober Elinor and the sprightly Marianne—on her sister and herself. Austen-Leigh demurred, but only in order to pay tribute to the novelist's superior moral insight: "Cassandra's character might indeed represent the *sense* of Elinor, but Jane's had little in common with the *sensibility* of Marianne. The young woman who, before the age of twenty, could so clearly discern the failings of Marianne Dashwood, could hardly have been subject to them herself." The entire family seems to have shared his not-so-secret preference for Jane over Cassandra: another Austen nephew, Henry, of whom Austen had been particularly fond in his teens, told a cousin after Austen's death that whenever he visited the house at Chawton—where Cassandra and Mrs. Austen lived on for some years—"he could not help expecting to feel particularly happy . . . and never till he got there, could he fully realise to himself how all its peculiar pleasures were gone."

Perhaps because of the ambivalence Cassandra inevitably inspires—implicit in everything everyone says about her is the unspoken question, why did Jane have to be the one to die?—biographers and critics have tended to downplay her centrality in Austen's life. Even the sympathetic Chapman sought to depersonalize the sororal relationship: defending the surviving Jane-Cassandra letters against charges of being "trifling" in subject and style, he asserted that the sisters' purpose in writing to each other was to exchange information not only "between themselves, but between two branches of a large family. There are indications that these letters and others like them were read by, and to, a number of people. Even if this had not been so, it would not have been consonant with the sisters' temperament, or with their way of life, to exchange letters of sentiment or disquisition." Le Faye suggests we consider Austen's letters to Cassandra "the equivalent of telephone calls between the sisters"—"hasty and elliptical," full of family news, but little more.

It is certainly true that the surviving letters contain their share of trivia. Whole passages can go by as a blur of names and now meaningless events:

Yesterday I introduced James to Mrs. Inman;—in the evening John Bridges returned from Goodnestone—and this morn before we had left the Breakfast Table we had a visit from Mr. Whitfield, whose object I imagine was principally to thank my Eldest Brother for his assistance. Poor Man!—he has now a little intermission of his excessive solicitude on his wife's account, as she is rather better. James does duty at Godmersham today.—The Knatchbulls had intended coming here next week, but the Rentday makes it impossible for them to be received & I do not think there will be any spare time afterwards. They return into Somersetshire by way of Sussex & Hants, & are to be at Fareham—& perhaps may be in Southampton, on which possibility I said all I thought right—& if they are in the place, Mrs. K. has promised to call in Castle Square;—it will be about the end of July.

Elsewhere we learn more than we want to know, perhaps, about the incessant visits of various collateral family members, the meals eaten and cups of tea drunk, whether fires have been necessary in the sitting room, the muddy state of nearby roads, and similar minutiae.

And yet reading through the correspondence now—especially in the light of recent historical findings about the psychic complexity of female-female relationships in late-eighteenth- and early-nineteenth-century Britain (the recently rediscovered diaries of Austen's lesbian contemporary, Anne Lister, are an example)—one is struck not so much by the letters' hastiness or triviality as by the passionate nature of the sibling bond they commemorate. Sororal or pseudo-sororal attachments are arguably the most immediately gratifying human connections in Austen's imaginative universe. It is a curious yet arresting phenomenon in the novels that so many of the final happy marriages seem designed not so much to bring about a union between hero and heroine as between the heroine and the hero's sister. At the end of *Northanger Abbey*, while the heroine, Catherine Morland, is clearly delighted to marry the entertaining Henry Tilney, the most intense part of her joy seems to derive from the fact that in doing so she also becomes "sister" to his sister Eleanor, whose subtle approbation she has sought—and glowingly received—throughout the novel. But even Austen's heroes are often more like sisters than lovers in the conventional sense. The soft-mannered Henry, for example, takes a feminine interest in fabrics, and "comforts" his female relations with his knowledge of muslins and chintzes; and he is repeatedly contrasted with his father, General Tilney—a far more domineering and stereotypically masculine type.

Reading Austen's letters to Cassandra, one cannot help but sense the primitive adhesiveness—and underlying eros—of the sister-sister bond. The first surviving letter dates from 1796, when Austen was twenty and Cassandra twenty-three. From the start the tone is rhetorical, literary (not like a phone call at all), and one of whimsical yet fierce attachment. Austen wants more than anything to make her older sister laugh. As in her novels, she uses first lines flirtatiously, like comic bait, to catch Cassandra in webs of mock-heroic invention. From 1801: "Expect a most agreeable letter, for not being overburdened with subject—(having nothing at all to say)—I shall have no check to my Genius from beginning to end." "This will be a quick return for yours, my dear Cassandra," she begins a missive from 1813. "I doubt its having much else to recommend it, but there is no saying, it may turn out to be a very long, delightful Letter." "Here I am, my dearest Cassandra, seated in the Breakfast, Dining, Sitting room, beginning with all my might." And again, from 1814: "Do not be angry with me for beginning another letter to you. I have read the Corsair, mended my petticoat, & have nothing else to do."

Once Cassandra is ensnared, Austen holds her fast with in-jokes and sisterly games of style, complete with lovable misspellings. For all the family gossip they impart, Austen's letters remain intensely scripted: full of parodic references to shared reading and the cherished (or maligned) books of female adolescence. "So much for Mrs. Piozzi," Austen concludes after a passage of ludicrous Miss Bates–like ramblings on the salutary effects of the Bath waters. "I had some thoughts of writing the whole of my letter in her stile, but I believe I shall not." She parodies Pope's comic catalogues ("In a few hours You will be transported to Manydown—& then for Candour & Comfort & Coffee & Cribbage"), Johnsonian lapidary pronouncement ("I am looking over Self Control again, & my opinion is confirmed of its' being an excellently meant, elegantly written Work, without anything of Nature or Probability in it"), the effusions of Mrs. Radcliffe ("the shades of Evening are descending & I resume my interesting Narrative"), and the fey Caledonian jests of Sir Walter Scott ("I do not write for such dull elves!"). Elsewhere she announces: "I am going to write nothing but short Sentences." The result—rather more uncannily—is like proto-Gertrude Stein:

> There shall be two full stops in every Line. Layton and Shear's *is* Bedford House. We mean to get there before breakfast if it's possible. For we feel more & more how much we have to do, And how little time. This house looks very nice. It seems like Sloane St moved here. I believe Henry is just rid of Sloane St—Fanny does not come, but I have Edward seated by me beginning a letter, which looks natural.

One can imagine the pleasure-addiction such writing engendered. For the reader, like Cassandra, is seduced by the constant foolery:

> I will not say that your Mulberry trees are dead, but I am afraid they are not alive.

> What dreadful Hot weather we have!—It keeps one in a continual state of Inelegance.

> So much for that subject; I now come to another, of a very different nature, as other subjects are very apt to be.

> Where shall I begin? Which of all my important nothings shall I tell you first?

And what *of* these important nothings? It is frequently said of Austen's letters that they "illuminate" the world of her fiction. This is certainly the case, though to say so is hardly to say very much. Sometimes, it is true, Austen comments directly on work in progress—in particular, on the earlier novels, *Sense and Sensibility*, *Pride and Prejudice*, and *Mansfield Park*. (In a famous letter written just after the publication of *Pride and Prejudice* in 1813, she tells Cassandra that she is "vain enough" over her book, but thinks it "rather too light & bright & sparkling;—it wants shade.") But what advocates of Austen's correspondence usually mean is that the letters deal in a general way with the same topics explored in the fiction: marriages and family life, parties and balls, domestic entertainments, and the now-antiquated courtship rituals of the early-nineteenth-century provincial English gentry.

Yet with Cassandra in mind, one wants to put a finer point on it. Both Austen and Cassandra received marriage proposals at different times in their lives; Cassandra was in fact engaged to be married in 1797, only to have her fiancé die of a fever in the West Indies. Austen received at least two proposals in her youth, both of which she turned down. Biographers have made much of a mysterious "gentleman" at Lyme Regis in 1804–5 who, according to Austen's niece Caroline (who heard about it from Cassandra), had "seemed greatly attracted by my Aunt Jane. . . . I can only say that the impression left on Aunt Cassandra was that he had fallen in love with her sister, and was quite in earnest. Soon afterwards they heard of his death." Whatever one makes of the story (and Austen's own part in it goes unrecorded), neither she nor Cassandra showed much real inclination for matrimony later in life. One can't help but feel that both found greater comfort and pleasure—more of that "heartfelt felicity" that Emma Woodhouse finds with Mr. Knightley, or Elizabeth Bennet with the handsome Darcy—in remaining with one another.

The letters from Austen that Cassandra allowed to survive testify to such a primordial bond. Virginia Woolf observed of Austen's fiction that "it is where the power of the man has to be conveyed that her novels are always at their weakest." Perhaps this is because men are inevitably inferior to sisters. Even more so than in the fiction, Austen displays a remorseless eye in the letters for male fatuousness. It is as if she were at once trying to reassure Cassandra—no one is good enough for me but you—and inviting her complicitous laughter. Men are fools and imaginists and know nothing of the droll, shared cynicism of intelligent women. Thus of one admitted suitor, gone out of Hampshire to practice law in London, she writes sardonically in 1798:

It will all go on exceedingly well, and decline away in a very reasonable manner. There seems no likelihood of his coming into Hampshire this Christmas, and it is therefore most probable that our indifference will soon be mutual, unless his regard, which appeared to spring from knowing nothing of me at first, is best supported by never seeing me.

"Your unfortunate sister was betrayed last Thursday into a situation of the utmost cruelty," Austen begins another letter from 1801; "I arrived at Ashe Park before the Party from Deane, and was shut up in the drawing-room with Mr. Holder alone for ten minutes." A flirtation with the silly, would-be alluring Mr. Evelyn is endured for the sake of his shiny new phaeton: "There is now something like an engagement between us & the Phaeton, which to confess my frailty I have a great desire to go out in;—whether it will come to anything must remain with him.—I really believe he is very harmless; people do not seem afraid of him here, and he gets Groundsel for his birds & all that." The comically appended "all that," with its sly echo of an appropriate line from *The Rape of the Lock* (*"Snuff,* or the *Fan,* supply each Pause of Chat, / With singing, laughing, ogling, and all that"), is Popean indeed in its brisk satiric dismissal.

When Austen encounters, rarely, a man who disturbs her sexual self-possession, her protestations of dislike are liable to become spinsterish and strident. The handsome, unfriendly Henry Wigram "is about 5 or 6 & 20, not ill-looking & not agreeable.—He is certainly no addition.—A sort of cool, gentlemanlike manner, but very silent. . . . I cannot imagine how a Man can have the impudence to come into a Family party for three days, where he is quite a stranger, unless he knows himself to be agreeable on undoubted authority." But for the most part she retains her levity—to the point of joking with Cassandra about various possible (impossible) matches. One James Digweed, she teases her sister, "must be in love with you, from his anxiety to have you go to the Faversham Balls, & likewise from his supposing that the two Elms fell from their grief at your absence." "Was it not a galant idea?" she asks. "It never occurred to me before, but I dare say it was so." She imagines herself married to certain literary men of the day. After reading of the death of the poet Crabbe's wife, she writes: "Poor woman! I will comfort *him* as well as I can, but I do not undertake to be good to her children. She had better not leave any." And elsewhere, listing some favorite comic fantasies—which include having her portrait painted for the Royal Academy—she announces she will marry "young Mr. D'arblay," the adolescent son of Fanny Burney.

If men are ultimately insignificant, women, by contrast, are a source of unending sisterly preoccupation. Austen's physical descriptions of women—their faces, voices, hair, clothing, comportment at balls and in sitting-rooms—are funny, complex, often poignant, and as exquisitely drawn as any in her fiction. Yet they inevitably reveal, too, what can only be called a kind of homophilic fascination. Unlike men, women have bodies—to be scrutinized and discussed, admired or found wanting. Thus Mrs. Powlett, seen at a dance in 1801, "was at once expensively & nakedly dressed;—we have had the satisfaction of estimating her Lace & her muslin." Of a Mrs. and Miss Holder: "it is the fashion to think them both very detestable," but "their gowns look so white & so nice I cannot utterly abhor them." "*Miss* looked very handsome," she says of another plausible young lady, "but I prefer her little, smiling, flirting Sister Julia." "I admire the Sagacity & Taste of Charlotte Williams," the novelist writes approvingly in 1813; "those large dark eyes always judge well. I will compliment her, by naming a Heroine after her."

At times the sexuality of women's bodies elicits oddly visceral effects: "I looked at Sir Thomas Champneys & thought of poor Rosalie; I looked at his daughter & thought her a queer animal with a white neck." "I had the comfort of finding out the other evening who all the fat girls with short noses were that

disturbed me at the 1st H. Ball. They all prove to be Miss Atkinsons of Enham."
"I have a very good eye at an Adultress," she boasts in 1801, after seeing a well-
known demirep at the Pump Room in Bath, "for tho' repeatedly assured that another in the same party was the *She*, I fixed upon the right one from the first."
Even unseen women can be arousing; witness the peculiarly proprietorial fantasy
inspired by the news that an Austen family friend is to marry a Miss Lewis at
Clifton. "I would wish Miss Lewis to be of a silent turn & rather ignorant, but
naturally intelligent & wishing to learn;—fond of cold veal pies, green tea in the
afternoon, & a green window blind at night." It is as if Austen were first conjur-
ing the woman up, then projecting herself, shamanistically, into the role of tu-
tor-husband.

Yet two female bodies are even more insistently "present" in the letters—
Austen's and Cassandra's own. The extraordinary number of passages in the letters devoted to clothing, for example—on her trips to London and Bath Austen
often bought fabric, pieces of trim, and other items to be used in the making or
refurbishing of her own or her sister's dresses—bespeaks the close terms of physical intimacy on which she and Cassandra lived and the intense psychic "mirror-
ing" that went on between them. A passage like the following, in which Austen's
wish to have Cassandra "see" a gown being made up for her in Bath—and by implication the body that will wear it—is so fantastically detailed as to border on
the compulsive:

> It is to be a round Gown, with a Jacket, & a Frock front, like Cath: Bigg's
> to open at the sides.—The Jacket is all in one with the body, & comes as
> far as the pocketholes;—about a half a quarter of a yard deep I suppose all
> the way round, cut off straight at the corners, with a broad hem.—No
> fullness appears either in the Body or the flap;—the back is quite plain, in
> this form;—☐—and the sides equally so.—The front is sloped round to
> the bosom & drawn in—& there is to be a frill of the same to put on oc-
> cassionally when all one's handkerchiefs are dirty—which frill *must* fall
> back.—She is to put two breadths & a half in the tail, & no Gores;—
> Gores not being so much worn as they were;—there is nothing new in
> the sleeves,—they are to be plain, with a fullness of the same falling down
> & gathered up underneath, just like some of Marthas—or perhaps a little
> longer.—Low in the back behind, a belt of the same;—I can think of
> nothing more—tho' I am afraid of not being particular enough.

Such passages remind us strikingly of how important a role clothes have
played in the subliminal fetish life of women—how much time women spend
looking at one another, dressing one another, and engaging in elaborate and mu-
tually pleasurable "grooming behavior." Austen and Cassandra were hardly exempt: the conventions of early nineteenth-century female sociability and

body-intimacy may have provided the necessary screen behind which both women acted out unconscious narcissistic or homoerotic imperatives.

But the desire to be seen and imaginatively embraced—to be held in Cassandra's mind's eye—is everywhere in Austen's letters. "Own-body" references (to borrow a term from the sociologist Erving Goffmann) are frequent in her correspondence and carry a powerful existential charge. She constantly invites her sister to think about her—about her precise location in space, or about the various physical sensations that either soothe or discomfit her. "I am in the Yellow room—very literally—," she tells Cassandra on arriving at their brother's estate in Kent, "for I am writing in it at this moment." "How do you do to day?" reads a somewhat plaintive missive from Bath; "I hope you improve in sleeping—I think you must, because *I* fall off;—I have been awake ever since 5 & sooner, I fancy I had too much cloathes over my stomach; I thought I *should* by the feel of them before I went to bed, but I had not courage to alter them." Far from being trifling, such details bring to life the phenomenology of the novelist's emotional world. Cassandra was indeed the person she slept with, we realize with a start, and without her sister's comfortable warmth, slumber itself was altered.

In their own way the letters to Cassandra may ultimately say more of Austen's fiction—the inner sensual content of the works—than other seemingly more relevant or better-known pieces of Austeniana. Besides the Cassandra letters, the new Oxford edition includes two famous shorter correspondences: a series of letters Austen wrote to her novel-writing niece, Anna Austen, in 1814 (Anna had sent some chapters-in-progress to her aunt for criticism) and a set from 1817 to another niece, Fanny Knight, who was debating over several marriage proposals. The former correspondence contains a number of much-quoted pieces of authorial advice ("3 or 4 Families in a Country Village is the very thing to work on") and displays all of Austen's characteristic humor and taste: "Devereux Forester's being ruined by his Vanity is extremely good; but I wish you would not let him plunge into a 'vortex of Dissipation.' I do not object to the Thing, but I cannot bear the expression;—it is such thorough novel slang—and so old, that I dare say Adam met with it in the first novel he opened." Yet the flippancy sometimes borders on condescension and was perhaps not entirely helpful: Anna ended up burning the work in question after developing a painful creative block.

As for the letters to Fanny, though one might expect them to shed light on the novelist's powers of empathy (Fanny's predicament is one that occurs often in Austen's fiction), they make for rather unpleasant reading. Were one wanting to make the vulgar case for Austen's homoeroticism, here would be the place to look: the tone is giddy, sentimental, and disturbingly schoolgirlish for a forty-two-year-old woman. Austen was infatuated with Fanny and slips often into embarrassing coquetries: "You are inimitable, irresistible. You are the delight of my Life. Such letters, such entertaining letters as you have lately sent!—Such a description of your queer little heart! . . . I shall hate you when your delicious play of Mind is all settled down into conjugal & maternal affections." As a love ad-viser she is dithery and contradictory—sometimes fearing the hold Fanny has over men ("Mr. J.W. frightens me.—He will have you"), at other times breath-lessly suggesting new lovers for her. She is rather like her own Emma Wood-house, who, in an excess of displaced amorosity in *Emma*, persuades her dim-witted little protégée, Harriet Smith, quite wrongly, that three different men are in love with her—with comically disastrous results.

What one ends up realizing is that more than anyone else Cassandra pro-vided the essential ballast in Austen's life—was the caretaker of her mind and body, and guarantor of her imaginative freedom. ("Aunt Cassandra nursed me so beautifully!" Austen wrote to Fanny near the end of her life. "I have always loved Cassandra, for her fine dark eyes & sweet temper.") It is always surprising to realize that Jane Austen had a mother, who indeed outlived her: when she is mentioned, rarely, in the letters, it is only as a kind of background presence—someone there, but half-forgotten. (The ailing Mrs. Austen is recorded as saying to a grandson some years after Austen's death: "Ah, my dear, you find me just where you left me—on the sofa. I sometimes think that God Almighty must have forgotten me; but I daresay He will come for me in His own good time.") Cassandra, one might say, was her real mother. And to the degree that Austen's fictions are works of depth and beauty and passionate feeling—among the supreme humane inventions of the English language—one suspects in turn it is because she loved and was loved by Cassandra.

Can we forgive Cassandra her jealousy? Reading the last, wrenching letters in the new Oxford collection—those written by Cassandra herself to their nieces after Austen's agonizing death from Bright's disease in 1817—there is nothing for it but to do so. Cassandra sat by her sister's bedside all of the long final evening and night, at one point supporting Austen's dying head, which was "al-most off the bed," in her lap for six hours. "Fatigue made me then resign my place to Mrs. J.A. for two hours & a half when I took it again & in about one hour more she breathed her last." "I *have* lost a treasure," she wrote to Fanny Knight a few days later, "such a Sister, such a friend as never can have been sur-passed.—She was the sun of my life, the gilder of every pleasure, the soother of every sorrow, I had not a thought concealed from her, & it is as if I had lost a part of myself." She had a ring made up with a lock of Austen's hair set in it—she wore it for the rest of her life—and dreamed of meeting her again: "I know the time must come when my mind will be less engrossed by her idea, but I do not like to think of it. If I think of her less as on Earth, God grant that I may never cease to reflect on her as inhabiting Heaven & never cease my humble en-deavours (when it shall please God) to join her there." If such prayers are ever answered, one can only hope that she did.

postscript

After its publication in the *London Review of Books* in August 1995, the fore-going essay prompted a veritable gaggle of attacks in the British and North American press. I was accused of "outing" Jane Austen, I was obviously both depraved and insane. I wrote the following letter—also printed in the *LRB*—by way of response:

There has been a spate of reports in the British press saying that in my essay about Jane Austen's letters I made the claim that Jane Austen "may have been gay" or may have had a "lesbian relationship" with her sister, Cassandra.

My comments have been grotesquely, indeed often comically, distorted. Nowhere in my essay did I state that Jane Austen was a lesbian—certainly not in the modern clinical sense of the word—or that she had sex of some sort with her sister. As a number of Austen scholars and biographers consulted about the matter have pointed out, there is no evidence suggesting that Jane Austen had sexual relations of any sort with anyone, let alone with her sister Cassandra.

I stand by what I *did* say in the piece, however: that Austen's relationship with Cassandra was unquestionably the most important emotional relationship of her life, that she lived with her sister on terms of considerable physical intimacy, and that the relationship—I believe—had its unconscious homoerotic dimensions. I am amazed, frankly, that in 1995 this should be considered so controversial and inflammatory a statement. Social historians have been writing for the past twenty years about the profoundly homosocial nature of middle- and upper-class English cultural life in the eighteenth and nineteenth centuries: The sexes were highly segregated, and powerful emotional (and sometimes physical) ties between persons of the same sex were both common in the period and often expressed in highly romantic or passionate terms. Unmarried women, especially siblings, frequently shared a bed—as Austen and Cassandra did for all of their adult lives. I have been accused of "not realizing" that such physical intimacy between women was in fact "normal" or "common" in the period, when that was precisely part of my point. The culture at large reinforced—far more than our own culture does today—same-sex intimacy of all kinds. To point to a "homoerotic" dimension in the Austen/Cassandra relationship is in one sense simply to state a truth about the lives of many English women in the early nineteenth century: that their closest affectional ties were with female relatives and friends rather than with men.

Elaborating on this fundamental point, I suggested that specific elements in Austen's letters (the many satires on men and marriage) and in her novels (the compelling emotional importance given to sororal and quasi-sororal relations) indicate that she and Cassandra lived out a particularly intense version of the sister bond. Once again, I did not say that I thought Austen necessarily acted out such feelings in any explicitly sexual way—only that I believe such feelings were there. I take it as a psychological given, obviously, that parental and sibling attachments have an erotic dimension—indeed provide the basic models for all of our subsequent affective attachments. Surely literary critics writing in the *London Review* are still allowed to speculate about such things.

Sadly, the hysterical reaction on the part of a number of press commentators—that I have somehow "polluted the shrine" by daring to reflect along these lines about Austen's emotional life—seems grounded in the most banal (and morally bankrupt) anti-homosexual sentiment. The question of Austen's "sexual orientation" is not the real issue here. No one—including the most well-informed Austen scholar—will ever be able to make more than an educated guess about that. What is disconcerting about the press reaction to my review is that so many people, apparently, still consider the mere suggestion that someone like Austen might have had homosexual feelings such an appalling slur that any hope for sensitive debate on the matter becomes impossible. It is neither a crime nor a sin to love—in whatever way one is able—a person of one's own sex.

note

1. Jane Austen, *Jane Austen's Letters,* ed. Deirdre Le Faye (Oxford and New York: Oxford University Press, 1995)

8

SUBLIMELY BAD

How bad are most of the novels produced by English women writers in the decades before Jane Austen? Sad to say, just when one thinks one has read the very worst of them, another comes along to send one's spirits plummeting further. Eliza Fenwick's excruciating pseudo-Gothic epistolary novel, *Secresy: or, The Ruin on the Rock* (1795), is hardly the first "lost" eighteenth-century woman's novel to be resurrected over the past decade by feminist literary historians.[1] Other recent finds include Eliza Haywood's snooze-inducing *The British Recluse* from 1722 ("a sad Example of what Miseries may attend a Woman, who has no other Foundation for belief in what her Lover says to her, than the good Opinion her Passion has made her conceive of him"); Sarah Fielding's deeply unpleasant *David Simple* (1744), in which characters with names like Spatter, Lady Know-All, and Mr. Varnish assail the gormless hero until he drops dead of despair; and Sarah Scott's thoroughly demoralizing *Millenium Hall* (1762), on the supposed consolations of living in a grim all-female community where one does nothing but sew all day and read aloud from Scripture with one's pious fellow virgins. Whether, given the competition, *Secresy* is so "sublimely bad"—in Pope's phrase—to take the crown of ultimate badness remains to be seen.

Which isn't to say, paradoxically, that works like Fenwick's are uninteresting or unimportant or—in a funny way—not worth reading. Badness often has its own somewhat decadent pleasures. For the reader effete enough to venture, the very ineptitude of much BJ (Before Jane) women's fiction can make for a certain supercivilized enjoyment. In *Secresy*, for example, connoisseurs of kitsch will undoubtedly take pleasure in the exquisite character of Nina—a Bambi-like "little fawn" who for long stretches of the novel is the orphaned heroine, Sibella's, only companion. (Fenwick's plot is a kind of knockoff of Bernardin de St. Pierre's *Paul et Virginie*: Sibella Valmont has been kept in semi-feral isolation since childhood by a cruel uncle obsessed with the educational theories of Rousseau; she will fall in love with—and be betrayed by—her uncle's natural son, the libertine Clement Montgomery.) When the other heroine of the novel, Caroline Ashburn, first comes across Sibella, she is perched like a "Wood Nymph" on a tree stump, with Nina curled in her lap "in an attitude of confidence and affection." Yet the tiny, sure-footed Nina is as helpful as she is devoted. When the plot veers into melodrama—which is almost right away—the plucky little beast carries letters back and forth between characters, shows Sibella where a supposed "Hermit of the Rock" is hiding, and alerts her to interlopers and would-be kidnappers by bounding meaningfully over various rocks and hillocks.

Yet one wants more in the end, perhaps, than silly-pastoral and the fleeting satisfactions of camp. The case for reading *Secresy* has to be made on more compelling grounds. One might begin by pointing, as Fenwick's editor Isobel Grundy does (somewhat briefly) in her Introduction, to *Secresy*'s broader historical significance: what it reveals about the rise of female authorship in eighteenth-century Britain. Problematic though works like *Secresy* may seem today, the enfranchisement of women writers was undeniably one of the great cultural achievements of the epoch. Thanks to gains in female literacy and the rapid expansion of the middle-class reading audience, more women than ever before began writing professionally in the eighteenth century, and by Fenwick's time (1766–1840), had come—despite the fierce misogynistic resistance sometimes marshaled against them—to dominate in the field of popular fiction.

Over the past twenty years, English and American scholars have documented, often poignantly, this remarkable, unprecedented coming into writing. Many female-authored poems, plays, essays, and novels have been restored to view—some for the first time since their original publication—and our general picture of eighteenth-century English literature has been transformed and enriched. Among cognoscenti, it is now considered intellectually backward, as well as a bit vulgar, to speak only of the period's male classics. Perhaps most strikingly, the novel—as the form overwhelmingly favored by female authors—has come increasingly into focus, far more than satire or the *Spectator*-style essay, as the preeminent literary genre of the century.

This still leaves the *Secresy* problem unresolved: why read *this* novel when there are others with more immediate appeal? Without much success either way, Isobel Grundy tries to make the case for *Secresy* on both ideological and artistic grounds. The Cornish-born Fenwick, about whose early life little is known, was active in her twenties and thirties in radical political circles, and along with her husband, John Fenwick, an Irish patriot and member of the London Corresponding Society, became friends with William Godwin and Mary Wollstonecraft around the time of the French Revolution. One of the few—haunting—pieces of biographical information we have about Fenwick, indeed, is that she was present at the birth of Wollstonecraft's daughter—the future Mary Shelley—and took charge of her for a time after Wollstonecraft's sudden death of infection a few days later. Grundy makes much of these personal and intellectual ties, and finds in Fenwick's novel a rousing assertion of themes—both feminist and freethinking—borrowed from her friend's notorious *Vindication of the Rights of Woman.*

Without a doubt, Fenwick's negative portrait of Sibella's uncle Valmont, the novel's Rousseau-reader-cum-Gothic-villain, owes much to Wollstonecraft's bitter critique of Rousseau and his disdainful dismissal of female intellect in *Émile.* In turn, when Fenwick assails the corrupting power of "secresy"—that "cankerworm" eating away at the sympathetic bonds between men and women—she echoes passages in the *Vindication* on the hypocrisy and duplicitousness fostered by sexual and social inequality. But Fenwick pays an even more direct homage to her friend—who lived openly with several lovers before marrying Godwin—by having her heroine reject the erotic self-denial enforced on women in patriarchal society. Not only does she show Sibella, innocent child of the forest, freely "giving" herself to the worldly Clement, she has her defend the union—which will result in pregnancy and her death in childbirth—with a strikingly Wollstonecraftian appeal to natural law. Society's petty rules do not apply to them, Sibella tells her lover before their coupling: "'tis our hearts alone that can bind the vow."

Out of such interesting but inconclusive detail, Grundy tries to convince us that *Secresy* is a great book. Fenwick's "artful" handling of the epistolary form is reminiscent of Richardson, she suggests; the novel's plot has an almost "Shakespearean" tragic force. Describing Fenwick's exorbitantly melodramatic final scenes, in which Sibella, having finally escaped from her uncle's castle, falls into a hysterical stupor on finding out that Clement has secretly married Caroline Ashburn's wealthy, dissipated mother, Grundy enthuses over the "sublime" handling of Sibella's breakdown and the "extraordinary emotional power" of the climactic tableau.

The boosterism here doesn't convince—will never convince—because too much else is ignored: the absurd plot, the incoherent characterization, the intrusive, often repellent didacticism (Fenwick also wrote rather grim children's books), the impossibly stilted prose. A less sentimental and more rewarding approach would have been to acknowledge the novel's awfulness at the start and go on from there; for it is precisely *Secresy*'s awfulness, paradoxically, that makes it—in a deep as well as a camp sense—worth reading. Not only is Fenwick's novel a veritable compendium of the imaginative and stylistic tics deforming so much early English women's fiction, and hence of diagnostic value, it starkly illuminates the larger individual and collective costs of "coming into writing": the psychological price women paid for their swift and subversive entry into the world of English letters.

Were Fenwick's novel a human being, one would be tempted to characterize it as autistic—as primitive and withholding in a profound sense. Its most striking feature is a kind of dissociation of sensibility. Within the novel certain characters are literally dissociated: Sibella, immured in the grounds of her uncle's estate, is cut off from human society; her pathetic attempts at liberation, including the ill-fated passion for Clement, result only in alienation and death. Yet she and her friend Caroline, through whose more jaded eyes we see most of the action, also seem like dissociated parts of one another. Like Marianne and Elinor Dashwood in *Sense and Sensibility* (though with none of their charm), Sibella and Caroline suggest twinned yet opposing styles of femininity—one spontaneous, sexual, and full of "natural" sensibility, the other reasonable, brittle, and unromantic. But Fenwick, unlike Austen, seems unable to imagine any deeper connection between them. Despite the "violent friendship" they are supposed to bear one another, they inhabit polarized fictional universes. Caroline, the rational one, is a supercilious bourgeois prig, given to eavesdropping and sententious comments on male moral turpitude; Sibella, the romantic one, is either weirdly exalted, a kind of Blakean pneumaton, or else like a crash victim or psychotic—glassy eyed, dumb, and inert. (In the novel's final pages, after she gives birth to a dead baby and is near death herself, she is "perfectly yet horridly calm.") So deep in the end is the sense of imaginative incoherence, one loses faith in the shaping consciousness behind the fiction; it's like trying to make eye contact with someone who can no longer recognize faces.

Yet this same psychic compartmentalization—the autistic "splitting up" of narrative and human function—is found everywhere in early female fiction. The melodramatic entombing of the heroine by a powerful, often paternal figure is a conventional, even obsessional topos in eighteenth-century women's writing; one sees it in novels by Maria Edgeworth, Ann Radcliffe, Sophia Lee, Mary Wollstonecraft, Elizabeth Inchbald, and numerous others. It is frequently amalgamated with a sort of Bluebeard motif: in Inchbald's *A Simple Story* the heroine is kept prisoner by her father, whom she has never seen, in his own country house. (She is not to enter his rooms, on pain of instant banishment.) Another common topos is the splitting up of emotional possibilities into different characters. Female characters are particularly prone to this schizoid reductionism: impossibly virtuous young heroines are made to coexist, for example, with spectacularly sinister or depraved older women—grotesque harridans like Madame Duval in Frances Burney's *Evelina*, or unpleasantly sexualized mother figures like Madame Montoni in Radcliffe's *The Mysteries of Udolpho*, or the disturbingly labile Lady Delacour in Edgeworth's *Belinda*.

Indeed, mothers and fathers seem to be at the root of the problem. Nowhere is the dissociated quality of early women's fiction more painfully apparent than in the appalling, seemingly pathological relations that obtain in such works between parents and children. Here again Fenwick's novel is exemplary. *Secresy* has two parental surrogates—Valmont, the entomber, and the squalid Mrs. Blackburn, seducer of Clement. Both are monsters: Valmont in the familiar Gothic bogeyman style (which Austen would slyly parody in the character of General Tilney in *Northanger Abbey*); Mrs. Ashburn in a rather more modern mode, as the mother who won't touch or let herself be touched. The generations are cut off from one another, and with such lethal finality—there is no question here of reconciliation—that one senses, at large in these novels, a kind of generalized psychic trauma: a feeling of authorial victimization so deep and disordering as to preclude the more familiar gratifications of fictional narrative.

To speak of a "dissociation of sensibility" is to bring to mind, of course, T. S. Eliot's classic deployment of the phrase in his famous essay on the metaphysical poets. At some point in the seventeenth century, Eliot argued, the ratiocinative and emotional functions were separated in English poetry: where there had once been integration and wholeness (Donne, Crashaw, and Herbert) came fragmentation and division (Milton through Tennyson). The poet's mind became increasingly like the ordinary man's—alienated, diffuse, unable to bridge the chasm between intellect and feeling:

> When a poet's mind is perfectly equipped for its work, it is constantly amalgamating disparate experiences; the ordinary man's experience is chaotic, irregular, fragmentary. The latter falls in love, or reads Spinoza, and these two experiences have nothing to do with each other, or with the noise of the typewriter or the smell of cooking; in the mind of the poet these experiences are always forming new wholes.

Whether or not one accepts the elegiac languor here, Eliot correctly identifies the anomie attached to writing in a modern age. What he left out was the fact that poets became like "ordinary men" in the seventeenth century precisely because ordinary men were now becoming poets: the "print explosion" of the late Renaissance had meant a wholesale increase in male literacy and a sweeping democratization of English literary culture, witnessed emblematically in the rise to prominence of deracinated figures like Milton and the radical pamphleteers. For women this coming-into-writing seems to have been delayed—women always lag about a century behind in the history of major cultural shifts—yet no less traumatic. For at the same time that it empowers, literacy inevitably brings with it self-division, ambivalence, and an infantile element compounded of fear and rage: fear that one's words may offend those who *own* writing already, rage at being cut off from discourse for so long. The wrenching Oedipal dramas played out in so much of modern literary history—for those who own writing already are always one's parents or surrogate versions of them—suggest as much: that it is potentially as alienating as it is exhilarating to make oneself known as text.

In women writers of the eighteenth century, for whom the anxieties of textuality would have been exacerbated both by the cultural contempt in which their productions were held and by the crippling contradictions of the female role itself (how do women reconcile reading Spinoza with the "smell of the cooking" when they are supposed to be *doing* the cooking?), the impetus toward paranoia and fragmentation is especially acute. The unwillingness of writers like Fenwick to "meet the eye," the psychic deadness and emotional rebuff one so often senses in their work (signaled in *Secrecy* by the title), the murderous, estranging hostility to parental figures—all, paradoxically, may be part of the pathology of beginning, of trying to get over the birth trauma of authorship itself.

How does one get over it? This is a miracle about which we know little: the outwitting of autism. Yet surely Austen—who invariably looks her reader in the eye—offers a key to the mystery. She seems to have overcome any sense of imaginative alienation early on: certainly by the age of five or six. Her disarming, affectionate, endlessly amusing juvenilia might indeed be seen as a kind of ritual exorcism of all the creative dead ends writers like Fenwick got stuck in. Witness "The Mystery—An Unfinished Comedy," one of several droll little playlets she wrote at the age of twelve or so and dedicated to her father:

> *Scene the first. A garden.*
> [*Enter* CORYDON.]
> CORY. But hush! I am interrupted.
> [*Exit* CORYDON. *Enter* OLD HUMBUG *and his* SON, *talking.*]
> OLD HUM. It is for that reason I wish you to follow my advice. Are you convinced of its propriety?
> YOUNG HUM. I am, sir, and will certainly act in the manner you have pointed out to me.
> OLD HUM. Then let us return to the house.
> [*Exeunt.*]
> *Scene the second. A parlour in* HUMBUG'S *house.*
> MRS. HUMBUG *and* FANNY, *discovered at work.*
> MRS. HUM. You understand me, my love?
> FANNY. Perfectly, ma'am. Pray, continue your narration.
> MRS. HUM. Alas! it is nearly concluded, for I have nothing more to say on the subject.
> FANNY. Ah! here's Daphne.
> [*Enter* Daphne.]
> DAPHNE. My dear Mrs. Humbug, how d'ye do?
>   Oh! Fanny 'tis all over.
> FANNY. Is it indeed!
> MRS. HUM. I'm very sorry to hear it.
> FANNY. Then 'twas to no purpose that I . . .
> DAPHNE. None upon earth.
> MRS. HUM. And what is to become of? . . .
> DAPHNE. Oh! that's all settled. [*Whispers* MRS. HUMBUG.]
> FANNY. And how is it determined?
> DAPHNE. I'll tell you. [*Whispers* FANNY.]

MRS. HUM. And is he to? . . .

DAPHNE. I'll tell you all I know of the matter.

> [*Whispers* MRS. HUMBUG *and* FANNY.]

FANNY. Well! now I know everything about it, I'll go away and dress.

MRS. HUM., DAPHNE. And so will I. [*Exeunt.*]

> *Scene the third.*
>
> *The curtain rises and discovers* SIR EDWARD SPANGLE *reclined in an elegant attitude on a sofa, fast asleep*
>
> [*Enter* COLONEL ELLIOTT.]

COLONEL. My daughter is not here I see . . . there lies Sir
Edward . . . Shall I tell him the secret? . . . No, he'll certainly blab
it . . . But he is asleep and won't hear me . . . So I'll e'en venture.

> [*Goes up to* SIR EDWARD, *whispers him, and exit.*]
>
> *Finis.*

Were it not for the fact that Austen wrote her little drama four or five years before Eliza Fenwick published *Secresy*, one might be forgiven for thinking that the precocious satirist had Fenwick's inept fiction in mind. It's all here: the assault on silly Gothic suspense-building, the anticipatory camp, the delightful adolescent-rococo send-up of exhausted conventions. But most important, perhaps, is the touch of grace, the inability to feel frightened, either of past or future. Parents here are humbugs—like oneself—but no more than that. One suspects that the admirable Reverend Austen, whose love for his brilliant daughter shines forth in all of her compositions, had something to do with this grace: did something well enough to make writing seem the most natural thing on earth.

note

1. Eliza Fenwick, *Secresy: or, The Ruin on the Rock*, ed. Isobel Grundy (London: Broadview Press, 1994).

9
RESISTING CASANOVA

ight one beg—with trepidation—to differ on Casanova? On the face of it he might seem to be the perfect nineties sort of guy. Unlike his strange coeval the Marquis de Sade, Casanova (1725–1798) was sexy without being scary: of the hundreds of female conquests commemorated in the twelve closely-printed volumes of erotic memoirs he composed at the end of his life, not one ended up garotted, chopped up into little pieces, hideously sodomized, or dumped in some horrid well. Like the gentlemanly seducers of today, Casanova was not only solicitous about his partner's pleasure—concerned to "perform the gentle sacrifice" without rudeness or roughness or unseemly dispatch—but careful to take hygienic precautions whenever any "voluptuous combat" was about to ensue. To minimize the risk of a "fatal plumpness" in his lovers, he tells us, he never hesitated to wear a "little garment of very fine, transparent skin, eight inches long, closed at one end, but resembling a purse and having at its open end a narrow pink ribbon." Way excellent!

And then there is the sex itself, which is often fashionably perverse—in a mild, postmodern, *Vanity-Fairish* sort of way. While willing to bed almost any unattached female he encountered, Casanova typically liked a little kink—whether numerical, sartorial, or familial. Having two women at once was good, for example—preferably sisters, like the naughty virgins Nanetta and Marta, whom he deflowered while a seminary student in his teens:

> I began with the one toward whom I was turned, not knowing whether it was Nanetta or Marta. I found her curled up and covered by her shift, but by doing nothing to startle her and proceeding step by step as gradually as possible, I soon convinced her that her best course was to pretend to be asleep and let me go on. Little by little I straightened her out, little by little she uncurled, with slow, successive, but wonderfully natural movements, she put herself in a position which was the most favorable she could offer me without betraying herself. I set to work, but to crown my labors it was

necessary that she should join in them openly and undeniably, and nature finally forced her to do so. I found this first sister beyond suspicion, and suspecting the pain she must have endured, I was surprised. In duty bound religiously to respect a prejudice to which I owed a pleasure the sweetness of which I was tasting for the first time in my life, I let the victim alone and turned the other way to do the same thing with her sister, who must be expecting me to demonstrate the full extent of my gratitude.

When only one woman was available, dressing up worked a charm: many were the young women whom Casanova disguised as boys or "sham nuns" in order to heighten subsequent "fits of rapture." A favorite amour of the 1740s was a Bolognesean opera singer whose particular quirk was to pass herself off as a castrato. At first glimpse of the doe-eyed "Bellino," Casanova writes, he knew at once—despite the singer's silken breeches and the dainty bump at the crotch—that "he" was really a "she." "His eyes were a woman's and not a man's." But the gender-bending nonetheless inflames him. After he and the singer strip down and consummate their passion, he asks her to demonstrate the "little apparatus" of gut with which she deceives those impolite enough to question her sex:

> She gets out of bed, pours water into a glass, opens her trunk, takes out her apparatus and her gums, dissolves them, and fits on the mask. I see something unbelievable. A charming girl, who looked it in every part of her body, and who, with this extraordinary attachment, seemed to me even more interesting, for the white pendant offered no obstruction to the well of her sex. I told her that she had been wise not to let me touch it, for it would have intoxicated me and made me become what I was not, unless she had instantly calmed me by revealing the truth.

So inspired is he by the sight of this adorable little fashion accessory he immediately commences a second love "skirmish" in which both he and his curious bedmate end up "victorious."

And incest too never failed to please. Encountering an old love, one Donna Lucrezia, eighteen years after their first meeting, Casanova finds that she has a beautiful daughter, Leonilda, of whom he is the father. After telling Lucrezia he will help with Leonilda's dowry (she is betrothed to an elderly marchese), he promptly gets in bed with them both and makes love first to the mother then to the daughter:

> But the moment which brings Lucrezia to the death of love is precisely the moment when, out of consideration for her, I think it is my duty to withdraw. Leonilda, stirred to pity, with one hand helps the passage of her

mother's little soul, and with the other places a white handkerchief under her father, who was ejaculating.

Twenty years later, in Prague, he meets by accident the handsome young Marchese della C.—Leonilda's son—who is both, he records with satisfaction, his son and his grandson.

But even without the sex, Casanova would seem to be the ultimate user-friendly, feel-good dude. There's the gabby, talk-show host manner (with celebrity appearances by Catherine the Great, Voltaire, Pope Benedict XIV, and countless others), the glitzy backdrops (Venice, Milan, Paris, Madrid, St. Petersburg, Naples), and the fact that he has been deemed *great literature* by various esteemed authorities. "Has any novelist or poet," gushed Edmund Wilson when Willard Trask's definitive English translation of the *History of My Life* first appeared in 1960, "ever rendered better than Casanova the passing glory of the personal life?" The late V.S. Pritchett saw him as Enlightenment culture hero. "Casanova is unsurpassed as the re-creator of the daily talking interests of 18th-century Europe. He ranges from slut to patrician, from closet to cabinet, waterfront to palace. He is superior to all other erotic writers because of his pleasure in news, in gossip, in the whole personality of his mistress." Such charmingly insouciant ways, one imagines, combined with a love of fine food and wine, compulsive social climbing, and an utter lack of any moral or political conviction—he once appeared at a Milan masquerade in a gorgeously ruffled velvet suit that had been slashed in pieces and patched up with expensive silk so as to resemble the costume of a "luxury beggar"—would seem to make Casanova ideally suited to life in the late twentieth century, home of Starbucks, *The Kiss*, lipstick lesbians, homeless people, and gourmet cigars.

One will find nothing to contravene such rosy impressions in *The Man Who Really Loved Women*, the Franco-Belgian analyst Lydia Flem's recent psychobiography of Casanova.[1] Written in the soulful, stylized, all-in-the-present-tense mode much in fashion among lit-crit types these days—the latest version of *Europrofondeur*—her book is a veritable love-poem to the sprightly snogger. He was a man "born to make people happy," she declares—a "friend and lover to women" whose overflowing memoirs are the crowning achievement of a life spent deliciously, even heroically, in a utopian quest for pleasure:

> Voluptuousness becomes memory. The unending repetition of his experiences is transcended by writing. The very act of writing allows this transcendence of self. Casanova enjoys the moment, and once it slips away, he enjoys remembering the moment, a moment that is enhanced by the precious feeling of transience. His pleasure in living is perpetuated as literary pleasure.

In writing it all down—every turn, twist, and tumble—Casanova achieved "not just a deepened sense of self but also a moral meditation on existence."

Obviously this is not biography in the conventional sense. For dates, places, or indeed a more linear approach in general, one must seek out the memoirs themselves, lately reissued in six elegant paperback volumes by Johns Hopkins University Press.[2] Instead, Flem offers a rambling, anecdotal meditation on certain prime Casanovan themes: his impoverished Venetian childhood, his idealization of his beautiful yet unavailable mother, his delight in outwitting elderly paternal figures, his rootlessness and constant search for novelty, his lifelong, often histrionic compulsion to prove he was "a boy and not a girl." The overall tone is hortatory and faintly sanctimonious: Casanova is the one whose "insolent legacy" is to show us the way to be happy.

What to do with it all? In some ways Flem's book succeeds, though not perhaps in the way its author intended. On matters nonsexual she can be illuminating and imaginative. She points up well, for example, the psychic effects of Casanova's humble origins—he was the eldest child of Venetian *commedia* actors who abandoned him to the care of strangers for much of his childhood—and how he sought, through canny self-improvement, to undo the double stigma of low birth and neglect. Casanova might be called the first great *parvenu* of Western culture: the first to see that in the new and increasingly fluid social world of eighteenth-century Europe knowledge itself could be a ticket to fortune. By recognizing that superficial cultivation and a certain intellectual flair might "[give] power to people who do not have it by birth as a privilege of caste," he managed to insinuate himself into the *beau monde* in his teens and stay there for the rest of his life. (A lifelong dabbler in history, alchemy, mathematics, and philosophy, he wrote novels, plays, and scholarly treatises, organized the national lottery in Holland, and ended his days as librarian to Count Waldstein of Bohemia.) He's the first "unplaceable" man of modernity; and figures such as Napoleon, or the heroes of Stendhal and Balzac, are unimaginable without him.

Similarly, Flem highlights interestingly some of his many idiosyncracies—such as his lifelong interest in physiology and the peculiar freaks of the body. After being arrested in Venice in 1755 for ostensibly practicing magic, he was flung into the worst of the republic's prisons, the infamous Piombi, or Leads, under the roof of the Doge's Palace. While waiting in an antechamber to be taken to his cell, he recalls, he experienced the contradictory urge to sleep and to micturate: "I spent four hours there during all of which I slept, waking every quarter of an hour to make water—a very strange phenomenon, for I had never suffered from strangury, the heat was excessive, and I had not supped; nevertheless I filled two large chamber pots with urine." "It had been my experience," he observes, "that surprise caused by an act of oppression produced the effect of a strong narcotic on me, but it was only now that I learned that it is highly diuretic." In later years, he prided himself on one-upping professional medical men; after hurting his hand in a duel—it had gone black with gangrene—he kept his doctor from amputating it by threatening to kill him. Unbeknownst to the physician, he had noticed that the wound was "red at the edges"—the first sign of healing. When the wound closed up, he brags, he was hailed as a genius.

But at the same time something troubles in Flem's account, and after a while one realizes it is Casanova himself. Flem's lack of distance on her subject—she often seems more than a little in love with "Giacomo" (as she calls him) herself—means that she ends up duplicating his own triumphalist vision of himself. So thoroughly indeed has she identified herself with Casanova's own narcissism—the root cause behind everything he said or did—she ends up playing the role of ventriloquist's dummy to his obliging ventriloquist. The fact that well over a third of *The Man Who Really Loved Women* is composed of verbatim quotations from the *History of My Life*—each one set off, like trendy ad copy, in "significant" italics—suggests how deeply the psychoanalyst has let herself be penetrated, so to speak, by the naughty Venetian.

The problem here is that Casanova was a severely damaged human being. Flem's claims to the contrary, he was *not* deeply interested in other people or in making them happy—especially not women—and in one way or another he exploited just about every person he ever met. Risible though his memoirs can be—and no one can deny that in small doses they make an utterly agreeable way of wasting one's time—they are also the record of an ultimately soul-deadening smugness and solipsism. Their significance as human testament and historical artifact is consequently limited. Far from ranking with the genuinely great autobiographies—whether Augustine's or Rousseau's or Frederick Douglass's or Violette Leduc's or Janet Frame's—the *History of My Life* remains in the end as emotionally impoverished, as irrevocably petty and banal, as its author was in life.

Women, of course, are at the heart of it. It's partly a matter of having no real "close-ups": the various women whom Casanova seduces—all the Teresas, Antonias, Marias, Cecilias, Amalias, and so on—tend to blur into one another after a while. Casanova's representational style might be compared to that of his eighteenth-century contemporary, the scene painter Canaletto. In the same way that in Canaletto's famous panoramas of Venice and London human figures are reduced to identical, barely individuated flecks of color—everyone seems to be seen from the same distance, about five hundred yards away—so Casanova's characters are, psychologically speaking, also "seen from a distance." They tend to resolve into crude *commedia* types—fools or knaves, slatterns or seductresses, helpers or obstacles. In the case of his lovers, this emotional distancing is particularly pronounced: at best we learn if a certain conquest is dark or fair, amenable or unwilling. When a woman reappears several times over the course of the narrative—as the incest-prone Donna Lucrezia does—the reader is often hard-pressed to recall who she is or why she originally had a claim on our attention. There is nothing of that intense cross-sex imaginative involvement we find, for example, in Byron's descriptions of his mistresses, or indeed in the reveries of later erotic memoirists, such as the anonymous author of the Victorian pornographic masterpiece *My Secret Life.*

Flem is convinced that there is "not a trace of misogyny in Casanova," and educes his passionate love for his mother, Zanetta—whom she calls the "*prima amorosa*" of his life—in support of this statement. Yet Zanetta, a leading lady in the Comici Italiani acting troupe, cared little for her son. He was stupid and unresponsive as a child, not speaking until he was eight, and suffered debilitating nosebleeds from which his parents seem to have hoped (none too secretly) that he would die. After her husband's death in 1733 Zanetta left her son with strangers, decamped for Verona, St. Petersburg, and Dresden, and seldom ever saw him again. The nosebleeds only ceased when Casanova's grandmother took him to a witch in Murano, who locked him in a chest for several hours and effectively scared them out of him. He learned to talk soon after, and immediately impressed everyone around him—he boasts—with his suddenly-revealed brilliance and precocity.

Flem suggests that these childhood experiences, resulting in a never-to-be-relinquished hope of pleasing an absent mother, prompted what she calls Casanova's extraordinary "generosity" as a lover:

> Never to harm a mistress, never to arouse her anger or disappointment, never to make her suffer from their affair in any way—this is what he consistently aspires to. Giacomo would never forgive himself for tormenting a woman with the slightest hint of tragedy. Though on several occasions he sincerely plans to marry a lover, he can never bring himself to give up his freedom. He knows he would make a bad husband. He dodges the law or only pretends to submit to it, he laughs at authority and religion, but he respects his women friends and he is careful not to be at fault where they are concerned. . . . There is nothing he dreads more than seeing a woman become his enemy.

But the memoirs at times tell a less pleasant story—of a lifelong ambivalence toward women that sometimes issued in vengeful furies. After La Charpillon, a courtesan in London, steadily refuses his advances, he is at first violent (he tries to rape her), then suicidal, until he has the gratifying idea of placing a parrot he has trained to say "Miss Charpillon is more of a whore than her mother" among the milling throngs at the Royal Exchange. In Aix, in 1768, he becomes enraged by a fourteen-year-old peasant girl who has the misfortune to hold herself in the "wrong posture" while he is trying to copulate with her: he should have "beaten her," he repines, "as I had done to one of her sort in Venice twenty-five years earlier." And whenever he is laid low with venereal disease—a not infrequent occurrence in the memoirs—he typically reviles the unlucky woman he believes to have infected him: numerous are the outbursts in the *History of My Life* against the "whores," "wretches," and "she-monsters" accused of passing on to him the Paphian disorder. (How many of them, one wonders, caught it from him?) Needless to say, he inevitably presumes his reader to be another jaded man of the world, like himself.

Granted, Casanova's usual way of relating his (real? made-up?) sexual adventures is droll: he has the faux-castrato "Bellino" declare after their tryst, for example, "I did not become truly a woman until I tasted the perfect pleasure of love in your arms." But his women remain soulless, precisely because he has no access to souls. He responds only to surfaces, fabrics, sheens, integuments. In this crippling absence of insight—a lack of what may only be called sensibility—Casanova shows himself, paradoxically, out of sync with the main tendencies of his epoch. The great imaginative discovery of the eighteenth century was, after all, female inwardness: the uncharted inner psychic realm of women's desires and fears, aspirations and antipathies. The discovery was registered in the lives of real women: in the fiercely unsentimental poems and letters of Lady Mary Wortley Montagu, in the grand social experiments of powerful *salonnières* such as Anne Thérèse de Lambert, Madame du Deffand, Julie de Lespinasse, and Suzanne Necker, in the moral, intellectual, and polemical ardors of Mary Wollstonecraft, Olympe de Gouges, Bettina von Arnim, and Germaine de Staël.

Above all the discovery was registered in the newly emerging novel—the first literary genre of Western civilization to devote itself, almost exclusively, to female dream-space. Casanova, as he tells us himself, disliked novels: even when desperate for books, while imprisoned in the Leads, he refused the novels offered him by a sympathetic prison guard. Perhaps they hit a little too close to home. For from its beginning the great cultural task of the novel has been to announce the end of libertinism. Not its literal end, of course: in Samuel Richardson's massive, magnificent *Clarissa* (1747–48), a novel with some claim to being the greatest piece of prose fiction ever written, the anguished heroine is first sexually humiliated, then destroyed, by a Casanova-like seducer. Richardson's handling of his tragic story in no way precludes sympathy for the villain; the seducer, Lovelace, is in many ways as noble, gifted, and heartbreaking a figure as the heroine. But what Richardson also makes stunningly clear, and this is the source of the cathartic pity and fear his novel evokes, is Lovelace's absolute and utter moral obsolescence. When women have souls, libertines become *de trop*.

Was Casanova *really* "the man who really loved women"? Such designations can only be tendentious, whether advanced by men or women. (Perhaps women are better judges of the matter, but to say that is not to say very much at all.) Still, reading Flem, and indeed Casanova himself, one is tempted to try to take the question seriously. Certainly there are other men—both of Casanova's own time and after—to whom the label may more fittingly apply. Mozart, for example, who cherished his wife Constanza to the death, even as his operas explore the themes of love and fidelity with ravishing and sometimes agonizing honesty. Or Keats, whose tender, virile, and lovable personality comes across in every word he wrote, but most unerringly in the letters to Fanny Brawne. And even in our own ghastly century, there is James Joyce, who in a spectacular imaginative collusion with the feminine—as *Ulysses* and *Finnegans Wake* bear out—found a permanent and glorious vitalization of his art.

In the 1950s, during the great intellectual renewal of interest in France and elsewhere in the writings of the Marquis de Sade, the feminist philosopher Simone de Beauvoir wrote a famous essay entitled "Must We Burn Sade?" We may not in the end wish to "burn" Casanova (or Sade either for that matter). If knowing something about the eighteenth century and its extraordinary artistic, cultural, and political legacy has become a mark of civility in the twentieth, then Casanova tells us something we desperately need to know. He will never go out of style as long as we retain our curiosity about the past, the vicissitudes of the erotic, and the tragicomic collisions of male and female.

And, it must be said, he holds a mirror up to our own age as well. The fact that he's back in fashion, in glossy covers, even as a new millennium begins, tells us something about the hollow mood of our own moment, in which superficiality reigns and a brazen use of "spin" can take the edge off the abominable. Casanova's renewed popularity in some quarters—Clive James recently anointed him a "great man" and "a kind of genius" in the pages of the *New Yorker*—suggests how profoundly the contemporary cult of self-congratulation has taken root. He'd undoubtedly make a great talking head. That has never been in question. But we need not love him either, even when we're told that he loves us.

notes

1. Lydia Flem, *Casanova: The Man Who Really Loved Women*, trans. Catherine Temerson (New York: Farrar, Straus and Giroux, 1997).

2. Giacomo Casanova, Chevalier de Seingalt, *History of My Life*, trans. Willard Trask, 6 vols. (Baltimore: Johns Hopkins University Press, 1997). All quotations are from this edition.

10
THE JUVENILIA OF CHARLOTTE BRONTË

nlike the more accommodating juvenilia of Jane Austen (in which the ease and high Mozartian humor of the later stylist are already plainly visible), the early writings of Charlotte Brontë have always proved a stumbling block to her devotees. Some of the difficulty has had to do with the freakish nature of the surviving manuscripts. "An immense amount of manuscript is an inconceivably small space" is how Elizabeth Gaskell described the "curious packet" of juvenilia that came down to her after Brontë's death; as if to mimic the inhuman density of print, the fourteen-year-old Brontë has written nearly all of her earliest stories and poems on tiny sheets of paper in a hand "almost impossible to decipher without the aid of a magnifying glass." The facsimile pages reproduced in Christine Alexander's new edition—some measuring only two inches by three inches—give a dizzying sense of the near-demoniacal physical labor that went into the originals and of the challenge they pose to anyone attempting to read through or transcribe them.

But the difficulty has had equally to do with the sheer strangeness of the juvenilia and the unusual (if poignant) circumstances in which they were composed. The story of life in the bleak Haworth parsonage is well known: thrown back upon themselves, the brilliant Brontë children, Charlotte, Emily, Anne, and Branwell, took refuge in a world of the imagination. In 1829, when Charlotte was thirteen, the four invented an imaginary West African kingdom (the Glass Town Confederacy) and began writing plays and stories about Verdopolis, the capital of Glass Town, and its inhabitants. Emily and Anne quickly broke off from the other two, inventing their own mythical country of Gondal. Charlotte and Branwell in turn developed the separate kingdom of Angria, adjacent to Glass Town, and devoted themselves to describing its history, wars, politics, social events, and scandals in a bizarre plethora of miniature novels, mock-newspapers, and poems. The so-called Glass Town Saga, jointly produced over the next ten years, was the result; an epic jumble of manuscripts, all complexly related, on Angrian life and manners, high and low.

The problem is not simply that it is difficult to separate Charlotte's contributions from Branwell's, though this is sometimes the case—even in the manuscripts in Charlotte's hand. The protagonist of most of Charlotte's stories is the charismatic duke of Zamorna (a.k.a. Arthur Wellesley), son of the duke of Wellington, would-be Byronic seducer, and ruler of Angria. Branwell's pet creation is "the former pirate Alexander Percy" (a.k.a. "Rogue"), who as the scheming Angrian prime minister becomes Zamorna's chief rival and enemy. The youthful coauthors frequently borrowed each other's characters, however, and a number of Charlotte's stories focus on Percy rather than Zamorna. Throughout their lengthy collaboration, moreover, both Charlotte and Branwell were continually adding new characters and killing characters off, only to revive them by joint fiat later. Familial and sexual relationships are as a result almost impossible to keep straight. (Both Zamorna and Percy have a host of legitimate and illegitimate offspring, including several sets of twins, by different wives and mistresses.) And over the course of the saga certain characters change names, titles, looks, and personalities with hallucinatory frequency. Zamorna himself appears in some stories as the heroic "Marquis of Douro," defender of the Glass Town Confederacy against the marauding Ashantees, and in others as the sinister "Adrian," who rules over Angria like an Oriental despot. The effect can be bewildering.

Until fairly recently, Brontë's editors and biographers have tried to make the Glass Town material accessible by excerpting drastically—the approach taken by Frances Beer in her 1986 Penguin edition of early writings. The results, while useful, have never been wholly satisfactory: Beer's selection—which by highlighting stories having to do with Zamorna's wives and lovers, charts Brontë's evolving treatment of her female characters—leaves so much else out as to be a distortion of the whole. Only with Christine Alexander's new complete edition-in-progress (two volumes have appeared; a third is on the way) are we beginning to see Brontë's juvenilia in its true light, as a work of dazzling, almost visionary grandiosity and brilliance, and surely one of the most astonishing productions ever to issue from an adolescent pen.[1]

Which isn't to say that anyone who picks up Alexander's exhaustively annotated volumes will instantly have an easy time of it. Adding to the intricacy of the Glass Town saga is the fact that Charlotte and Branwell composed the different parts of it under different authorial personae. Most of the manuscripts that Charlotte produced between 1833 and 1835 are supposedly the work of Lord Charles Albert Florian Wellesley, Zamorna's "literary" younger brother and self-appointed chronicler of Angrian affairs. At least one text, however, is attributed to the antiquarian "Captain Tree," Lord Charles's main rival on the Verdopolitan literary scene. In his preface to "The Foundling" (1833)—a story he offers as a "plain relation of facts"—Tree accuses Lord Charles of perpetrating "vile and loathsome falsehoods" about Zamorna and his circle. Lord Charles responds (in "The Green Dwarf") by accusing Tree, somewhat improbably, of being an evil midget who once plotted against the Angrian ruler. The effect is of a kind of Nabokovian textual labyrinth, which the valiant editor does her best to clarify in a series of amusing yet also mind-bending footnotes.

For the reader willing to plunge wholeheartedly into Brontë's convoluted imaginary world, however, the rewards are great. Not least is the insight that the Angrian cycle offers into the writer's later work. To move through the multifarious universe of the Glass Town stories is to watch Brontë—as if through a magic optic—inventing the very themes that would later sustain her. In the dark-haired, ambiguous Zamorna, for instance, the noble, "bewitching," yet also "barbarous" figure to whom virtually everyone in Angria yields up in hopeless fascination, there are clear (though sometimes comical) intimations of Rochester, Monsieur Paul, and even Robert Moore. Like Brontë's later heroes, and especially Rochester, Zamorna is an alluring yet enigmatic figure, who owes much of his strange charm to his handsome "fixed sneer," his occasional brutality, and the Byronic mysteries surrounding his past. (More than one wedding in Glass Town will be shockingly interrupted at the moments of the vows.) He is typically heartless and brusque to women, yet draws them ineluctably toward him—as in "High Life in Verdopolis" (1834) or "The Spell, An Extravaganza" (1834)—like "the Grand Sultan of Turkey surrounded by his seraglio."

Unlike Branwell's tales, which tend to focus on Angrian politics and military affairs, Charlotte's tales are almost all romantic intrigues of one sort or another, with Zamorna figuring prominently. Thus in "Lily Hart" (1833), Zamorna—in disguise—helps arrange the clandestine marriage of his noble friend John Augustus Sneachie to the impoverished yet beautiful Lily Hart; in "The Spell," he changes places with his secret twin brother in order to confound Percy; in "My Angria and the Angrians" (1834)—once again in disguise—he flirts with his neglected third wife, Mary Henrietta, to test her fidelity.

Brontë is hardly uncritical of her hero, however, and even in the earliest stories one finds numerous instances of that exhilarating sarcasm—a kind of visionary flippancy—that is so much a part of her later style. She had not at this point located this sardonic power in a female narrator: the women of the Glass Town saga, including Zamorna's wives, are on the whole a rather dispiriting lot—willing to put up with "Zamorniac" posturings in the hopes of receiving one of their idol's "peculiar smiles." The only exceptions are his Scottish mistress, Mina Laury, who manages to fend off a tiger attack on his behalf, and the majestically turbaned Zenobia, "the Verdopolitan de Staël," who harbors an adulterous passion for him. Unhappily married to Zamorna's rival Percy, the handsome Zenobia is a bluestocking and a coquette, a student of Angrian poetry and languages, and a noted pugilist who frequently spars with her piratical husband. (Like Fielding before her and Compton Mackenzie after, Brontë shows an unexpected interest in *les boxeuses*.) At her celebrated Glass Town salon, surrounded by "a knot of beaux esprits, the very flower of Africa's geniuses," Zenobia often succeeds in cowing Zamorna with "conversazione" of fascinating brilliance.

Instead it is Lord Charles Wellesley, the "small imp of a brother" through whose jaded eyes we usually see Zamorna, who emerges as Brontë's first truly captivating character. The elfin Lord Charles is a born snooper: he spies on his great sibling (of whom he is madly jealous) by rummaging through his letters and hiding behind curtains in various Verdopolitan ballrooms. (Though Lord Charles's age and size shift from story to story, he is apparently diminutive enough—even as an adult—to hang from chandeliers in order to eavesdrop.) With his fey, cynical, and recessive nature—he is usually seen, like Jane Eyre, observing his brother from a window seat or other dark corner—he suggests both the adolescent author herself and the mordant, watchful heroines she would soon create. Certainly in Lord Charles's ambivalent view of Zamorna, whom he regards with a mixture of veneration and contempt, one finds anticipations both of Jane Eyre's satirical, slyly vaunting attitude toward Rochester and Lucy Snowe's moody private joking at the expense of M. Paul.

The most exciting aspect of the Glass Town material, however, is the measure that it gives of the sheer prodigiousness of Brontë's literary imagination. The youthful author borrowed incessantly, of course, from favorite sources: from Byron and the Romantic poets, Sir Walter Scott and Ann Radcliffe, the Bible and *Paradise Lost*. She had also read precociously in parliamentary reports and newspapers and modeled many of Angria's leading personages on contemporary English political figures. (Not always exactly: Castlereagh appears as an Angrian dandy with a strange "lolling" tongue.) But the result is more, finally, than the sum of the parts. Brontë imagines her fanciful civilization so thoroughly, and in such precise and uncanny detail, that to read of its complex affairs is to enter a surreal alternative universe, akin to the fabulous world of the *Arabian Nights*, Lewis Carroll's Wonderland, or the strange mirror-universes of Borges and Calvino.

The African setting contributes to the hallucinatory effect: though supposedly situated in the Gold Coast region, Angria bears little resemblance to any actual West African locale. The indigenous Ashantees, it is true, constantly threaten Glass Town's mostly English- and Scottish-descended inhabitants, but they are only fleetingly—and crudely—depicted. The future creator of Bertha Mason sheds few tears here for the "savage" victims of British imperialism. Instead, the juvenile Brontë regales her reader with a series of extravagant dream landscapes in which tropical, Mediterranean, and Lake District elements are freely mixed. Angria's pleasant "glens" are dotted with palmettos and tamarind trees; the valley of the Niger is full of moldering Gothic ruins. Verdopolis, the great capital, is a kind of Palladian dream city, filled with palaces and elegant marble buildings, such as one might see, through a visionary golden haze, in a canvas by Claude or Poussin. When we view Zamorna riding in triumph through its wide city streets, or disporting with his fellow "African" aristocrats in exquisitely appointed rococo drawing rooms (with Ashantees distantly clamoring in the background), the effect is almost of a kind of subequatorial camp. Indeed, though in a somewhat more juvenile vein, Brontë offers the same zany exoticism that one finds in Beckford's *Vathek*, Firbank's *The Flower Beneath the Foot*, and some of the more recherché fictions of Brigid Brophy.

The human scene is as rich and varied as the geography. Besides its politicians and aristocrats, Angria has its poets and painters, its architects and historians, its lawyers and mill owners, its "rare-lads" and great beauties. Sir Edward de Lisle is "the eminent Verdopolitan portrait painter"; Alexander Soult its leading bard; and Sir John Leaf "the Glass Town Thucydides." The ancient and mysterious Crashie, who lives in a tower and seldom comes out, is the confederacy's revered spiritual leader. Next to Zenobia, the glamorous Lady Maria Sneachie (of Sneachie's Land, the misty region to the north of Verdopolis) is the chief Glass Town flirt; and Mr. Myrtillus Ellrington, who sports salmon-pink "cambric trowsers," one of its leading fops. By contrast, the austere Prince John Sneachie, duke of Fidena and counselor to Zamorna (and an early version of *Jane Eyre*'s St. John Rivers), represents the less frivolous side of Angrian social life.

Angrian villains include the ominously named Robert Sdeath, who plots with Percy against Zamorna; Pigtail, a repulsive creature from Frenchy's Land (to the south of Angria) who kidnaps Verdopolitan infants using a huge hook; and Young Man Naughty, a "middle-aged giant man with grey hair," who is one of the leaders of Percy's Great Rebellion of 1831. Giantism and dwarfism, interestingly enough, seem to be rampant in the Glass Town world; besides Maimoune, "the great fairy," and the evil splay-footed dwarf Finic (supposedly Zamorna's son by his Ashantee mistress Soffala), there are the strange inhabitants of Stump's Island, who are four feet high, speak in incomprehensible dialect ("Daw mun boy for t'saak and kluke"), and wear "one great round wooden shoe on which they shuffle about with great rapidity." Even General Leaf, Angria's military hero, is pixieish in stature: in "The Green Dwarf," he appears, somewhat ludicrously, as "a little personage with jointless limbs, a chubby face and a pale pink wig of frizzled silk surmounted by a tall black hat on which was an ornament of carved wood."

One can only regard with awe, as Gaskell did, the isolated and untraveled teenager who, along with her brothers and sisters, could invent such a world and populate it so fully and idiosyncratically. Reading through the juvenilia, one has constantly a sense of imaginative confidence, of glorious vistas and plenitudes, as in the following panorama of Verdopolis seen from afar:

Its stately towers and turrets shone like fairy buildings of gold. Ships crowded the distant harbour. Magnificent barges and yachts were skimming with spread sails over its deep blue bosom, while the oar-chant of the rowers and the louder voice of commerce came with such distinctness through the calm clear atmosphere that the words they uttered might have been heard by an attentive listener.

The lonely Brontë loved equally imagining crowds: when Zamorna arrives at the stadium in Verdopolis for a great horse race and celebration, a "huge unbroken mass of human faces" slopes far above him, "upwards like a living hill almost to the very clouds."

One must also regard with something close to awe Christine Alexander's detailed annotations, which are tactful yet helpful throughout. Some, like the series of footnotes in which she traces Brontë's peculiar interest in "resuscitation"—the revival of characters after seemingly fatal accidents and illnesses—prompt deeper reveries. When we see Zamorna recover from an apparently mortal disease in "The Spell, An Extravaganza," or Percy revive after being shot in "Arthuriana: Brushwood Hall" (1833), it is hard not to think of the interesting "reprieves" granted so many of Brontë's later characters: Rochester, alive after the fire in *Jane Eyre*; M. Paul saved from drowning (perhaps) at the end of *Villette*. Even Lord Charles Wellesley's comical reawakening ("in my own warm bed") after a stunning blow to the head in "Corner Dishes: A Day Abroad" (1834) anticipates those near blissful moments, particularly in *Jane Eyre* and *Villette*, in which the narrator "comes back to life" after some terrible trauma or calamity. Brontë is one of the great poets of suffering and melancholia—witness the drawn-out agony of Caroline Helstone in *Shirley*—but such scenes remind us that she was equally drawn to the imagery of healing and recuperation.

Alexander underplays the pathos: she doesn't mention, for instance, that at the time Brontë began "resuscitating" characters, she had already lost her mother and two older sisters to tuberculosis, and would later lose her two younger sisters as well. Yet one cannot help but sense the element of wish fulfillment in these marvelous revivals. Brontë had discovered at an early age that the writing of fiction was a way of making the dead live again—if only on the page. All the more poignant, then, the setting of "A Leaf from an Unopened Volume," one of the last Angrian tales from 1834, "in the Year 1858." Zamorna still reigns as Adrian the Magnificent; Percy, Zenobia, Lord Charles, and the rest of the Angrian aristocracy carry on their flaunting, wooing, and scheming. Yet Brontë herself was already three years dead in 1858: a victim of tuberculosis and puerperal fever, brought on by complications associated with her first pregnancy.

note

1. Christine Alexander, ed., *An Edition of the Early Writings of Charlotte Brontë*, 2 vols. (Oxford: Blackwell, 1987).

SHUT UP, SWEET CHARLOTTE

n the recently published letters of Vita Sackville-West to Virginia Woolf, there is an entertaining missive from 1927 in which Vita, recovering from a Christmas flu, describes a "delightful" dream induced by aspirin:

> I dreamt that I dined with Eddy Sackville-West, a party consisting of Eddy, Charlotte Brontë, you, and me. Eddy seemed vexed and anxious, and after dinner took me aside to say, "Vita, you must find me very attractive to put up with such a dull party on my account?"

The silliness of the dream is mighty, of course: the campy Eddy, Vita's cousin, was homosexual and hardly contending for her passions; the flamboyant Vita, besides, was having an affair with Woolf. But the crowning absurdity, of course, is Brontë—whose bizarre materialization in the midst of a Bloomsbury dinner party makes one want to laugh aloud. That such an evening might be "dull"— Woolf and Brontë together—seems patently ludicrous.

From another angle, though, it's a sad business, all this Charlotte-longing. For that is what Sackville-West's dream is also about: bringing back—and feeding and reviving and making glad—the saddest, hungriest, most appallingly deceased woman in English literature. For who doesn't feel sympathy for Charlotte Brontë? Ever since the publication of Mrs. Gaskell's *Life of Charlotte Brontë* in 1853, two years after Brontë's death at thirty-eight, the elements of her story have been all too familiar: the motherless childhood at the bleak parsonage at Haworth on the Yorkshire moors; the stern, reclusive, half-mad clergyman-father; the semistarvation at the Cowan Bridge School for Clergymen's Daughters (model for the ghastly Lowood School in *Jane Eyre*); the deaths of her two elder sisters from consumption in 1825; the lonely sojourn in Brussels and unrequited love for a married man; the stagnant, empty years as a schoolteacher and governess; the alcohol-sodden death of her feckless brother, Branwell, in 1848; the deaths of her sisters Emily and Anne, their literary dreams mostly unrealized, only a few months later; her own brief fame as a novelist cut short by illness and depression, and an agonizing death during pregnancy—less than a year after her marriage to her father's curate—just when happiness seemed at last within reach.

What makes Charlotte Brontë's story all the more heartbreaking is how close she came to escaping it all—to fleeing Haworth and the death-in-life it represented. Reading Juliet Barker's monumental biography of the Brontës—surely the most exhaustive, thoughtful, and profoundly researched book anyone has ever written about the family—the most exhilarating passages are those in which Barker, like Gaskell before her, describes Brontë's brief taste of freedom after the spectacular success of *Jane Eyre* in 1847.[1] As Brontë's identity gradually became known to the public—she had submitted her novel under the masculine pseudonym "Currer Bell," and not even her publishers, Smith, Elder & Co., knew who she was until some months after its appearance—a new world seemed miraculously to open up for her: trips to London, parties in her honor, the acclaim of the rich and famous, and best of all, the approbation of literary idols such as Thackeray, Gaskell, Harriet Martineau, G. H. Lewes, and Leigh Hunt.

For a moment Vita's dream doesn't seem so farfetched, or the world of Bloomsbury dinner parties so far away. We, too, find ourselves fantasizing: had Branwell not languished and died, had Emily and Anne not fallen prey to the terrible family curse of consumption, had Brontë herself not felt obliged to return to her ailing yet resilient father in Yorkshire (outliving his wife and five other children, he would outlive her by six years), we can easily see her moving across the decades—vibrant, enriched, increasingly cosmopolitan, a marvel of rebound and rehabilitation—to the very edge of the twentieth century.

It is no wonder that Brontë inhabits the dream life of modern women writers. She comes so close, only to fall back, irretrievably, into family and death and the past. One wants to save her from Fate itself. "It is strange to reflect," wrote Virginia Woolf on the centenary of Brontë's birth in 1916, "what a different image we might have of her if her life had been a long one":

She might have become, like other writers who were her contemporaries, a figure familiarly met with in London and elsewhere, the subject of anecdotes and pictures innumerable, removed from us well within the memory of the middle-aged, in all the splendour of established fame. But it is not so. When we think of her we have to imagine someone who had no lot in our modern world; we have to cast our minds back to the fifties of the last century, to a remote parsonage upon the wild Yorkshire moors. Very few now are those who saw her and spoke to her; and her posthumous reputation has not been prolonged by any circle of friends whose memories so often keep alive for a new generation the most vivid and most perishable characteristics of a dead man.

In the absence of such contacts, Woolf says, one can only turn back to the astonishing, rebarbative, strangely consoling novels—each one "a superb gesture of
defiance, bidding her torturers depart and leave her queen of a splendid island of
imagination."

It will come as a shock to Brontë's many admirers to find Juliet Barker's biography so resistant to this peculiar and abiding pathos. Indeed, the book is revisionism on a grand scale. Not only does Barker wish to shift attention away from
the author of *Jane Eyre* and *Villette* back toward the other Brontës—this, more
than any previous Brontë book, is intended as a family portrait—she also wishes
to rearrange our sympathies: to undo what she sees as the distorting effects of the
"poor Charlotte" school of biography so skillfully propagated by Gaskell and her
successors. As Barker announces in a brisk introduction, a chief goal of her
1,000-page work is to dismantle the popular perception of Brontë as "the long-
suffering victim of duty, subordinating her career as a writer to the demands of
her selfish and autocratic father." Instead, we are to see her as no better or worse,
no more a victim of Fate, than her equally pitiable parent or siblings.

In purely practical terms the task is an ambitious one, if only because so
much surviving Brontë material is so Charlotte-centered. It is not simply that
she left more in the way of manuscript material and correspondence than anyone else in her family, or that Gaskell—as Woolf observed—has indeed
"stamped our minds with an ineffaceable impression" of her. Her writings themselves seem to assert her preeminence. Unlike the novels of Emily and Anne,
which can seem strangely dissociated from the little we know about their authors' personalities—*Wuthering Heights* has the stark, autonomous quality of
myth—Charlotte's novels have a fiercely intimate, self-dramatizing feel.

Both *Jane Eyre* and *Villette* are fraught, claustrophobic first-person narratives:
the thematic links with Brontë's own life (exile, loneliness, poverty, sexual longing) are obvious. Yet even the more spacious *Shirley*, set in rural Yorkshire against
the backdrop of the Luddite rebellions of 1811–12, seems to allegorize its author's state of mind. In the excruciating rendering of the nearly book-long
melancholia of its heroine, Caroline Helstone, Brontë gives one of the more
vividly personal accounts of chronic inward sadness since Burton's *Anatomy of
Melancholy* or the journals of Cowper. No wonder biographers since Gaskell
have fallen under her spell.

Despite these obstacles, Barker, it must be said, comes close to achieving her
goal—at least in the first, more limited part of her endeavor. A one-time curator
of the Brontë Parsonage Museum at Haworth, she has turned up masses of new
Brontë material, particularly having to do with Patrick Brontë, the much-ma-
ligned father; Branwell, the ill-fated brother; and Anne, the youngest of the siblings. (She is less successful with Maria Brontë, the dead mother, and with the
elusive Emily, who remains, Barker admits, largely a cipher.) She has been ingen-

ious in seeking out new sources of information about the lesser-known members of the family.

Astonishing though it may seem, Barker is the first biographer to read systematically through contemporary Yorkshire newspapers such as the *Halifax Guardian* or *Bradford Observer*, despite the fact that Patrick Brontë is known to have corresponded regularly with several of them. Uncovering his contributions, she is able to demonstrate that far from being the brooding madman of legend, shut up in his study while his motherless children wandered the moors, he was in fact deeply involved in local political and religious affairs, an energetic reformer on behalf of the poor, and, ironically—given the legend that the family tuberculosis was the result of drinking water contaminated by the fetid runoff from the graveyard next to the Haworth parsonage—an agitator on behalf of public sanitation and a safe water supply.

But Barker has also returned to neglected private sources, with similarly illuminating findings. Her thorough rereading of the juvenilia—in childhood and adolescence the younger Brontës jointly produced a phantasmagoric trove of stories about two imaginary kingdoms known as Angria and Gondal—prompts a reevaluation, in particular, of Branwell's thwarted talents: Barker is convinced that he originated much of the so-called Angrian material and could have been as significant a writer in adulthood as any of his sisters had he lived. Perusing the school essays that Charlotte and Emily wrote during their sojourn in Brussels for the formidable Constantin Heger—the married teacher with whom Charlotte fell in love and later memorialized as M. Paul in *Villette*—Barker finds fascinating insights into each sister's personality and (in Charlotte's case) the evolution of her literary style. And having trawled through hundreds of forgotten letters, diaries, and notebooks, Barker is able to shed light on a number of misunderstood or misrepresented matters: the development of Branwell's alcoholism, the identity of the illegitimate child he fathered in 1840, the nature of the religious crises experienced by Anne Brontë in 1837 and 1849, Charlotte's infatuation with her publisher George Smith.

The result of such sleuthing is unquestionably the most detailed account ever of the month-by-month—and in some cases day-by-day—activities of the Brontë clan. One suspects that Barker has learned a great deal from the extraordinary, even visionary biographical techniques developed over the past two decades by Richard Holmes. As in Holmes's remarkable studies of Coleridge and Shelley, or his recent double portrait *Dr. Johnson and Mr. Savage*, there is a phenomenological density about *The Brontës*—a wealth of recovered sensuous detail—that brings the departed world of its subjects alive in an almost kinesthetic fashion. Whether she is describing the bell-ringing competitions held in Haworth Church, the Brontës' dogs and cats, or the consternation caused by the explosion of a local bog in 1824, Barker exhibits, like Holmes, a visceral alertness to the way in which the so-called background experiences of life shape private and collective awareness.

This alertness can make for moments of exquisite biographical empathy—as when she notices, for example, that the fatal illness of the Brontës' mother, Maria, in August 1821 coincided with the death of Queen Caroline, the much-loved wife of George IV. For the Brontë children and their grief-stricken father the timing could not have been worse: "the paraphernalia of public mourning were everywhere to be seen and even Patrick's pulpit had to be draped in funereal black as if in preparation for the death that had to come." Later, describing Patrick's removal of the parsonage piano from the parlor into an unused upstairs bedroom after the deaths of Branwell, Emily, and Anne—an act that irritated Charlotte, who thought its absence added to the sepulchral gloom of the house—Barker is no doubt correct to see "that the presence of the silent piano in the room where Patrick spent most of his time must have been a painful daily reminder of his three children who had all loved to play it."

But when it comes to Barker's other goal—the demythologizing of Charlotte—the biographer cannot be said to succeed. The problem is in part one of clashing temperaments: Brontë is precisely the sort of person a scholar as meticulous as Barker might be expected to dislike. Brontë herself could never have written a 1,000-page biography. Her recklessness, her anger, her impatient aversion to anything or anyone contravening her own passionate vision of life inevitably disqualified her for any career other than the one she chose: that of genius. The creator of *Jane Eyre* was not fastidious or painstaking or fair. She was only great.

But Barker, too, has her limitations. Her disaffection for Brontë's magnificently troubled personality results in its own kind of unfairness—manifest at times in the crudest anti-Charlottism. Massively articulated though the biography is, its emotional subtext can be boiled down to a single issue: Was it right for Charlotte to rebel? For rebel she did—by despising Haworth, by yearning for an education and economic independence, by loving the wrong people, and above all by writing. Writing for Brontë was a form of metaphysical complaint. Her novels are complaints in the sense that Sophocles' plays or the Book of Job are complaints—not niggling or negative, but cries of rage directed at evil gods who murder souls. The savage indictment in *Jane Eyre* of Lowood School—that vile substation of hell where children inhale their death at every breath and the adults cannot be bothered to look in on them—is simply the first of Brontë's many salvos against the satanism of everyday life.

Barker consistently disparages these acts of resistance. In the process she drains Brontë's life of any moral dimension. Brontë's heroic intransigence is recast as so much grumbling and selfishness, her dark perception of human life as masochism and hysteria. A petty judgmentalism, a kind of Head Girl goody-

goodyism, seems to overtake Barker whenever she feels obliged to comment on Brontë's inner life. Brontë is invariably in the wrong. Thus her desperate push to improve her own and her family's lot by going abroad to study in Belgium—she took Emily with her so that the two of them might learn enough French and German to open a school of their own and thereby relieve the strain on their father's small income—is described as "ruthless" and "an entirely selfish pursuit of learning." Her dislike of the ill-paid, exhausting task of governessing (she wrote in disgust to her friend Ellen Nussey that not only was she supposed to teach her infant charges, "but wipe the children's smutty noses or tie their shoes or fetch their pinafores or set them a chair") is attributed to her "snobbishness" and "recalcitrance." ("Charlotte's attitude," Barker calmly reports later, "alone had been responsible for her unhappiness as a private governess.") Elsewhere she is described as "sour," "jaundiced," "venomous," "wallowing in self-pity," or pathologically "jealous"—as when she complains to Nussey that one of her father's curates, William Weightman, is flirting rather heartlessly with several Haworth young ladies and intends to marry none of them.

In the symbolic battle of fathers and daughters, Barker inevitably sides with the fathers. The desire to humanize Patrick Brontë may be a laudable one, but Barker's special pleading on his behalf—against Charlotte—borders at times on the grotesque. Though hardly the ogre of repute, Patrick Brontë was not a particularly easy or empathetic man: his fundamentalist religion made him cold, unimaginative, repressive. (In 1816, in a didactic book for children, he excoriated the "sensual novelist and his admirer" as "beings of depraved appetites and sickly imaginations," and on another occasion he cut up one of his wife's dresses because he disapproved of the cut of the sleeves.) And he could be childish in the extreme. He refused to attend Charlotte's wedding to his curate, Arthur Bell Nichols, out of senile rage at her for discomposing his household.

Yet Barker gives him the benefit of the doubt at every turn. The decision to send his daughters to the Cowan Bridge school (Branwell was allowed to stay at home) is supposedly explained away by the fact that the school had wealthy patrons who had been friendly to him, and that he had no knowledge of the conditions there. We are advised to take Charlotte's attack on the school in her fiction as a piece of embittered exaggeration after the fact: "Lowood (Cowan Bridge) is seen through the eyes of the child suffering there, not the dispassionate adult." As if to model how a dispassionate adult might better understand matters, Barker then lays out, like one of Swift's Laputan scientists, some reassuring statistical information showing that, yes, a number of girls indeed died of typhoid and consumption there every year from the miserable treatment, but there were other schools in England at the time where even more died.

Gaskell, who knew Charlotte well, is traduced because she supported Charlotte over her father. Lambasting the hostile portrait of Patrick in the *Life of Charlotte Brontë*—Gaskell reported that he seldom allowed his children meat at

their meals and would terrify them by firing guns off out the parsonage windows—Barker blames Gaskell for listening too readily to malicious rumors
spread by a one-time Brontë nurse. (The nurse in question had described the
Brontë children as "spiritless" and "noiseless" and "different to any children I had
ever seen.") Barker suggests that the nurse was dismissed under a cloud, thus explaining the negative comments. But the only evidence educed in support of this
theory is a passing and rather inconclusive comment made by the Brontë family
cook—who would have had her own reasons for not wanting people to think
the Brontës had grown up half-starved—many years later. "Perhaps, like Mrs.
Gamp," Barker then goes on to fantasize, "[the nurse] had helped herself too frequently to the beer which Aunt Branwell kept under lock and key in the cellar."
And what begins as speculation soon becomes accepted truth: several hundred
pages on, Barker refers to the "sacked nurse" (who surely tippled) as the source of
all stories about Patrick's peculiarities. Left out entirely is the possibility that
Charlotte might have told Gaskell herself about her father during the visits she
paid to her fellow novelist in the early 1850s—or that the stories might have
been true.

Perhaps the most Gothic of Barker's anti-Charlottisms is her contention that
Charlotte destroyed the manuscript of a second novel left by Emily after her
death. That such a manuscript existed, even Barker admits, is questionable. The
only evidence that it may have is a letter to Emily from her publisher in 1848, in
which he says merely he would "have great pleasure in making arrangements for
your next novel." Yet the same publisher had notoriously confused Emily with
Anne in an advertisement the previous month, and may have been referring to
Anne's second novel, *The Tenant of Wildfell Hall*, then in progress. No extant
Brontë diary or notebook refers to Emily working on another novel after
Wuthering Heights.

Undaunted, however, Barker elaborates the theory that Charlotte found her
sister's manuscript and—out of pique or high-handedness—consigned it to the
flames. As a theory this is marginally allowable. Charlotte was concerned that
Emily's reputation not suffer after her death, and an inferior work might have
challenged the public's view of her as a budding genius cut off in her prime. But
what disturbs, again, is the way Barker's theory so quickly hardens into fact. Describing Charlotte's reluctance later to let certain unpublished poems by Emily
appear in a posthumous edition of *Wuthering Heights*—on the grounds that her
sister had not thought them worthy of inclusion in the book of poems the three
sisters had published jointly as "Currer," "Ellis," and "Acton Bell" in 1846—
Barker darkly connects this hesitation with "what happened to Emily's second
novel."

Her superb research notwithstanding, Barker's achievement is marred by
what one could call a piety about piety. It has become fashionable lately to praise
the pious and damn the naysayers; and Barker has predictably harsh words for

those "feminists" who have blamed "the men in Charlotte's life" for holding her back and possibly stunting her talent. As a fine old Christian gentleman, she suggests, Patrick Brontë deserves our sympathy. At the same time, she argues, Charlotte herself was fatally lacking in piety. Had she accepted her lot as meekly as her sister Anne did, had she performed her duties as daughter and woman with a little more enthusiasm and esprit de corps, much of her suffering—her biographer thinks—might have been avoided.

This may be true, but it also misses the point. Charlotte Brontë was not a saint; few people of her extraordinary talent are. It might seem anachronistic, as well as peculiar, to connect Charlotte Brontë with Ludwig Wittgenstein, but the comparison may be instructive. Both were the products of—and at odds with—strange, charismatic families. Both were schoolteachers who hated teaching. (It is one of the great myths of the pious that everyone should enjoy teaching the young and that those who don't are morally defective.) Both were critical and charmless and miserable most of the time. And both were geniuses of the first rank. A recent biographer of Wittgenstein appositely subtitled his book "The Duty of Genius," to convey the idea that for Wittgenstein there was something beyond the performance of conventional virtues. Though female, poor, and shell-shocked by loss—Gaskell spoke of her "constitutional absence of hope"—Charlotte Brontë, too, recognized the duty of genius. That is why we care about her.

note

1. Juliet Barker, *The Brontës* (London: Weidenfeld and Nicolson, 1994).

12

ALWAYS THE BRIDESMAID, NEVER THE GROOM

Perhaps the most embarrassing consequence of reading *Victorian Sappho*—Yopie Prins's impressive account of how Victorian poets over the course of a century envisioned, exploited, and distorted the mysterious figure of Sappho—is being forced to confront one's own mental images of the long-dead Greek poetess.[1] My own most cherished notions of her, I find, are at once detailed, puerile, and unbending—a strange hodgepodge of Baudelaire, Mary Barnard, and Ronald Firbank, all colored still by the prejudicial fancies of a flannel-shirted, late-1970s lesbian adolescence:

> SAPPHO: short, dark in appearance, teensiest hint of a moustache—a cross between Mme. Moller (high school French teacher) and a slightly defective but still gorgeous Audrey Hepburn. More femme than butch in style (favours flowing chitons, the odd bangle, funny sandals with lots of straps) but good too at outdoorsy things, such as pounding in tent pegs and spotting constellations. Sings and dances, always ready with a hymn to Aphrodite, but gets mopey at weddings (always the bridesmaid, never the groom!). Dynamite in bed, of course, and *totally* gay: that stuff about being in love with Phaon and jumping off a cliff *just not true*! Ovid all bollocks. Would have been in love with me, had I lived in ancient Greece. May in fact have been referring to me in Wretched Tatty Papyrus Fragment No. 211 (Lobel-Page):
>
> > Come [Terry?]. . . .
> >   cast off your [air-cushioned?] Nikes
> > the [?] nightingale [?]. . . .

Sappho of Lesbos has always seemed more phantasm than historical personage, of course: we know so little of her life and have so precious little of her poetry that editors and biographers over the centuries have more or less had to invent her. At least since the Renaissance, when the first fragmentary pieces of her writings began to circulate again in Europe after nearly two thousand years of neglect, she has been an object of unrelenting speculation, scandal, and interpretive projection. As Yopie Prins puts it in her austerely poststructuralist idiom, to the extent that Sappho "survives," she does so primarily as a "trope" or rhetorical vessel, a linguistic figment or "ungrounded proper name" endlessly available for imaginative occupancy by others. Hence Audrey Hepburn and the chitons.

What *is* known of her? Lauded throughout classical antiquity as the "Tenth Muse" and greatest poet next to Homer, Sappho is believed to have lived on the Greek island of Lesbos some time around 600 B.C. Plato and Aristophanes mention her; in ancient Rome, Horace and Catullus wrote famous imitations of her verses. Some six hundred years after her death, her renown was such that there was an attempt at a collected edition of her songs: a group of Greek scholars at Alexandria are said to have gathered together all of her known lyrics, organized them according to metrical scheme into nine books, and transcribed them onto papyrus scrolls.

Most records of Sappho disappeared, however, after the fall of Rome. During the Middle Ages both she and her work were largely forgotten. (According to one legend, the Christian patriarch Gregory of Nazianzos, offended by the licentiousness of her themes, put her books to the torch in A.D. 380) Neither Dante nor Chaucer refers to her. Only with the recovery and translation of certain ancient texts in the Renaissance—Longinus's *On the Sublime*, for example, in which the famous and much-admired Fragment 31 ("He seems to me equal to the gods") appears as a quotation—were bits and pieces of her poetic corpus gradually reassembled. The salvage operation has continued ever since, with several Sapphic fragments reappearing only in this century. The sum total of surviving texts, however, remains pitifully small: just one complete poem (the so-called "Hymn to Aphrodite") and about two hundred tiny scraps of verse, many of them—agonizingly—only a word or two long. Sappho still seems more "lost" than found, and barring any extraordinary archaeological discoveries, appears likely to remain so permanently.

The notorious controversy (now many centuries old) over Sappho's sex life is related to these gaps in the historical and textual record. Ancient writers often spoke of her as a homosexual libertine: the early Christian writer Tatian described her as a "love-crazed female fornicator who even sings about her own licentiousness." And indeed as more poem fragments surfaced after the Renaissance—many addressed to beautiful girls and suffused with cryptic erotic fervor—she came to be regarded in sophisticated quarters as indisputably a lover of women. By the seventeenth and eighteenth centuries, she was a stock character in Latin, French, and English pornography, and the term *Sapphist* (later followed by *Lesbian*) began to circulate as a popular synonym for tribade.

Seemingly at odds with the homosexual identification, however, was the curious legend of Sappho's disastrous passion for Phaon, a handsome young ferryman whose rejection of her is said to have prompted her suicide. (In the classic account she is supposed—beset by love-anguish—to have leaped from the Leucadian cliffs into the roiling sea below.) Ovid dramatized the suicide story in his influential *Heroides*, a best-seller of the sixteenth and seventeenth centuries, and ever after poets, scholarly commentators, and ordinary readers struggled to reconcile Sappho-the-apparent-lesbian with Sappho-the-despondent-lover-of-Phaon. Early English imaginative writers seemed able to absorb the disparity relatively calmly: both Donne, in his "Sapho to Philaenis" (1633), and Pope, in "Sappho to Phaon" (1712), for example, presented Sappho as bisexual. But later, more prudish commentators were disturbed by the whole messy situation. Uncomfortable in particular with the long-standing rumors of Sappho's homosexual "impurity"—as indeed with homoerotic readings of her verse in general—eighteenth- and nineteenth-century editors and translators fixed on the Phaon legend as a convenient way of debunking the Sappho-as-lesbian tradition. To focus on her fatal leap was one way of asserting the poet's erotic "normalcy" even in the face of scattered, often obscure, yet mounting textual evidence to the contrary.

Modern classicists have yet to resolve the biographical enigmas, though most, it must be said, now recognize a homoerotic content in the Sapphic corpus and view the Phaon story as apocryphal (and alien) accretion. Some have argued there may have been two "Sapphos" in antiquity—one a poet and one a courtesan—and that their legends became somehow mixed up. Others suggest that the Phaon suicide story may hint at some archaic sacrificial ritual—even that Sappho may have been *pushed* off a cliff, perhaps as punishment for nameless (homosexual?) debaucheries. Still others, such as Joan McIntosh Snyder, speculate that the Phaon myth may have arisen from an ancient exegetical slip; for "given the obvious mythological and metaphoric implications of the story, it is likely that if Sappho ever did refer in her songs to leaping off the White Rocks of Leukas, she meant the phrase in a nonliteral way, perhaps as a metaphor for falling into a swoon. Eventually, it may be that later writers interpreted the phrase (if indeed she used it) as referring to a literal leap, thus giving rise to the suicide legend."

The controversy is worth mentioning because it turns out to be so central to Prins's new book—might indeed be said to haunt it at a fairly deep level. *Victorian Sappho* deals with that period in Sappho's modern reception history—the nineteenth century—when the interpretive battle over the poet's libidinal orientation was at its height. From one angle Prins's book seems a mostly straightforward, if somewhat cool, exercise in historical demystification. Her overriding goal, Prins asserts in the introduction, is not to adjudicate between conflicting Sapphic myths, but to show how by the end of the century "Sappho had become a highly overdetermined and contradictory trope within nine-teenth-century discourses of gender, sexuality, poetics, and politics." Drawing an analogy from case grammar, she describes her aim as one of exposing how differ-ent Victorian writers "declined" the "name" of Sappho—i.e., by fabricating un-real identities for her:

> Each chapter of *Victorian Sappho* proposes a variation on the name, demonstrating how it is variously declined: the declension of a noun and its deviation from origins, the improper bending of a proper name, a line of descent that is also a falling into decadence, the perpetual return of a name that is also a turning away from nomination.

Yet even as she claims *not* to be taking any point of view on Sappho's mixed-up legend—merely exposing a "declension" or "decadence"—she manages to do a little improper bending of her own, and, hugger-mugger, ends up throwing in her lot with Sappho the Phaon-obsessed: the one who leaps from the cliff. (The cover of *Victorian Sappho* not so secretly suggests as much: it reproduces Charles-Auguste Mengin's ghastly-glorious 1877 painting of the poet, bare-breasted beneath a swirling black sky, gazing mournfully down at the Aegean.) Watching Prins make this particular plunge, postmodern tresses lifting in the wind, is to be struck again by how difficult it is, in life or literary criticism, to avoid the classic Sapphic double bind: take the girls or take the jump.

None of which is to say this isn't an arresting book—the most penetrating on the poet since Anne Carson's *Eros the Bittersweet* (1987) and Joan DeJean's *Fic-tions of Sappho* (1989). Prins's immersion in the Victorian art and literature of Sappho is deep, the sophistication of her approach formidable. And as her open-ing remarks suggest, the topic of Sappho's nineteenth-century reception is in-deed multifaceted enough to allow for intense meditation on a host of crucial literary-historical issues: the evolution and ideology of women's writing, the problem of translation, the uses of Hellenism, the history of English metrics, the nature of lyric. By any measure this book (Prins's first) is a debut of major ambi-tion and considerable achievement.

Still, Prins's concerns are rhetorical—even deconstructionist—rather than psychobiographical, and she pursues them in a manner that the sapphically in-clined Sapphist will no doubt find off-putting. The study is divided into four parts, each representing a distinct aspect of the poet's nineteenth-century legacy. In the first section, "Sappho's Broken Tongue," Prins provides a useful potted chronology of English translations of Sappho, up to and including Dr. Henry Wharton's highly influential *Sappho: Memoir, Text, Selected Renderings, and a Literal Translation* (1885). The much-translated (and notoriously strange) Frag-ment 31—quoted below in Anne Carson's closely literal modern version— comes in for particular attention:

He seems to me equal to the gods that man
whoever he is who opposite you
sits and listens close
to your sweet speaking

and lovely laughing—oh it
puts the heart in my chest on wings
for when I look at you, a moment, then no speaking
is left in me

no: tongue breaks, and thin
fire is racing under skin
and in eyes no sight and drumming
fills ears

and cold sweat holds me and shaking
grips me all, greener than grass
I am and dead—or almost
I seem to me.

Confronted by this arousing yet mutilated utterance—almost certainly only the beginning of a much longer poem—English readers such as Wharton, writes Prins, found in the very ambiguity and truncation of its lines an "ideal medium" for "sublime transport."

Yet already Prins shows her hand. What interests her most about Fragment 31 is not the apparently homoerotic situation—the poet seems to address a young woman with whom she is infatuated—or indeed the way that English translators, well into the nineteenth century, chose either to emphasize or to obfuscate that fact. (One masterpiece of dishonest revisionism, John Hall's translation of 1652, begins

He that sits next to thee now and hears
Thy charming voyce, to me appears
Beauteous as any Deity
    That rules the skie.

How did his pleasing glances dart
Sweet languors to my ravish'd heart
At the first sight though so prevailed
    That my voyce fail'd.

—precisely so as disguise the female object of the speaker's yearning.) What pre-occupies her instead is what she sees as the fragment's allegorical significance—

the way it dramatizes through the metaphor of the "broken tongue" a powerful yet paradoxical conception of lyric poetry itself.

The argument here is not for the faint of heart. Critics since Longinus, Prins observes, have often fixed on a psychokinetic paradox at the heart of the fragment: the poet "is simultaneously losing composure and composing herself, falling apart *in* the poem and coming together *as* a poem that seems to speak, with heightened eloquence, to the reader." For Prins, the "self-defacing" logic of Fragment 31—the poet's tongue is "broken," yet through the art of the translator, who reconstitutes and reorganizes her scattered parts, we seem nonetheless to hear her "voice"—haunts Sappho's literary afterlife as well as the Western lyric tradition she is said to initiate:

> What makes Sappho sublime is the mutilation of the Sapphic fragments, allowing her to be simultaneously dismembered and remembered, in a complex mediation between corpse and corpus: the body of the poet is sacrificed to the body of her song, and this body of song is sacrificed to posterity, which recollects the scattered fragments in order to recall Sappho herself as the long-lost origin of lyric poetry.

Sappho, for Prins, is in the end a mere "name"—the proper name of someone who says, oddly enough, that she cannot speak. With each new appropriation of the Sapphic name, she is written back into being, but falsely. She remains the quintessential lyric poet precisely because whatever "subjectivity" she models is merely the accumulated effect of countless lyric misreadings and mistranslations.

I *think* I understand this: if I've got it right, it's rather like listening to a recording of Patsy Cline singing "I Fall to Pieces." Even though Cline died in a plane crash nearly forty years ago, to hear her sing about falling to pieces ("each time I see you walk by") is to experience the fantastical illusion that she is present. The fact that she is dead and literally in pieces (one presumes) is a paradoxical boon, for we are thus free to envision her—as Prins suggests various Victorian poets did with Sappho—"as an imaginary totalization, imagined in the present and projected into the past." Each time we turn on the CD player, "Patsy" opens herself up to our fantasy—thanks to the revivifying fakery of electronically reconstituted sound.

Whatever one makes of the Derridean turns in Prins's argument, the moody preoccupation with Sapphic absence—with the notion that no one who claims to speak "in the name of Sappho" ever really does—undoubtedly shapes the rest of *Victorian Sappho*. In remaining sections Prins looks closely at three of the more spectacular instances of nineteenth-century Sapphic impersonation. First is the strange case of "Michael Field"—a pair of homosexual female lovers, aunt and niece, whose jointly authored, Sapphically-inspired verses in *Long Ago*

(1889) set the stage for later lesbian appropriations of the poet. Second up is Swinburne, whose outrageously sadomasochistic imitations of a Sapphic "voice" in "Anactoria" and other poems of the 1860s and 1870s led to his work being dubbed "the *reductio ad horribilem* of . . . intellectual sensualism." And last but not least Prins examines a number of now mostly forgotten "English Sapphos": early nineteenth-century female poets such as Letitia Elizabeth Landon and Caroline Norton, whose kitsch setpieces on the theme of Sappho's suicide ("The Last Song of Sappho," "The Picture of Sappho," etc.) at once confirmed Sappho's heroic status as originary "Poetess" and sent her—repeatedly—to a vertiginous yet mysteriously seductive death.

Prins's poststructuralist allegiances, it must be said, make for some absorbing close readings. A crucial theme of the book is how in order to create something "in the name" of Sappho a writer must also "forget" something about her—willfully blind himself to some critical aspect of her legacy. Out of this self-inflicted purblindness comes an intensification of vision—along whatever privileged line the poet-imitator has chosen to preserve. In the case of Katherine Bradley (1846–1914) and Edith Cooper (1862–1913), the two women who together made up the authorial phenomenon of "Michael Field," the strategic forgetting, as it were, of the Ovidian Sappho—of the Sappho who dies out of love for Phaon—made it possible for them to exploit various Sapphic fragments collected in Wharton as "prompts" for a delicately homoerotic, collaboratively authored love verse:

> Αυταρ οραιαι στεφανηπλοκευν
> They plaited garlands in their time;
> They knew the joy of youth's sweet prime,
>   Quick breath and rapture;
> Theirs was the violet-weaving bliss,
> And theirs the white, wreathed brow to kiss,
>   Kiss, and recapture.

Phaon, Prins notes, is mentioned in some of the first poems in *Long Ago* as a figure for "the ravages of heterosexual desire," but banished from later poems, as Bradley and Cooper attempt to reclaim between them an all-female imaginary space, or textual "field," in which love between women can flourish. In this curiously double, testosterone-free projection of Sapphic "voice," Bradley and Cooper—who always maintained they were so *"closely married"* that after bouts of composition they knew not who had written what lines—found the perfect metaphor for their own sensuous and creative "interlacing." "Composing poems for *Long Ago*," writes Prins, "Bradley and Cooper enact the very premise of their collaboration, the mutual implication of each in the writing of the other and the eroticizing of that textual entanglement by turning it into an infinitely desirable feminine figure." Most of the poems, admittedly, are a bit drippy—an odd mixture of flowery neoclassical pastiche and 1890s-ish lezzie soft-core:

> What praises would be best
> Wherewith to crown my girls?
> The rose when she unfurls
> Her balmy, lighted buds is not so good,
> So fresh as they
> When on my breast
> They lean, and say
> All that they would,
> Opening their glorious, candid maidenhood.

Still, one suspects the girl-shaken Sappho of Fragment 31 might have approved.

In the case of Swinburne (1837–1909) the process of strategic forgetting took a far kinkier turn. In "Anactoria," a dramatic monologue from 1866 in which Sappho is overheard addressing her young lover Anactoria, Swinburne ignores both the Ovidian Sappho and the avatar of "Michael-Field"–style homosexual *tendresse* in order to re-create *his* Sappho as monstrous (even cannibalistic) sexual sadist:

> Ah that my lips were tuneless lips, but pressed
> To the bruised blossom of thy scourged white breast!
> Ah that my mouth for Muses' milk were fed
> On the sweet blood thy sweet small wounds had bled!
> That with my tongue I felt them, and could taste
> The faint flakes from thy bosom to the waist!
> That I could drink thy veins as wine, and eat
> Thy breasts like honey! that from face to feet
> Thy body were abolished and consumed
> And in my flesh thy very flesh entombed!

Here Prins is brilliant, linking Swinburne's Venus-in-Furs treatment of the poetess both with his well-known flagellation mania—around the time he was writing "Anactoria" he was also working on a volume of "bum-tickling" pornographic eclogues known as *The Flogging Block*—and his obsession with poetic form. Swinburne inevitably associated the metrical rhythms of poetry, she suggests, with imaginary scenes of beating. His elaborate experiments with the so-called Sapphic stanza (three five-stress lines with a fourth half-line at the end of the stanza) were not simply attempts to find in the English accented line an equivalent for Sappho's Greek, in which meter is determined by the length of vowel, but a way of commemorating fetishistically the primitive, smarting rhythm he mentally connected with lyric verse and his own art. Given such a fantasy scenario, the vulnerable, tongue-tied Sappho of Fragment 31 was of little use. He preferred to envision her—his favorite poet—as an eager, schoolmistressy dominatrix, instilling the sacred rhythms of verse in her Swinburnean poet-pupils by way of the birch:

> Would I not hurt thee perfectly? not touch
> Thy pores of sense with torture, and make bright,
> Thine eyes with bloodlike tears and grievous light
> Strike pang from pang as note is struck from note,
> Catch the sob's middle music in thy throat,
> Take thy limbs living, and new-mould with these
> A lyre of many faultless agonies?

Ultimately, Prins suggests, in complex later poems such as "On the Cliffs" (1880), examined here with intricate care, Sappho became an even more abstract presence in Swinburne's poetic imagination—a kind of "rhythmicized body" or corporeal pattern, ardently craved, which he sought to reinscribe, ever more perversely, in the exquisite perturbations of his own beat-driven verses.

The horde of female poets taken up in the final chapter, Mary Robinson (1758–1800), Felicia Hemans (1793–1835), Letitia Elizabeth Landon (1802–1838), Caroline Norton (1808–1877), Christina Rossetti (1830–1894), and Mary Cowden Clarke (1809–1898), are hardly as daring but equally morbid. Lesbianism (nice or nasty) be damned—they "remember" Sappho solely as the maundering, soul-baffled lover of Phaon. This, for Prins, is the most retrograde, yet also most revealing "declension" of Sappho's name in the nineteenth century: her portrayal as love-struck *heterosexual* suicide in a gaggle of terminally dreary death-leap poems authored by women.

Though composed at the very end of the eighteenth century, Mary Robinson's "Sappho to Phaon" (1796) is typical, alas, of this otiosely feminine genre:

> Oh! can'st thou bear to see this faded frame,
>> Deform'd and mangled by the rocky deep?
>> Wilt thou remember, and forbear to weep,
> My fatal fondness, and my peerless fame?
> Soon o'er this heart, now warm with passion's flame,
>> The howling winds and foamy waves shall sweep;
>> Those eyes be ever clos'd in death's cold sleep,
> And all of Sappho perish but her name!

Prins herself gets a bit morbid here, citing poem after poem to make the same point: that such self-abnegating verse expressed a deep-dyed anxiety about assuming visionary authority in a male-dominated poetic world. Sappho is indeed the primordial woman writer—the greatest "Poetess" ever—but the only way to imitate her, it seems, is by bungee jumping without a cord. Even as female poets try to "ground" their accession to poetry by impersonating Sappho, it also "falls to [them] to perform this foundational claim as itself an act of falling or continually losing ground." The result is a killing paradox: "women poets rise to authorship only by falling [into] the abyss of female authorship, where the Poetess proves to be the personification of an empty figure." It is no surprise, given Prins's slightly dizzying logic here, that with the exception of the grave and great Rossetti, most of these excruciating "English Sapphos" have themselves been forgotten, and their wretched poems likewise.

Prins's obsessiveness is compelling—even too compelling. For it is at this point one begins to feel something is *wrong* with *Victorian Sappho*—indeed, has been wrong all along, despite how good it is. Some obvious line of thought is being resisted; things seem oddly back to front. It is not simply that Prins herself "forgets" works—or historical contexts—that weaken her thesis. The argument that Victorian women writers imagined themselves as so many Sapphos-about-to-commit-suicide in order to symbolize a feminine sense of poetic disenfranchisement would seem to be compromised, at the least, by the existence of numerous male-authored eighteenth- and nineteenth-century poems that appear to do something similar. What of Cowper's "The Castaway" (1799), in which the speaker is likewise poised on the edge of some self-imposed lyric dissolution? The famous tolling, final lines ("We perished, each alone; / But I beneath a rougher sea, / And whelmed in deeper gulfs than he") are as self-evacuating as anything in Robinson or Hemans. In Matthew Arnold's droogy play-in-verse "Empedocles on Etna" (1852), the main speaker is the slave-philosopher, expatiating on his misery and about to plunge into the fiery volcano to his death ("Take thy bough, set me free from my solitude; / I have been enough alone!"). Given what appears to be a fad in the period for such I'm-just-about-to-kill-myself poems, how specifically female is the sensation of disenfranchisement?

A deeper problem, however, lies in Prins's attitude, which I use here in the slang American sense: she is like the brooding, jagged hostess in the hip urban restaurant who doesn't want anyone to have any fun (let alone feel nourished) despite all the glamorous people and interesting food. A powerful oddity of *Victorian Sappho* is that it works backwards chronologically. Prins admits as much in her epilogue: "I might have started with the final chapter, tracing the emergence of Sappho as proper name for the Poetess within sentimental women's verse of the early Victorian period, setting the stage for Algernon Swinburne's sensational reappropriation of this lyric figure for high Victorian poets, and continuing with the conversion of Sappho of Lesbos into a lesbian Sappho by

Michael Field toward the end of the century." She has refused the obvious chronological ordering, she says, in order to keep her readers from assuming any "progress" or development in the evolution of Sapphic iconography. She is particularly concerned that we *not* latch on to the notion (which she then perversely elaborates) that "while earlier versions of Sappho are primarily mediated by Ovid," later ones give way to "a Sapphic corpus reconstructed from Greek fragments," which is in turn read by Michael Field, John Addington Symonds, and countless others as explicitly lesbian.

Surely this is cutting off one's nose to spite one's corpus? The self-conscious maneuvering here suggests how deeply Prins holds to a view of literary history at once fashionably postmodern and painfully anorexic: that literature is nothing more—can be nothing more—than a system of endless displacements, cheats, and losses. The more we try to grasp someone named Sappho, the more she eludes us. The one we had hoped to embrace falls away from us. Prins's backwards ordering (which is at least as artificial an arrangement as any chronological one) seems designed to instill this sense of loss in the reader by way of an almost kinesthetic dysphoria—a continuous sense of everything "declining," falling, and getting worse. Thus we go from Michael Field (pretty poems about hugging and kissing) to Swinburne (weird poems about whipping and hurting) to the "English Sapphos" (gormless poems about lying all dead and mangled in the seaweed). A feeling of overkill sinks in as Prins describes yet another Sapphic suicide poem, as if pleasure—charmingly homosexual—had to be transformed into fatality—agonizingly heterosexual—over and over again. Go straight and die, Sappho! It's a desolating outlook—as if Prins were saying, Look where our attempts to recognize the literary past take us: straight to the bottom of a cliff, again and again.

And is it true? At the risk of revealing one's Audrey Hepburnism as incurable, one might wish to demur. We *have* gotten somewhere—and something—over the long process of Sapphic recovery and reception. We have more fragments than we used to; we understand them better. And surely it is not pure fancy to read into them a homosexual dimension? Given that all truths remain approximate truths, might one not argue, still, that Michael Field's lesbian image of Sappho is closer to the view of her held by present-day classicists—indeed is more *accurate*—than that of the tedious "English Sapphos"? Might not the image of Sapphic girl-loving have something more to it than mere wishful projection? The story of how scholars as well as ordinary readers came to accept the Sapphic fragments as love poems addressed to women is one of the most fascinating and checkered stories in all of literary reception history. (And contrary to Prins's assertion that the poet's "association with lesbian identity is a particularly Victorian phenomenon," the coding of Sappho as Sapphist has a complex seventeenth- and eighteenth-century genealogy as well, as work by Harriette Andreadis, Elizabeth Wahl, and Emma Donoghue has shown.) Yet none of this history carries any ultimate weight in *Victorian Sappho*. All representations of Sappho are equally false—mere figments or "translation effects," written over poor old Sappho's dead body.

But even if this were the case, so what? One might still argue for a more forgiving view of human image-making. Prins is as scathing as any Yale-school deconstructionist of the late 1970s in her contempt for the rhetorical maneuver known as *prosopopoeia*—more commonly known as personification: "the figure that gives face by conferring speech upon a voiceless entity, yet in so doing also defaces it." Yet what is life itself but an endless series of acts of personification? Every time we think about other people—attribute motives, assume traits, try to understand what they are saying or wanting to say—we engage in personification. It is easy enough to say the resulting image is false, but it is also all we have. There is no other point of access—no other "person" (in literature or life) than the one we're forced to come up with.

Given the fragmentary nature of the record, most of our presumptions about Sappho must inevitably be hesitant, hedged round, imperfect. The incompleteness of the poems themselves must likewise frustrate mightily, just as it frustrates us to hear about other wonderful lost things: Homer's comic epic, the vast majority of Monteverdi's operas, Old Master paintings destroyed in wars, the Mozart or Debussy (or Kurt Cobain) songs that never got written because the composer died prematurely. But there is always room to rejoice in what does survive, however compromised or partial its form. Sappho, whoever she was, left an extraordinary amount of beauty in her wake, precisely in the shape of her imitations—the touching, provocative, endlessly gorgeous body of translation she inspired. One would never know it from reading the melancholy Prins, however—nor that some of Sappho's fragments are as funny and joyful as they are lovely:

> Now to delight my women friends
> I'll make a beautiful song of this affair.
> > (Fragment 160)

> certainly now they've had quite enough
> of Gorgo
> > (Fragment 144)

> Though it isn't easy for us to rival
> goddesses in the loveliness of their figures [
> > (Fragment 96)

> I think that someone will remember us in another time.
> > (Fragment 147)

These are translations, of course, from Jim Powell's *Sappho: A Garland* (1993). I'm sure some things have gone missing, but I don't really care. She sounds like someone I would like.

note

1. Yopie Prins, *Victorian Sappho* (Princeton, N.J.: Princeton University Press, 1999).

13
FLOURNOY'S COMPLAINT

The dilemma: it is 1892, you are a thirty-year-old female shop assistant in a small silk manufacturing concern in Geneva, the city of your birth. You live with your parents in a modest but pleasant suburban house; you travel to work on the streetcar. You have no suitors, but don't really mind: you have a spiritual protector named "Léopold," a reincarnation of the eighteenth-century magician Cagliostro, who appears to you in visions in the long brown robe of a monk, offering advice and emotional solace. Your main hobbies are embroidery—of mystic shapes and patterns bearing no resemblance to anything in the visible world—and the obsessive cultivation of states of "obnubilation," during which "strange multicoloured landscapes, stone lions with mutilated heads, and fanciful objects on pedestals" float before your eyes.

Yet life is tedious beyond words. Your parents' provincial ways annoy you (you're not convinced they really are your parents); the gray Genevan skies oppress. You hate being a "little daughter of Lake Léman"; you feel yourself born for a higher sphere. Above all, you have an overweening desire to enthrall, to exhibit "the magnificent flowering of that subliminal vegetation"—your inner life—before a throng of enraptured admirers. But how to get the attention you deserve?

If you are "Hélène Smith"—the shop girl in question and subject of the Swiss psychologist Théodore Flournoy's sensational 1899 case history, *From India to the Planet Mars*—you solve the problem in classic nineteenth-century female-monomaniac fashion: by becoming a spirit medium. Initiated into table-rapping in the winter of 1891–92, Smith—whose real name was Elise Müller—progressed quickly from bouts of automatic writing and glossolalia to extended trance states in which she revealed that she had lived a number of glamorous past lives: as "Simandini," a beautiful Hindu princess forced to commit suttee in the early fifteenth century; as Marie Antoinette, doomed queen of France; and perhaps most intriguingly, as a visitor to Mars, whose inhabitants, language, and customs she was able to describe in phantasmagoric detail. At weekly séances over the next few years Smith produced an array of "proofs" of these past existences and simultaneously enlisted a doting crowd of followers convinced of her psychic powers.

It was Smith's triumph—and subsequent misfortune—to attract the attention of Théodore Flournoy (1854–1920), professor of psychophysiology at the University of Geneva, friend of William James (and later Carl Jung), and enthusiastic debunker of putatively occult phenomena. Since the late 1880s Flournoy, whose deceptively chivalrous, self-effacing manner concealed a penetrating forensic intelligence, had eagerly sought a medium on whom to test his evolving theories about the relationship between trance phenomena and the psychopathology of the unconscious. Introduced to Smith in 1895, he at once struck up a friendship with her and asked if he could study her in action. Exalted by his interest and avid to convert him to the "beautiful doctrine of spiritism," Smith not only welcomed him at sittings for the next four years, but permitted him to subject her to various uncomfortable physical experiments, including pressing on her eyeballs and sticking her with pins during trance states to test for localized anaesthesia and absent or impaired reflexes.

Flournoy's professional curiosity at once inspired the excitable seeress to new mystic heights. Smith was what Flournoy would dub in *From India to the Planet Mars* a "polymorphous, or multiform, medium"—that is, a medium subject to a diverse, highly theatrical range of automatisms while in the trance state. Not only was she able to receive messages "through the table" from beings such as her spirit guide Léopold, who frequently manifested himself during sittings as a kind of disembodied play-by-play commentator on what was going on; she could gabble in mysterious tongues, write and draw in hands other than her own, and drastically alter her voice and physiognomy as she gave herself up to various spirit "controls." By far the most impressive demonstrations of her mediumship, however, were what Flournoy called her "somnambulistic romances"—the grandiose, quasi-mythopoetic fantasies of having lived at other times, in other worlds.

It is hard to say which of her "romances" was the most bizarre; each was a marvel of intricate, exfoliating absurdity. A set of "Martian" visions witnessed by Flournoy in 1896, for example, began with the entranced medium speaking to "an imaginary woman who wished her to enter a curious little car without wheels or horses." After pantomiming the act of climbing into a car Smith performed a series of contortionist gestures indicative of extraterrestrial travel:

Hélène . . . mimics the voyage to Mars in three phases, the meaning of which is indicated by Léopold: a regular rocking motion of the upper part of the body (passing through the terrestrial atmosphere), absolute immobility and rigidity (interplanetary space), again oscillations of the shoulders and bust (atmosphere of Mars). Arrived upon Mars, she descends from the car, and performs a complicated pantomime expressing the manners of Martian politeness: uncouth gestures with the hands and fingers, slapping of the hands, taps of the fingers upon the nose, the lips, the chin etc., twisted courtesies, glidings and rotation on the floor etc. It seems that is the way people approach and salute each other up there.

Such rituals completed, Smith would then exclaim over the odd sights before her—Martian men and women in "hats like plates," peach-colored earth, tree trunks that widened as they ascended, pink and blue canals filled with "horrid aquatic beasts like big snails," and so on—and hobnob with various Martian personages. Chief among these was a wizardlike being named Astané who was inevitably accompanied by a creature with the head of a cabbage, a big green eye in the middle, and "five or six pairs of paws, or ears all about." Sometimes Astané took hold of Smith's index finger and made her write Martian words, such as *dodé né ci haudan té mes métiche Astané ké dé mé véche*, later translated through the table as "This is the house of the great man Astané, whom thou hast seen." On awakening, Smith—who claimed not to remember what she said or did while entranced—would examine with amazement the errant bits of "Martian" thus produced.

The "Hindoo" and "Royal" fantasies were equally colorful. Under the sway of her Hindoo vision Smith reenacted episodes from her life as the unfortunate Simandini: her betrothal to the handsome Prince Sivrouka; their courtship in the splendid palace gardens at Tchandraguiri; the happiness of married life, complete with cavorting handmaidens and pet monkey; her anguish at her husband's premature death; her frightful despair as she mounted the funeral pyre on which she was bound to perish. Flournoy himself was often roped into these tragicomic tableaux: after the table revealed that he was himself the reincarnation of Sivrouka, Smith quickly incorporated him into the fantasy mise-en-scène as "her lord and master in the flesh," showering him with caresses and "affectionate effusions" in a weird pseudo-Sanskrit.

As Marie Antoinette, Smith would flutter an imaginary fan, mimic taking snuff and throwing back a train, and address Flournoy and his fellow sitters as if speaking to members of her court. A sitter named M. Demole was recognized as the current reincarnation of Philippe d'Orléans, another as that of Mirabeau. Each then had to improvise witty repartee while Smith-as-Antoinette discoursed on eighteenth-century fashion and politics. Her demeanor during these confabs was appropriately regal—her innate taste for everything that is "noble, distinguished, elevated above the common herd," Flournoy wrote, lending each gesture a perfect "ease and naturalness."

Granted, there were occasional cock-ups. "Her Majesty" sometimes fell into the verbal booby traps her interlocutors set for her—as when words such as *bicycle, tramway,* or *photography* were introduced into supposedly eighteenth-century conversations. Not recognizing the anachronism at first, "Marie Antoinette . . . allows the treacherous word to pass unnoticed, and it is evident that she perfectly understood it, but her own reflection, or the smile of the sitters, awakens in her the feeling of incompatibility; she returns to the word just used, and pretends a sudden ignorance and astonishment in regard to it." In one unfortunate instance she calmly smoked a cigarette—proffered by a sly Mirabeau—before realizing with a grimace that she did not understand "the use of tobacco in that form."

But little seemed to faze the medium in the grip of such fancies—not even the grotesque irruption of yet another retroactive personality. It was one of Smith's pet notions that her spirit control Léopold, in his earlier incarnation as the magician Cagliostro, had been Marie Antoinette's lover in the years before the French Revolution. Thus even as she performed her royal part, she might suddenly be "taken over" by Léopold, who assuming his former identity would expatiate on his passion for the tragic queen. "Her eyes droop," Flournoy wrote; "her expression changes; her throat swells into a sort of double chin, which gives her a likeness of some sort to the well-known figure of Cagliostro." After a series of hiccoughs and sighs indicating "the difficulty Léopold is experiencing in taking hold of the vocal apparatus," the "deep bass voice of a man" would issue from her throat "with a pronunciation and accent markedly foreign, certainly more Italian than anything else."

When Flournoy—who candidly admitted the surreal fascination Smith's performances held for him—began writing up *From India to the Planet Mars* in 1898, the besotted medium seems to have assumed, with more vainglory than sense, that he would champion her supernatural lucubrations. Certainly she responded helpfully to his scores of seemingly innocent questions about her early life, peripheral daydreams, reading, knowledge of foreign languages, and the like. But any satisfaction at being the object of such scrutiny vanished once the book itself appeared. For Flournoy had launched a devastating assault on her claims. Her tales of past lives were simply unconscious projections, he wrote, "subliminal poems," akin to "those 'continued stories' of which so many of our race tell themselves in their moments of *far niente*, or at times when their routine occupations offer only slight obstacles to day-dreaming, and of which they themselves are generally the heroes." Down to the most freakish detail, every element contained in them, he proposed, could be explained by purely psychological mechanisms.

Crucial to Flournoy's explication was the phenomenon of cryptomnesia: the process by which forgotten perceptions, relegated to the unconscious, undergo "subliminal elaboration" and return to awareness in an estranged yet vivid form. What Smith claimed to experience as memories of past lives, he suggested, were in fact bits and pieces out of her own psychic past—remnants of earlier perceptions, now disguised and incorporated into extended narcissistic fantasies.

For every feature of Smith's "romances" Flournoy set out some unexceptional, even banal, unconscious etiology. Her descriptions of Martian flora and fauna derived, he thought, from a "buried" acquaintance with Camille Flammarion's best-selling book *La Planète Mars et ses conditions d'habitabilité* (1892), a volume of fanciful speculations about life on Mars popular in spiritualist circles. The name Simandini—which came through the table first as "Simadini"—was a "hypnoid distortion," he proposed, of Semadeni, the name of a long-established family of Genevan dry-goods merchants. Smith's descriptions of Sivrouka and his palace followed almost verbatim passages from "De Marlès's history of India"—a book conveniently located on the shelves of the Geneva Public Library. The romantic fantasy about Cagliostro and Marie Antoinette was "probably inspired" by an engraved illustration from a Dumas novel about the French Revolution hanging in the home of one of Smith's friends—and so on.

Most damningly, with the help of Saussure, his colleague at the University of Geneva who was not only a linguist but a Sanskritologist, Flournoy demonstrated that the glossolalic scraps of Martian and pseudo-Sanskrit Smith disgorged while entranced—the feature of her mediumship most baffling and impressive to lay observers—were nothing more than "infantile" imitations of French. However exotic-seeming individual words, the grammar and syntax were "puerile counterfeits" of Smith's mother tongue. Like her other fabrications, these uncanny mock-languages were "subliminal creations"—the fantastic by-product of a personality profoundly, exorbitantly, at odds with the real.

Smith's reaction to all of this was predictably explosive; Flournoy had cheated and traduced her. When *From India to the Planet Mars* became both a popular and a critical success—it went through numerous editions and was hailed by *Mind* as a classic of psychological inquiry—the outraged medium demanded (and received) half of Flournoy's royalties. But neither the psychologist's money, nor that of an adoring American benefactress whose assistance allowed her to devote herself to séances full-time, seemed to salve her wounded spirit. Her confidence in her spirit guides faltering—she would later renounce her belief in the reality of the Martian and Hindoo visions—she became convinced that Flournoy was spying on her and railed about him to friends. She took up religious painting but in a fit of paranoia refused to let any of her paintings be exhibited or photographed. Claiming to have "suffered much" from the perfidy of men—she never married and (apart from Léopold) seems to have had a loathing for the sex in general—she died in 1929 at the age of 68.

What to make of it all a hundred years later? In his elegant, erudite, intermittently irritating Introduction to the new Princeton edition of *From India to the Planet Mars*, Sonu Shamdasani, historian of psychoanalysis and editor of several works by Jung, presents the story of Flournoy and Hélène Smith as a kind of postmodern allegory of a fascinating yet ultimately malign encounter between mental science and spiritualism at the turn of the century.[1] In their "encounter with the séance," he suggests, male scientists like Flournoy discovered both a sexual and an epistemological threat. Precisely because the spirit medium challenged patriarchal protocols so thoroughly—claiming powers of insight and self-expression conventionally granted to men alone—she had to be "contained" within the evolving masculinist discourse of psychiatry. In the ensuing confrontation between the adepts of the new psychology and the (mostly) female proponents of spiritualism, women like Hélène Smith, whose subversive shape shifting made a mockery of business as usual, could hardly escape undamaged.

True, Shamdasani is willing to credit Flournoy with some striking achievements: with developing a model of the unconscious that at once antedates and complements some of the better-known formulations of Freud, and with articulating the concept of a "hidden creative self" that greatly impressed the Surrealists, and Breton in particular. And he acknowledges that clinicians have come in recent years to value the originality and brilliance of the Swiss psychologist's speculations on cryptomnesiac memories, even as the peculiar mental aberration known as Multiple Personality Disorder reaches epidemic proportions in contemporary Western society. If Hélène Smith were alive today she would undoubtedly be classified, *pace* Ian Hacking, as a "multiple"—with Léopold, Simandini, Marie Antoinette, and the rest as secondary personalities actualized by some mysterious concatenation of intrapsychic causes.

But Flournoy is also in some degree the villain of the piece: an archetype of the Arrogant Psychologist, obsessed with a Helpless Woman, onto whom he projects his own unresolved conflicts about sex and the psyche. Thus we learn that Flournoy may have "failed to comprehend" his own emotional transference onto Smith, or the manifold ways that he perhaps exploited her in his ambitious quest for knowledge. He sought to "taxonomise" the "museum of all possible phenomena" he found in her, Shamdasani writes; yet when she resisted, he was "haunted," even unmanned, by her enigmatic image. At the end of *From India to the Planet Mars* Shamdasani appends a fiercely hostile essay by the French feminist writer Mireille Cifali, who accuses Flournoy (along with another male colleague, Lemaître) of pushing the entranced Smith—by dint of incessant, neurotic questioning—into increasingly distressed and dissociated states. "By reading the minutes of the séances," Cifali intones, "we remain struck with astonishment" as Flournoy and crony seek to make of the medium "a true puppet, a pure object of observation."

The famous image of the French psychiatrist Charcot grotesquely manipulating the body of a swooning female patient before a crew of male students—or of a gloating cartoon-Freud tormenting a befuddled and resentful Dora—seems to hover over the proceedings here, prompting Shamdasani toward the inevitable postfeminist, post-Foucauldian conclusion: in the pitched battle between male empirical science and female occultist rebellion, women like Smith were essentially victims, their fragile dreams of transcendence obliterated under the cruel, analytic, masculine gaze.

Yet the work itself resists such fashionable circumscription. After reading

From India to the Planet Mars William James told its author that "you and Delboeuf are the only worthy successors to Voltaire." The compliment is apt, for Flournoy's book is fundamentally a work of satire—an ironic assault on human pretension in the great Enlightenment tradition of *Candide* or *Micromégas*. To ideologize over it is to miss its central charm: that while launched as scientific case history, it is also a brilliant and uncompromising salvo against unreason. Perhaps the most meaningfully "feminist" response to it in the end is simply to acknowledge it as such, even as we see Smith's visions for what they were: the nonsensical divagations of a psyche puffed up with conceit and self-deceiving to the point of monstrosity.

The work operates as a mock-encomium or "praise of folly," with Flournoy himself an ironically self-deprecating narrative presence throughout. Absent here is the sometimes cheerless dogmatism of Freud: even in the most devastatingly sceptical sections, Flournoy's manner is one of exaggerated courtesies and arch feigned deference to the "ladies and gentlemen" of the "spiritist" persuasion. Explaining the "psychogenesis" of Léopold, he warns readers averse to such speculations simply to "skip" the offending passages. Accused of being unable to see "the supernormal . . . plainly before my eyes," he politely acknowledges that "it is, of course, to be regretted, but then it is I alone who will be in disgrace on the day when the truth shall be made manifest." And he positively revels in pretended embarrassment when forced to allude to his own starring role in some of Smith's séance-dramas. Conscious of the "honour" of being appointed the uncouth yet impressive "Asiatic potentate," Prince Sivrouka, he asks the reader's pardon for calling attention to "the immodest role which has been imposed upon me in this affair against my will."

Yet his greatest ironies are reserved for Smith herself, whose grand "subliminal romances" supposedly rival the visionary creations of the ancient bards and hierophants. Smith is repeatedly described as a "genius" and "poet" (during certain trances, she "feels compelled to speak in distinct rhymes of eight feet, which she does not prepare, and does not perceive until the moment she has finished uttering them.") She is a maker of semidivine "comedies" and "beautiful subliminal poems"; and the scraps of strange handwriting she produces are like passages out of long-lost mystic "books."

Breton took such comments seriously, educing a connection between Smith's automatisms and the experimental arts of the Fin de Siècle and beyond. "What is Art Nouveau," he asked in *The Automatic Message*, "if not an attempt to generalise and adapt mediumistic drawing, painting and sculpture to the art of furniture and decoration?" And at times one can see—just barely—what he means. Smith's hallucinatory paintings of various Martian scenes—one is reproduced on the cover of *From India to the Planet Mars*—have the effulgent color schemes, flattened perspective, and burgeoning floral devices of turn-of-the-century poster art; her rendering, while entranced, of the abstract, curliform Martian alphabet looks like a kind of goofy imitation Klee. In turn, the entire Martian tableau, with its fanciful rocket cars, wizards in funny hats, and flimsy theatrical "extraterrestrial" backdrops, sometimes brings to mind certain pioneering cinematic images of the period, such as the playful, intentionally hilarious moon-landing sequence in Georges Méliès's 1902 *Le Voyage dans la lune*.

Yet it's impossible to take Flournoy straight, and not only because he so often casts doubt—delicately yet damningly—on Smith's veracity. After asking her about De Marlès's history of India, the book in which he finds several Hindoo visions reproduced almost word for word, he praises the "indomitable and persevering energy" with which she denies any knowledge of the book or its contents:

> It must indeed be admitted that the idea of the passage in question having come before the eyes or ears of Mlle Smith through any ordinary channel seems a trifle absurd. I only know in Geneva of two copies of the work of De Marlès, both covered with dust—the one belonging to the Société de Lecture, a private association of which none of the Smith family nor any friend of theirs was ever a member; the other in the Public Library, where, among the thousands of more interesting and more modern books, it is now very rarely consulted. It could only have happened, therefore, by a combination of absolutely exceptional and almost unimaginable circumstances that the work of De Marlès could have found its way into Hélène's hands; and could it have done so and she not have the slightest recollection of it?
>
> I acknowledge the force of this argument, and that the wisest thing to do is to leave the matter in suspense.

What he really thinks of Smith's disavowal is glintingly apparent: in the exquisite "almost" slipped in before "unimaginable circumstances," in the quaintly anthropomorphized image of the book somehow "finding its way" into Smith's hands, in the parody of pedantic retreat in the last sentence.

For all of her stunning "artistry," Flournoy intimates, Smith is a colossal waster of her own and everyone else's time. She aspires to a kind of Wagnerian gigantism: individual séances go on for an exhausting six or seven hours (she is likely to extend them further if sitters dare to fidget or wonder aloud about getting their suppers); she likes to work in a Wagnerian multiplicity of expressive forms—babbling, crying, gesticulating, scrawling messages and drawings, singing snatches of "Indian" melody and so on. Yet the somnambulistic *Gesamtkunstwerk* is really a *Gesamtkitschwerk*. After a while, Flournoy hints, the "sham" Orientalism begins to cloy; the visions of Marie Antoinette start to look like the "plotless" maunderings of a not-too-bright schoolgirl; and even mysterious Mars begins to pall:

All things become wearisome at last, and the planet Mars is no exception to the rule. The subliminal imagination of Mlle Smith, however, will probably never tire of its lofty flights, in the society of Astané, Esenale and their associates. I myself, I am ashamed to acknowledge, began, in 1898, to have enough of the Martian romance.

Ars est longa—but vulgarity is even longer.

Visions such as Smith's, Flournoy insinuates, clog up the human field: solipsistic in essence, they leave no room for authentic dialogue or connection. They are an affront to empathy: a parody of communication rather than the real thing. Flournoy was prepared to go a long way on a human level with Smith, and some of his comments on her overwhelming emotional neediness—as in the following passage on the Marie Antoinette fantasy—are undeniably touching:

> In themselves, Mlle Smith's royal somnambulisms are almost always gay and joyous; but, considering their hidden source, in so far as they are the ephemeral and chimerical revenge of the ideal upon the real, of impossible dreams upon daily necessities, of impotent aspirations upon blind and crushing destiny, they assume a tragic signification. . . . The daily annihilation of the dream and the desire by implacable and brutal reality cannot find in the hypnoid imagination a more adequate representation, a more perfect symbol of an emotional tonality, than her royal majesty whose existence seemed made for the highest peaks of happiness and of fame—and ended on the scaffold.

Yet even for Flournoy, one suspects, Smith remained profoundly unlovable. Infatuated with her own "gift"—by which she made herself into a grotesque—she had nothing left to give.

Henry James, who may have known of Hélène Smith through his brother's interest in her case, saw a kind of obscenity in the lurid maneuvers of the somnambulist; his depiction in *The Bostonians* (1886) of the young "seeress" Verena Tarrant convulsing subtly, almost orgasmically, before a group of fascinated observers is one of the most troubling images of female self-degradation in nineteenth-century literature. James also knew what many recent social historians of the period seem determined to disallow: that spiritualism—from Katie King and the Fox sisters to Eusapia Paladino and Madame Blavatsky—was a moral, political, and aesthetic disaster for women. Rather than prompting any new respect for women's rights or capabilities, as some scholars have suggested, the spiritualist movement simply reinforced age-old stereotypes about female childishness, irrationalism, and emotional opportunism. Women, like Smith, who turned to the spirit world out of a narcissistic craving for attention, ended up making everything worse for the rest of us.

There are no photographs of Smith in *From India to the Planet Mars*: as Flournoy notes, she refused to allow any pictures of herself "either in her normal state or in that of Léopold" to appear in the book. This is to be regretted, although she was surely wise (for once) to do so. Has anyone ever noticed the sheer squalor of the mediumistic performances captured in late-nineteenth- and early-twentieth-century séance photographs? In many of these photos, such as those showing the famous Boston medium "Margery" (later exposed as a fraud by Houdini) materializing pieces of fake ectoplasm, the effect is almost pornographic. Margery's face is puffy and contorted, her body grossly distended, the placenta-like substance that is supposed to be the ectoplasm a disgusting rubbery white blob emerging from under her dress. Hélène Smith knew better, but still not well enough.

note

1. Théodore Flournoy, *From India to the Planet Mars: A Case of Multiple Personality with Imaginary Languages*, ed. Sonu Shamdasani, trans. Daniel B. Vermilie (Princeton, N.J.: Princeton University Press, 1994).

14
PIPE DOWN BACK THERE!

First, a fiery allegory—the reviewer's house is burning down! After tossing the cats out the window, she has time only to save one object before fleeing: either a CD of Sarah Bernhardt declaiming from *Phèdre* or an old sepia-tinted postcard of Eleonora Duse in D'Annunzio's *La Città morta*. Quick! which to choose? The Bernhardt has always been a source of deep hilarity: given the primitive acoustic equipment (the original recording was made in 1903), the fabled French actress sounds like Minnie Mouse on speed. She gabbles her way through "Oui, Prince, je brûle pour Thésée" at a mad, cartoonish pace, *r*'s unrolling wildly in every direction. (Watch your head!) The reviewer dotes on her deranged-chipmunk tones, and has even been known to mimic them—along with accompanying pops and blops and funky squeaks—for the enjoyment of select companions. How to live without her?

Yet the *carte postale* of Duse might seem even more cherishable. Despite her postmodern household location—propped up like a jokey little icon next to the Body Shop bottles on the bathroom shelf—Duse exudes, well, a certain *sublimity*. She's all in black, in some kind of elegant, judicial-looking, Portia-like robe, and leans against a Greek column on a terrace, head tilted up to the heavens. She's obviously standing on a stage—there's a pale cardboard mountain and painted cataract in the far distance—but something in the mute classicism of her pose undoes any sense of theatricality. She doesn't lend herself to parody in the way that Bernhardt does; she's austere, pure, removed. Nor does she need to reel off alexandrines to make an effect. You can tell just by looking she's One Tragic Babe. What to do? (*Gasp, splutter, cough cough!*)

It is clear what Willa Cather—lifelong connoisseur of big-bosomed *tragédiennes*—would have done: snatch up La Duse and let gabbly old Bernhardt go to hell. In her recent book on the novelist, Joan Acocella speaks with some reverence of Cather's "Duse revelation": the young writer's precocious verdict, having seen both actresses perform onstage in the 1890s, that Duse was the superior artist because of the classical restraint she invariably brought to her roles.[1] Bernhardt "expressed" tragic emotion, wrote Cather in a newspaper review, whereas Duse "almost concealed" it: "She takes her great anguish and lays it in a tomb and rolls a stone before the door." Cather gravitated toward Duse, Acocella suggests, because the Italian actress's understated style came closest to expressing Cather's own evolving impulse as a novelist: to convey meaning subtly, through oblique hints and indirection rather than romantic grandstanding. When Cather came to compose the great, limpid narratives of Midwestern prairie life that made her famous—*O Pioneers!* (1913), *The Song of the Lark* (1915), *My Ántonia* (1918), *One of Ours* (1922), *A Lost Lady* (1923), and *The Professor's House* (1925) among them—it was exactly this quality of noble withholding that she sought to achieve.

Cather's preference may have been shaped by a certain emotional identification. Unlike Bernhardt, whose love affairs were notorious, the real-life Duse seemed to have no husband and no friends: "She is utterly alone upon the icy heights where other beings cannot live." Cather was only twenty-two when she wrote this, Acocella notes, "but she seems to have seen her life before her: strait is the gate. Like Duse, she will not marry, not dissipate. And her art will be like Duse's. She will not express things, but contain them." And indeed, like her chosen idol, Cather made a fetish out of proud self-concealment. She never married, and despite the tremendous popular success of her work—she won the Pulitzer prize in 1922 and had her picture on the cover of *Time* magazine in 1931—she became reclusive and incommunicative in later years. She regularly refused interviews and before her death in 1947, at the age of seventy-four, made sure that all of her private papers were burned. About the two major emotional relationships of her life—the first with Isabella McClung, a Pittsburgh heiress and the beloved "best companion" to whom she dedicated *The Song of the Lark*; the second with Edith Lewis, a fellow spinster from Nebraska with whom she lived in New York from 1913 to her death—we know next to nothing. The elusive Duse, one feels, would have approved.

The same preference for austerity informs Joan Acocella's view of Cather and her critics. Brief though it is (only ninety-four pages of full-blown text) *Willa Cather and the Politics of Criticism* is a sort of gleaming, double-edged thing: both a brisk appreciation of Cather's artistic achievement and a stern, even cutting assault on modern Cather scholarship. It grows out of a controversial article that Acocella, a well-known dance critic, published in *The New Yorker* in 1995. The original article was a fairly devastating attack on the various ways in which Cather—in Acocella's view the only American novelist besides James to rival Tolstoy and Flaubert for beauty of style and moral depth—had been manhandled by contemporary academic critics. The story Acocella told was one of noble articulation—Cather's poised, pared-down imaginative utterance—overwhelmed by idiotic jabber. Starting sometime around 1980, she opined, Cather studies had been hijacked by a group of academic feminists, queer theorists, and multiculturalists, all determined to subject her to various grotesque and self-serving ideological "paradigms." So incessant (and obnoxious) the resulting critical din, Cather's true greatness as a writer was in danger of being obscured. Against the pretentious gibberish of the academy, Acocella presented her own cool, plain-speaking account of Cather's genius as a necessary (if lonely) rescue operation: she would save Willa Cather from her critics. The piece was at once an elegant piece of satire (almost Swiftian at times in its own mordant understatement) and a powerful valuation of Duse-like reserve over gabbly Bernhardt *noise*. Shut up, everybody, Acocella seemed to be saying: let Cather be Cather—in all of her so-briety, reticence, and artistic self-possession.

Acocella's targets were predictably outraged, but she garnered admirers too—including numerous mutinously inclined academics. The mid-nineties were an especially fraught and exhausting time in the so-called culture wars in American universities, and for many professional literary scholars—myself included—Acocella's essay registered as brusque and fierce and timely, and relievingly free of cant. By taking as her test case an author whose work was spectacularly resistant to the kinds of critical depradation then in fashion (being neither overtly politi-cal in its themes nor garrulously "postmodern" in narrative mode), she seemed to point up the inadequacy of the critical models themselves. With a few sharp strokes, Acocella cut through the verbiage to offer a purified, if somewhat old-fashioned, model of literary appreciation, one distinguished, like Cather's fiction itself, by modesty, tact, and unshakable common sense.

If it all seems slightly less exhilarating now, it is not simply because a lot of the twanging and the racket seems to have died down. Acocella is the same lucid, ob-durate force—an intelligent outsider challenging the norms of a somewhat deca-dent and in-grown professional clique. She is also a marvelous, canny writer. But in its new and expanded version (she has added a fuller account of Cather's criti-cal reception in the twenties and thirties and a concluding reflection on her "tragic sense of life"), her essay must also disquiet even the most jaded anti-aca-demic. Were *all* the critical maneuvers executed by Cather scholars over the past two decades as foolish as Acocella makes them sound here? Was everyone so dumb and self-serving? And even if they were, shouldn't literary critics be allowed to take their inevitable (yet often illuminating) wrong turns? Do we not want *any* noise? Duse-like gravitas is all very well, but at times one craves a bit of babble and gabble and silly flamboyance—someone to career around the stage like a banshee and stir everybody up. At the heart of Acocella's enterprise—and this fea-ture seems somehow more noticeable the second time around—is the satirist's morbid intolerance for human error, the very kind of error so necessary, paradox-ically, to intellectual exchange. This intolerance gives her argument its delectable polemical edge (what a glorious bunch of dunces inhabit English departments!) but also limits her ability to compel unalloyed assent. That Bernhardt CD, after all, was an awful lot of fun; can't we make one last foray into the flames to get it?

None of which is to say that Acocella's central points have lost either their charm or their satiric force. She is in many ways perfectly positioned to unfurl a modern lampoon on academic folly, being both involved and not involved, close but not too close. An intriguing if fanciful essay might be written about the "symbolic distance" at which individuals instinctively wish to place themselves when called upon to examine or describe something. The distance (metaphorically speaking) an observer is inclined to choose can often be related to the intensity of his or her need for psychological intimacy with others. The painter Canaletto—hardly known for emotional depth—typically views his human beings from about five hundred yards away; seen against his panoramic Venetian backdrops, his people are often little more than dots or tiny blobs. One suspects, in consequence, that he cared more for water, sky, and architecture than people. By contrast, Ingres, in his uncannily absorbing portrait sketches, typically places himself (psychically as well as literally) a mere one or two feet from his subjects—close enough to capture the very warmth radiating from their skin. Novelists such as Henry James and Proust seem to want to reduce the distance between themselves and their characters virtually to nothing—to bore into their characters' skulls and take us with them. Cather, rather more conservatively, typically locates herself about four or five feet from her characters—near enough to tell us what we need to know about Ántonia or Jim or the professor, Godfrey St. Peter, but not so near as to infringe upon their privacy or essential dignity. She observes her characters respectfully, as if across the width of a farmhouse supper table, or from a distance equivalent to that between one furrow and the next in a neatly ploughed field.

Perhaps because of her background in dance—she has written a wonderful book on Mark Morris and edited an unexpurgated version of Nijinsky's diaries—Acocella locates herself, figuratively speaking, at a kind of middle distance from her subjects, as if she were watching them from a well-placed seat (perhaps thirty or forty feet away?) in a spacious auditorium. This vantage point, it is true, allows for an occasional focus on individuals, but what come across far more strikingly are larger, more abstract patterns of movement—a choreography, so to speak, of human effects. Reviewing the history of Cather scholarship over the past seventy-five years, Acocella tracks the shifts of critical fashion almost diagrammatically—as a set of temporary formations, each with its distinctive advances and retreats, signature turns, and obsessional gestures, all kinesthetically linked to social and intellectual changes in American culture at large.

The story she tells is one of increasingly loopy, enfoliated movement. Once a sober pavane, Cather criticism has gradually degenerated, she suggests, into a kind of nutty St. Vitus's dance—even as popular interest in Cather's life and work has grown. (Like Haworth, the Yorkshire home of the Brontës, Red Cloud, Nebraska, the small Midwestern prairie town where Cather spent most of her early years and adolescence, has become a popular destination for tourist buses:

Willa-embossed mugs and T-shirts proliferate.) It was not always such. Cather's early commentators were admiring to the point of boosterism, yet recognized, even so, what was original and distinctive about her work. In the first flush of her career, following the huge public success of *O Pioneers!* and *My Ántonia,* both tales about life in little Nebraska farming towns, patriotically minded reviewers such as H.L. Mencken and Van Wyck Brooks hailed what they saw as her heroic break with effete European fictional models. "In their view," writes Acocella, "American fiction was choking to death on well-made plots about the suppressed emotions of wealthy people in Boston. The time had come for novelists to shove the teacups aside and give the country a 'literature of youth,' about ordinary people—poor people, people outside the cities—experiencing real emotions and expressing them in plain American language." In the stark realism of *My Ántonia,* about an illiterate Czech hired girl who bears and loses an illegitimate child yet struggles on to become the hardworking wife of an immigrant farmer, Cather took a story of "poor peasants"—Mencken wrote approvingly in 1919—and drew from it "the eternal tragedy of man." Reviewing her early novels in the *New Republic,* Carl Van Doren praised both her democratic outlook and "elemental" vision of human suffering. "Passion blows through her chosen characters," he enthused, "like a free, wholesome, if devastating wind."

Yet already by the mid-1920s, Acocella suggests, Cather's critics had begun to execute some dubious trips and turns. Even as Cather continued to produce brilliant, irreproachable, often deeply intransigent fictional works—Acocella judges the haunting problem novel of 1925, *The Professor's House,* about an aging college teacher trapped in a loveless marriage, the most metaphysical and "terrifying" of all Cather's books—certain commentators seemed determined to misunderstand her. Some of this misunderstanding, it is true, had to do with Cather's own refusal to cater to what she saw as the trivialization of artistic and intellectual life after World War I. Firmly anchored in the moral and stylistic conventions of nineteenth-century realism, she was largely impervious to the avant-garde experiments of writers like Joyce or Woolf. Nor, for all her bleakness, was she interested in conveying that spirit of sophisticated cultural malaise and psychosexual malfunction so palpable in Hemingway or Fitzgerald. As Acocella puts it: "Cather went on giving [readers] stories about noble-minded people living in small towns, often in the past. She did not examine her characters' stream of consciousness or, for the most part, their sex lives. She examined their ideals, which she took seriously. And she wrote about them in a prose that looked decidedly nonexperimental—pure, classical, like something carved from white marble."

Even so, a host of critics (mostly male) simply missed the point. Among other things, the decidedly odd and unsexy "Miss Cather" was deemed to be insufficiently engaged with Big Social Issues. During the Depression she came under violent attack from left-leaning reviewers for attributing (as they saw it) the sufferings of her rural working-class characters to some "timeless tragic principle" rather than to forces of social and economic disenfranchisement. Thus, when she evoked the harshness and sadness of American prairie life, wrote the Marxist critic Newton Arvin in 1931, she did so as if "mass production and technological unemployment and cyclical depressions and the struggle between the classes did not exist." Set against the fierce muckraking of Theodore Dreiser or Sherwood Anderson, another critic complained, Cather's fiction was "harmless stuff that 'could be read in schools and women's clubs.'" Her Flaubertian classicism (and concomitant moral irony) went mostly unrecognized, and despite her huge popularity with general readers—her 1931 novel *Shadows on the Rock* was the most widely read book in the United States in the year following its publication—even such serious-minded critics as Edmund Wilson and the young Lionel Trilling regularly disparaged her as spinsterish, middlebrow, and reactionary, a kind of tiresome maiden aunt in the back parlor of American letters.

True, Cather had her defenders—but as Acocella grimly notes, they were prone to loading up her novels with "pious readings completely out of line with the text." "The great shame of the left-wing attack on Cather in the thirties," she suggests, "is not just that it removed her from serious consideration by some of the best minds (Wilson, Trilling), but that it polarized the discussion of her work. The more she was senselessly dismissed by the Left, the more she was senselessly exalted by the Right and used as a stick to beat the Left—indeed, to beat anything that the Right disliked." Social and religious conservatives sought to corral her. Though Cather was herself a kind of doom-blasted Episcopalian—the kind that Sophocles might have been, had he been born in Red Cloud in the 1870s rather than fifth-century Athens—Catholic commentators in particular sought to make her over as sentimental coreligionist. Thus according to a writer in *Commonweal*, *Obscure Destinies*, the best-selling book of stories she published in 1932, radiated "a living light, like candles on an altar in a shrine dedicated to human pity and love." Cather, for her part, didn't seem to mind playing along: in various essays published toward the end of her life, she freely lambasted Freud, Marx, Roosevelt, the New Deal, and all politically or ideologically motivated art: "An artist should have no moral purpose in mind other than just his art. His mission is not to clean the Augean stables; he had better join the Salvation Army if he wants to do that."

Yet far worse was to come in subsequent decades—notably in the misplaced piety department. If critics during Cather's lifetime mostly failed to register what was centrally and supremely important about her—her majestically unillusioned vision of human experience—those who came along after her death claimed to find virtues in her work by which the novelist herself would have been shocked and appalled. And here is where Acocella, the dance aficionada-cum-satirist, really gets her mojo working: in her ghoulishly funny account of the feminist "rediscovery" of Cather in the 1970s, 1980s, and 1990s. This (for Acocella) comically wrong-headed project—launched by a veritable Maenad-horde of American academic feminists sometime around 1975—was in itself hardly un-expected. One of the much-bruited goals of the new Anglo-American feminist literary scholarship of the 1970s, after all, was precisely to recover neglected women authors and restore them to prominence within a gloriously "female-centered" literary tradition. That Cather—a novelist of undoubted genius and appeal whose rightful place in American letters had somehow been subverted by male critics (Trilling et al.)—should become a candidate for such rehabilitation will surprise no one who lived through those heady days. (Bliss was it in that dawn to drink herbal tea, read Adrienne Rich, and have no penis!) The time seemed ripe for a major reevaluation of a pioneering woman writer.

There was only one problem, as Acocella, now gimlet-eyed, points out. Cather herself was a full-bore raving misogynist—at least on the subject of fe-male authorship:

> "Sometimes I wonder why God ever trusts [literary] talent in the hands of women, they usually make such an infernal mess of it," she wrote in 1895. "I think He must do it as a sort of ghastly joke." Female poets were so gushy—"emotional in the extreme, self-centered, self-absorbed." As for female novelists, all they could write about was love: "They have a sort of sex consciousness that is abominable.". . . "If I see the announcement of a new book by a woman, I—well, I take one by a man instead. . . . I pre-fer to take no chances when I read."

Unlike Virginia Woolf, she saw no point in identifying herself polemically with any sort of second-rate "female" literary tradition: she preferred real writers, like Virgil and Tolstoy. True female genius, she thought, was a *rara avis*. Perhaps be-cause her own earliest intellectual mentors had been male—a music teacher in Red Cloud, an English professor at the University of Nebraska—she held fairly unabashedly to the idea that whatever intellectual or artistic gifts a women might happen, freakishly, to possess inevitably came down to her from some pa-ternal source. Even the great Duse, she believed, was first and foremost a "daughter of Dante."

Cather scorned the idea that being a woman novelist meant she was confined to dealing primarily with female characters or conventionally "feminine" topics such as love and courtship. Some of her best novels (*The Professor's House, One of Ours, Death Comes for the Archbishop*) have no memorable female characters at all. In *My Ántonia*, she devotes far more attention to the male narrator—the elu-sive, artistic Jim Burden—than she does to the eponymous, somewhat stolid heroine. That buoyant structuring device of so much female-authored fiction since the eighteenth century—the marriage plot—held little interest for her. (She is, on the contrary, one of the great poets of failed marriage, as the marvelous, catastrophic, strangely neglected novel of 1922, *One of Ours*, suggests. The death of love in that work is like the slow, sad seepage of air out of a balloon.) And even when she probes, ever so delicately, some of the more intimate turns in her characters' emotional lives, a fierce sense of decorum kept her from any kind of sexual candor. She remains by far the most Tiresian, androgynous, and erotically remote of all the great female novelists. Austen seems positively sluttish in comparison, Ivy Compton-Burnett a bedizened Jezebel. On the rare occasions when Cather does focus on a major female character, as in *The Song of the Lark,* heterosexual love barely figures in the story at all. A flawed, off-kilter, yet absorbing Bildungsroman about a Swedish-American girl from the plains who dreams of becoming an opera singer, the novel is Cather's sole portrait of female artistic ambition triumphantly fulfilled. Well into her career as an internationally celebrated Isolde, the book's heroine, Thea Kronborg, marries her loyal suitor-manager—the somewhat bathetically named Fred. But if you blink your eyes, you are likely to miss the happy nuptials altogether. No humpy Tristan he.

How did "the feminists" manage to drag the incorrigible Willa over onto their side? According to Acocella, by way of some wishful, even prurient biographical manipulations. She reserves the central and most caustic satire of her book for one of the blockbusters of 1980s Cather criticism—Sharon O'Brien's influential *Willa Cather: The Emerging Voice*, a massive, often ponderous study of the writer's early life and career published by Oxford in 1987. O'Brien's claim to fame, put somewhat cartoonishly, is that she was the first major scholar to "out" Cather—to take up the issue of the novelist's sexuality (long-rumored to be lesbian) and relate it directly to her creative enterprise. Though deeply closeted, Cather was patently homosexual, O'Brien argued, and her secret homosexuality explained much—not only about her fiction, but also about her misogynist attitudes. In love for years with Isabelle McClung, the "garden fair" who had spurned her by marrying in 1916, Cather remained enthralled by—yet deeply conflicted over—the power of the feminine. While longing all her life for some primal "maternal-erotic" figure to whom to cleave, she also despised her own yearnings, and sought to identify herself, self-protectively, with boys and men. Much of the strange reticence of her fiction, its odd peripatisms and withdrawals, could be attributed, O'Brien ventured, to this impacted authorial ambivalence. Cather both ached for and feared her "maternal goddess"; she found psychic refuge in a pose of virile detachment and intermittent hostility toward other women.

In fact, O'Brien went on to claim, precisely by recognizing Cather's lesbianism openly and forthrightly, it became possible for the modern reader to regard her sympathetically—as a kind of underground feminist-in-the-making. Cather was a victim of patriarchal attitudes, to be sure, but in that her deepest emotional commitments were to women, and her fiction full of the coded signs of hidden "gynocentrism," she might be forgiven her less flattering comments on her own sex. One could even consider her, paradoxically, a sort of sexual heroine: someone who sought, courageously, to channel unorthodox erotic yearnings into artistic creativity of the highest order. "Her love of women was a source of great strength and imaginative power to her," O'Brien concluded, but "she feared misunderstanding and repudiation if this love were to be publicly named." (As a cub reporter in Pittsburgh in the 1890s, Cather had covered the Wilde debacle—with horrified revulsion.) She loved in secret, but love she did, and like a hidden flame, her surreptitious devotion to members of her own sex both animated and refined her art.

However turgidly rendered, O'Brien's psychosexual portrait of Cather was not without its compelling features—nor, one felt, entirely off the mark. One of O'Brien's biographical coups was to include among her book's illustrations an extraordinary set of studio photographs (now in the Nebraska State Historical Society archives) of the fourteen-year-old Cather dressed as "William Cather, Jr." For four years of her adolescence—even as bewildered relatives and neighbors looked on—the tomboyish Cather doggedly adopted this male alter ego as her primary public identity. She cut her hair short, wore boys' jackets, ties, and caps around town, and regularly signed herself "William Cather, M.D." in friends' albums and yearbooks. The denizens of Red Cloud were agog at the pubescent cross-dresser among them. As late as the 1970s, civic folk legend held that the intrepid young Cather had been a "hermaphrodite" and wore men's shoes—indeed "had 'em made special."

The pictures themselves are fabulously bizarre. In one, "William Cather" wears a jaunty Civil War cap embroidered with his/her initials; in another, a kind of miniature porkpie hat, shiny cravat, and goofy, insouciant smile. In perhaps the most startling of the photographs, Cather sports, anachronistically, the same brusque, perfectly manicured flattop last seen (by this reviewer) on the lesbian folksinger Phranc, a minor musical cult figure of the 1980s. As images go, these juvenile self-portraits are full of charm and aplomb and baby-butch esprit; they are also inutterably weird. At the very least, they allow one to imagine for the strange boy/girl who chose to present herself thus an *interesting*, if not uncanny, sexual future.

But Acocella will have none of it. It was not "that remarkable," she tells us, for rebellious adolescent girls in the nineteenth century to wish to escape the burdens of femininity through such role playing: witness the tomboy Jo, who cuts off her hair and dresses as a boy in Louisa May Alcott's *Little Women*. "Those were the days before such sentiments placed one under suspicion of being a lesbian." And Cather's masquerade was after all only temporary; she went back to a conventionally feminine appearance as soon as she left for college. Nor is Acocella convinced, more broadly, that one can—or should—make knowing pronouncements about Cather's sexuality. The jury is still out, she suggests, on the question of whether Cather was homosexual; even the impassioned relationship with McClung may simply have been one of those fervent "romantic friendships" so common between women in the late nineteenth century. Her own best guess on the subject, reluctantly proffered, is that the adult Cather may have been "homosexual in her feelings and celibate in her actions." Which is not to say, she hastens to add, that the novelist suffered from any sexual "complex" or that her love life (or lack of one) had any deducible impact on her work. "Many of the notable women writers of the nineteenth century were celibate— 'spinsters and virgins,' as Ellen Moers calls them. If Emily Brontë and Jane Austen managed without having sex, why not Cather? Because we think she was homosexual?" To appreciate a great book, she asserts, we need not gossip, like silly adolescents, over its author's life between the sheets. To subject someone as dignified as Cather to such treatment seems particularly demeaning and beside the point.

Having chastized O'Brien—not just for overreading but for nosiness and vulgarity as well—Acocella proceeds to let rip, satiric afterburners on high, at just about everybody who has written about Cather in O'Brien's wake. Following O'Brien's putative revelations, "the feminists now had what they needed, the hidden conflict. Since it was homosexuality, it had to be very heavily defended. Hence the surface of Cather's fiction could no longer be taken literally; it had to be read *through*." Among those "reading through" in this manner—with mostly foolish results—Acocella finds not only the usual academical drones and poseurs, but some touted names in contemporary North American literary criticism and theory: Eve Sedgwick, Judith Butler, Jonathan Goldberg, Judith Fetterley, Jean Schwind, Elizabeth Ammons. Acocella takes no prisoners. She is queen of the devastating citation, and more than happy to let the jargon-mad professors hang themselves.

Thus poor Robert J. Nelson, author of a 1988 book on the novelist, gets mercilessly dinged for writing about Cather's oscillation between a "phallocentric hegemony" and a "vaginocentric" one. (According to Nelson, as cruelly quoted by Acocella, Thea Kronborg, standing "in erectile sublimity" on a peak in Panther Canyon in *The Song of the Lark,* "is, symbolically, . . . the linear and upright form of the male phallus.") She wickedly lampoons Ammons and Patrick Shaw for finding lurking sexual symbols, such as giant wombs and fallopian tubes, in Cather's frequent descriptions of Midwestern scenery. ("No tree can grow, no river flow, in Cather's landscapes," notes Acocella, "without this being a penis or a menstrual period.") And she has morbid fun at the expense of those commentators—fairly numerous lately, it is true—who have attributed secret homosexual feelings to various Cather characters:

Not just Ántonia and Jim [in *My Ántonia*], but most of Cather's main characters are shown to be "masked" homosexuals: Alexandra in *O Pio-*

neers!, Thea in *The Song of the Lark*, Claude Wheeler and David Gerhardt in *One of Ours*, Euclide Auclair in *Shadows on the Rock*, and of course those two priests in *Death Comes for the Archbishop*. In *The Professor's House* we hit pay dirt: according to various commentators, not just Professor St. Peter and Tom Outland and Roddy Blake, but also Louie Marsellus and Lillian, the professor's son-in-law and wife, respectively, are homosexuals. Another lurking invert is Sapphira Colbert, the paralyzed old woman in *Sapphira and the Slave Girl*. You can tell, says Robert J. Nelson, because her name is close to Sappho's.

Acocella's most magnificent potshot is reserved for Eve Sedgwick, reigning doyenne of "queer" literary studies in the United States and occasional commentator on the new crypto-homo Cather. In a 1989 essay on *The Professor's House*, Sedgwick argued that while the novel might seem painfully "heterosexist" on the surface, a queer-friendly reader could nonetheless discern in it its author's powerful covert rebellion against hegemonic "heteronormativity." Sedgwick's signal piece of evidence (alas) was the multisyllabic name that Cather bestowed—in the last sentence of the novel—on the ship on which the professor's wife and daughter sail home from Europe: the *Berengaria*. Deconstructing this odd nautical monicker, Sedgwick finds it burgeoning with erotic puns and Gertrude Steinian word-play:

> *Berengaria*: ship of women: the {green} {aria}, the {eager} {brain}, the {bearing} and the {bairn}, the {raring} {engine}, the {bargain} {binge}, the {ban} and {bar}, the {garbage}, the {barrage} of {anger}, the {bare} {grin}, the {rage} to {err}, the {rare} {grab} for {being}, the {begin} and {rebegin} {again}.

Such readerly *jouissance* proves costly, however. Zeroing in on this ballast-heavy, deliciously listing target, Acocella does not hesitate to blow Sedgwick out of the water:

> This list of anagrams, which must have taken a while to work out, supposedly reveals the maelstrom of lesbian energies churning beneath the surface of *The Professor's House*, energies that Cather was venting when she gave the ship that strange name. Yes, Sedgwick says, the name has a historical meaning—Berengaria was the wife of Richard the Lion-Hearted—but otherwise it is a "nonsense word." She apparently does not know that it was the name of a real ship, a famous Cunard ocean liner, on which Cather had returned from Europe immediately before starting work on *The Professor's House*.

Amusing enough, to be sure. Yet after a while one begins to view some of the torpedoing with mixed emotions. True, Acocella's satire has its wholesome, head-clearing, "tough love" aspect. Like a good cop on the beat, she is not going to put up with any more juvenile mischief making at a great writer's expense. You kids! Pipe down back there! And drop those spray paint cans right now! When she itemizes—sardonically—just what makes Cather so unfit for "politically correct" analysis, one may find oneself going all weak and wobbly and compliant in the presence of such steely-eyed moral authority:

> Nina Baym has written with discouragement of the tendency for feminist theorists to 'excoriate their deviating sisters,' the ones who do not toe the theoretical line. Nowhere is this tendency more prevalent than in Cather studies, and for obvious reasons. Other women writers uphold the feminists' description of what it means for a woman to try to enter the patriarchal literary tradition. Emily Dickinson cowering in her room, Mary Shelley trying to work between pregnancies, Kate Chopin hounded out of print, Harriet Beecher Stowe writing with one hand while holding a baby with the other: these women tell the story the feminists are trying to tell. But Cather? If anything, she is a rebuke to the feminists. All the things they say a woman can't do—learn to write from men, create a life centered on writing, with no intrusions—she did them, and with very little wear and tear. No alcoholism, no abortions, no nervous breakdowns. She jumped the gate, and therefore she makes the gate look perhaps not so high after all. Add to this her other crimes: her male identification, her attacks on Kate Chopin, on Harriet Beecher Stowe. Finally, keep in mind that she was a strong, bossy woman, one who cowed people, scared people. Isn't this somebody the feminists might want to bring down a peg? And if she, this flinty old Republican, this staple of Catholic school curricula, should turn out to be a closet lesbian, a frightened person, a person whose most intimate secrets we know and, from our comfortable, post-gay liberation perspective, can understand, even as we express our regret over her lack of courage—if, in other words, we were superior to Willa Cather—wouldn't that be nice?

No, it w-w-wouldn't be nice, we whimper. You're right, Joan! Willa's great! We're rotten little punks in comparison! And the cowardly baby-tears start to flow . . .

But while it's a relief not to find oneself in Acocella's index—*thank God I never wrote about Cather; Jane Austen was bad enough*—one can still have a twinge of sympathy for the unfortunate souls who do. Acocella is not always fair, and once she's pegged you, she is seldom forgiving. You would not know from her account that the hapless Sharon O'Brien is actually fairly illuminating on Cather's early career, nor that O'Brien writes clearly and interestingly on

Cather's complicated, often rivalrous literary relations with male novelists such as Henry James. Nor would you know that Judith Butler—caricatured here as a critic who leaves Cather "bound and gagged" in the coils of Lacanian theory—can be as witty and grown-up as Acocella herself, as when she analyzes the various linguistic and sexual inversions in Cather's 1896 short story "Tommy the Unsentimental." In this comically surreal tale—about an eccentric country spinster who changes her name from Theodosia to Tommy, wears men's trousers, and likes to perform chivalric love-errands on behalf of pretty young neighborhood lasses—the usually lugubrious Cather comes shockingly close to a kind of dadaist, Firbankian camp. Acocella never mentions this story—in part, one suspects, because lurking within it is precisely the sort of flip, self-ironizing joke that the serious-minded Cather she reveres should not have been capable of making: *this funny old gal is a whopping dyke!* Butler both gets the joke and parses it nicely.

On Cather and homosexuality, Acocella is too grim by half. Is it really so vulgar or inane to be curious about a great writer's erotic life? A case might be made that the most significant methodological development in Western biography since Boswell has in fact been precisely the attempt to correlate the intimate, even psychosexual aspects of an individual's character with his or her public achievements. The older one gets the more one realizes how deeply everything that one is—everything one believes oneself to be—is bound up with whom one loves. Most of the world-class biographies written in English over the past fifty years—Leon Edel's James, George Painter's Proust, Michael Holroyd's Strachey and Shaw, Richard Ellmann's Joyce and Wilde, John Richardson's Picasso, Maynard Solomon's Mozart, Ray Monk's Wittgenstein and Russell, Hermione Lee's Woolf, Judith Thurman's Dinesen and Colette—have been distinguished by their intense, liberating attention to sexual-emotional themes. It may be true that Cather's peculiar, mysteriously configured homoeroticism has not yet had the sort of intelligent analysis it demands, but that is no reason to exempt her from inquiry of this kind.

Indeed, with Cather's sexuality ruled out of bounds as a topic, whole swatches of her work become unnecessarily opaque. Again, one would not know it from Acocella but Cather was one of the great, over-the-top diva "groupies" of the late nineteenth century: a woman who seldom went for long without an ardent adolescent crush on some touring opera singer or actress. No reticence here: her newspaper articles of the 1880s and 1890s are full of engorged love paeans to Nellie Melba, Emma Calvé, Olive Fremstad, and Lillian Nordica—not to mention the redoubtable Clara Butt, best known for her foghorn renditions of "Land of Hope and Glory." (The boomiferous Butt possessed an "ocean of voice," Cather rhapsodized, "like the moan of the sea or the sighing of the forest in the night wind.") The displacement of homoerotic emotion onto female performers was a common phenomenon among cultivated women in the nineteenth and

early twentieth centuries: George Sand and Queen Victoria had similar serial
pashes. But the psychic mechanism seems especially strong in Cather. To dismiss
this giddy, enraptured side of her—simply because it makes her seem undigni-
fied, or because Outing People Is Wrong—is to miss an important and fascinating element in her imaginative response to the world. *The Song of the Lark*—that
curious soul kiss of a novel—makes little sense without it. Great women artists
clearly intoxicated Cather, and however subtly, she sought to pass on to her
reader the lovely poison she imbibed from them.

Which brings us back, perhaps not so circuitously, to Bernhardt and Duse.
Even as one finds oneself agreeing with Acocella about many things—for example, that much of what passes for academic literary criticism today is indeed a
kind of self-indulgent, histrionic "noise"—one resists the slightly apocalyptic
(and repressive) drift in her argument: that for the sake of Cather's reputation,
the noise should stop. At her direst moments, Acocella is a pull-the-plug sort of
person; she wants rackety Bernhardt brought down off the stage, and Duse,
moody model citizen, put up in her stead once and for all. Enough with the p.c.
tirades about Cather and patriarchy, Cather and Native Americans, or Cather's
views on the "economic exploitation of Nebraska farmers by 'larger corporate
entities.'" "How wearying," Acocella exclaims, "is the *tone* of recent political criticism of Cather, so aggressive, so righteous, calling her to the dock to answer
whether she is as good as the critic." How much better simply to absorb Cather's
"tragic sense of life" with the appropriately humble and silent awe.

But criticism—in order to be anything at all—needs its noisemakers and vul-
garians as well as its noble and refined types. The People Who Get It Wrong,
paradoxically, are as necessary to the enterprise as the People Who Get It Right.
Criticism is an ongoing negotiation between truth and error, and sometimes, by
an irritating yet ultimately productive dialectic, error is for a while in the ascen-
dant. "In academic criticism," as W. K. Wimsatt once delicately put it, "you see
less genius than in some other kinds, but more deliberacy, self-consciousness,
program, literalism, and repetition." To put it more bluntly: sometimes even
professional literary critics (most of whom are not geniuses) say dumb, pretentious, and off-the-track things.

Yet without such error, no critical dialogue. And without such dialogue, now
to quote Kundera, "the discoveries effected by art go unnamed and thereby remain absent from the history of art, for a work enters history and becomes *visible* there only if its discoveries, its innovations, are specified and recognized.
Without the meditative background that is criticism, works become isolated gestures, ahistorical accidents, soon forgotten." Interestingly, while Cather (the
critic) preferred Duse, she was open-minded enough to recognize—and
honor—Sarah Bernhardt's very different mode of artistic expression. Bernhardt
had an uncanny power, she wrote, to project feelings "more lifelike than life."
She was heroic, grandiose, and in her very excess, blasphemously present—

someone who by "a thousand little things" could unleash dizzying emotions in her audience. Even as she prepared to do something different in her own art—and in that difference resides our gain, as Acocella points out so well—Willa Cather was willing for a while to let go, to drift in the noise, and let the strange importunate sounds roll over her.

note

1. Joan Acocella, *Willa Cather and the Politics of Criticism* (Lincoln: University of Nebraska Press, 2000).

15

VERY FINE IS MY VALENTINE

Nearly a century has gone by since Gertrude Stein began the extraordinary work of "taking apart language" in order to remake the world. Between 1903, when she began *The Making of Americans*, a heroic, intransigent, 1,000-page "history of everything that ever was or is or will be them, of everything that was or is or will be all of any one or all of them," and her death in 1946, Stein produced a body of experimental writing that in pathos, scope, and splendor surpasses that of any other American writer of her generation. The monumentality of this literary achievement comes increasingly into focus as the sentimental cult of her personality begins to wane. Numerous memoirs and biographies over the years have borne witness to Stein's comical, beguiling, richly cultivated nature. "A rose is a rose is a rose" has found its way on to notepaper and embroidered knickknacks, and women's bookstores display rack upon rack of Stein postcards, calendars, and stuffed toys. But as the decades pass, and the golden, involving afternoons at the salon on the rue de Fleurus gradually recede into the distance, Stein's real accomplishment stands out: she "changed language and writing," her latest editor, Ulla Dydo, observes, "for us all."

Yet anyone who admires Stein must at some point deal with the inevitable embarrassing question: will we ever find the time to read her? Edmund Wilson, though a booster of sorts, was doubtful. While recognizing in Stein a "literary personality of unmistakable originality and distinction" (and admiring the early story collection, *Three Lives*), he admitted to finding her avant-garde writings, with their coy aberrations of syntax and weird, painstaking repetitions, impossible to get through. "I confess that I have not read [*The Making of Americans*] all through," he wrote in *Axel's Castle*, "and I do not know whether it is possible to do so." "With sentences so regularly rhythmical, so needlessly prolix, so many times repeated and ending so often in present participles, the reader is all too soon in a state, not to follow the slow becoming of life, but simply to fall asleep."

Wilson quotes a representative passage:

> Some are needing themselves being a young one, an older one, a middle-
> aged one, an older one, an old one to be ones realizing what any one
> telling about different ways of feeling anything, of thinking an older one,
> an old one to be ones realizing what any one is telling. Some are needing
> themselves being a young one, an older one, a middle-aged one, an old
> one to be one being certain that it is a different thing inside in one being
> a young one, from being an older one, from being a middle-aged one,
> from being an older one, from being an old one.

Confronted with such "queer and boring" stuff, he opined, "most of us read her
less and less." Less and less, echoes the pigeon-hearted reader—alas alas.

Against such familiar grousing, Ulla Dydo issues a passionate cry on Stein's
behalf. Her marvelous *Stein Reader*, containing a wealth of neglected Stein plays,
portraits, poems, and stories—many of which have never been published before
or only in corrupted forms—is above all a kind of exhortation: that we read *all*
of Gertrude Stein, and read her intensely, word for word, with the same complex
attention we might devote to Woolf or James or Flaubert, or indeed, Mallarmé,
Pound, or John Ashbery.[1] That Dydo herself has done so is not to be doubted:
she describes, mind-bogglingly, reading aloud (with two fellow scholars) "every
word, every spelling and every punctuation mark of every text in this book" at
the Yale library in the summer of 1990. Certainly she is the first scholar to try to
reproduce Stein's texts exactly as Stein wrote them. She is scathing about the
slovenly editorial practices of earlier anthologists—of Carl Van Vechten, whose
Selected Writings of Gertrude Stein (1946) reproduced numerous textual errors introduced by Stein's companion, Alice B. Toklas, when she retyped Stein's manuscripts in 1937, and Richard Kostelanetz, who based the texts in *The Yale
Gertrude Stein* (1980) on eight posthumous (and error-laden) volumes published
by Yale in the 1950s. Instead of relying on existing printed versions—even those,
such as in *Operas and Plays* (1932), that Stein herself proofread—Dydo has returned whenever possible to the earliest manuscripts and typescripts. She has, in
addition, arranged Stein's works in order of date of composition rather than of
publication, so that the reader can track, as best as he or she is able, the evolution
of Stein's strange, Lego-like, yet imperishable style.

Dydo speaks of her anthology as a "primer" for learning to read Stein, and
indeed it is—in an almost kinesthetic sense. "It returns us," she says in her introduction, "to the schoolroom where Stein asks what the three Rs are and teaches
us to read in ways more fundamental than we had thought possible, more literal
than we had known." Like the eponymous subject of "Sitwell Edith Sitwell"
(1926), the reader must sit well, sit still, and learn "when to look when to look
up and around when to look down and around when to look down and around
when to look around and around and altered." The fact that Stein's experimental
writing is, as Dydo admits, a "hard school"—that it's difficult at times not to

fidget—does not concern her; only through an unflinching confrontation with "Stein the modernist innovator," not "Stein the personality," she repeatedly admonishes us, is anything worthwhile to be gained. Thus she eschews Stein's popular works, like *The Autobiography of Alice B. Toklas* (1933) and *Lectures in America* (1935)—in which Stein set out to explain her writing "from the outside," through anecdotes and simplified example—in favor of such dense "language inventions" as "A Long Gay Book" (1911–12), "Pink Melon Joy" (1915), "Capital Capitals" (1922), "Saints and Singing" (1923), and the recursive, brain-addling "Business in Baltimore" (1925).

Even when certain writings ("Two Women," "He and They, Hemingway," "How She Bowed to her Brother") seem to hold out some private reference, Dydo argues, we are not to regard them—at least at first—as part of a personalized mise-en-scène. The proper way to approach Stein's portraits is "through the words, not through what we know of the subject." She quotes Stein's baffling four-line sketch of the poet Apollinaire from 1913:

> Give known or pin ware.
> Fancy teethe, gas strips.
> Elbow elect, sour stout pore, pore caesar, pour state at.
> Leave eye lessons I. Leave I. Lessons. I. Leave I lessons, I.

The first sentence, Dydo observes, "appears to make no sense. Singly or grammatically, the words refer to nothing in the world that we recognize. So we return to the work as words or even to the letters that make them up. Reading aloud, we gradually begin to hear not the words we see in print but others immediately behind them. Eventually the two sets of spoken words collapse into one: 'Give known or pin ware' sounds 'Guillaume Apollinaire.' The four English-looking words turn into two French-sounding words, a name written as Stein heard it, transliterating and translating it separately into English sounds and words."

Dydo pauses for a brief tutorial on referentiality:

Of course, Guillaume Apollinaire is not even the real name but the pen name of Wilhelm Apollinaris Albertus de Kostroitzky (1880–1918), a Pole, not a Frenchman. In 1913, when this portrait was written, anyone hearing the Wilhelm behind Guillaume might also have heard the name of the German Kaiser Wilhelm, which now also enters this strange scenario of French and English word formations. The poet's and the kaiser's foreign name is transcribed by a foreigner into a foreign language that puts before the reader the subject-as-name, or the subject-as-words. Most of us say who we are by jumping from our name to a reference—a picture, a description, a photo, an anecdote. But Stein repeats the name as homophone until it puns and plays in the ear. Referentiality is back in a transcription more literal than we thought possible and more essential to the art of writing than visual appearances.

—then illustrates the kind of multilingual close reading that the portrait demands:

> Stein wrote in English, but around her was French, which she spoke, as she also spoke German. Her work, even in erroneous formations and misspellings, always includes possibilities of French and even German play extending the verbal world. The words "lesson," "leave," *leçons*, *laissons* are examples. Other French words perhaps segregating into English ones are *surtout*, an adverb meaning "chiefly" but also a noun meaning "overcoat"; *pour*, a preposition meaning "for" but also becoming the adjective or noun "poor," which translates into *pauvre*. Both these groups are behind "sour stout pore, pore caesar." That "pore caesar, pour state at" echoes *pour l'état* is easy to hear. And behind Caesar marches kaiser.

She concludes with a short clinic on Steinian grammar and the problem of exegesis:

> Grammar also determines understanding. The second line as printed in the *Reader*, relying on the manuscript rather than the typescript, reads "teethe," not "teeth." Did Stein want the verb or did she misspell the noun with a final -e? Did she revise, forget, or carelessly proofread her original word? Did Toklas in typing err or correct Stein's spelling? We cannot know. But if the word is "teethe," then "fancy teethe" becomes not an adjective and a noun but two verbs, unless it becomes the sentence "infants (or Fr. *enfants*) teethe." The readings we adopt here—perhaps more than one—affect the next syntactic configuration, "gas strips." Stein plays endlessly, but always with a purpose and always with her subject in her eye and ear.

By way of such freewheeling verbal associationism—akin to its subject's own formal experiments with language—the Apollinaire portrait becomes "a bilingual eye lesson that is also an ear lesson in new reading." "The anecdotes in the *Autobiography*," Dydo warns, "will not help us read it."

Yet this is hardly the whole story—as Dydo herself elsewhere seems to acknowledge. The schoolroom, with its atmosphere of high seriousness and occasional moral reprimand, inevitably gives way to the seductive pleasure world of the salon, and of the sunny French countryside around Bilignin, where Stein and Toklas summered between the wars. Perhaps the greatest strength of Dydo's collection, paradoxically, is how *sociable* it makes Stein seem, how approachable and informal and rusticated a writer—and how vivid a reporter on human life—even in her most rigorously avant-garde pieces. This is almost entirely due to Dydo's sympathetic editorial approach (little theoretical jargon, lots of contextual information) and richly informed sense of Stein's imaginative world. Stein the "personality" comes back here—with a charming, voluble vengeance—but in a manner that illuminates rather than distracts.

The process isn't entirely painless, of course: contending at the outset with a chunk of *The Making of Americans* (Dydo includes almost a hundred pages of it), the reader may decide that Edmund Wilson was right—it *is* unreadable. And there are moments at which one finds oneself temporarily blinded by what Dydo calls Stein's "wallpaper" effects, as in this sentence (taken at random) from "Business in Baltimore":

And yes and yes and and more and better and yes and yes and better and yes and yes and more and yes and yes and better and and yes and yes and better and yes and yes and more and yes and yes and best and better and yes and yes and most and more and yes and yes and yes and yes and better and yes and best and most and better and more and best and better and yes and yes and yes and yes and yes and yes and more and yes and yes and better and yes and yes and more and yes and yes.

But what strikes one most is how flexible and beautiful Stein's writing so often is, and how different—in mood and feeling—individual Stein pieces are from one another. There is a constant modulation in tone and scope. Some of the pieces here are little-known masterworks: the brooding, mysterious "Portrait of Constance Fletcher," with its intense reflection on family life and its limitations; the fanciful domestic farce "A List," with its references to tableware and fruit names and adulterous couples; the political satire, "Accents in Alsace," written in Alsace-Lorraine in the immediate aftermath of the First World War; the astonishing late drama, *Doctor Faustus Lights the Lights*, with its literary-philosophical tone and reverberant, choric, almost medieval plainsong effects. But every selection in one way or another reveals Stein's uncanny linguistic gift. Stein's great aim, writes Dydo, was to reproduce the world in language as intensely and accurately as possible: "Stein always wrote about real things. She did not arbitrarily compose words apart from actuality." The laborious grammatical convolutions, the obsessive reiteration, the perplexing non sequiturs, must all be read as revivifying gestures, as ways of forcing the reader to "begin again," to see the world in a new and more immediate way. What Dydo's anthology conveys so remarkably is precisely this: how grounded in actuality Stein's descriptive language was, and how many different effects—visual, musical, cognitive, and emotional—she was capable of producing with it.

Witness, for example, the lightsome, fluid uplift of "Orta or One Dancing"—Stein's tribute to her friend Isadora Duncan:

> In dancing she was dancing. She was dancing and dancing and in being
> that one the one dancing and dancing she was dancing and dancing. In
> dancing, dancing being existing, she was dancing, and in being one danc-
> ing dancing was being existing.

Or the parched evocation of summer heat in "Mildred's Thoughts," dedicated to Mildred Aldrich, an American journalist living on an old farm over-
looking the Marne valley:

> I have thought very much about heat. When it is really hot one does not
> go about in the day-time. It is just as well to drink water and even to buy
> water if necessary. So many people diminish. And flowers oh how can
> flowers be north. They are in the air. How often do we air everything.
> Seem to me sing to me seem to me all safe. Seem to me sit for me to me
> all Wednesday. I do not mind July. I do not mind Thursday or Friday or
> Saturday. I do not mind breath of horses. We know what we think.

Or the old-fashioned, discursive mode—turning to a kind of impromptu
nursery tale—of the final section of "A Valentine to Sherwood Anderson":

> Let us describe how they went. It was a windy night and the road al-
> though in excellent condition and extremely well-graded has many turn-
> ings and although the curves are not sharp the rise is considerable. It was
> a very windy night and some of the larger vehicles found it more prudent
> not to venture. In consequence some of those who had planned to go
> were unable to do so. Many others did go and there was a sacrifice, of
> what shall we, a sheep, a hen, a cock, a village, a ruin, and all that and
> then that having been blessed let us bless it.

Stein could be marvelously satirical at times, as in the comic, colloquial par-
ody of British speech inflections in "Pink Melon Joy," written in 1915, when
Stein and Toklas, stranded by the war, spent several months as house guests of
Alfred North Whitehead and his wife:

> We were right. We meant pale. We were wonderfully shattered. Why are
> we shattered. Only by an arrest of thought. I don't make it out. Hope
> there. Hope not. I didn't mean it. Please do be silly. I have forgotten the
> height of the table.
> It's infamous. To put a cold water bottle in a bed. It's steering.

And startlingly graphic—as in the voluptuous mimicry of the rhythms of lovemaking and release in "As a Wife Has a Cow—A Love Story," one of Stein's numerous love poems to Toklas:

> Have it as having having it as happening, happening to have it as having, having to have it as happening. Happening and have it as happening and having it happen as happening and having to have it happen as happening, and my wife has a cow as now, my wife having a cow as now, my wife having a cow as now and having a cow as now and having a cow and having a cow now, my wife as a cow and now. My wife has a cow.

Yet the brilliance of such effects notwithstanding, Stein's writing is something more than just an experiment in description. It is also inevitably a self-transcription. The autobiographical impulse is strong in Stein's writing—may in fact be its quintessential feature. And even Dydo, for all her hard-nosed strictures against reading for "personality," is forced to concede this. Her headnotes to each piece are masterworks of concise yet revealing biographical contextualization. She is illuminating on Stein's relationships with Hemingway, the Cone sisters, William James, Carl Van Vechten, Picasso, Juan Gris, Constance Fletcher, and the rest— and shows how these friends and associates make their appearances, like brightly colored effigies, in composition after composition. She is sympathetic to Stein's artistic struggles and her attempts to explain herself to an often uncomprehending world. ("A paragraph is why they went where they did.") She is informative about Stein's reading, and how surprisingly allusive much of Stein's writing is. (Shakespeare, Goethe, Dickens, Alexandre Dumas, Henry James, Mark Twain, and Henry Adams are only a few of the classic authors Stein cites or parodies.) Most important, she calls our attention to the ways in which Stein's writing is a kind of ongoing lyrical tribute to the muselike Alice Toklas, and to the passionate, if sometimes stormy, love that Stein and Toklas shared.

> Very fine is my valentine.
> Very fine and very mine.
> Very mine is my valentine, very mine and very fine.
> Very fine is my valentine and mine, very fine
>   very mine and mine is my valentine.

Toklas, Dydo repeatedly affirms, was the "one who made writing possible"—the secret addressee of virtually every Stein work.

The writer who comes most often to mind as one reads *The Stein Reader*, oddly enough, is Montaigne. Not only because Stein's work, like Montaigne's, so frequently evokes the French countryside. For someone so associated with modernist fragmentation, Stein is also the most pastoral of writers:

Look down and see a blue curtain and a white hall. A horse asleep lying surrounded by cows.

She is very happy and a farm. She is very happy and a farm. She is very happy and a farm. She is very happy and a farm. She is very happy and a farm.

One thinks of each writer inhabiting a peaceful, sun-drenched landscape—the Dordogne for Montaigne, the Rhône valley for Stein. Such places, in the 1570s and the 1930s, turn out not to be that far apart. In Stein, as in Montaigne, the same fondness for anecdote and curious lore, the same love of painting and color, the same enriching homoeroticism, the same sympathy for animals. And at times Stein seems to echo Montaigne directly, "When I play with my cat," Montaigne asked, "who knows whether she isn't amusing herself with me more than I am with her?" "I am I," Stein responds, "because my little dog knows me."

But the comparison also seems just because Stein, like Montaigne, is one of the great self-revealers of Western literature.

When I say that introductions mean that, when I feel that I have met them, when I am out aloud and by spacing I separate letters when I do this and I am melancholy I remember that rivers, only rivers have suppressed sounds. All the rest overflow. Piles are driven. Ice is free. Changes are by little spools, and toys are iron. Toys are iron whether or not they are Italian. This is so far. Please be at rest. I shall. I shall not speak for anybody. I shall do my duty. I shall establish that mile. I shall choose wonder. Be blest.

Each work of Stein's, like each of Montaigne's, is an exhilarating investigation of self, to the point that writing and personality, grammar and life, become indistinguishable, "Mon métier et mon art c'est vivre," wrote Montaigne. "I do not despair," wrote Stein in 1921; "read me easily." Dydo indeed shows us how to read her—if not always easily—with pleasure and gratitude.

note

1. Ulla E. Dydo, *A Stein Reader* (Evanston, Ill.: Northwestern University Press, 1993).

16

IF EVERYBODY HAD A WADLEY

hangelings, centaurs, ogres, and elves may no longer inhabit the earth,
but occasionally we run into their descendants: people so monstrous, in-
candescent, or freakishly *themselves* that only a quasi-supernatural description
seems to do them justice. In the twentieth century they come in all shapes and
sizes—from the obvious ghouls and werewolves (Rasputin, Adolf Hitler, Idi
Amin, Jeffrey Dahmer); to various midrank demigods and unicorn-people (T. E.
Lawrence, Ludwig Wittgenstein, Che Guevara, Greta Garbo, Edith Sitwell, JFK,
Maria Callas, Howard Hughes, Andy Warhol, Glenn Gould, the late Princess of
Wales); down to minor bog sprites such as Eartha Kitt, Cher, or Quentin Crisp.
(Such lists are infinitely expandable.) What links each of these disparate individuals is a singularity so tangible as to border on the uncanny. We register each as a
unique assemblage of moral and psychic tics: and each, in turn, seems to connect
us to some alternative world. We are deeply impressed when one of them weakens and dies.

The sort of singularity I am talking about is often accompanied by celebrity:
one's palpable strangeness makes one famous. Not always, of course; certain
mute inglorious oddballs no doubt spend all their days in obscurity—Una-
bombers without typewriters—while others flash out for a time then disappear.
Marion Barbara ("Joe") Carstairs, the subject of Kate Summerscale's vastly entertaining recent biography, *The Queen of Whale Cay*, would seem to fall into the
latter category.[1] In the twenties, Carstairs (1900–93) was briefly yet wildly celebrated as the "fastest woman on water"—Britain's premier speedboat racer, win-
ner of the Duke of York's Trophy, and world record holder in the
one-and-a-half-liter class. Voraciously homosexual in private life, Carstairs
dressed like a beautiful man, smoked cigars, and was pursued from race to race
by a gaggle of female fans. (Sir Malcolm Campbell of *Bluebird* fame called her—
apparently without irony—"the greatest sportsman I know.") Special "friends"
included the lesbian actresses Tallulah Bankhead and Gwen Farrar; and as the

Evening News reported in 1925, Carstairs could "dance a Charleston which few people can partner."

By 1934, however, Carstairs had almost completely fallen from view. With several helpful millions inherited from her American mother, scion of the Standard Oil Company, she bought a sparsely populated island in the outer Bahamas and ruled over it for the next forty years in magnificent yet near-total isolation. True, a few celebrities continued to visit: the duke and duchess of Windsor, Marlene Dietrich (Carstairs's lover in 1938–39), and the cabaret singer Mabel Mercer, along with the occasional reporter from *Life* or the *Saturday Evening Post*. But by the 1960s Carstairs was all but forgotten—known only, outside the Bahamas, to a handful of British and American lesbians, in whose doting hearts, pumping away like so many little speedboat engines, her glamorous feats were kept alive. I first read about her in a ragged back number of *The Ladder*, the pioneering lesbian magazine published privately in the United States in the 1950s and 1960s. There, in a breathless personality profile ("Her Own Private World") she was described as "possibly the 20th Century's most fabulous woman." Even then, however, one had the sense of a mythical-beast-sighting, which the accompanying grainy photographs—showing Carstairs playing tennis, riding a motorcycle, and patroling the solitary reaches of her island, like a blonde Adonis in shorts—did little to dispel. As Kate Summerscale puts it, there was something so odd about Carstairs it was almost as if she *had* to be forgotten: "her projects were so outlandish that they took her beyond fame and notoriety to obscurity."

Summerscale's own interest in Carstairs was sparked, she tells us, when she was assigned to write Carstairs's obituary for the *Daily Telegraph* in 1993. (Carstairs almost lived out the century; she was born in 1900.) Conversations with Carstairs's surviving friends, lovers, and relations led Summerscale to a set of tape recordings that Carstairs made in the 1970s when she was contemplating having someone ghostwrite her autobiography. That project came to naught—Carstairs was resistant to any real self-examination—but the tapes convinced Summerscale that even after this "self-made man" had retreated from the public eye, she still longed for applause and commemoration:

> I imagined that Joe Carstairs hoped on her death to be left, like the island, to return to wilderness. Yet I also knew that Joe had wanted her extraordinary exploits to be celebrated. As much as she sought exile, she sought recognition. I thought she would be glad to have a book written about her; it was a question of what kind of book.

The "kind of book" Summerscale has produced is perhaps not what Carstairs would have relished—*The Queen of Whale Cay* is as sly, delicate, and probing as its subject was unsubtle, butch, and incurious—but it is nonetheless an eloquent tribute to Carstairs's weird, larger-than-life, even *daemonic*, persona.

The book succeeds so well, paradoxically, precisely because the biographer does not attempt to naturalize or explain away her subject's manifold eccentricities. Certainly the elements of mystery, omen, and arabesque were there from the beginning. No one is quite sure who Carstairs's father was: he may or may not have been Albert Carstairs, a Scottish army officer who disappeared before her birth in London in 1900. Her volatile, oil heiress mother—subsequently a heroin addict and dabbler in bizarre rejuvenation therapies—seems not to have paid much attention to the odd little homunculus to whom she had given birth. ("I was never a little girl," Carstairs said later; "I came out of the womb queer.") And hardly surprisingly Carstairs grew up with a changeling indifference to her wealthy family. In 1905, while still a toddler, she was flung from the back of a bolting camel in the London Zoo, knocked out, and after regaining consciousness, nicknamed "Tuffy." As an adult she liked to speak of this deliverance as a kind of symbolic death and rebirth—the moment at which her real life began. By way of such personal mythmaking, Summerscale suggests, Carstairs "threw off the feminine, proper names of the old century and of her family's choosing," undid "the bonds of parentage and gender," and assumed "the power of self-creation." Later in life Carstairs claimed not to know her father's name and strangely mistook her mother's. After christening a series of record-setting speedboats after her in the 1920s—*Estelle I, II,* and *III*—Carstairs announced that she had belatedly discovered that her mother's name was really Evelyn.

After a brief period at a boarding school in Connecticut, Carstairs experienced her first real liberation. Financed by the family trusts, she made her way in 1916 to the battlefields of France, where she drove an ambulance for the American Red Cross. Between runs to the trenches she shared a flat in Montparnasse with several other girl drivers, one of whom, Dolly Wilde, louche niece of Oscar and member of the expatriate lesbian circle around Natalie Barney, became an early and important love. Wilde introduced "Joe" (as she was now known) to European art and culture, though it must be said that the ultra-athletic Carstairs remained throughout her life largely indifferent to mental or aesthetic exercises. Her personality was basically feral and unlettered, and despite a short introspective phase in her forties when she collaborated with another of her lovers on some moody sapphic verses—

> The lustful lungings of the masses
> Trundling home perambulators,
> Striving to increase the nation—
> Indiscriminate copulators.

is a representative sample—"Joe" was to remain all her life a creature of action and not words.

Following the Armistice and a stint driving lorries for the British forces in

Ireland, Carstairs returned to northern France, where she assisted in the grisly work of reburying thousands of British soldiers who had been killed in the war and placed in temporary graves. This horrifying task seems not to have affected her spirits adversely; on the contrary, like many rebellious women of her era, she seems to have been curiously enlivened by the spectacle of mass (male) destruction. "If the men who had served in the Great War were exhausted and depleted," observes Summerscale, women like Joe "returned replenished, brimming with vigour and ambition." For Carstairs the war was a kind of *donnée*, the necessary catastrophe upon which much of her subsequent career—as sporting rival to men and virile lover of women—depended.

In 1920, upon receiving an inheritance of $200,000 a year, Carstairs opened the X Garage, a fashionable London chauffeur service, the gimmick of which was to use all female drivers. When not driving her clients around, she was busy consolidating her reputation as she-male-about-town. She cut her hair in an Eton crop and took to wearing ties and cufflinks and the loose men's trousers known as Oxford bags. Several notable women succumbed to her at this time—notably Bankhead, about to star in Noël Coward's *Fallen Angels*, and the exotic Argentinian-American revue performer Teddie Gerard. The comedian Bea Lillie, then making her name as a male impersonator on the London stage ("I was known as the best-dressed man in London") was another close friend.

A lover of the mid-1920s, a hard-drinking, "tough-faced" young secretary named Ruth Baldwin, was responsible for what is unquestionably one of the most peculiar elements in Carstairs's story. Around the same time that Carstairs began to take an interest in speedboat racing—she closed the X Garage and commissioned her first hydroplanes in 1925—Baldwin gave Carstairs a weird little man-doll, just over a foot long, made out of leather by the German toy-makers Stieff. Dubbing him "Lord Tod Wadley," Carstairs immediately made him the object of an extraordinary, often comical, private cult. She spoke of Wadley as her dearest friend; had expensive outfits made for him on Savile Row; ordered tiny leather shoes for him from Italy; and placed his name, along with her own, on a plaque over the front door of her flat in Chelsea. After her racing exploits had made her internationally famous, she posed for publicity photographs with the quizzical "Lord Tod" perched dashingly on her shoulder.

Wadley soon developed his own mock-life, which ran in tandem with Carstairs's own. The admirably deadpan Summerscale reports that in 1929 one of Carstairs's friends "dummied up a magazine feature in which Wadley was pictured yachting, riding, taking cocktails, writing a novel and sitting for a studio portrait"—

In one photograph he is depicted reclining among foliage, spectacles perched on the top of his head, empty bottles strewn about him and an open book lying by his side. Beneath runs the caption: "I am a thorough student, and when I feel I must have solitude, I take a day in the country—with my books." Another caption reads: "'Hullo! My dear fellow': Lord Tod Wadley greets a friend."

Wadley functioned for Carstairs as mascot, fetish, and alter ego—as a miniature externalization of her own glamorous, if cartoonish, nature. "'We're like one,' Joe said. 'He's me and I'm him. It's a marvellous thing. If everybody had a Wadley there'd be less sadness in the world.'"

Though Wadley was too precious to be taken on the water, Carstairs held him responsible—totemlike—for all of her racing victories, beginning with the one that made her name: the duke of York's race in 1926. This was a brilliant win: in a heroic finish, during which her propeller got accidentally caught by a submerged rope and she had to cut herself free while also controlling her wildly juddering balsa wood craft, she defeated the world-class German racer Krueger and became an instant national heroine. ("Shingled Girl Beats German," was the *Daily Mail*'s headline the next day.) As she piled up victory after victory over the next two years—the Royal Motor Yacht Club International Race, the *Daily Telegraph* Cup, the Bestise Cup, and the Lucina Cup—the press had a heyday celebrating "a new type of river girl . . . keen-eyed and close-shingled," "Miss M.B. Carstairs, foremost motor-boat enthusiast in Britain."

Yet these triumphs, though spectacular, were relatively short-lived. In 1928 Carstairs commissioned an exorbitantly expensive speedboat, the *Jack Stripes,* which she hoped to race across the Atlantic at 50–60 mph. (As Summerscale reminds us, setting speed and distance records on land, air, and water had become a kind of international mania in the 1920s; Carstairs was undoubtedly inspired in part by Lindbergh's monoplane crossing the previous year.) The *Jack Stripes* foundered on its first run in the English Channel, however ("bucking like an insane bronco"), and the plan had to be scrapped. This disappointment was subsequently compounded by three successive losses in the Harmsworth British International Cup, the most prestigious of all motorboat races. In one of these trials Carstairs and her engineer were thrown from their plunging boat and nearly killed. Carstairs maintained her usual aplomb—when she surfaced after the crash she was still chewing her gum—but the danger had been great. "Other racing boats were coming at us," she later said; "I thought we'd get our heads taken off." By 1930 not even the adoring women who sent her provocative pictures of themselves seemed enough to assuage her professional frustration.

At the same time it was becoming more and more difficult to be what she was: an imperturbably mannish woman. In the wake of the obscenity trial of Radclyffe Hall's lesbian novel *The Well of Loneliness* in 1928, there was widespread public backlash against supposed "inverts" and sex deviants. The editor of the *Sunday Express* publicly excoriated homosexuality as a pestilence threatening to destroy social life. In the new repressive moral climate, Carstairs, like other unconventional women of the time, came increasingly under suspicion. Reporters began to comment critically on her tattoos and swearing and indelicate mannerisms: "she smokes incessantly," wrote one in 1930, "not with languid feminine grace, but with the sharp decisive gestures a man uses." The last straw seems to have come for her during the run-up to her final Harmsworth race, when an American newspaper disparaged her pet, Lord Tod Wadley, as "an absurd manikin."

Escape from such trials came dramatically. In 1933 Carstairs spotted an advertisement for Whale Cay, a tiny island in the British West Indies thirty miles northwest of Nassau and ninety miles east of Miami. After visiting and chatting with its two residents—a black lighthouse keeper and his wife—she bought the island outright for $40,000. "I am going to live surrounded only by coloured people," she told the press: "I am not even taking a motor car, for when I bought the island there were no roads. Now I am building roads and a residence, but my only means of transport will be two ten-foot dinghies. The island is about 1,000 acres in extent and is nine miles long. I cannot say if I will ever return."

She did not. And hence the most uncanny of Carstairs's changeling turns: her transformation into the self-appointed "Boss" of Whale Cay. The island had beckoned to her, she said, in a kind of sublime vision ("When I saw the island I thought this is what I must do. . . . Something great will come of it") and she threw herself into rescuing it. With the help of cheap labor from nearby islands—unemployment was endemic in the pre-tourist West Indies of the 1930s—she cleared the land of its dense vegetation, laid out a lavish plantation for herself and her lovers (the Great House), and built cottages for her workers and their families. The local population grew to several hundred residents. She built a dock, a school, a church, a fish cannery, and a general store. In the late thirties she bought several neighboring islands too—primarily to serve as markets for the various goods produced by Whale Cay farmers and craftsmen.

Like a female Kurtz, Carstairs dominated her black subjects by sheer force of personality. Many of them were believers in *obeah*, a form of voodoo religion brought by African slaves to the Caribbean in the eighteenth and nineteenth centuries. On one occasion, while clearing a road with some of her men soon after her arrival on the island, Carstairs killed a snake by hurling her knife at it. "And by God I cut that goddamn snake's head right off." The feat was taken as an omen and ever after, she told friends later, the native men followed her with unstinting devotion. Lord Tod Wadley's conspicuous presence in her life—he sat on her lap as she tooled around the island on her motorbike—likewise encouraged popular faith in her magical powers. As Summerscale reports, the residents of Whale Cay believed the perky little doll to be her "witchcraft man, able to discover and disclose their secrets." With Wadley's help, Carstairs made laws and delivered judgments (adultery and alcohol were banned on the island); officiated at marriages and births (she assumed the privilege of naming all children born on Whale Cay); established youth camps; and detained island miscreants with the help of a private militia, which she had had outfitted with uniforms and machetes.

For the most part the colonial authorities in Nassau regarded Carstairs's seigneurship with complacency: in 1940, the duke of Windsor, recently appointed wartime governor of the Bahamas to keep him as far away from Europe and real power as possible, paid an official visit to Whale Cay and was received by Joe with gratifying pomp. He was accompanied by his duchess, in whom the renegade Carstairs seems to have found a kindred spirit:

> Joe showed them her boats in the dock, and while the Duke was on the deck of one of the yachts she took the Duchess into the cabin. The Duchess saw Wadley. "Who is *that?*" she asked (Joe was impressed that she said "who" rather than "what"). Joe introduced her: "That's my boy, that's Wadley." "My God," said the Duchess, "he's just like my husband."

Which isn't to say all was sobriety on Whale Cay. Up at the Great House (where the adultery and alcohol ban was decidedly not in effect), Carstairs continued to entertain friends and paramours and carry on much as she had done in London. Dietrich visited several times around 1940; though they parted acrimoniously, Carstairs left her a Whale Cay beach in her will. A succession of other girlfriends came and went: Charlotte, Blanche, Helen, Jackki, Jorie, and the exquisite Mabs, "a manicurist with a small green scorpion tattoo." Several of Carstairs's lovers were black, though none, as it happened, Bahamian; in her intimate life Carstairs preferred the sophisticated women she encountered on annual holiday trips to New York and the Riviera to local beauties. No such scruples inhibited Father Julian Henshaw, the Firbankian priest Carstairs brought in from Capri to preside over the spiritual life of the island: on his merry way to drinking and fox-trotting himself to death, he delighted in pederastic idylls with his Whale Cay choir boys.

As the years wore on, however, Carstairs began to retreat more and more into reclusive eccentricity. In the 1950s, as her health broke down, she became increasingly unable to sustain the illusions of intransigent manliness. Perhaps by way of compensation Wadley's exploits became more and more grandiose. In the 1960s Carstairs claimed that Wadley had known Jack Kennedy ("They went to the Bay of Pigs together. . . . He had a *tremendous* liking for him"), had been a moon astronaut, and had had numerous wives, mistresses, and children. Yet even these fancies failed to stop the clock. With the rise of Bahamian nationalism Carstairs became disenchanted with her Whale Cay subjects, who were turning restive and disobedient. (While taking a walk one day she was horrified to see two of them copulating openly under a palm tree.) In 1975 she sold the island for $1 million and moved to Miami. There and on Long Island she lived out the rest of her life, watching wild animal shows and boxing on television (she idolized George Foreman), writing checks for obscure philanthropic causes, and tending to Wadley and his friends and associates—a vast army of dolls and stuffed animals given to her over the years by various girlfriends. When she died in 1993 she and Wadley were cremated together and their ashes placed in a single grave.

Why commemorate the life of such a hallucinatory being? Summerscale, as noted, refrains from analyzing Carstairs overmuch; nor does she try to extract from her life any larger cultural meaning or sociopolitical message. What commentary Summerscale provides is understated and of a literary and mythopoetic cast—as if she were describing a character out of Ovid's *Metamorphoses* or Perrault's fairy tales. Thus she explicates Carstairs's fixation on Lord Tod Wadley by way of a suitably creepy passage from Djuna Barnes's 1936 lesbian novel *Nightwood*:

> In *Nightwood*, the narrator reflects on the significance of the doll given to her by her girlfriend, Robin. "When a woman gives [a doll] to a woman," she writes, "it's the life they cannot have, it is their child, sacred and profane. . . . Sometimes if [Robin] got tight by evening, I would find her standing in the middle of the room, in boy's clothes, rocking from foot to foot, holding the doll she had given us—'our child'—high above her head."

Like the doll in Barnes's novel, Summerscale suggests, Wadley too was "a mock-child," a "sacred and profane earnest" of the love between Carstairs and her lover of the 1920s, Ruth Baldwin, whose death by drug overdose in 1937 seems to have affected Carstairs more than any other private loss.

Elsewhere Summerscale compares Carstairs to the hero of J. M. Barrie's *Peter Pan*, finding in her dream of perpetual boyishness—she exercised fiercely all her life to "ward off womanliness"—and yearning for a secret hideaway a connection with Barrie's fantastic sprite:

> As Wadley was an image of her soul, Whale Cay was its map. The island, Joe believed, was her own creation: "I didn't make improvements," she pointed out impatiently. "There was nothing there. I made just what I wanted." By inventing a counter-kingdom, a fantasy world in which to live, she defied the censures and strictures of the adult world. In 1941 she was shunned against by that world [she had offered to help with the war effort and had been refused] and once again she retreated to her Neverland. Whale Cay was a region of her self, and so it had no chronology. Here she could be a boy who never had to grow up.

Summerscale's point is bizarrely reinforced by Carstairs's startling resemblance in photographs to the musical comedy star Mary Martin—the first screen Peter Pan and Hollywood's reigning sapphic icon, with Garbo and Dietrich, in the 1940s and 1950s.

Perhaps most interestingly Summerscale refuses to read any kind of heroism—mock or otherwise—into Carstairs's sexual dissidence. She is not concerned with rehabilitating Carstairs for potential groupies, whether feminist or lesbian or both. Carstairs was hardly a feminist, she avers: "after all, the principle by which she defined herself was male." But neither should her life be treated as an exemplary lesbian story: "Joe Carstairs was too singular and strange to be representative of anything other than herself."

One might challenge Summerscale on this last: surely the first half of Carstairs's life offers a revealing glimpse, at the very least, into the largely unexplored world of wealthy Anglo-American lesbian culture between the wars. However intermittently, Carstairs was part of an international lesbian clique—*soignée*, impudent, privileged, and eminently creative—becoming ever more visible in Britain, France, Italy, and the United States in the 1920s and 1930s. The links between Carstairs and various prominent figures in this extraordinary sapphic society—Radclyffe Hall, Natalie Barney, Vita Sackville-West, Gertrude Stein, Mercedes de Acosta, Gluck, Djuna Barnes, Ida Rubinstein, Romaine Brooks, Elsie de Wolfe, Eileen Gray, Wanda Landowksa, Winaretta Singer, Rose O'Neill, Violet Trefusis, Janet Flanner, and numerous others—demand further investigation.

And odd as it might sound, one might wish to register Carstairs's audacious achievements as lesbian seductress. Summerscale estimates that Carstairs had some 120 lovers, many of whose photographs are reproduced in *The Queen of Whale Cay*. Some of these women were undoubtedly brief flings ("You let them sleep in the *bed* with you afterwards?" she once asked a male friend). Yet when pressed, she would acknowledge she had always been sensational between the sheets: "I was made to think so. Everybody else thought so, so I thought so too. *I* would have liked me." Our culture has no term of awe for women who make love *heroically*: Don Juan and Casanova remain strictly masculine archetypes. Needless to say, heterosexual women get scant public appreciation for their erotic talents: the most gifted Venus or *grande horizontale* receives ambiguous praise at best. Lesbians fare even worse: no woman in Western culture, including the great Sappho herself, has ever won popular acclaim for her skill at bringing other *women* to sexual ecstasy.

With Carstairs, however, we are in the presence of world-class charm: Bedroom Eyes for the Ages. Of extraordinary interest is the as-yet unwritten history of twentieth-century lesbian libertinism: witness the tantalizing vignettes we have of the young Elizabeth Bishop on Key West, for example, in bed with Billie Holiday; or Natalie Barney, who took her last lover at the age of eighty; or Vita

Sackville-West, one of whose lovers cherished the marks on her inner thighs left by Vita's earrings. Carstairs would undoubtedly figure nobly in such a history—that is, if the history itself were considered noble. Her true artistry, one suspects, lay in her amorosity, which she approached as a vocation, with something akin to genius.

Yet perhaps Summerscale is right in the end not to turn her subject into allegory. The value of a life such as Carstairs's lies ultimately in its preposterousness—the sheer exuberance of its strangeness and distance from the everyday. A figure as singular as Carstairs assails one's sensibilities the way the god Pan might were he suddenly to materialize in one's back garden. One would be tempted to pretend one hadn't seen him, to explain him away as some kind of optical illusion—a trick of light against the shrubbery. For sanity's sake, one might even decide to forget him. But such luminescent creatures have a way of returning to view—of reminding us, in their pathos, of all the things we haven't done, and the things we never will.

note

1. Kate Summerscale, *The Queen of Whale Cay: The Eccentric Story of "Joe" Carstairs, Fastest Woman on Water* (London: Fourth Estate, 1997).

17

NIGHT AND DAY

Was Cole Porter human? Friends (and enemies) often spoke of him as if he were something else—a kind of Puck or sprite or wind-up toy, possessed of eerie and mischievous gifts. After spotting him in the bar of the Paris Ritz, sipping Pernod and composing "his devastating little rhymes," Beverley Nichols, who didn't like him, compared the songwriter to a "startled leprechaun." Moss Hart, his collaborator on the musical *Seven Lively Arts*, found him "impish." "A little human music box" was Ben Hecht's phrase, while Agnes de Mille, choreographer of *Nymph Errant*, spoke of the strange, mincing way Porter walked ("very gingerly, with tiny steps") and thought his head looked like a doll's. Even Robert Kimball, editor of *The Complete Lyrics of Cole Porter*, speaks of the composer's "mascot-like head," as if he were a ventriloquist's dummy.

This last image—of a miniature man-doll, perched uncannily on someone's lap—seems painfully apt. After a near-fatal riding accident on Long Island in 1937, in which a frightened horse rolled on him and crushed both his legs, the permanently lamed Porter had to be carried virtually everywhere by his valet Paul Sylvain. Several photographs of Porter from the 1940s and 1950s, reproduced in William McBrien's new biography, show him being hefted about—a tiny monkey in a tuxedo—by the beefy, black-haired manservant.[1]

For all his brilliance, his success, and his charm—Oscar Levant called him the "rich boy who made good"—Porter himself seems to have wondered at times about his own humanity. Many of his songs are autobiographical—and as starkly self-interrogating as anything by Schubert. One of the more disturbing has to be "I'm a Gigolo," a frigid little ditty that Porter recorded in New York in 1935:

> I should like you all to know,
> I'm a famous gigolo.
> And of lavender, my nature's got just a dash in it.
> As I'm slightly undersexed,

> You will always find me next
> To some dowager who's wealthy rather than passionate.

The composer's famously arch declamation and twinkling arpeggios cannot hide, however, a growing malaise:

> Go to one of those nightclub places
> And you'll find me stretching my braces
> Pushing ladies with lifted faces
> 'round the floor.
> But I must confess to you
> There are moments when I'm blue.
> And I ask myself whatever I do it for.

With the turn to the refrain, the music shifts abruptly to the minor and gets slow and creepy and harmonically unsettled—like something, indeed, out of *Winterreise*. The piano tapping out a sinister chromatic bass, Porter's voice takes on a spectral, whited-out quality, even as he limns his character's moral emptiness:

> I'm a flower that blooms in the winter,
> Sinking deeper and deeper in "snow."
> I'm a baby who has
> No mother but jazz,
> I'm a gigolo.
> Ev'ry morning, when labor is over,
> To my sweet-scented lodgings I go,
> Take the glass from the shelf
> And look at myself,
> I'm a gigolo.

A wan thought of "stocks and bonds" from "faded blonds"—"ev'ry twenty-fifth of December"—cheers the singer momentarily, but he quickly falls back into psychic desuetude:

> Still I'm just a pet
> That men forget
> And only tailors remember.

In the song's finale, when he declares, unconvincingly, how glad he is to be a gigolo, the tinny music seems to mock him, winding down slowly, like a failing clock as it weakens and stops.

The song is full of self-revelation—from the incriminating "dash" of lavender to the prodigal faded blondes. In 1919, as he was launching his career as a song-writer and a playboy in the ballrooms and the cafés of postwar Paris, the twenty-eight-year-old Porter, the Yale-educated scion of a well-to-do family in Peru, Indiana, had married Linda Lee Thomas, an invalidish, exorbitantly wealthy society divorcée fifteen years his senior. Theirs was the classic marriage of convenience. He was homosexual, promiscuously so; she was lonely and apparently asexual. (Despite popular rumors to the contrary, says William McBrien, there is no evidence that Linda was herself a lesbian.)

At the time of their marriage he was already syphilitic. To say that Linda bought Porter outright puts it too strongly; they seem genuinely to have loved each other, even as each sought in the other a desirable fashion accessory. Yet it is undoubtedly the case that Linda's millions brought Porter a far greater social prominence than he might have achieved on his own, along with a constant supply of houses, cars, swimming pools, and handsome young masseurs. And he had plenty of dough—his and hers—left over for "snow," the high-grade cocaine that he was wont to snort between glasses of champagne and frenetic spells at the piano.

Also palpable in "I'm a Gigolo," however, is the narrator's chilly awareness of his own monstrosity. He is unnatural (a flower that blooms in the winter), motherless, sexually abject. When he looks at himself in the mirror, after a night of fulsome labors, he seems to ape, grotesquely, a host of female mirror-scenes in European literature and art: the bemused looking-glass gaze of the Rokeby Venus; the glance of self-appraisal that the heroine Belinda casts upon herself as she completes her toilette in the opening verses of *The Rape of the Lock*; the Marschallin's poignant self-inspection, in the famous scene in *Der Rosenkavalier*, in which she realizes that she is growing old and will inevitably lose her handsome young lover. When Porter's narrator looks in the mirror, however, there is nothing human to be seen—no man nor woman either—just a petted, peripheral, and hybrid thing: halfway to human, but always falling short.

As the song, so the man. Even in the somewhat occluded version provided by McBrien, Porter's life story exposes a spirit haunted by a comparable sense of incompleteness, superfluity, and marginality. "I'm a toy balloon that's fated soon to pop," goes one of Porter's most celebrated lyrics, and he went about life with the brittle incertitude of one fundamentally unsure of his place in the world.

The malaise seems to have been established early on. Porter's childhood was pampered, but a possessive mother and distant father set up a contradictory rhythm in his soul. His mother, "the Great Katie," doted on him, and would treat him as her personal emotional appendage until her death at ninety in 1952. In painful contrast, his father, a stolid Midwestern businessman, seemed altogether unmoved by his son's obvious, if forward, gifts. (Watching a silent film at the cinema at the age of eight, the pixieish Porter climbed uninvited onto the stage during a melodramatic scene and played a bouncy honky-tonk number on the stage piano until he was ejected.) After being packed off to boarding school in Worcester, Massachusetts, in 1905, Porter had little to do with his father, who died in 1927, having never, it seems, gotten the point. The bored, jaded, too-tired-to-be-bothered speakers who inhabit so many of Porter's songs may owe something to Sam Porter's killing lack of interest in his strange yet musically prodigious offspring.

Porter tried to resolve the psychic unease of family life through performance—by turning himself into the life of the party. From adolescence onward he was attracted by loud, boisterous groups and attached himself to them with antic sociability. He had begun performing in public as a child; his summer job, in his teens, was singing and playing the piano on a steamship that plied the waters of Lake Maxinkuckee, a resort near his home in Peru. (Later in life, one of Porter's friends advanced the curious theory that the exaggerated, even clumsy piano rhythms found in Porter's recordings of his own songs—the right hand in his 1934 version of "You're the Top" is positively hiccupy in its syncopation—came from the fact that he learned to project his songs to the accompaniment of pounding steamship engines.)

At Yale, where he matriculated in 1909, Porter studied little—preferring instead to produce college theatricals, frolic with the cheerleading squad, and concoct fizzy pep songs for the football team. However risible or camp, the very titles of his songs from this period bespeak a yearning for corporate acceptance and connection—"I Want to Be a Yale Boy," "If I Were Only a Football Man," "I Want to Be Married (To a Delta Kappa Epsilon Man)." To be at the center of things, even if it meant serving as boy-mascot or male cocotte, was to feel part of a living and breathing human enterprise.

The same impulses animated him as he moved forward into the most volatile and momentous period of his life. After graduation from Yale and an unsuccessful stint at Harvard Law School (his father had hoped he would go into mining or farming), he occupied himself with party-going, jaunts to Europe, and writing amateur musical revues for the Yale Dramatic Association. In 1916, at the suggestion of the pioneering Broadway producer Bessie Marbury, who had recognized his budding talents, he collaborated on his first full-scale musical, the now-obscure *See America First*. Despite droll song lyrics reminiscent of Gilbert and Sullivan—an obvious and early influence on Porter—the show closed after fifteen performances. Soon after this humiliation—the critics had written "Don't see *America First*"—Porter decamped for France, then in the throes of war, as a soldier-volunteer.

Legend has it that Porter served during World War I in the French Foreign Legion, though his new biographer suggests that whatever army service he actually performed (he seems to have worked mainly for a Franco-American relief agency) was hardly onerous. And even before he was out of uniform Porter was making the rounds of cafés, supper clubs, and Parisian drawing rooms, using his piano playing as an entrée into fashionable society. After the Armistice, marriage to Linda, and on into the mid-1920s, he continued this somewhat feckless existence, shuttling back and forth between Paris and the Lido in Venice, where he was part of a fast-living set that included the celebrated decorator Elsie de Wolfe (later Lady Mendl), Gerald and Sara Murphy, the Princess di San Faustino, Diana Vreeland, Consuelo Vanderbilt, the actor Monty Woolley, the black cabaret singer Bricktop, and the bizarre Elsa Maxwell—an obese, mustachioed lesbian from California who parlayed a brazen skill for social climbing, party organizing, and gossip-mongering into fortune and fame as a society columnist and a life-long celebrity-chaser.

After contributing songs to various revues in London and New York, Porter had his first big break in 1928 with the "musi-comedy" *Paris*, starring Irene Bordoni. Critics went gaga, and the show's celebrated signature tune, "Let's Do It, Let's Fall in Love," became a smash hit. (The latter—in which centipedes, kangaroos, schools of cod, guinea pigs, giraffes, and "pekineses at the Ritz" all "do it" with aplomb—was the first in a series of what one critic later dubbed Porter's "habits of rabbits" songs.)

Over the next decade this starry triumph was repeated many times, as Porter tossed off a string of masterpieces for various hit shows in London and on Broadway: "Let's Misbehave," "Looking at You," "What Is This Thing Called Love?" (*Wake Up and Dream*, 1929); "You Do Something to Me" (*Fifty Million Frenchmen*, 1929); "I'm Getting Myself Ready for You," "Love for Sale" (*The New Yorkers*, 1930); "After You, Who?" "Night and Day" (*The Gay Divorcee*, 1932); "I Get a Kick Out of You," "All Through the Night," "You're the Top," "Anything Goes" (*Anything Goes*, 1934); "Don't Fence Me In" (*Adios, Argentina*, 1934–35); "When Love Comes Your Way," "Begin the Beguine," "Just One of Those Things" (*Jubilee*, 1935); "Easy to Love," "I've Got You Under My Skin" (*Born to Dance*, 1936); "Down in the Depths," "It's De-Lovely" (*Red, Hot and Blue*, 1936); "In the Still of the Night" (*Rosalie*, 1937); "Get Out of Town," "My Heart Belongs to Daddy" (*Leave It to Me*, 1938); "I Concentrate on You" (*Broadway Melody of 1940*, 1939).

In 1937, with rumors of a European war intensifying, the Porters sold the lavish apartment in Paris where they had lived for over a decade and moved back to New York. Porter threw himself again into nonstop composing and socializing. Following his terrible horse-riding accident—he would undergo thirty operations on his legs before finally submitting to the amputation of his right leg in 1958—his creative pace slackened slightly, but only temporarily. Within a few months he was back at the piano, producing songs for *Du Barry Was a Lady* (1939), *Panama Hattie* (1940), *You'll Never Get Rich* and *Let's Face It* (1941), and *Something for the Boys* (1943). He continued to write for musicals into the 1950s. The late yet still ebullient *Kiss Me, Kate*, which Auden thought superior to the work on which it was based—Shakespeare's *The Taming of the Shrew*—was in fact Porter's greatest box-office success, running for 1,077 performances between 1948 and 1951.

Starting in the early 1940s Porter also worked in Hollywood, composing scores for films such as *Something to Shout About* (1943), *The Pirate* (1948), and *High Society* (1956). Hollywood, in the form of Jack Warner, repaid the compliment by making *Night and Day* (1946), a stilted, fanciful, and utterly mawkish biopic about him, starring Cary Grant and Alexis Smith. The timing of this sentimental fable could hardly have been more ironic. Even as the film idealized the cozy domestic life of Cole and Linda, the principals (who spent most of their time apart anyway) were now permanently estranged and living in separate residences: Porter in Los Angeles, where he presided over weekly pool-and-sex parties for young actors and off-duty servicemen at his house on Rockingham Drive, Linda in New York, where she was spending increasing amounts of time—on account of her worsening emphysema—in an iron lung at the Waldorf. Out of this she would clamber periodically in order to smoke cigarettes, drink martinis, and have her gowns fitted by Mainbocher.

Porter's last years were sad. The neurotic desire to be surrounded by others never left him. He had the means to make such conviviality possible, of course: "Porter always paid for sex," one friend reported after his death. And he continued to have poolside dinner parties for eight almost nightly, complete with Baccarat crystal and a servant with a flit gun to ward off insects. But age, poor health, and incorrigible alcoholism took their toll. In 1950 he became convinced, irrationally, that he had lost all his money, and he underwent electric shock treatments for depression and paranoid delusions. Linda, increasingly ill, died in 1954, leaving him morose and guilty. The composer retreated further into drink and various kinds of obsessive-compulsive behavior.

After the amputation of his leg in 1958 Porter lamented that he was "only half a man," but he spent much of his time narcissistically browning himself under a tanning machine. Nor was this his only Aschenbach-like regimen: he also dyed his hair, had his body hair shaved every week, and regularly applied witch-hazel potions to his eyelids to keep his skin youthful-looking. A buxom masseur named Richard tended to these and other tasks behind closed doors.

Porter's end was piteous and squalid. When, in the early 1960s, the now-incontinent composer was unable to find anyone to spend weekends with him, he would insist that his butler Burke pretend to be his guest, even while continuing to wait on him. Thus the embarrassed factotum, writes McBrien, "would alternate between serving Cole his meals as an employee and then joining him at the dining table as his guest." Ultimately dinner itself became a mere charade. At Porter's death in 1964, after surgery to remove a kidney stone, he was indeed only half a man: owing to malnutrition and alcohol poisoning, his weight had dropped to eighty pounds. He literally shriveled up. His last request after the

operation was that a friend go to his house and destroy his collection of pornographic photographs.

What to do with such a rebarbative—often disturbing—personality? One
might be tempted to search for Porter's absent humanity in his oeuvre, were it
not, at first glance, so inhumanly good. A Shakespearean fluency of output (he
wrote over eight hundred songs), combined with seemingly miraculous lyric and
melodic gifts, set him oddly apart from composing contemporaries—even such
profound talents as Irving Berlin, Jerome Kern, Lorenz Hart, and Billy Stray-
horn. At times his songs can seem almost too clever, too inevitable, too delectably right in their eerie fusion of word and musical accompaniment. We seem
to be in the presence of a kind of songwriting demiurge.

Contemporaries marveled at the ease with which Porter composed. A host of
legends and "creation myths" (usually apocryphal) sprang up around his most
popular lyrics. He is supposed to have written "Night and Day" one rainy week-
end at Newport, after his hostess, Mrs. Vincent Astor, remarked during a
lunchtime downpour, "I must have that eave mended at once. That drip, drip,
drip is driving me mad"—thus prompting the song's famous repeated-note
opening, "Like the drip, drip, drip of the raindrops." The inspiration for "You're
the Top" is said to have come when Porter and Mrs. Alistair Mackintosh began
making up a list of rhyming comic superlatives during dinner at Boeuf sur le
Toit. And Joan Fontaine always claimed that she was in on the epiphanic moment that led to "Don't Fence Me In": overhearing Porter on the phone with his
wife, she remembered him suddenly saying, "Linda, please don't fence me in."
(Porter's women friends, interestingly, are often involved in these origin-myths,
functioning like traditional muses or handmaidens of genius.) To admiring acquaintances Porter seemed indeed a kind of necromancer or alchemist, able to
turn the dross of everyday chitchat into the gold of art.

Nor are such tales of fantastical creativity entirely off the mark. There can be
no mistaking the dashing sublimity of Porter's gift. The lyrics of his songs alone
might qualify him for a place in the pantheon—in the burnished satiric tradition of English poets such as Dryden, Pope, and Byron. Like the great versifiers
of the Restoration and the early eighteenth century (not to mention the madcap
lord), Porter endowed a compulsive verbal facetiousness—wrenched rhymes, incongruous syntactical and semantic juxtapositions, comic enjambements—with
a ribald yet coruscating glory:

> In olden days, a glimpse of stocking
> Was looked on as something shocking,
> But now, God knows,
> Anything goes.
> Good authors too who once knew better words

Now only use four-letter words
Writing prose,
Anything goes.
If driving fast cars you like,
If low bars you like,
If old hymns you like,
If bare limbs you like,
If Mae West you like,
Or me undressed you like,
Why, nobody will oppose.
When ev'ry night, the set that's smart is intruding
    in nudist parties in Studios,
Anything goes.

As in *The Dunciad* or *Don Juan*, celebrities of the day (usually the composer's friends) appear as characters in his verses, transmogrified into mock-heroic actors in a spry pageant of folly and caprice:

Farming, that's the fashion,
Farming, that's the passion
Of our great celebrities of today.
Fannie Hurst is haulin' logs,
Fanny Brice is feedin' hogs,
Garbo-Peep has led her sheep all astray.
Singing while they're rakin',
Bringing home the bacon,
Makes 'em feel more glamorous and more gay.
Miss Elsa Maxwell, so the folks tattle,
Got well-goosed while dehorning her cattle
Farming is so charming, they all say.

To be sure, Porter's satire was always light. Apart from keeping up a general assault on sexual prudery (numerous lyrics in his shows, such as "Love for Sale," had to be changed or dropped at the demand of censors), he never bothered with larger social or political issues. Still, there is depth there nonetheless, hauntingly so; and when he veers toward melancholy, as in many of the classic ballads, no songwriter of the past one hundred years is more adept at evoking, by lyric alone, what Pope once called the moving toyshop of the heart;

In the roaring traffic's boom,
In the silence of my lonely room,
I think of you, night and day.

Porter's tunes have, if anything, an even greater stand-alone power: witness seventy years of gorgeous appropriations by jazz instrumentalists as varied as Lester Young, Django Reinhardt, Charlie Parker, Lee Konitz, John Coltrane, and Cecil Taylor. (Parker used the erotically throbbing minor chords of "What Is This Thing Called Love?" in both "Hot House" and "Fats Flats.") From the start Porter's admirers were wont to compare his unusual harmonic language and un-expected melodic turns with those of Schubert, Schumann, and other masters of the nineteenth-century lied. "'So in Love'," wrote one critic, "is as neatly worked out as a *lied*: far from being in the 32-bar mold that marks most 'hits,' its melody extends itself and glides to an end in a way that only an artist could manage." The composer and conductor Leo Smit thought the startling intervals and circuitous musical line of "Night and Day" reminiscent of Schumann's "The Lotus Flower."

Yet it is unquestionably in the dazzling conjunction of lyric and melody that Porter's ineffability lies. And here the most apt comparison might be with great masters from the late seventeenth and eighteenth centuries—with Purcell, Handel, and the magnificent word-setters of the High Baroque. In "I Get a Kick Out of You"—

> I get no kick in a plane.
> Flying too high with some guy in the sky
> Is my idea of nothing to do,
> Yet I get a kick out of you.

—the melody climbs vertiginously upward as the lyric begins its own dizzying ascent on the word "flying." Such mannerist interplay between lyric and *melos* is everywhere in the songs. It is in the exquisite "Love for Sale," in which the sound of slowing footsteps in the opening recitative—

> When the only sound in the empty street
> Is the heavy tread of the heavy feet
> That belong to a lonesome cop
> I open shop.

—is mimicked in the spare and ponderous melody to which the lines are set; and in "Just One of Those Things," where a madly propulsive, hell-for-leather tune seems to underscore the singer's urge to break free from the sexual snares in which he or she is entangled; and in the astonishingly beautiful "Ev'ry Time We Say Goodbye," when the singer intones the famous lyric—

> There's no love song finer
> But how strange

> The change
> From major to minor

—and Porter's melody does exactly that. Word and music fall exquisitely together, like figments of a dream, even as Porter himself comes to seem more un-
fathomable and Puck-like: a weird little Jazz Age *daemon*, with martini glass in
hand and genius to spare.

William McBrien does little, unfortunately, to humanize Porter or to make
him seem less strange and doll-like. This is not for want of confidence. "Was it
Hippolyte Taine who said success in writing came from a felicitous conjunction
of *l'homme, moment, et milieu?*" McBrien asks in his opening acknowledgments.
"I believe, as do my publishers, that this book represents such a conjunction."
But the result belies such authorial amour propre. Despite having had the bless-
ing of the Porter estate and access to various new archives, McBrien cannot be
said to have produced a satisfying book. The story that he tells is often confused
and elliptical. The narrative of Porter's courtship of Linda (if so calculated an enterprise may be called that) is related in clumsy fits and starts; Porter's nervous
breakdown in the 1950s is passed over, mystifyingly, in a paragraph or two.

The charged subject of the composer's homosexuality enters, as it were, entirely through the back door, when McBrien, having said nothing at all to prepare the ground, shifts abruptly from a discussion of Porter's marriage to a
gossipy account of his 1925 affair with the poet Boris Kochno, régisseur for Diaghilev's Ballets Russes. No explanation is forthcoming for this turn of events—
no reference backward, say, to adolescent experiments; nor does McBrien ever
manage to put Porter's sexuality into any coherent psychological or historical
context. Major loves—Kochno, the architect Ed Tauch, the dancer Nelson Bar-
clift, the actor Robert Bray (who later played the forest-ranger father on television's *Lassie*)—remain largely ciphers, part of a depressing parade of big-legged
hunks who seem entirely without charm or inner lives of their own.

Still more off-putting is McBrien's tone, which oscillates between the dire
savoir faire of the small-town college professor ("the couplet is proof that Porter
was *au fait* with the world of Diaghilev") and a kind of gossip-columnist fatuousness when he is simply overcome by the fabulosity of it all: "The languorous
Venetian summer of 1926 was punctuated by the arrival of many guests:
Dorothy Oelrichs, wife of Herman, his friend from Yale; Dorothy "Dickie" Fel-
lowes-Gordon; Noël Coward and his lover, John C. "Jack" Wilson; Lady Abdy;
the Duke of Verdura; Monty Woolley; Lady Diana Cooper; Jean Bouvier; the
Mendls; Countess de Frasso; and Countess di Zoppola (the former Edith Mortimer)." Dickie! Lady Abdy! The former Edith Mortimer! Well, did you evah!

How to turn a gigolo back into a human being? Perhaps no biography will
ever make Porter seem other than a wintry flower. Still, just as the fading beauty
is restored (if briefly) to a sense of life and vibrancy in the gigolo's presence, so

Porter, one might argue, has been humanized by his performers—by those who have infused his songs with their own breath, flesh, and blood. Porter's most humanizing talent, paradoxically, was his power to make others human: by giving them songs so perfect—so luminous, forgiving, fateful, and profound—that they have had no choice, whatever their individual technical or moral resources, but to sound more fully alive in the singing and the playing of them. Performers typically surpass themselves when singing Porter. To listen to Ethel Merman, usually maligned as an unsubtle belter, delicately wend her way through "I Get a Kick Out of You" on a 1934 recording with Johnny Green and his Orchestra is to hear a mistress of sensuous phrasing, as elegant, subtle, and seductive as Madame de Maintenon.

Is there any more joyful human legacy of our otherwise ghastly waning century than the magnificent cornucopia of Porter performances now surviving on record and compact disc? One has one's private touchstones, of course: Libby Holman's wild, moonstruck vibrato in "Love for Sale"; Mabel Mercer's epicene goofing on "Where Oh Where" and "Ace in the Hole"; Julie Wilson's cigarette-ravaged versions of "My Heart Belongs to Daddy" and "Easy to Love"; Chet Baker's intoning "Ev'ry Time We Say Goodbye" as if exuding beautiful amber. Nor have Porter's tunes been entirely co-opted by the nostalgia industry: one of the most telling musical enterprises of the 1980s was *Red, Hot and Blue*, a collection of Porter classics performed by Annie Lennox, Salif Keita, the Pogues, Iggy Pop, the Cocteau Twins, and other rock icons. In the context of a plague-ridden postmodernity—profits from the sale of the recording went to AIDS research—songs such as "I've Got You Under My Skin" took on new and ever more poignant resonances.

In this warm and engaged munificence, the living, pulsing breath of those who sing him, Porter himself lives on—far more than in lyric sheet or photograph or indeed life story, especially one as desultory as McBrien's. Only there, perhaps, do we find the human face in the mirror, the gigolo with a day job, the manikin with a soul and a tiny, beating heart. He's a Popeye, he's a panic, he's a pip—but he's also strangely de-lovely.

note

1. William McBrien, *Cole Porter: A Biography* (New York: Knopf, 1998).

18

THE WILL TO WHIMSY

s it possible for an author to be too delightful? In Claire Harman's excellent biography of the English novelist and short-story writer Sylvia Townsend Warner, published in 1989, there is a remarkable photograph of Warner in be-whiskered old age: laughing, intelligent eyes shining out behind huge, comical horn-rimmed spectacles, man's jacket, stub of cigarette held gaily in hand, a charming rakish smile. It is precisely the sort of image—so happy, leering and indomitable—that makes one want to run away screaming and hide one's head under a pillow.

Reading through Harman's fascinating recent volume of Warner's diaries—Warner began keeping a daybook in 1927, just after the success of her first novel, *Lolly Willowes*, and carried on with it, with a few significant interruptions, until her death at eighty-seven in 1978—one sometimes has the same sense: of an almost inhumane chipperness, of a sensibility so resilient and ironical and civilized, one can hardly imagine the event, mighty or mundane, that could disturb such ineffable self-possession.[1] Warner knew that she was a brilliant, fantasticating writer and discovered, rejoicingly, in the vicissitudes of daily life a constant inspiration for her intensely self-conscious and self-pleasuring art. Yet as a diarist (and even as a novelist she is an acquired taste) she can come close at times to wearing the reader down with a kind of Nietzschean Will to Whimsy.

Warner had a compulsively capering imagination and was inevitably drawn to the stylish or fanciful turn. (When her friend David Garnett gave her the notebook in which she began keeping her first diary, she headed it "Apocrypha.") Like her contemporary, Virginia Woolf, she is one of the great transmogrifiers—of the ordinary into the surreal, of the boring or otiose into the archly or grandly facetious. Much of this reflexive preciosity was due, one suspects, to the joyfully spirited education she received from her father, George Townsend Warner, a distinguished master at Harrow School from 1891 to 1916. Warner was raised in an atmosphere of competitive male intellectual preening, and something of the precocious schoolboy manner that she absorbed in adolescence never completely left her. Witness the pedantic drollery of this early entry from 1929, when she was still living a bohemian life in London and working on *Tudor Church Music*, a scholarly compendium she coauthored with an erstwhile lover, the elderly musicologist Percy Buck:

> Today I saw an advertisement of water-cress—a picture of a little girl thrusting some into the maw of her grand-papa at table. Underneath were these mysterious words: A True Incident. And in the Times was a snip about some workmen repairing a church in Gosport who broke unwittingly into a vault. Smoke was seen coming from it, the fire-engine sent for. When the vault was opened a coffin burst into flames and vanished in ashes and powder. Things like this make life very pleasant.

Or this from 1931, describing an absurd exhibition of Russian ballet–style dance at the home of Ursula Nettleship, Augustus John's sister-in-law:

> I had to go to Nettleship's awful party. All the women sitting silent on the window seats, with their feet tucked in as though there had been a mouse, while a plump young woman in scarlet pajamas did acrobatic dances. Her first entry, feet over hands from between curtains, was accompanied by a crash of broken glasses. No one spoke to me except a Danish lady who asked twice—"Who is she?" and then, for variety's sake, pointing to one of the few men, "How old is he?" Home with hysteria, and early to bed.

Producing similes—fantastical or jocose—was as easy for her as breathing. The widow of Thomas Hardy, met at a party in 1930, is "like a very sad subdued seal, looking out of her face and then diving under again." Three ironwork lawn chairs in the garden at Frankfort Manor—the Norfolk house she rented with her companion, the poet Valentine Ackland, in the early 1930s—"lean forward over the white table like three surrealist spinsters in ardent destruction of someone's character." A bare-chested workman digging a well is "like a Norfolk garden god," and Valentine "by lamplight . . . in her silk dressing gown, with her long legs up, just like a Cruikshank debauchee."

At times, Warner uses the simile to put the cap on some more extended piece of comic observation. Coventry Patmore, Warner decides, after reading him aloud with Valentine, "is better than one thinks, but not so good as he thinks himself":

> To be so very pure and at the same time so very rich in language is rather too like bathroom tiles of a grand description to be perfectly comfortable.

Benjamin Britten has "a head with no chin, a pounce like a weasel, and a total attentiveness with the music. He has a goblin look, like a child in the Carpaccio Annunciation who peeps down when she ought to have been at her lessons." And the epicene scholar and translator Enid Starkie, who comes to visit an antique shop run by Valentine in the 1950s, inspires the following:

> Mrs. King rang up to ask if she could bring Enid Starkie to see the shop. I pared my nails and flattened my hair and walked in on a backview, childishly short and bulky, of bright blue trousers, very baggy, a baggy scarlet duffle-coat, a red beret, too large and some bunches of red-gold hair, falsely bright. It turned round, and the face was Rimbaud: the oddest mixture of thwarted childish brilliance & profound nervousness. If she has never acted a vice in her life, she is still vicious. Very shy; grunts like a guinea-pig; very ill, I surmise. Very much a don, though Valentine was not prepared to believe this, holding more subfusc views of dons.

The grunting guinea pig (in blue trousers) with the face of Rimbaud is like something out of Grandville or a decadent E. H. Shepard: a discomfiting vision of the female-juvenile perverse.

Such satiric fantasia will not surprise admirers of Warner's fiction. The inventiveness of the diaries is entirely of a piece with that found in a more developed form in her best writing—in *Mr. Fortune's Maggot* (1927), say, in which a pious English missionary falls ludicrously (and homosexually) in love with one of the faun-like South Sea islanders he is contriving to convert, or *The Corner That Held Them* (1948), about Richelieu-like maneuverings among a group of nuns in an obscure fourteenth-century English convent, or the remarkable *Kingdoms of Elfin* (1977), a series of exceedingly grown-up fairy stories about the political, sexual, and aesthetic lives of a group of articulate elves.

The danger in such a style is great, of course—of falling into a kind of self-parodying, ultimately soulless affectation. At times, Warner does come over as a trifler, especially in her attempts at political commentary. (She was an ardent if sentimental Communist, and her grotesque paeans to Stalin, whom she continued to admire well into the 1970s, make for embarrassing reading.) But at the deepest level she was aware of the danger in the flippant mode. Reflecting in her diary in 1964 on a "nice calm story about incest" she was then writing, "The Love Match"—about a brother and sister who live together as man and wife in a rural village after the First World War—she was stern with herself: "NO FRISKS OR QUIPS, my old girl." The style was to be as "flat as flat, and dry as dry." "I must strangle all my imps."

What saved Warner from herself—and in turn saves her for us—was the relationship with Ackland, with whom she lived as lover and companion for thirty-seven years until Ackland's death from cancer in 1968. Warner herself seems to have recognized as much. After Valentine's death, when the elderly novelist boasted to her young friend Soo Pinney that "before V. I was exceedingly sophisticated & worldly" (she had met Ackland in the late 1920s when both began moving in the fashionable artistic and literary circle around the writer T. F. Powys), Pinney was moved to remark, "A good thing you loved each other. Otherwise you'd be intolerable by now." For which rejoinder, Warner noted in her diary, "I was loving & grateful."

Ackland saved her, paradoxically, not because they were happy together or even particularly well suited to each other. On the contrary, as the diaries make painfully clear, theirs was a relationship founded in deep misery: in Ackland's seemingly intractable lifelong sadness and depression. Alienated in youth from her wealthy, philistine family, sexually restless, a poet whose ambitions always outstripped her very limited gifts, Ackland seems to have suffered from incurable emotional wounds. Yet her very desolation made her curiously attractive. Warner was first drawn to her—literally into her bed—after hearing Ackland call out, from the room next to hers in the summer cottage they were sharing in Dorset in 1931 near the Powys's, "I think I am utterly loveless." This "forsaken grave wail" and the impulsive act of comfort-giving that followed quickly turned to rapturous sexual pleasure for them both, and Warner was hooked for life—into an ultimately masochistic psychic dyad in which the handsome and gloom-ridden Ackland, self-absorbed to the last, relentlessly tested her devotion and abused her love. Ackland's first defection occurred in 1938, when she became obsessed with an American woman, Elizabeth Wade White, and started an affair with her that lasted, off and on, until 1949. A still more protracted emotional ordeal began in the early 1950s when Ackland (to Warner's agnostic horror) became a grim, contentious, rosary-clutching convert to Roman Catholicism, openly mourning Warner's refusal to follow her into the faith.

Yet the torment with Ackland, and one suspects the impossibility of ever fulfilling her complex needs, also humanized Warner's imagination. Ackland was the perfect antidote to archness and affectation; the recurrent metaphysical sadness that was a part of their life together added a moral seriousness to Warner's temperament and imbued her writing with much-needed gravitas. The magnificent historical novel, *The Corner That Held Them*, written during the emotional turmoil of the 1940s, is a good case in point: the "rockets and Catherine wheels" are all here—the novel is a Gothic-comic masterpiece—but the comedy seems born out of underlying sorrow, and is tempered with an almost Shakespearean grace and pathos.

Even with some regrettable excisions (Warner destroyed most of the notebooks she kept during the Wade White affair), the diaries document this crucial relation—and Warner's corresponding emotional and artistic transformation—in moving, sometimes shattering detail. The diaries have their own cumulative intensity (thanks in part to Harman's tactful editing) and testify powerfully to Warner's unflinching emotional honesty. To be sure, there are funny moments amid the misery: reading through an "Elizabethiad" (a love letter from Wade White that Valentine shows her in a fit of remorse) Warner cannot resist a mordant *explication de texte*:

> It was full of reproaches, and grandeurs—and like some sort of salade russe in aspic, or fruits in ice, because of the long elaborately conducted and eloquent sentences, so much glaze that what was to be said seemed little more than the pretext of the sentence. In the evening I happened to read Proust's letters—they seemed positively spontaneous in comparison.

But the overall effect is of deepening suffering—and of a chastening, ultimately unrecuperable loss. In the entries from the 1940s, Warner is eloquent in her pain and bitterness over Ackland's faithlessness ("my hair is burned black as Dante's with hellfire, and I wonder why it will not lie down in a graceful wave") and grief-stricken when she realizes that the sexual love between them is at an end. In one poignant entry from September 1949, after they have ceased to sleep in the same room, she describes Valentine, druggy on phenobarbitol, "sleepwalking" into her bed: "I tried to warm her; and as she warmed to, the smell of love came from her, that smell of corn and milk that I shall never smell from her again except love for another causes it." The body of that other also haunts her dreams: she dreams of Wade White, in the foyer of a concert hall, "inordinately tall, and in black, as massive as an up-ended coffin."

Entries from the 1950s and 1960s tell a similar tale: with Ackland's retreat into religiosity, Warner experienced an almost physical disgust, and a renewed sensual longing for her friend that at times makes for painful reading. ("The physical repulsion I feel at the thought that she sticks out her tongue and has a wafer planted on it came up in a dream where I found I had a limp white disk in the palm of my hand and said to it—But I wouldn't harm you—Which indeed is true. I don't want to harm anything—only to escape uncompromised, uninvolved.") Small things, like her cat Niou "with his wild-silk head," brushing her leg affectionately as she talks with Valentine in the garden, inspire anguished asides: "Cats & roses—it should be enough. But I sometimes pine to be found worth eliciting, to be found enjoyable." And at times she is moved by her suffering to a sort of grand polyphonic grief, as in the following dense, excruciating vignette of love gone dead:

> A conversation that almost approximates to the former estate, so nearly that it gives an illusion of being the real thing, though on a post-earthquake site, or more exactly, taking place in a dream that is almost like life only the view out of the window is Africa—that concludes as a conclu-

sion, not as an intermission, rather solemnly—and later on the revived warmth is gone, and a feeling of even greater hopelessness & frustration whelms one: I thought of this, watching Valentine trying to make a fancy clock go; and the strike rang out, and there was that little chirp & mutter of machinery, and the pendulum wagged & the clock ticked; and while we were talking, the pendulum wobbled, weakened, and the clock was ticking no longer.

All the more wrenching, then, the final pages of this volume, containing the diaries written between Ackland's death and Warner's own in 1978. Warner's brilliance never left her, only redoubled, so to speak, under the pressure of an unassuageable sorrow. While mourning Ackland with an intensity and self-reproach unknown to those who love without ambivalence, she kept in these last ten years a curious double diary—recording the same events simultaneously in both a printed diary and a lined notebook. These parallel entries differ in interesting ways; those from the lined notebook seem far more intimate and distraught—almost like a secret voice emanating from below. (Harman marks the difference by printing the lined notebook entries in italics.) The effect is brilliant and heartbreaking, not least because one senses Warner's yearning—in this fragmentary split conversation with herself—for the fleshly interlocutor she had lost:

Jean translated *sciolta* for me.
And I listened to Brigg Fair.
But, having been filled with pure emotion, an essential,
I waned and went early to bed.
. . . I listened to Brigg Fair: the first hearing since, another cuckoo. It did not need to come back, it is as fresh as ever, that morning when I came back from walking on the drove, & stood at the gate of [our cottage] *hearing her play it, sharing her listening unbeknown, and realising the intensity of what she was to me. I was as fresh as ever, fresher than my sense of loss. My emotion was so pure that it was like a pure alcohol: not a trance for it did not remove me; not a heightening for there was no acceptance on my part; I was* inside *acceptance.*
"There I stood, leaning against you, listening—"
"I have never been away" is the nearest I can come to it. It still encloses me. It was physical, too, for I had that penetrated feeling in my heart.

Perhaps the closest thing to this in modern literature is Mallarmé's *Pour un tombeau d'Anatole*—the series of anguished poetic fragments Mallarmé wrote after the death of his eight-year-old son. Indeed, as the final entries take Warner toward her own much-longed-for death, we forget the all-too-witty woman of the late photographs and listen instead to the noble redeeming accents of love and solitary grief.

note

1. Claire Harman, ed., *The Diaries of Sylvia Townsend Warner* (London: Chatto and Windus, 1994).

19
TERROR ON THE VINEYARD

When slave girls rebel, boss ladies, watch out! In literature as in life, the revenge of a female underling on a female superior can be a messy business—with limbs, eyeballs, breasts, and other detachable body parts left dripping in gore around the house. A variety of situations may propel such fury. In Euripides' *Electra*, Western civilization's mythic prototype for female-on-female mayhem, the rebel is an Outraged Daughter and the boss lady her Wicked Old Mother: Clytemnestra's doom is sealed when she puts her sex life ahead of her daughter's. At other times it's a matter of plain old class rage: a put-upon servant who's had enough of a tyrannical mistress. In France in 1933 the notorious Papin sisters—real-life models for the homicidal domestics in Genet's *The Maids*—disemboweled their bourgeois mistress and her daughter in a fit of bestial frenzy after the unfortunate Mme Lancelin complained once too often about a blown fuse on her steam iron.

In women's fiction, the heroine's simmering hatred for an older woman—often resolving into psychic violence—has long been a classic theme. Brontë's excoriating portrait of Mrs. Reed in *Jane Eyre* is undoubtedly an attack on some detested female oppressor of her youth: Brontë's description fairly seethes with murderous venom. Edith Wharton's heroines, steely girls on the make such as Lily Bart or Undine Spragg, routinely anathematize the hypocritical society matrons who obstruct their passage to wealth and status: *their* aversion seems grounded in Wharton's own polite loathing of her grand yet self-absorbed mother. In the mordant sapphic novels of Elizabeth Bowen, older women are depicted as seductive and treacherous—enchanting sociopaths who leave the younger women who fall in love with them both shell-shocked and vengeful. (See in particular Bowen's brilliant first novel, *The Hotel*, from 1927.) In Muriel Spark's *The Prime of Miss Jean Brodie* vengeance is taken—when the teenage heroine Sandy, the complicated pet of the charismatic Miss Brodie, provokes her teacher's destruction by informing school authorities about Brodie's fascist sympathies. Similar acts of girlish *ressentiment* roil the works of Katherine Mansfield,

Sylvia Plath, Daphne du Maurier, Ivy Compton-Burnett, Iris Murdoch, Elizabeth Jolley, Sybille Bedford, and many others.

Female autobiographers have likewise been forthright about such hatreds—if less so about the pleasures of posthumous retribution. When a famous and idealized older woman fails to live up to the needs of a younger protégée, it is de rigueur nowadays for the latter to rage in print at the cruelty of her faithless idol. *Mommie Dearest* (1978), Christina Crawford's high-kitsch account of her wretched childhood with her adoptive mother, Joan Crawford, is the archetype here—the first and most spectacular of real-life *She was mean!* books. Yet so many exposés of this kind have appeared over the past twenty years they might be said to constitute a popular mini-genre. Angelica Garnett's 1984 *Deceived by Kindness: A Bloomsbury Childhood*, with its quietly devastating portrait of her mother, Vanessa Bell, is fairly subtle; more tendentious is Maria Riva's *Marlene Dietrich* (1992)—another mother-daughter horror story—or Bianca Lamblin's *Mémoires d'une jeune fille dérangée* (1993), translated into English in 1996 as *A Disgraceful Affair: Simone de Beauvoir, Jean-Paul Sartre and Bianca Lamblin*. While professing to be a kind of perverse tribute, the Lamblin book is actually a deeply morbid recounting of its author's adolescent love affair with Simone de Beauvoir, who first seduced her then passed her over—with chilling sang froid— to her lover Sartre.

It is somehow not surprising that with the publication of Rosemary Mahoney's memoir, *A Likely Story*, the celebrated American writer Lillian Hellman (1906–84) should sustain a similar assault.[1] Over the course of a long and controversial life Hellman herself was hardly a stranger to same-sex animus. Her first play, *The Children's Hour* (1934), about a malicious young girl who accuses two female teachers at her boarding school of conducting a lesbian relationship, is often taken retroactively as a political parable—an attack on those in the McCarthy period who "named names"—yet the heart of the drama lies in its depiction of the girl's shocking misogyny and its dire consequences. (One of the teachers commits suicide.) In the early 1980s Hellman got embroiled in her own ugly mess when she engaged in a vicious public feud with Mary McCarthy, who had attacked her on television. (McCarthy's ever-quotable judgment on Hellman's memoirs: "Every word she writes is a lie, including 'and' and 'the.'") When asked by a friend why she had filed a lawsuit against the younger writer, Hellman responded, "I can't let Mary's poisonous nonsense go without taking a stand, can I?" Her words uncannily echo the play of fifty years earlier—not least because the evil girl against whom the teachers seek to defend themselves is also named Mary.

Mahoney is a Rosemary, not a Mary, but her memoir—a moody, lavishly worked account of a miserable summer she spent as a teenager working as Hellman's housemaid on Martha's Vineyard in 1978—is a *She was mean!* book with bells on. It has received unusual praise in the United States—even in such genteel quarters as the *New York Times*—largely, one suspects, because its author fulfills the expectations of the genre so well. In these blithe postfeminist times, everyone, it would seem, enjoys the spectacle of a famous old dead lady humbled—especially one as wrinkly, foul-mouthed, and imperious as Hellman. Three cheers for the slave girl! Go get 'em, Rosemary!

Yet huzzahs notwithstanding, something about Mahoney's bravado troubles. The author of two successful story collections—*The Early Arrival of Dreams* (1990) and *Whoredom in Kimmage* (1993)—Mahoney goes about her indictment of Hellman with a novelist's artfulness and skill. But even as one admires the precocious mastery with which she crafts her ignoble tale—and the tale is in parts undeniably compelling—one feels less than at ease in Mahoney's still-embarrassingly raw emotional world. The memoir is doomed, not only by its author's resentment, still smoldering ominously after twenty years, but also by her cloying sentimentality about her younger self.

Both the resentment and the sentimentality are present from the outset. *A Likely Story* begins in 1984, with an airless, slightly hysterical scene of discovery. Mahoney is helping her artist-sister strip and paint an old industrial loft space in a grimy part of Los Angeles. As the sun beats in and the paint fumes become more and more oppressive, her eye falls on the headline on a piece of old newspaper on the floor—*Lillian Hellman, Playwright, Author, and Rebel, Dies at 79.*

> Seeing these words was like discovering that the cool, slippery object you've crushed beneath your bare foot in the garden is a large pus-colored slug. I recoiled instinctively and my face tightened and my free hand flew up to cover my mouth. For several years I had supposed that Lillian Hellman was already dead, perhaps because for years I had been killing her off in my imagination. But the newspaper was only a few days old. I looked at the headline again to be certain I had read it correctly, then heard myself mutter, "Thank God." I called out to my sister that Hellman was dead. Lillian Hellman was good and dead. I clapped my dirty hands and made cracks about the pieties that were sure to be scattered about at her funeral.

After Mahoney's first exultation is over, the news of Hellman's death prompts a painful memory of herself, six years earlier, in the claustrophobic little bedroom off the kitchen at Hellman's summer home on the Vineyard: "I remembered lying miserably awake in that small bed thinking that if I were a bolder person, I would find a way to repay all Hellman's strictures and stridor; maybe lacing her beloved, fussed-over wine bottles with vinegar, or switching her medicines, or rearranging her furniture in the middle of the night so that she, nearly blinded by glaucoma, would become mazed in her own living room."

Writing in the late 1990s, the thirty-something Mahoney is careful to distance herself from her timid yet tricky 1978 self: "I wasn't in the least aware that such malevolent thoughts might be harmful to my soul or that they reflected a frustration and vindictiveness that bespoke only my own unhappiness." Indeed, what affected her most in the end about Hellman's death, she concludes, was an unexpected "feeling of sorrow."

These older-but-wiser sentiments seem strangely undone, however, as she begins her narrative proper. This, despite the breezy Cape Cod setting, reads like a kind of misfiring Gothic novel. At the center, in the role of vulnerable heroine, is the seventeen-year-old Rosemary—youngest of seven Irish-Catholic siblings, daughter of a doctor (who is dead) and a mother (alcoholic) whom she adores. Swept away by Hellman's memoirs in high school—she regards the older woman as "brave and strong and full of noble ideals"—she forms a desperate wish to meet her. She writes her a letter, asking if she can work for her for the summer, and to her amazement Hellman accepts the offer. All then is giddy alacrity. Like Jane Eyre setting off for Thrushcross Grange, or the excitable Governess departing for Bly at the opening of James's *The Turn of the Screw*, Mahoney promptly leaves her parents' house in dreary Milton, Massachusetts, and heads for the sundappled Vineyard, reveling in fantasies about the marvelous experiences awaiting her in her new post.

Alas, the portents are wrong from the start. Teachers and friends who have heard about her job with Hellman have taken to muttering things like "They say she's a pretty tough dame," and Mahoney's mother worries about her sensitive daughter's well-being. Stopping at the local grocery store after arriving on the Vineyard, Mahoney notices that the clerks and bag boys shudder and make obscene gestures when "old Lilly baby's" name is mentioned. Hellman herself, bored and magisterial at their first interview, is nothing less than terrifying—an uncanny mixture of artifice, decrepitude, and grotesque, idol-like force:

> Through the furry veil of my nervousness I noted how Hellman sat in her chair, her slippered heels just reaching the floor, how she laid one bonethin arm across the convex bowl of her belly while the other lifted a cigarette to her lips. She smoked in a thoughtful, nibbling way, and when she paused to carry the cigarette to her mouth, her chin rose in preparation, as though someone else's hand were feeding it to her. She looked vulnerable and girlish sitting there. She had large, flat thumbnails. I stared at her; no Eskimo icon could be more imposing. She blew smoke into the air and looked back at me, her cloudy eyes not seeing me clearly, as was obvious by the tilt of her head and the amused expression on her face, which I came to learn was not amusement at all but strain. The way her mouth settled when she was thinking, she seemed to be tasting her own large teeth, gauging their size and shape with her tongue. Her mouth was a wide, thin-lipped line that turned down slightly at its corners. Her face

was a pattern of downward-slanting flesh, like cake batter running down the side of a mixing bowl, and that day her skin, like the furniture and the wood floors, glistened in the humidity. Her eyes had a faintly Asian slant that made her look almost seductive. Her face was narrower, longer, than it had seemed in pictures, and her nose in profile was colossal and angled in the middle. She had a broad and rather handsome forehead with the faintest suggestion of a widow's peak. But the most remarkable thing about her, aside from the complicated pattern of wrinkles, was her hair: it was beautiful, thick and soft and wavy and tinted a summery wheaten color. It was the hair of a girlish young woman, the sort of rich pelt that on an older woman inevitably prompts the observer to think *wig*. It wasn't a wig.

When Mahoney is shown around by the housekeeper she is replacing—a goggle-eyed Hispanic woman named Marta who warns her in a furtive whisper that "Hellman is no nice lady. You look out!"—one can almost hear the dank organ chords sounding.

Over the three months that follow—cast abruptly into the role of live-in cleaner, dresser, cook, errand-runner, and maid-of-all-work to the ailing, seventy-four-year-old Hellman—Mahoney undergoes a kind of emotional shock therapy as humiliating (in her eyes) as any indignity perpetrated on one of Mrs. Radcliffe's insipid heroines. With her weird, unsteady gait, reeking tobacco breath, and lipstick "the color of dried blood," Hellman perambulates the house like an elderly Mother of Frankenstein, oscillating between bossy tantrums, purblind inanities, and a near-total indifference to the sensibilities of her youthful factotum. (When not in a senile rage over Mahoney's deficiencies as a servant—the tomboyish Mahoney is unable to cook anything more than boiled eggs, for example—Hellman seems to forget all about her existence.) Cheated of the attention for which she yearns, Mahoney retreats into turgid adolescent angst—sulking, pining, brooding over her absent mother (to whom she writes pathetic letters), and counting up the wrongs.

Twenty years on Mahoney recollects these wrongs as if they had happened yesterday. And hence the gory vignettes on which American reviewers of the book have fastened so gleefully. A harridan-like Hellman fumes at Mahoney for spilling a few drops of coffee. She humiliates her for neglecting to put the bathmat back in the right place after scrubbing the tub. She fixes her with a basilisk stare ("thin lips clapped together like a cartoon clam's") for forgetting to put her nightly eyedrops on ice. Whenever Mahoney fetches the wrong food item from the store or makes the beds incorrectly She-of-the-Pelt-Like-Copper-Hairdo blows her stack. She demands that Mahoney wear a frilly uniform while dusting. (Mahoney for once refuses.) The meager paychecks she hands over turn out to be uncashable. She creeps up behind Mahoney and scares her out of her wits when she is polishing the furniture. She never apologizes for anything. She is in short one hell of a bitch, with cigarette-tainted, "warm tarry breath" to boot.

Mahoney exposes instances of Hellman's venality with near-photographic recall: the way she forces her to funnel "a bottle of Jim's vodka, the cheapest brand available on the island, into the empty Smirnoff bottle in the living room"; her floridly racist vocabulary ("she was always saying *Chink* and *Jap* and *nigger*, which in *Pentimento* she claimed she would never say"); her cheating at Scrabble (during games with her neighbor Rose Styron she routinely peeks at Styron's letters whenever Styron leaves the room); the malicious remarks she makes about friends and houseguests as soon as they are out of earshot (Joseph Alsop, she tells Mahoney, "is a fag. . . . There's no reason for my liking him except that he was very good during the McCarthy period").

Some of this tartufferie, one must confess, is good for a hollow laugh—or even two or three. Bad behavior by the eminent, especially those who preen themselves on their moral or intellectual superiority, is always enjoyable to contemplate, and the gossip quotient in Mahoney's book is high. Hellman is not the only snotty famous person to fall under her jaded eye. James Taylor and Carly Simon, Hellman's guests one sunny afternoon, "smile stiffly" at Mahoney when she brings coffee in on a serving tray, but otherwise ignore her. Mike Nichols and John Hersey win grudging approval—the former for giving her a nice tip, the latter for his kindly, slightly alcoholic smile ("He had the look of a person who understood other people, who wanted to hear what they had to say"). Joseph Alsop, making chitchat with her in the kitchen, speaks with such a ludicrously fake British accent that he reminds her of Thurston Howell III on *Gilligan's Island*. William Styron is almost as monstrous as Hellman herself—self-centered, nervy, and savage with contempt for anyone who gets in his way. When he accidentally burns up the fancy pan-fried quail he is preparing for Hellman and her friends in Hellman's kitchen one night, he blames the resulting mess on Mahoney and her fellow cook, who have been helping out by chopping vegetables for him: "My apologies for the few that are singed," he says to the assembled guests; "The girls lost control of a burner."

And Mahoney, it must be allowed, has a gift for a certain cruel situation comedy—as when she records Hellman's ponderous attempts to instruct her in the use of the Cuisinart:

> Hellman tugged a Cuisinart out from its spot in the corner of the counter. It was new, she told me. Someone had given it to her as a gift. It was a terribly fancy gadget. She hadn't used it much. Its blades were terribly, terribly sharp. We must use extreme caution. She fussed over the plastic machine, removing fittings and containers and putting them on again, feeling their shapes with her fingers, bending over to inspect the handle, the electrical cord. Her long fingernails clicked on the hard plastic, and

her hands hovered gingerly over the pieces, as though the machine were a fancy pipe bomb.

After she and Hellman manage to reduce some sorrel leaves to a "thrashing green potion," Mahoney turns off the machine and tries to pry free the blade in order to wash it. When it suddenly pops up in the air and lands harmlessly on Hellman's foot, the scene turns to geriatric slapstick:

> Her head tipped forward, seemed to wobble on her neck. "Oh! Oh! Jesus Christ!" she yelped. Magnified through her eyeglasses, her lashes fluttered wildly, her face a map of tension and fear. "Oh, my God! Jesus Christ!" she gasped. "Am I all right?" Her lips trembled and she clutched at her own hands and stared down at her green-stained sneaker. She took a tiny step, a kind of test to see if her foot was still there. She looked up at me. "Are you all right?"
>
> "Oh, fine," I said. My heart pounded with confusion and fear. I saw no blood on the floor or on either one of us, so I concluded aloud again that we were both all right. I picked up the Cuisinart blade by its little knobbed handle and held it up for Hellman to see, perhaps hoping that the sight of it in my hand would provide further evidence that we were not hurt. . . .
>
> "Jesus Christ. It nearly took my head off." Her mouth hung open in fright. Her lips trembled. "My God, that fuckin' thing is a menace. I've got to have Melvin take a look at it."
>
> She went to the table, stabbed her cigarette into the ashtray, snatched up a pack of cigarettes, fished a fresh one out with trembling fingers, fitting it into her mouth, and lit it with her palm cupped protectively around the match, as if the room were subject to a howling wind.

Yet Mahoney's depiction of Hellman disturbs more than it amuses—indeed often repels—mainly because Mahoney pretends to a self-knowledge that her narrative itself does little to endorse. A crucial background element in *A Likely Story* is Mahoney's relationship with her widowed mother, Nona, whom she adores with a mixture of veneration and panic. Nona wears a leg brace (the result of polio) and moves about with difficulty—a fact that fills her daughter with both anxiety and loverlike solicitude. Mahoney's early adolescence, we learn, has been taken up with caring obsessively for Nona, trying to ease her burdens, yet also coping with her "stuporous disappearances"—the times when she comes home drunk and Mahoney has to help her stagger to bed to sleep it off. (Mahoney's numerous older siblings mostly ignore the situation.) At the time Mahoney takes the job with Hellman she is still deeply and slavishly embroiled with Nona. When mother and daughter reunite they conduct strange little rituals of absorption and interdependence. Mahoney will massage her mother's "dead leg," as if to bring it magically back to life, or help Nona practice taking her leg brace on and off at high speed, just in case she ever has to flee a burning house or swim free from a submerged car.

Two decades later Mahoney clearly wants her readers to draw the obvious parallel between the relationship with Nona and the relationship with Hellman. Both women are seductive and powerful yet physically enfeebled; both induce in the youthful Mahoney the same embarrassingly masochistic attitudes. Each seems rich in "adult" experience: Hellman is a famous writer and presence in the world; and even Nona, despite disability, alcoholism, and murky bouts of depression (Mahoney's father may have committed suicide), reads lots of books and manages to support her numerous children as a high school English teacher. The teenaged Mahoney inevitably sees herself as impoverished in comparison— compelled as if by destiny into the role of juvenile dogsbody and emotional supplicant.

What disturbs, however, is that Mahoney, even now, seems not to grasp any deeper psychic link between her feeling for her mother and her feeling for Hellman. While recognizing some of her mother's failings Mahoney presents Nona for the most part with saccharine, even sickly forbearance—as a kindly, Dickensian parent, unhappily prone to a few dipsomaniacal lapses. Yet what sensitive female child enjoys looking after a crippled and inebriated mother? Mahoney clearly yearned for her mother to look after *her*, and resented her fiercely when she did not. Only such resentment can help explain, one feels, the wildly rebounding fury at Hellman. Yet *A Likely Story* lacks any such retrospective authorial insight. Despite maudlin attention to her adolescent vulnerability—she is endlessly keen to tell us how gauche she was as a young woman, how lacking in confidence, how unprotected, weak, and shy—Mahoney seems unable, after twenty years, to relate the towering enmity toward Hellman to what was patently, at the time, a profound sense of being unmothered, *un ours mal léché*. The link is there; it is palpable in the narrative; but the crucial emotional synapses never seem to fire.

This failure of insight seems in turn connected with the most disquieting aspect of *A Likely Story*—Mahoney's painfully elaborate descriptions of Hellman's aging, raddled, all-too-human body. Mahoney's renderings—as when she describes watching Hellman through binoculars strip naked for a swim on the little private beach below her house ("a skeletal figure with two pendulous bosoms dangling from her rib cage like white leather wineskins two-thirds empty; her pruny arms and legs the color of butterscotch in the bright light")—seem infused at once with moral disgust and an almost erotic disappointment. She is particularly transfixed by Hellman's huge pillowy breasts ("like sloping cushions stuffed into her dress"), which seem to promise a maternal nurturance that never comes. Hellman's voluminous bra-cups, fondled as they emerge from the washing machine, are so "copious and solid they reminded me of quahog shells."

Yet Mahoney is fey when it comes to taking responsibility for her own not-too-subtle symbolism. Recollecting an annoying day when Hellman demanded that she make cookies from scratch rather than simply picking some up from the store, she remembers rebelliously thinking to herself that "I had never tasted a homemade cookie as good as an Oreo." When her favorite edible turns up later, however, it is in a strangely fraught, if not primal, context. Finding the drunken, snoring Hellman stretched out naked on her bed upstairs during a bibulous evening with the Styrons, Nichols, Peter Mathiessen, and the rest, Mahoney comments—with the bizarre know-nothingism of the amnesiac—that her "nipples were the size of Oreos."

This culminating image of the postprandial, brown-nippled Hellman—comatose, alone, exposed, and snuffly—is not only the cruelest in the book, it is also a fitting emblem of what is wrong, ethically and rhetorically, with Mahoney's enterprise.

> Her twisted toes poked up out of the ruffle of the sheets. She breathed softly, dead to the world, rib cage rising and falling, while her fancy guests laughed and chattered downstairs, smoking and enjoying her wine. She was the oldest person in the house by nearly ten years. She was like a wayward granny. Her body was so skinny and old it was like a scientific event looking at it in this way, like finding a large fragile fossil embedded in stone, or the mummified remains of a three-thousand-year-old man preserved in a bog, his prunish face flattened and smeared and warped, like a face pressed against a windowpane. I had once seen one of these men stretched out in a museum, and looking at him in his glass box, every joint visible beneath his dusty film of skin, I half expected him to sit up, with the floppy, corky creak of folding leather, and say, *Yes. Here I am. Again.*

Fine writing, yes (almost too fine)—but Mahoney can't resist layering on "significance" with rich, self-consciously artful strokes:

> Anyone leaving by the formal second-floor entry that night would have to pass her door and see their famous hostess dumb and naked, snoring and muttering on her bed. I stood there staring, floating in a wave of scorn and pity. I could punish her, leave the door open, and let people catch the terrifying sight. Or I could close it and protect her. I argued with myself. She had been so hard and unwelcoming. She hadn't allowed me in and had forced me to block her out. Everything here seemed bitter

and sour to me. It wasn't what I had expected, wasn't what I had wanted. And I felt embarrassed and angry for not having been wiser, for not having anticipated how complex it would be, how marginal my person was in this place. I hated surprises. I hated not knowing things.

After a last cool look at Hellman's wrinkled face, the lips "hanging loose in her oblivion," the made-up eyebrows "stuck up in spikes and spears" and hair "a glossy jumble on the pillow," Mahoney throws a sheet over her and gently pulls the door shut.

At such moments Mahoney's story seems to resolve into allegory—a kind of hortatory tableau, like one of those strange, northern, early Renaissance paintings in which a young girl and old crone, emblems of Youth and Age, confront each other in a landscape, the one glowing in her naked youthful beauty, the other withered and hideous. (Mahoney frequently comments on her own prettiness, and how much Hellman resents her for it.) As much as a Cranach or Memling, Mahoney seems to want to convey a message here about youth and age, beauty and *vanitas*, life and death.

The problem is that Hellman is not the archetypal crone of fable or allegory, despite the sinister boiled sweets she offers Mahoney upon their first meeting. By all accounts Hellman *was* difficult and contentious and abominable to those she disdained, but she was also as complex and soulful a human being as anyone else on the planet. One can't help feeling, even after reading Mahoney, that she deserves to be treated as such. Mahoney's central complaint is that Hellman never bothered to find out who she (Mahoney) was. Yet the most telling feature of Mahoney's book is its own tit-for-tat emotional logic. Just as Hellman, through her indifference, treats Mahoney as a thing, Mahoney does the same in reverse to Hellman. The Hellman of *A Likely Story* is not so much a real woman as a puppet or voodoo doll or primitive icon: "a cloth stitched around a skeleton or whittled sticks and twisted wire hangers, a piece of Peruvian handicraft." She has no inner life, no humane dimension—is set up instead as a sort of effigy in training. The clinical descriptions of her body, sunken in boggy sleep, hint at the further dissolution to come: Hellman is indeed halfway to corpse. And thus Mahoney distances herself—and us—from any identification with her target. Her portrait of Hellman is strictly from the outside—and willfully so—for it is by staying outside, remorselessly, that Mahoney is able to exact her vengeance.

Sadistic impulses are hardly to be disavowed, of course, least of all by churlish reviewers. A favorite poem of mine has always been Eileen Myles's divinely boorish "On the Death of Robert Lowell"—

> O, I don't give a shit.
> He was an old white haired man
> Insensate beyond belief and

Filled with much anxiety about his imagined
Pain. Not that I'd know
I hate fucking wasps.
The guy was a loon.
Signed up for Spring Semester at MacLeans
A really lush retreat among pines and
Hippy attendants. Ray Charles also
Once rested there.
So did James Taylor . . .
The famous, as we know, are nuts.
Take Robert Lowell.
The old white haired coot.
Fucking dead.

Cruel, indeed: but as anyone familiar with Myles's precocious, punked out, ex-quisitely risible oeuvre will know, her aggression is inevitably tempered by a par-adoxical fellow feeling. The poet's own histrionic travails—with alcoholism, abusive homosexual relationships, mental institutions, and the ravages of a Boston Irish working-class childhood (a childhood similar in many ways to Ma-honey's)—link her with the coots and the loons. Impertinence is merely a sally, a way of saying hello across the generations.

Mahoney has no such amiability, however—no saving urge toward comic self-incrimination. One finishes her book not with any sense of catharsis but with the decidedly less-than-momentous feeling that it was all rather a shame—all the bickering and bullying and loathing—but hardly cataclysmic. And with-out cataclysms, who cares? The promised Gothic horror, the much-vaunted Terror on the Vineyard, turns out to be nothing more than a feeble old woman drinking Scotch and a girl moping in a spare room. It's a kind of low-rent *Northanger Abbey*, without Austen's (or even Hellman's) genius. One ends up feeling hard and impatient and sorry for Hellman. Indeed, the more Mahoney tries to make us identify with her own youthful pain, the more the socked-in rages of adolescence and young adulthood—one's own—seem merrily to fly out of the windows of memory. Surely, one finds oneself thinking, Clytemnestra wasn't *all* bad. . . . It's hard being a boss lady! And thus "old Lilly baby," dead to the world, may get the last laugh after all: however much it hurt at the time, the children's hour is over at last.

note

1. Rosemary Mahoney, *A Likely Story: One Summer with Lillian Hellman* (New York: Doubleday, 1998).

20

YES, YOU, SWEETHEART

W ho more omnivorous—not to mention lewd—than Colette, the friz-
zle-headed Cat Woman of twentieth-century French writing? Shocking still the sheer salaciousness of the prose, even in the works of her
apprenticeship, written in the days when ladies wore bustles and carried parasols.
Take the following scene from the autobiographical *Claudine à Paris* (1901) in
which the precocious yet virginal seventeen-year-old heroine, recently arrived in
the capital with her dreamy widower father, is flirting with her "uncle" Renaud,
a handsome older friend of the family by whom (though she hasn't realized it
yet) she desperately wants to be fucked. She tells him a titillating story about one
of her schoolmates in the country village of Montigny:

> 'Take Célénie Nauphely, for example . . .'
> 'Aha! Let's hear what Célénie Nauphely did!'
> 'Well, Célénie Nauphely used to stand up—she was a big girl of four-
> teen—at half past three—half an hour before it was time to go . . . and
> say out loud, looking very serious and self-important, "Mademoiselle, can
> I go, please? I've got to go and suck my sister."'
> 'Merciful heavens! Suck her sister?'
> 'Yes. Just imagine, her married sister, who was weaning a child, had
> too much milk and her breasts hurt her. She pretended she used to spit
> the milk out again but, all the same, she must have swallowed some of it
> in spite of herself. Well, the girls used to fuss over her with admiring envy,
> this suckling infant. The first time I heard her telling all about it, I could-
> n't eat my next meal. Doesn't it have any effect on you?'
> 'Don't press the point or I think it most certainly will have an effect
> on me. You certainly open strange vistas on the Fresnois institutions,
> Claudine!'

The prurience here, as elsewhere in Colette, is breathtaking: a lasciviousness
so direct, rosy, and dizzying that even the bantering, ultracivilized Renaud dis-

solves into hard quiet jerks of voyeuristic delight. Yet there's also something upsetting about Colette's rude daring: something in the very unflinchingness of the primitive association of sexual pleasure with feeding at the breast that disturbs as much as it arouses. We know—but also don't want to know—how good it feels to suck. Colette, writes her new biographer Judith Thurman, invariably connected human happiness with "a voluptuous, feminine pliancy, and with the power of domination—a pleasure that became purer for her with age, and toward which she expresses an infant's sense of entitlement."[1] She reveled, in other words, in the frank, regressive seizure of the breast—in going after what she wanted without shame or *pudeur*. To read about her life—the prodigal literary gifts, the fearsome productivity, the exotic lovers (male and female), the emotional gourmandizing, the sheer untrammeled aggressiveness of her search for sensual and imaginative fulfillment—can be at once exhausting and unsettling. She's scary because she challenges us to a kind of psychosexual wrestling match: who will be the one who gets to suck?

For a female biographer—not to mention female reader—the challenge must be especially hot and fierce. Assuming the impossibility of ever pinning Colette herself to the mat, how to wriggle safely out of her Protean grasp? How to escape being immobilized and sucked dry? As is the case with so many famous and gifted French people, the sex business alone is enough to give one a *mégrim*. Colette's energetic yet intelligent libertinism inevitably puts one's own, actual or merely mental, in the darkest of dark shades. Like the beautiful-to-raddled leading lady in some fantastical Ages of Woman (she died at an empresslike eighty-one), Colette lived out virtually every sexual permutation known to woman with both gymnastic gusto and a sophisticated *bon goût*.

There was the Plump and Horny Older Man, of course: the notorious hack writer and journalist, Henry Gauthier-Villars, better known to posterity as "Willy," whom Colette married in 1893 soon after coming to Paris from her native Burgundian village of Saint-Sauveur-en-Puisaye. Willy (as his nom de plume suggests) was both comic menace to virgins and magnificent virile gift: he initiated Colette sexually, gave her the obligatory Belle Époque wives' case of gonorrhea, exploited her financially and professionally, but also got her—feverishly and fluently and brilliantly—to write. (All four of the wildly popular *Claudine* novels were written at Willy's instigation and published under his name. After a protracted legal battle, Colette regained the copyrights when she divorced him in 1910.) She would ultimately roll over him by becoming, along with her friend Proust, one of the two greatest of all twentieth-century French novelists. "Those girls who dream . . . of being the erotic masterpiece of an older man," she would write coolly after deserting him: "It's an ugly desire which they expiate by fulfilling."

Then there was the Plump and Horny Older Woman: the eccentric Mathilde de Morny, marquise de Belboeuf, the aristocratic cross-dresser and she-bachelor with whom Colette had a six-year lesbian affair upon leaving Willy. A descendant, thanks to a dizzying set of by-blows across the centuries, of Louis XV, the Empress Josephine, *and* Talleyrand, the mannish "Missy" (as she was known to friends) helped finance the strangest turn in the writer's early life: her debut on the popular stage. (Colette's knockabout career in French music hall, vaudeville, and pantomime—which lasted from 1906 to 1913—is unforgettably documented in her wonderful 1910 novel, *La Vagabonde*.) At the height of their liaison Missy and Colette starred together at the Moulin Rouge in an orientalist panto-concoction entitled *Rêve d'Égypte* in which Missy played an archaeologist and Colette a beautiful mummy who "comes back to life in a jeweled bra, slowly and seductively unwinds her transparent wrappings, and at the climax of the dance, passionately embraces the archaeologist." Their onstage kiss on the mouth on opening night started a riot, and the show shut down after two performances. A startling publicity photograph from around this time (not, alas, reproduced in Thurman) shows a bare-naveled Colette being carefully divested of a silk skirt by the ponderous, Dracula-like, astonishingly masculine Missy: surely one of the more peculiar author-consort photos ever.

In the second half of her life, following her marriage in 1913 to the newspaper editor Henry de Jouvenel, the birth of her daughter, Bel-Gazou, and the beginning of her gradual transformation from scandalous cocotte into France's most celebrated and respected woman writer, Colette moved on to a complicated series of Younger Women and Younger Men. Among the gals: Lily de Rême, the flirty, capricious model for May in the 1913 novel *L'Entrave*, about a bisexual *ménage à trois*; Musidora, the early cinema star (and one-time mistress of Willy) who became famous as the kohl-eyed darling of the Surrealists; the promiscuous Parisian *salonnière* Natalie Barney ("the Pope of Lesbos"); and, when Colette was in her fifties, the travel writer and explorer Renée de Hamon, the "little corsair" who wooed Colette by sending her dwarf azaleas and rare tropical plants as "discreet emissaries" of her passion.

The guys ranged from brainless young studs such as Auguste Hériot, playboy heir to the Magasins du Louvre department store fortune ("a mustachioed Child with an innocent gaze and an erection," in Thurman's memorable phrase) to the druggy, morphine-addicted Georges Kessel, known as "Smoke." Hériot was undoubtedly one of the models for Colette's most celebrated male character— Chéri—the beautiful young man adored and repudiated by the middle-aged heroine in the exquisite postwar novels *Chéri* (1919) and *La Fin de Chéri* (1926). Yet even more important to Colette's imaginative life, however, was her stepson—the shatteringly handsome sixteen-year-old Bertrand de Jouvenel, her husband's son by his first marriage, whom Colette promptly seduced when the boy came, Cherubino-like, to pay his respects to her at her seaside country house in 1919. Thurman's arousing vignette of the forty-six-year-old Colette stalking her young prey among the beach huts like a kind of Jazz Age Phèdre is ingratiating enough to bear quoting in full:

One day, Bertrand was coming back from his regular training run on the beach when he realized Colette had been watching him. She was wearing her bathing costume—one of those tight-fitting black jersey tank suits of the 1920s—and it clung to a body which by modern standards would be called obese. But fat women, when they are fit, are often much sexier half-naked than dressed, and Colette was still limber and superbly muscled, with Venusian breasts and the biceps of a discus thrower. "She passed her arm around my waist," he wrote. He trembled "uncontrollably."

Colette's gesture was a question too delicate or too indecent to be spoken. Bertrand's flesh gave her the response of which his voice would have been incapable. She rephrased it a few nights later when she intercepted him on the stairs as he was going up to bed. He offered his cheek for a goodnight kiss, but she insisted on his mouth. Again he shook violently and almost dropped a kerosene lamp he was carrying. Colette said nothing except "Hold [it] steady."

Though the affair with Bertrand soon came to an end—upon discovering his wife's relationship with his son, Henry de Jouvenel made sure that Bertrand was married off to a suitable nearby heiress—the Younger Man remained a staple of Colettean existence. Her last husband, Maurice Goudeket, whom she met in 1925 and married in 1935 at the age of sixty-two, was seventeen years her junior. That Goudeket, a handsome, deracinated, somewhat obscure Jewish dealer in pearls with a "subdued fire that bored matrons . . . found beguiling" was immediately nicknamed "Mr. Goodcock" (by Colette's friend Paul Valéry) suggests that he too—at least at the outset of the relationship—bore all the requisites of the type.

Demoralizing, indeed, these clinging jersey bathing suits, Venusian breasts, and bobbing male appendages. Yet the Colette biographer faces myriad other challenges too: hundreds of famous friends to be brought back to life (Marguerite Moreno, Anna de Noailles, Marcel Schwob, Francis Jammes, Renée Vivien, André Gide, Maurice Ravel, Jean Cocteau); a host of gorgeous houses and flats to be described; a small army of doted-on cats and dogs to itemize (Fanchette, Sidi, Kiki-La-Doucette, Saha, Gamelle); and last but not least, the monstrous, labyrinthine, seemingly inexhaustible Colettean oeuvre itself, which like a kind of hallucinatory, Art Nouveau-ish life-form continued proliferating new vinous shoots, brusque outgrowths, and curling tendrils for over five decades. As Thurman notes in the preface to *Secrets of the Flesh*, by the time of Colette's death in 1954 she had published "nearly eighty volumes of fiction, memoirs, journalism, and drama of the highest quality. Her published correspondence fills seven volumes, and at least three important collections of letters remain unedited." For any ambitious woman writer—not least the one setting out to write her biography—Colette can be nothing at first but a slithery, outrageous, potentially engulfing rival. If she cannot be dominated she must be out-witted—at all costs.

Judith Thurman, it must be said, puts up an extraordinarily good fight—with some of the best (and sexiest) feints, dodges, and near-takedowns this reader has ever seen. We live indeed in a Golden Age of female literary biography. Thurman's life can easily slide in alongside Hermione Lee's recent biography of Virginia Woolf as a somewhat unlooked-for end-of-century masterwork, being vital, absorbing, delectably written, and psychologically astute beyond anything anyone had any right to expect, especially given the mass of books (many excellent) already devoted to her subject's life and career. (Thurman's bibliography lists twenty-three other Colette biographies published since the 1950s—the most recent in English being Herbert Lottmann's from 1991.) Thurman seems to have a thing, it is true, for scary, sensual, heavily made-up female geniuses—her first book was a prize-winning life of Isak Dinesen, another fabled monster of *maquillage*. But she also has the sure sense of self required to meet them head on. Thurman must be considered, above all, the *wiliest* of Colette biographers: the most adept at playing Colette's own game, which is all about love, power, and the desire to feed off others. "Convention," she writes at one point, "presses against the character of an outsider like the weight of the ocean pressing against a diving bell. It takes an equal presence, a kind of single-mindedness, to resist it." She is speaking here of Colette's rebellious strength of character. But the passage applies equally to Thurman herself. If she does not escape each and every one of her subject's boa constrictor–like squeezes, or the occasional lift and drop, she comes as close as anyone has—achieving a portrait of quite naked intimacy and emotional honesty in the process.

Out of necessity many of Thurman's cagiest gambits are defensive ones. She is skeptical, even heretical, for example, when it comes to Colette's own personal mythmaking. Colette is one of the great narcissistic self-fashioners of modern literature, of course, and virtually all of her writing is autobiographical in some degree. (She once wrote that she was unable to "invent" her fictional material in the sense that a Gothic novelist might: "maybe what I lack is reverie, or a sense of the fantastic.") She writes always of herself: the oeuvre *is* the life. But as Thurman shows, she often engaged in a certain poetic revisionism, if not in outright fantasy-building. Witness the voluptuous memoirs of childhood, *La Maison de Claudine* (1922), *La Naissance du jour* (1928), and *Sido* (1929). In these lush, meditative souvenirs—among the most gorgeous outcroppings of her mature style—Colette describes an idyllic infancy and youth in the Burgundian countryside, ruled over by an adored and adoring mother: the formidable countrywoman and amateur botanist known as "Sido" (1835–1912), whose brisk yet vivifying interest in children, animals, fruits, and flowers undoubtedly shaped her daughter's consciousness in profoundly enriching ways. Reading Colette's memoirs in a feminist reading group in the late 1970s (*ubi sunt . . .* etc.), I and my T-shirted girl-cronies inevitably sighed longingly over the marvelous Sido, while also carping about the fact that none of *us* had been blessed with such an all-nourishing Earth Mother of a parent.

Thurman's view is more jaded. Though soulful, complex, and strong, she suggests, Sido could also be neglectful, jealous, bossy, and occasionally vicious. She left her daughter—paradoxically—with both a fierce receptivity to the world and a lifelong horror of intimate attachment. Colette inherited her cruel, epigrammatic, sometimes Nietzschean vein of humor. (After the death of Colette's father, a retired captain in the Zouaves, Sido described widowhood: "a black veil, and underneath a monkey's smile." Her daughter would later describe the curtains in a hotel room in which she was staying with Willy as "fit for wrapping up fetuses in.") Colette also absorbed Sido's basically godless and appalled sense of life as a lethal struggle in which one became either predator or prey. This bleaker side of Sido—whose "essential light" Colette nonetheless both craved and feared all her life—informs one of Thurman's early and most devastating assessments of Colette's character:

> For Sido's daughter and Willy's child-wife, there was no middle ground between her terror of abandonment and her fear of being consumed. . . . The lack of a sympathetic imagination tends to reproduce itself in the next generation, and Colette was a tyrant to her own child. She broke free of her servility through writing, and she eventually outgrew her need for a master, but what she couldn't transcend was the scenario of domination and submission. There is only one kind of love missing from the exhaustive, wise, and often revolutionary exploration of the subject contained in her oeuvre, and that love is mutual.

Sido was an earth mother whose cthonic charm could turn deadly: an off-kilter Ceres. She nourished those who wooed her properly, yet was hostile and unforgiving to those who disobeyed. Her daughter was ultimately the same.

If Sido emerges from Thurman's account as a far stranger and more nihilistic presence than she does in Colette's own memoirs, some of the supposed villains and dark horses in Colette's life story come across as unexpectedly likable and even good. Confronted by her subject's hypnotic rearrangements of reality Thurman's tactic is to deflect and triangulate—to give the missing third party, as it were, a chance to speak in his or her own voice. The chief beneficiaries here are Willy ("the pudgy erotomane"); Bel-Gazou, the much-abused only child to whom Colette gave birth at the age of forty; and Maurice Goudeket, the husband of Colette's old age. Thus Willy, whom Colette excoriates in *Mes Apprentissages* (1936) as a fat, vainglorious cheat and liar, addicted to young girls and *le vice paternel*, whose sexual and financial depredations left her broken in health and near despair before she finally summoned up the courage to leave him, comes across here—if not as entirely harmless—as surprisingly jolly and resplendent. He was funny and Parisian and incorrigible: one can see why the teenaged Colette ("mean and avid for emotions") fell for him. Before the bloat and the grossness set in, Thurman ventures, Willy was even a bit of hunk. She ponders his appeal in a characteristically frank, slightly kinky moment of sexual connoisseurship:

> [The] naked Willy, or nearly naked Willy, comes as a revelation, and must have been so to his many mistresses. In an album of photographs that belonged to Madeleine de Swarte, Willy's last companion, there is a snapshot of him on the beach at Cabourg dated August 1890, exactly a year after he met Colette. He is wearing a knitted bathing suit and a big straw hat. He has his arms crossed over his chest. He's paunchy, it is true, but he has a virile, confident body—a body all the more surprising be- cause the head on its shoulders looks much older in comparison.
>
> Thirty-five years later, Colette would be photographed on the beach at Saint-Tropez, in a similar pose, in a similar bathing suit. She was living, at the time, with a lover fifteen years her junior. She was quite tremen- dous. They had the same kind of allure.

In turn Thurman challenges some of the hoariest details in Colette's mon- ster-bating accounts of him: that Willy supposedly "locked her up," Bluebeard- like, until she produced the various *Claudine* novels (he probably didn't); that she was tormented by his many mistresses (she slept with some of them herself); that she had broken with him definitively by 1905 (she continued to ghostwrite books and articles for him and seems to have colluded with him behind the scenes during their very public divorce proceedings so that neither would lose too much money by the separation). It would be foolish to try to rehabilitate Willy completely—he was a raunchy old stegosaurus indeed—but Thurman makes us able to enjoy him, both as fin de siècle type and as an influential source of energy, daring, and worldliness in Colette's early life.

In the case of Bel-Gazou and Goudeket, Thurman's moral sympathies are quickened. Each suffered from Colette's casual will-to-power ethos. Bel-Gazou's story is a shocking one: Colette, the lyrical celebrant of motherhood and Sido's nurturing power, virtually abandoned her own infant daughter—leaving her first with a series of wet nurses, and then with a nervy English governess who tyrannized the child mercilessly for a number of years. Bel-Gazou grew up al- most feral, a kind of wild, sad, unruly parody of her mother. Like her mother, she became a sexual rebel, living most of her adult life as a lesbian. It is disillu- sioning to learn that Colette disapproved of this aspect of her daughter's life—es- pecially in light of her own sapphic attachments and arresting depictions of female homosexuality in *Le Pur et l'impur* (1932). (Thurman, it might be noted, is the first Anglo-American biographer to treat Colette's affairs with women with both an informed sense of period and a civilized respect for their meanings: her snapshots of Parisian lesbian life in the 1920s and 1930s have a Brassaï-like clarity and lack of sentiment.) Though in many respects a thwarted personality, Bel-Gazou developed a hook-or-by-crook kind of strength: she later served dangerously and honorably in the Resistance; and one ends up feeling proud of her, even if her mother didn't.

Goudeket is the secret hero of Thurman's biography: the last and best husband, the one who put up with his wife's lovers, intransigence, and gradually diminishing range of emotional and physical responses. (The crippling arthritis of Colette's later years was a special curse, given the buoyant athleticism of her youth, yet coincided with a certain ethical sclerosis as well.) As a Jew he had to absorb Colette's on-again, off-again anti-Semitism—another legacy from Sido. Thurman treads delicately here, but there is much to disturb. Nothing she quotes from Colette's letters is more repellent than the description of Maria Falconetti, luminous star of Carl Dreyer's *Passion of Joan of Arc*, who was engaged in 1923 to play in a theatrical version of *The Vagabond*: "Falconetti is a pain in the ass. She's doing her Duse number. No makeup, a horrible old neck. . . . Let her drop dead. She's now asking a thousand francs for a rehearsal. She must be a sordid old jewess who never washes." During the Second World War, Colette refused to speak out against the Vichy government and regularly published stories and articles in leading pro-German journals. Her novel *Julie de Carneilhan* (1941) contains a virulently anti-Semitic portrait of one of its central female characters. She may have intended by such acts to shield Goudeket, of course: he was interned by the Gestapo for seven weeks in the winter of 1941–42, then released after Colette persuaded the French wife of the German ambassador to convince her husband to let him go. Still, given Goudeket's gallantry and devotion to Colette throughout the war—he wore the yellow star and refused to leave her despite the extreme personal danger to which such uxoriousness exposed him—it is unsettling to read about her seemingly untroubled contributions to pro-Nazi newspapers such as *Combats* and *La Gerbe,* or works like *From Joan of Arc to Philippe Pétain*, a collection of sickly propagandistic essays on French culture edited by the actor and Vichy yes-man Sacha Guitry.

Not only does Thurman, in such malign passes, successfully defend against the coiling, morally ambiguous Colette persona, she also manages throughout her study to marshall her own elegant counteroffensive—through a sensuous (sometimes comic) mobilization of style. What she says of her subject might once again apply to herself. Colette's ability to compose exquisite prose, she writes, never faltered: even with the morbid *Julie de Carneilhan*, it's not the writing that dismays, Thurman argues, for "by now Colette could beat an old carpet and make it shed gold dust." Thurman is herself a mistress of style, and game enough to challenge Colette in her best and deepest place. One reads *Secrets of the Flesh*, above all, as a ravishing *exercice du style*—an experiment, at points (yes) almost rivaling Colette's own, in the fruitful, titivating, and ultimately profound arrangement of words.

Some of Thurman's rhetorical ploys, it is true, like the caperings of a precocious child, can be irritating—until one just gives in and says, laughingly, *Okay! You win! I'm impressed!* A favorite device is the blatantly anachronistic turn of phrase. Describing Colette's life in the 1890s, Thurman frequently uses hip urban slang—Manhattan/L.A. variety—to wrench her subject straight into the late 1990s. Thus Colette, visiting her native village six years after her marriage to Willy and the scandalous success of the *Claudine* novels, is described, somewhat goofily, as a naughty "homegirl." Lesbians are edgily yet affectionately referred to as "dykes," as in the ironic synopsis of Jean Lorrain's "comic horror story" *Âme de boue*, "in which a sinister dyke poses as a corpse to inspire the pity of a former girlfriend." The decadent fin de siècle novelist Rachilde—partial in her old age to "nightclubbing in flamboyant dress with a band of beautiful and predominantly gay young protégés who resembled the characters in her novels"—is dubbed a "geriatric clubrat." In Thurman's somewhat Starbucks-fueled account of life in the Belle Époque, Colette and Willy come across the quintessential *latte*-quaffing, bad-girl-bad-boy urban couple: she's got a home gym where she works out and checks out her "muscle tone" when she's not screwing around; he, like Warhol, has a "factory" of "groupies, wanna-bes, and druggies" around him—all the various assistants, ghostwriters, and hangers-on who help him churn out "product" and feed his vanity. Unlike Andy, though, Willy prefers compulsive "girlizing" to cruising cute boys.

Such moments are funny and one of the ways Thurman flexes her own authorial muscle against Colette's: I'm alive *now* and you're not. But she challenges her on other fronts as well. Colette-as-sexual-philosopher comes in for sly and insistent parody. Aphoristic *pensées*—on love and eros especially—are a Thurman speciality:

> Physical disgust can't be compromised with, but neither can its opposite, the *coup de foudre*. A woman still privately shuddering at an unwelcome sexual advance is all the more susceptible to an electric mutual attraction.

> It is certainly dangerous to take the word or trust the memory of anyone about the character of a former spouse. Indignation matures slowly, and sometimes the fruit is ripe only when the tree is dead.

> Her first much younger lover is a revelation no middle-aged woman whose senses have been numbed by rejection can ever forget.

If the enjoyment of an exciting sex life has never been incompatible with the production of a distinguished oeuvre, motherhood is a different matter.

It was love, it was France, so everybody was lying.

At times Thurman's fondness for the *aperçu* leads to comic pomposity, as when she twice quotes admiringly a French biographer's description of Colette's father (who lost a leg fighting in Italy for Napoleon III) as "a droll man with the melancholy gaiety of amputees and Southerners." This is the sort of thing one might find in Flaubert's "Dictionary of Received Ideas" ("Amputees: Known for their melancholy gaiety"). Yes, Judith, it's my wrinkly leg-stump that gives me my moody charm! Oh, those sexy amputees! Still, we forgive her in the end: the writing is so sheerly alive and goes so far toward illuminating Colette's own mercurial life-turns.

And by the end, Thurman achieves something quite special—a transformation of the wrestling match, that all-girl fight to the death, into a kind of witty erotic dance. For despite its rivalrous energies, this is ultimately a deeply sympathetic and engaged portrait of its subject. Granted, Cocteau's observation that "everything in art is monstrous" and "Madame Colette does not escape this rule" is taken on board and judged correct, but Thurman never lets mere monstrosity get in the way of her sense of what is fine, human, and profound about Colette's achievement. It is clear how much the biographer relishes that emotional intelligence born out of honesty and vulnerability, and she is appreciative of those who bravely espouse it. She has words of praise for Bertrand de Jouvenel—the stepson-lover of Colette who later himself became a distinguished man of letters—precisely, one suspects, because his humane understanding of psychological conflict, evidenced in an ability to absorb contradictions in others without panic, so exactly mirrors her own. (The stunning compliment Thurman pays the grown-up Bertrand: "An unusual capacity for transgression in a conscientious personality seems to be prerequisite for those who, like Bertrand de Jouvenel, achieve some form of greatness.") "Love," wrote Jouvenel in a memoir of his famous stepmother, "has two faces, *agape* and *eros*, a deep understanding and appreciation of the lovable, and a petulant wilfulness to seize it. It is not easy to divorce them. Colette was immensely rich in the former, and therein resides her greatness; for the latter, she suffered ample retribution."

However painful Colette's inability to separate the "two faces" of love in her own life, Thurman persuades us nonetheless that her subject grasped her limitations consciously and courageously—and by way of such awareness was able to turn them to magical account. Even as Colette failed (perhaps) in the real-life task, in the oeuvre, Thurman suggests, she bore plangent and ennobling witness to a lifelong effort to resolve her own most anguishing psychic contradictions.

The problem of intimacy is central in Colette's writing, of course, and the fraught influence of Sido on her affective life cannot be ignored. Excruciating indeed to anyone with a heart must be the stage direction she included in the libretto for *L'Enfant et les sortilèges*, the opera she wrote with Maurice Ravel in 1915, in which she called for "a ballet of little figures who express, in their dance, the grief of being unable to unite."

Yet Thurman is fierce in her defense of Colette against those who would accuse her of either soullessness or solipsism. Her "body-bound characters," writes Thurman, "[struggle] to preserve 'the capacity for excited love' in the face of inhibitions from without, and fears of ruthlessness and aggression toward the beloved object from within." The struggle is indeed a primordial one:

> It is not that Colette's characters lack an inner life: they suffer, if any-
> thing, from having too much interiority. Her work preserves the legacy of
> a child's earliest thinking about self and other—self and mother in partic-
> ular—whether the mother is absent, like Claudine's, or all too present,
> like Léa [the older woman in *Chéri*] or Sido. Whatever the story, and
> however frivolous or anecdotal its surface, Colette reminds us of that lost
> age at which we had not yet categorized desire into good or bad, male and
> female, real and imagined, passive and aggressive. She writes from the
> point of view not of the analytic adult but of the child first "sorting out"
> her paradoxical interests and experience.

"A coherent personality," writes the biographer, "aspires, like a work of art, to contain its conflicts without resolving them dogmatically." And certainly her own portrait of the artist is as far from dogmatical as it is possible to be. Colette's contradictions are acknowledged, but always with a sense of the exorbitant creative gift they made possible. Thus even as she registers Colette's "ancient and guiltless instinct for survival"—that rampant authorial will to seize at the breast and suck—Thurman is acutely aware of how, in the paradoxical coils of desire, someone who puts her own pleasure first can also bring exquisite delight to another: "Insatiable and untrusting, she sees to her own nourishment and becomes a glutton for but also an inspired dispenser of warmth, fullness, beauty, and pleasure." If it feels good to suck, it also feels good to be sucked, and like a mother cat voluptuously yielding to her kittens, Colette surrenders all to us in the work. Sex—that "mysterious despair that I seek and fear"—may have driven her toward promiscuity in life, but also provided her with an imagery for that miraculous conjunction of body and soul, self and other, which is the core vision of her art. As Thurman notes in one of her own lyric Colettean turns, such clarifying hedonism was in the end equivalent to an ethics: "a credo without a god, or an afterlife, but with the power of all true faith to inspire ecstasy, and reverence for creation, and to console."

Colette is the sort of writer it is easy to feel, perhaps, one has grown out of—that one already knows her too well, that one long ago took from her all that one could. Perhaps because something about her inevitably conjures up the embarrassing daydreams of youth—all those thoughts of love and France and food and being sophisticated and not oneself (those books! those billets doux! that blue lampshade!)—it is easy to assume she has no new news to impart. Yet one finishes reading Thurman's life impatient to go back to her—to commit oneself yet again to her strange, witty embrace and swirling, florid gravitas. (Even in English the prose staggers: Colette has always been blessed with magnificent translations.) And when one does, the ancient feline magic is instantly revivified. Has there ever been any more slangy and free and wickedly comic rendering of the female adolescent psyche than *Claudine à l'école*? Any more lavishly botanical rendering of what it's like to kiss—yes, you, sweetheart—than the following passage from *La Vagabonde*?

> I move my head imperceptibly because of his moustache which brushes against my nostrils with a scent of vanilla and honeyed tobacco. Oh! . . . suddenly my mouth, in spite of itself, lets itself be opened, opens of itself as irresistibly as a ripe plum splits in the sun. And once more is born that exacting pain that spreads from my lips all the way down my flanks to my knees, that swelling as of a wound that wants to open once more and overflow—the voluptuous pleasure I had forgotten . . . his mouth tastes of mine now, and has the faint scent of my powder. Experienced as it is, I can feel that it is trying to invent something new, to vary the caress still further. But already I am bold enough to indicate my preference for a long, drowsy kiss that is almost motionless—the slow crushing, one against the other, of two flowers in which nothing vibrates but the palpitation of two coupled pistils.

My favorite Colette book when I was young was her most homosexual—the ravishing tome first published as *Ces Plaisirs* in 1930, then later retitled *Le Pur et l'impur* in 1932. (She has something for everyone.) It's a weird one: a drifting memoir of various Sapphists and she-men known in the early Willy-days—from the tormented expatriate poetess Renée Vivien, all absinthe and Baudelaire and masochistic sex, to the handsome young invert, "ghost-secretary to Monsieur Willy," who visited the young Colette Willy in her flat and regaled her with tales of the boxers and Paris firemen with whom he consorted. As narrator, Colette keeps a discreet, dispassionate, retrospective distance, though one of the characters recollected is indeed her own former lover, the cross-dressing Missy, here disguised as the noble yet wistful "Chevalière":

The seduction emanating from a person of uncertain or dissimulated sex is powerful. Those who have never experienced it liken it to the banal attraction of the love that evicts the male element. This is a gross misconception. Anxious and veiled, never exposed to the light of day, the androgynous creature wanders, wonders, and implores in a whisper. . . . There especially remains for the androgynous creature the right, even the obligation, never to be happy. If jovial, the androgynous creature is a monster. But it trails irrevocably among us its seraphic suffering, its glimmering tears. It goes from a tender inclination to maternal adoption. . . . As I write this, I am thinking of La Chevalière. It was she who most often bruised herself in a collision with a woman—a woman, that whispering guide, presumptuous, strangely explicit, who took her by the hand and said, "Come, I will help you find yourself . . ."

"I am neither that nor anything else, alas," said La Chevalière, dropping the vicious little hand. "What I lack cannot be found by searching for it."

One might moon over such passages endlessly (and did) while waiting for life to begin. Yet perusing the book now, in the same tattered old paperback of daydreams past, I find my eye caught by the last paragraph. While I know whole swatches of this book by heart, I have no memory of it at all. Colette is describing a conversation with an unnamed older woman, who has lost her female companion of many years. The woman tells Colette, "we were joined in an infinity so pure that I never thought of death."

As that word "pure" fell from her lips, I heard the trembling of the plaintive "u," the icy limpidity of the "r," and the sound aroused nothing in me but the need to hear again its unique resonance, its echo of a drop that trickles out, breaks off, and falls somewhere with a plash. The word "pure" has never revealed an intelligible meaning to me. I can only use the word to quench an optical thirst for purity in the transparencies that evoke it—in bubbles, in a volume of water, and in the imaginary latitudes entrenched, beyond reach, at the very center of a dense crystal.

Faced with such perfect, lapidary, and truth-bearing sentences, one's only appropriate response is indeed to fall to one's knees in surrender. About the "secrets of the flesh," as Judith Thurman reminds us so well, Colette still seems to say it all.

note

1. Judith Thurman, *Secrets of the Flesh: A Life of Colette* (New York: Knopf, 1999).

selected
bibliography

Acocella, Joan. *Willa Cather and the Politics of Criticism.* Lincoln: University of Nebraska Press, 2000.

Adburgham, Alison. *Women in Print: Writing Women and Women's Magazines from the Restoration to the Accession of Victoria.* London: Allen and Unwin, 1972.

Addison, Joseph. *The Spectator.* Edited by Donald F. Bond. 5 vols. Oxford: Clarendon Press, 1965.

Alexander, Christine, ed. *The Early Writings of Charlotte Brontë.* 2 vols. Oxford: Blackwell, 1987.

Andreadis, Harriette. *Sappho in Early Modern England: Female Same-Sex Literary Erotics, 1550–1714.* Chicago: University of Chicago Press, 2001.

Arendt, Hannah. *Rahel Varnhagen: The Life of a Jewess.* Edited by Liliane Weissberg. Translated by Richard and Clara Winston. Baltimore: Johns Hopkins University Press, 1997.

Armstrong, Nancy. *Desire and Domestic Fiction: A Political History of the Novel.* Oxford and New York: Oxford University Press, 1987.

Austen, Jane. *Emma.* Edited by James Kinsley, with an introduction by Terry Castle. Oxford and New York: Oxford University Press, 1995.

_____. *Jane Austen's Letters.* Edited by Deirdre Le Faye. Oxford and New York: Oxford University Press, 1995.

_____. *The Juvenilia of Jane Austen and Charlotte Brontë.* Edited by Frances Beer. Middlesex, Eng.: Penguin Books, 1986.

_____. *Love and Freindship* [*sic*] *and Other Early Works.* Edited by Geraldine Killalea. New York: Harmony Books, 1981.

_____. *"Northanger Abbey"; "Lady Susan"; "The Watsons"; and "Sanditon."* Edited by John Davie, with an introduction by Terry Castle. Oxford and New York: Oxford University Press, 1990.

_____. *The Novels of Jane Austen.* Edited by R. W. Chapman. 3d ed. 6 vols. Oxford and New York: Oxford University Press, 1973–75.

Austen-Leigh, James Edward. *A Memoir of Jane Austen by her Nephew James Edward Austen-Leigh.* Edited by R. W. Chapman. Oxford: Clarendon Press, 1926.

Baillie, Joanna. *A Series of Plays: in which it is attempted to delineate the Stronger Passions of the Mind, Each Passion being the Subject of a Tragedy and a Comedy.* London, 1798.

Baker, E. A. *The Novel of Sentiment and the Gothic Romance.* Vol. 5 of *The History of the English Novel.* London: Witherby, 1929.

Ballard, George. *Memoirs of Several Ladies of Great Britain, who have been Celebrated for their Writings or Skill in the Learned Languages, Arts and Sciences.* London, 1752.

Barbauld, Anna Laetitia. *The Works of Anna Laetitia Barbauld.* 2 vols. London, 1825.

——————, ed. *The British Novelists; with an Essay, and Prefaces, Biographical and Critical.* 50 vols. London, 1810.

——————, ed. *The Correspondence of Samuel Richardson.* 6 vols. London, 1804.

——————, ed. *The Female Speaker.* London, 1811.

——————, ed. *The Pleasures of Imagination by Mark Akenside, M.D. To which is prefixed a critical essay on the poem, by Mrs. Barbauld.* London, 1795.

——————, ed. *The Poetical Works of Mr. William Collins. With a prefatory essay by Mrs. Barbauld.* London, 1797.

Barbauld, Anna Laetitia, and John Aikin. *Miscellaneous Pieces in Prose.* London, 1773.

Barker, Juliet. *The Brontës.* London: Weidenfeld and Nicolson, 1994.

Barker-Benfield, G. J. *The Culture of Sensibility: Sex and Society in Eighteenth-Century Britain.* Chicago: University of Chicago Press, 1992.

Beckford, William. *Vathek.* Edited by Roger Lonsdale. Oxford and New York: Oxford University Press, 1983.

Beer, Frances, ed. *The Juvenilia of Jane Austen and Charlotte Brontë.* Middlesex, Eng.: Penguin Books, 1986.

Behn, Aphra. Preface to *The Dutch Lover.* London, 1673.

——————. Preface to *Sir Patient Fancy.* London, 1677.

——————. *The Works of Aphra Behn.* Edited by Montague Summers. 6 vols. London: W. Heinemann, 1915.

Bender, John B. *Imagining the Penitentiary: Fiction and the Architecture of Mind in Eighteenth-Century England.* Chicago: University of Chicago Press, 1987.

Berger, Morroe, ed. and trans. *Madame de Staël on Politics, Literature, and National Character.* Garden City, N.Y.: Doubleday, 1964.

Birkhead, Edith. *The Tale of Terror: A Study of the Gothic Romance.* London: Constable, 1921.

Blewett, David, ed. *Reconsidering the Rise of the Novel.* Special Issue, *Eighteenth-Century Fiction* 12 (January–April 2000). Hamilton, Ont.: McMaster University, 2000.

Bloom, Harold, ed. *Jane Austen's "Emma": Modern Critical Interpretations.* New York: Chelsea House, 1987.

Blunt, Reginald, ed. *Mrs. Montagu, "Queen of the Blues,"—Her Letters and Friendships from 1762 to 1800.* 2 vols. London: Constable, 1923.

Bowyer, John Wilson. *The Celebrated Mrs. Centlivre.* Durham, N.C.: Duke University Press, 1952.

Brandon, Ruth. *The Spiritualists: The Passion for the Occult in the Nineteenth and Twentieth Centuries.* New York: Knopf, 1983.

Braverman, Richard. "'Dunce the Second Reigns Like Dunce the First': The Gothic Bequest in *The Dunciad.*" *ELH: A Journal of English Literary History* 62 (Winter 1995): 863–82.

Brewer, John. *The Pleasures of the Imagination: English Culture in the Eighteenth Century.* New York: Farrar, Straus and Giroux, 1997.

Brink, J. R., ed. *Female Scholars: A Tradition of Learned Women Before 1800.* Montreal: Eden Press, 1980.

Brontë, Charlotte. *The Early Writings of Charlotte Brontë.* Edited by Christine Alexander. 2 vols. Oxford: Blackwell, 1987.

_____. *The Juvenilia of Jane Austen and Charlotte Brontë.* Edited by Frances Beer. Middlesex, Eng.: Penguin Books, 1986.

Brooke, Frances. *The Old Maid by Mary Singleton, Spinster.* Rev. ed. London, 1764.

Brooks, Chris. *The Gothic Revival.* London: Phaidon Press, 1999.

Brooten, Bernadette J. *Love Between Women: Early Christian Responses to Female Homoeroticism.* Chicago: University of Chicago Press, 1996.

Brophy, Brigid. *Baroque-'n'-Roll: and Other Essays.* London: Hamish Hamilton, 1987.

_____. *Don't Never Forget: Collected Views and Reviews.* New York: Holt, Rinehart and Winston, 1967.

_____, Michael Levey, and Charles Osborne. *Fifty Works of English and American Literature We Could Do Without.* New York: Stein and Day, 1968.

Brown, Julia Prewitt. *Jane Austen's Novels: Social Change and Literary Form.* Cambridge, Mass.: Harvard University Press, 1979.

Burke, Edmund. *A Philosophical Enquiry into the Origin of Our Ideas of the Sublime and Beautiful.* Edited by J. T. Boulton. London: Routledge and Kegan Paul, 1958.

Burney, Frances. *Evelina: or, The History of a Young Lady's Entrance into the World.* London, 1778.

Butler, Judith. "'Dangerous Crossing': Willa Cather's Masculine Names." In *Bodies That Matter: On the Discursive Limits of "Sex,"* 143–66. New York and London: Routledge, 1993.

Butler, Marilyn. *Jane Austen and the War of Ideas.* Oxford: Clarendon Press, 1975.

_____. "The Woman at the Window: Ann Radcliffe in the Novels of Mary Wollstonecraft and Jane Austen." *Women and Literature* 1 (1980): 128–48.

Calloway, Stephen, Michael Snodin, and Clive Wainwright. *Horace Walpole and Strawberry Hill.* London: London Borough of Richmond-on-Thames, 1980.

Canetti, Elias. *Crowds and Power.* Translated by Carol Stewart. New York: Continuum Press, 1978.

Carson, Anne. *Eros the Bittersweet: An Essay.* Princeton, N.J.: Princeton University Press, 1986.

Carter, Elizabeth. *Letters from Mrs. Carter, to Mrs. Montagu, between the years 1755 and 1800, chiefly upon literary and moral subjects. Published from the originals in the possession of Montagu Pennington.* 3 vols. London, 1817.

_____. *A Series of Letters between Mrs. Elizabeth Carter and Miss Catherine Talbot, from the year 1741 to 1770.* 4 vols. London, 1809. Rpt. New York: AMS Press, 1975.

_____, ed. and trans. *All the works of Epictetus which are now extant; consisting of his Discourses, preserved by Arrian, in four books, the Enchiridion, and fragments. Tr. from the original Greek...with an introduction and notes, by the translator.* London, 1758.

Carter, Margaret L. *Specter or Delusion? The Supernatural in Gothic Fiction.* Ann Arbor: University of Michigan Press, 1987.

Casanova, Giacomo, Chevalier de Seingalt. *History of My Life.* Translated by Willard R. Trask. 6 vols. Baltimore: Johns Hopkins University Press, 1997.

Castle, Terry. *The Apparitional Lesbian: Female Homosexuality and Modern Culture.* New York: Columbia University Press, 1993.

_____. "Spectral Politics: Apparition Belief and the Romantic Imagination." In *The Female Thermometer: Eighteenth-Century Culture and the Invention of the Uncanny,* 168–89. Oxford and New York: Oxford University Press, 1995.

_____. "The Spectralization of the Other in *The Mysteries of Udolpho.*" In *The Female Thermometer,* 120–39.

Cather, Willa. *Early Novels and Stories (The Troll Garden, O Pioneers! The Song of the Lark, My Ántonia, One of Ours).* New York: Library of America, 1987.

_____. *The Kingdom of Art: Willa Cather's First Principles and Critical Statements, 1893–96.* Edited by Bernice Slote. Lincoln: University of Nebraska Press, 1967.

_____. *Later Novels (A Lost Lady, The Professor's House, Death Comes for the Archbishop, Shadows on the Rock, Lucy Gayheart, Sapphira and the Slave Girl).* New York: Library of America, 1990.

_____. *Stories, Poems, and Other Writings.* New York: Library of America, 1992.

_____. *Willa Cather: 24 Stories.* Edited by Sharon O'Brien. New York: Penguin, 1987.

Cavendish, Margaret, duchess of Newcastle. *Nature's Pictures Drawn by Fancies Pencil to the Life.* London, 1656.

_____, *CCXI Sociable Letters.* London, 1664.

Cecil, Lord David. *A Portrait of Jane Austen.* London: Constable, 1978.

Centlivre, Susannah. *Love's Contrivance; or, Le Médicin Malgré Lui.* London, 1703.

_____. *The Perjur'd Husband.* London, 1700.

_____. *The Platonick Lady.* London, 1707.

Chapman, R. W. *Jane Austen: Facts and Problems.* Oxford: Clarendon Press, 1948.

Clark, Sir Kenneth. *The Gothic Revival: An Essay in the History of Taste.* 1928. Rpt. Middlesex, Eng.: Penguin Books, 1964.

Clery, E. J. Introduction to *The Castle of Otranto,* by Horace Walpole. Oxford and New York: Oxford University Press, 1996.

_____. *The Rise of Supernatural Fiction, 1762–1800.* Cambridge: Cambridge University Press, 1995.

_____, and Robert Miles, eds. *Gothic Documents: A Sourcebook 1700–1820.* Manchester and New York: Manchester University Press, 2000.

Coleridge, Samuel Taylor. "General Character of the Gothic Literature and Art." In *Coleridge's Miscellaneous Criticism,* edited by Thomas Middleton Raysor, 11–17. London: Constable, 1936.

_____. "General Character of the Gothic Mind in the Middle Ages." In *Coleridge's Miscellaneous Criticism,* ed. Raysor, 6–10.

Colette. *The Claudine Novels.* Translated by Antonia White. London: Penguin Books, 1987.

_____. *The Pure and the Impure.* Translated by Herma Briffault, with an introduction by Janet Flanner. New York: Farrar, Straus and Giroux, 1967.

Colley, Linda. *Britons: Forging the Nation 1707–1837.* New Haven and London: Yale University Press, 1992.

Cooper, Elizabeth, ed. *The Muses' Library: or, A Series of English poetry, from the Saxons, to the reign of Charles II, being a general collection of almost all the old valuable poetry extant.* London, 1737.

Crawford, Christina. *Mommie Dearest.* New York: William Morrow, 1978.

Crosby, F. A. *Une Romancière oubliée, Mme Riccoboni, sa vie, ses oeuvres.* Paris, 1924.

Cross, Wilbur. *The Development of the English Novel.* New York, 1899.

Curtis, Judith. "The *Epistolières.*" In *French Women and the Age of Enlightenment,* edited by Samia I. Spencer, 226–41. Bloomington: Indiana University Press, 1984.

Dacier, Anne Lefèvre. *Homère défendu contre l'Apologie du R.P. Hardouin; ou suite des causes de la corruption du goust.* Paris, 1716. Rpt. Geneva: Slatkine Reprints, 1971.

_____, ed. and trans. *L'Iliade d'Homère, traduite en françois, aves des remarques par Madame Dacier.* Paris, 1711.

_____, ed. and trans. *L'Odyssée d'Homère, traduite en françois, avec des remarques par Madame Dacier.* Paris, 1711.

_____, ed. and trans. *Les Poésies d'Anacréon et de Sapho, traduites de grec en françois, avec des remarques. Par mademoiselle Le Fèvre.* Lyon, 1696.

Davenport-Hines, Richard. *Gothic: Four Hundred Years of Excess, Horror, Evil and Ruin.* New York: North Point Press, 1998.

Davis, Lennard J. *Factual Fictions: The Origins of the English Novel.* New York: Columbia University Press, 1983.

Day, William Patrick. *In the Circles of Fear and Desire: A Study of Gothic Fantasy.* Chicago: University of Chicago Press, 1985.

De Bolla, Peter. *The Discourse of the Sublime: Readings in History, Aesthetics and the Subject.* Oxford and New York: Oxford University Press, 1989.

Defoe, Daniel. *Roxana: or, The Fortunate Mistress.* Edited by Jane Jack. Oxford and New York: Oxford University Press, 1981.

DeJean, Joan. *Fictions of Sappho, 1546–1937.* Chicago: University of Chicago Press, 1989.

Demay, Andrée. *Marie-Jeanne Riccoboni: ou de la pensée féministe chez une romancière du XVIIIième siècle.* Paris: La Pensée universelle, 1977.

Dennis, John. "The Grounds of Criticism in Poetry." In *Eighteenth-Century Critical Essays,* edited by Scott Elledge, vol. 2, 121–22. Ithaca, N.Y.: Cornell University Press, 1961.

DeSalvo, Louise, and Mitchell A. Leaska, eds. *The Letters of Vita Sackville-West to Virginia Woolf.* New York: William Morrow, 1985.

Dijkstra, Bram. *Defoe and Economics: The Fortunes of "Roxana" in the History of Interpretation.* London: Macmillan, 1987.

Ditchfield, Peter Hampson. *English Gothic Architecture.* London: J. M. Dent, 1920.

Donoghue, Emma. *Passions Between Women: British Lesbian Culture, 1668–1801.* London: Scarlet Press, 1993.

_____. *We Are Michael Field.* Bath: Absolute Press, 1998.

Doody, Margaret Anne. "Deserts, Ruins and Troubled Waters: Female Dreams in Fiction and the Development of the Gothic Novel." *Genre* 10 (1977): 529–72.

_____. *The True Story of the Novel.* New Brunswick, N.J.: Rutgers University Press, 1996.

Drake, Nathan. *Literary Hours, or Sketches Critical and Narrative.* 2 vols. London, 1800. Rpt. New York: Garland, 1970.

DuBois, Page. *Sappho Is Burning.* Chicago: University of Chicago Press, 1995.

Duckworth, Alistair M. *The Improvement of the Estate: A Study of Jane Austen's Novels.* Baltimore: Johns Hopkins University Press, 1971.

Duffy, Maureen. *The Passionate Shepherdess: Aphra Behn, 1640–89.* London: Jonathan Cape, 1977.

Duncombe, John. *The Feminiad: A Poem.* Edited by Jocelyn Harris. Los Angeles: William Andrews Clark Memorial Library, University of California, 1981.

Eaves, T. C., and Ben D. Kimpel. *Samuel Richardson: A Biography.* Oxford: Clarendon Press, 1971.

Echlin, Elizabeth, Lady. *An Alternative Ending to Richardson's "Clarissa."* Edited by Dimiter Daphinoff. Bern: Francke, 1982.

Eden, Anne. *A Confidential Letter of Albert; from his first attachment to Charlotte to her death. From the Sorrows of Werter.* London, 1790.

Edgeworth, Maria. *Letters for Literary Ladies.* London, 1795.

Edmundson, Mark. *Nightmare on Main Street: Angels, Sadomasochism, and the Culture of Gothic.* Cambridge, Mass.: Harvard University Press, 1997.

Elias, Norbert. *The Civilizing Process: Sociogenetic and Psychogenetic Investigations.* Rev. ed. Translated by Edmund Jephcott. Edited by Eric Dunning, Johan Goudsblom, and Stephen Mennell. Oxford: Basil Blackwell, 2000.

_____, and Eric Dunning. *Quest for Excitement: Sport and Leisure in the Civilizing Process.* Oxford and New York: Basil Blackwell, 1986.

Eliot, T. S. *The Letters of T. S. Eliot.* Edited by Valerie Eliot. 2 vols. San Diego: Harcourt Brace Jovanovich, 1988.

Ellis, Kate Ferguson. *The Contested Castle: Gothic Novels and the Subversion of Domestic Ideology.* Urbana: University of Illinois Press, 1989.

Elstob, Elizabeth. *An English-Saxon Homily, on the birth-day of St Gregory: Anciently used in the English Saxon Church. Giving an Account of the Conversion of the English from Paganism to Christianity, Translated into Modern English with Notes, etc.* London, 1709.

_____. *The Rudiments of Grammar for the English-Saxon Tongue, first given in English, with an apology for the study of northern antiquities.* London, 1715.

Elwood, Anne Katharine. *Memoirs of the Literary Ladies of England, from the Commencement of the Last Century.* 2 vols. London, 1843.

Ezell, Margaret J. M. *Writing Women's Literary History.* Baltimore: Johns Hopkins University Press, 1993.

Fenwick, Eliza. *Secresy: or, The Ruin on the Rock.* Edited by Isobel Grundy. London: Broadview Press, 1994.

Ferguson, Frances. *Solitude and the Sublime: Romanticism and the Aesthetics of Individuation.* London and New York: Routledge, 1992.

Ferguson, Moira. *Eighteenth-Century Women Poets: Nation, Class, and Gender.* Albany: State University of New York Press, 1995.

_____, ed. *First Feminists: British Women Writers 1578–1799.* Old Westbury, N.Y.: Feminist Press, 1985.

"Field, Michael" [Katherine Bradley and Edith Cooper]. *Long Ago.* London: George Bell and Sons, 1889.

_____. *A Selection from the Poems of Michael Field.* London: The Poetry Bookshop, 1923.

_____. *Underneath the Bough: A Book of Verses.* London: George Bell and Sons, 1893.

_____. *Works and Days: From the Journal of Michael Field.* Edited by T. and D. C. Sturge Moore. London: John Murray, 1933.

Fielding, Henry. *"The Covent-Garden Journal" and "A Plan of the Universal Register-Office."* Edited by Bertrand A. Goldgar. Middletown, Conn.: Wesleyan University Press, 1988.

_____. *Tom Jones.* Edited by John Bender and Simon Stern, with an introduction by John Bender. Oxford and New York: Oxford University Press, 1996.

Fielding, Sarah. *Remarks on "Clarissa."* Edited by Peter Sabor. Los Angeles: William Andrews Clark Memorial Library, University of California, Los Angeles, 1985.

Fleenor, Juliann E., ed. *The Female Gothic.* Montreal and London: Eden Press, 1983.

Flem, Lydia. *Casanova: The Man Who Really Loved Women.* Translated by Catherine Temerson. New York: Farrar, Straus and Giroux, 1997.

Flournoy, Théodore. *From India to the Planet Mars: A Case of Multiple Personality with Imaginary Languages.* Translated by Daniel B. Vermilye. Edited by Sonu Shamdasani, with a commentary by Mireille Cifali. Princeton, N.J.: Princeton University Press, 1994.

Fothergill, Brian. *Beckford of Fonthill.* London: Faber and Faber, 1979.

Francis, Ann. *A Poetical Epistle from Charlotte to Werther.* London, 1788.

_____, ed. and trans. *A Poetical Translation of the Song of Solomon, From the Original Hebrew, with a Preliminary Discourse, and Notes, Historical, Critical and Explanatory.* London, 1781.

Freud, Sigmund. "Psychoanalytic Notes upon an Autobiographical Account of Paranoia." In *Three Case Histories,* edited by Philip Rieff, 103–86. New York: Macmillan, 1963.

Gallagher, Catherine. *Nobody's Story: The Vanishing Acts of Women Writers in the Marketplace, 1670–1820.* Berkeley: University of California Press, 1994.

Garnett, Angelica. *Deceived with Kindness: A Bloomsbury Childhood.* London: Chatto and Windus, 1984.

Gaskell, Elizabeth. *The Life of Charlotte Brontë.* Edited by Angus Easson. Oxford and New York: Oxford University Press, 1996.

Gelder, Ken, ed. *The Horror Reader.* London and New York: Routledge, 2000.

Genlis, Stéphanie Ducrest de St. Aubin, comtesse de. *De l'Influence des femmes sur la littérature française, comme protectrices des lettres et comme auteurs; ou Précis de l'histoire des femmes françaises les plus célèbres.* Paris, 1811.

Goldberg, Jonathan. *Willa Cather and Others.* Durham, N.C.: Duke University Press, 2001.

Graffigny, Françoise d'Issembourg d'Happoncourt, Madame de. *Lettres d'une péruvienne.* Paris, 1752.

Graham, Kenneth W., ed. *Gothic Fictions: Prohibition/Transgression.* New York: AMS Press, 1989.

Grant, Aline. *Ann Radcliffe: A Biography.* Denver: Swallow, 1951.

Green, Mary Elizabeth. "Elizabeth Elstob: The Saxon Nymph." In *Female Scholars: A Tradition of Learned Women Before 1800,* edited by J. R. Brink, 137–60. Montreal: Eden Press, 1980.

Grey, J. David, A. Walton Litz, and Brian Southam, eds. *The Jane Austen Companion.* London: Athlone Press, 1986.

Grierson, Constantia, ed. *Afer Publius Terentius, Comoediae, ad optimorum exemplarium fidem recensitae. Praefixa sunt huic editioni loca Menandri et Apollodori, quae Terentius Latine interpretatus est. Accesserunt emendationes omnes Bentleianae.* Dublin, 1727.

_____, ed. *Cornelius Tacitus, Opera quae exstant, ex recenscione et cum animadversionibus Theodori Ryckii.* 3 vols. Dublin, 1730.

Griffith, Elizabeth. *The Morality of Shakespeare's Drama Illustrated.* London, 1775.

Grundy, Isobel. *Lady Mary Wortley Montagu.* Oxford and New York: Oxford University Press, 1999.

Grunenberg, Christopher, ed. *Gothic: Transmutations of Horror in Late Twentieth-Century Art.* Cambridge, Mass.: MIT Press, 1997.

Guibert, Hervé. *To the Friend Who Did Not Save My Life.* Translated by Linda Coverdale. London: Quartet Books, 1991.

Haggerty, George. *Gothic Fiction/Gothic Form.* University Park: Pennsylvania State University Press, 1989.

_____. "Literature and Homosexuality in the Later Eighteenth Century: Walpole, Beckford and Lewis." *Studies in the Novel* 18 (1986): 341–52.

Halperin, John. *The Life of Jane Austen.* Baltimore: Johns Hopkins University Press, 1984.

Halsband, Robert. "Addison's *Cato* and Lady Mary Wortley Montagu." *PMLA* 65 (1950): 1112–29.

_____. "Ladies of Letters in the Eighteenth Century." In *Stuart and Georgian Moments,* edited by Earl Miner, 271–91. Berkeley and Los Angeles: University of California Press, 1972.

Harman, Claire. *Sylvia Townsend Warner: A Biography.* London: Chatto and Windus, 1989.

_____, ed. *The Diaries of Sylvia Townsend Warner.* London: Chatto and Windus, 1994.

Harris, Jocelyn. *Jane Austen's Art of Memory.* Cambridge: Cambridge University Press, 1989.

Harrison, Elizabeth. *A Letter to Mr. John Gay, on His Tragedy Call'd "The Captives."* London, 1724.

Harrison, Lucy. "Ann Radcliffe—Novelist." In *A Lover of Books: The Life and Literary Papers of Lucy Harrison,* edited by Amy Greener. London: J. M. Dent, 1916.

Haywood, Eliza. *The Female Spectator.* 3d ed. 4 vols. London, 1750.

Hazlitt, William. "On the English Novelists." In *Lectures on the English Comic Writers.* London, 1818.

Hellman, Lillian. *Four Plays by Lillian Hellman. The Children's Hour. Days to Come. The Little Foxes. Watch on the Rhine.* New York: Modern Library, 1942.

_____. *Pentimento.* Boston: Little, Brown, 1973.

Honan, Park. *Jane Austen: Her Life.* London: Weidenfield and Nicolson, 1987.

Honour, Hugh. *Horace Walpole.* London: Longman, Green, 1957.

Hume, Robert D. "Gothic Versus Romantic: A Reevaluation of the Gothic Novel." *PMLA* 84 (1969): 282–90.

Hunter, J. Paul. *Before Novels: The Cultural Contexts of Eighteenth-Century English Fiction.* New York: Norton, 1990.

Hurd, Richard. *Letters on Chivalry and Romance.* In *The Works of Richard Hurd, D.D.* 8 vols. London: Cadell and Davies, 1811.

Inchbald, Elizabeth, ed. *The British Theatre; or, A Collection of Plays, which are acted at the Theatres Royal, Drury Lane, Covent Garden and Haymarket. Printed under the Authority of the Managers from the Prompt Books. With Biographical and Critical Remarks by Mrs. Inchbald.* 25 vols. London, 1808.

Irwin, Joyce L. "Anna Maria van Schurman: The Star of Utrecht." In *Female Scholars: A Tradition of Women Scholars Before 1800,* edited by J. R. Brink, 68–85. Montreal: Eden Press, 1980.

James, Henry. "Mary Elizabeth Braddon." In *Literary Criticism: American Writers, English Writers,* edited by Leon Edel, 741–43. New York: Library of America, 1984.

Janowitz, Anne F. *England's Ruins: Poetic Purpose and the National Landscape.* Oxford: Blackwell, 1990.

Johnson, Claudia L. *Equivocal Beings: Politics, Gender, and Sentimentality in the 1790s—Wollstonecraft, Radcliffe, Burney, Austen.* Chicago: University of Chicago Press, 1995.

──────────. *Jane Austen: Women, Politics, and the Novel.* Chicago: University of Chicago Press, 1988.

Johnson, Reginald Brimley, ed. *Bluestocking Letters.* London: J. Lane, 1926.

Johnson, Samuel. *The Adventurer,* no. 15, December 11, 1753. In *The Yale Edition of the Works of Samuel Johnson,* edited by W. J. Bate, John M. Bullitt, and L. F. Powell, vol. 2, 456–61. New Haven: Yale University Press, 1963.

Kahane, Claire. "The Gothic Mirror." In *The (M)other Tongue: Essays in Feminist Psychoanalytic Interpretation,* edited by Shirley N. Garner et al., 334–51. Ithaca, N.Y.: Cornell University Press, 1985.

Kavanaugh, Julia. *English Women of Letters: Biographical Sketches.* 2 vols. London, 1863.

Keats, John. *The Letters of John Keats.* Edited by Hyder Edward Rollins. 2 vols. Cambridge, Mass.: Harvard University Press, 1958.

Kelly, Gary. *English Fiction of the Romantic Period, 1789–1830.* London and New York: Longman, 1989.

Kemp, Peter, ed. *The Oxford Dictionary of Literary Quotations.* Oxford and New York: Oxford University Press, 1997.

Kiely, Robert. *The Romantic Novel in England.* Cambridge, Mass.: Harvard University Press, 1972.

Kilgour, Maggie. *The Rise of the Gothic Novel.* London and New York: Routledge, 1995.

Kimball, Robert, ed. *Cole.* With a biographical essay by Brendan Gill. New York: Holt, Rinehart and Winston, 1971.

──────────, ed. *The Complete Lyrics of Cole Porter.* With a foreword by John Updike. New York: Knopf, 1983.

Kirkham, Margaret. *Jane Austen, Feminism and Fiction.* Brighton: Harvester Press, 1983.

Kliger, Samuel. *The Goths in England: A Study in Seventeenth- and Eighteenth-Century Thought.* Cambridge, Mass.: Harvard University Press, 1952.

Kramnick, Jonathan Brody. *Making the English Canon: Print-Capitalism and the Cultural Past, 1700–1770.* Cambridge: Cambridge University Press, 1998.

Labalme, Patricia H., ed. *Beyond Their Sex: Learned Women of the European Past.* New York: New York University Press, 1980.

Lamblin, Bianca. *A Disgraceful Affair: Simone de Beauvoir, Jean-Paul Sartre, and Bianca Lamblin.* Translated by Julie Plovnick. Boston: Northeastern University Press, 1996.

Lanser, Susan S., and Evelyn Torton Beck. "Why Are There No Great Women Critics?" In *The Prism of Sex: Essays in the Sociology of Knowledge,* edited by Julia A. Sherman and Evelyn Torton Beck, 79–91. Madison: University of Wisconsin Press, 1979.

La Roche, Sophie von. *Pomona für Teutschlands Töchter.* Munich and New York: K. G. Saur, 1987.

Lascelles, Mary. *Jane Austen and Her Art.* Oxford and New York: Oxford University Press, 1939.

Lawson, Dominic. "Hold On, the PC Lot May Be Right." *Daily Telegraph*, September 2, 1995, 15.

Lecky, W. E. H. *The History of the Rise and Influence of the Spirit of Rationalism in Europe.* 2 vols. New York: D. Appleton, 1919.

Lee, Hermione. *Virginia Woolf.* New York: Random House, 1996.

Lennox, Charlotte. *The Female Quixote.* Edited by Margaret Dalziel, with an introduction by Margaret Doody. Oxford and New York: Oxford University Press, 1989.

_____. *Shakespear Illustrated: or the Novels and Histories, on which the Plays of Shakespear are Founded, Collected and Translated from the Original Authors, with Critical Remarks.* 2 vols. London, 1753. Rpt. New York: AMS Press, 1973.

Lewis, Matthew. *The Monk.* Edited by Howard Anderson. Oxford and New York: Oxford University Press, 1973.

Lewis, W. S. *Horace Walpole.* New York: Pantheon Books, 1961.

Lipking, Lawrence. "Aristotle's Sister: A Poetics of Abandonment." In *Canons,* edited by Robert von Hallberg, 85–106. Chicago: University of Chicago Press, 1983.

Littlewood, S. R. *Elizabeth Inchbald and Her Circle 1753–1821.* London: D. O'Connor, 1921.

Lonsdale, Roger, ed. *Eighteenth-Century Women Poets: An Oxford Anthology.* Oxford and New York: Oxford University Press, 1989.

Lynch, Deidre, ed. *Janeites: Austen's Disciples and Devotees.* Princeton, N.J.: Princeton University Press, 2000.

Macaulay, Catherine. *Letters on Education: with Observations on Religious and Metaphysical Subjects.* London, 1790.

Madan, Judith. "The Progress of Poetry." In *The Flower-Piece: A Collection of Miscellany Poems.* London, 1731.

Mahl, Mary R., and Helene Koon, eds. *The Female Spectator: English Women Writers Before 1800.* Old Westbury, N.Y.: Feminist Press, 1977.

Mahoney, Rosemary. *A Likely Story: One Summer with Lillian Hellman.* New York: Doubleday, 1998.

Mailer, Norman. *Advertisements for Myself.* New York: Putnam, 1959.

Makin, Bathsua Pell. *An Essay to Revive the Antient Education of Gentlewomen, in Religion, Manners, Arts & Tongues. With an Answer to the Objections against this Way of Education.* Edited by Paula L. Barbour. Los Angeles: William Andrews Clark Memorial Library, University of California, 1980.

Maturin, Charles Robert. *Melmoth the Wanderer.* Edited by Victor Sage. London: Penguin Books, 2000.

McBrien, William. *Cole Porter: A Biography.* New York: Knopf, 1998.

McDowell, Paula. *The Women of Grub Street: Gender, Press, and Politics in the London Literary Marketplace, 1688–1730.* Oxford and New York: Clarendon Press, 1998.

McIntyre, C. F. *Ann Radcliffe in Relation to Her Time.* New Haven: Yale University Press, 1920.

McKeon, Michael. *The Origins of the English Novel, 1600–1740.* Baltimore: Johns Hopkins University Press, 1988.

McMullen, Lorraine. *An Odd Attempt in a Woman: The Literary Life of Frances Brooke.* Vancouver: University of British Columbia Press, 1983.

Mereau, Sophie. *Kalathiskos.* Berlin, 1801–2. Rpt. Heidelberg: L. Schneider, 1968.

Miles, Robert. *Ann Radcliffe: The Great Enchantress.* Manchester and New York: Manchester University Press, 1995.

_____. *Gothic Writing 1750–1820: A Genealogy.* London and New York: Routledge, 1993.

_____, and E. J. Clery, eds. *Gothic Documents: A Sourcebook 1700–1820.* Manchester and New York: Manchester University Press, 2000.

Miller, D. A. *Narrative and Its Discontents: Problems of Closure in the Traditional Novel.* Princeton, N.J.: Princeton University Press, 1981.

Miller, Nancy K. *Getting Personal: Feminist Occasions and Other Autobiographical Acts.* New York: Routledge, 1991.

_____. *The Heroine's Text: Readings in the French and English Novel, 1722–1782.* New York: Columbia University Press, 1980.

_____. "Men's Reading, Women's Writing: Gender and the Rise of the Novel." *Yale French Studies* 75 (1988): 40–55.

_____. *Subject to Change: Reading Feminist Writing.* New York: Columbia University Press, 1988.

Moers, Ellen. *Literary Women.* Garden City, N.Y.: Anchor Press, 1977.

Monaghan, Peter. "With Sex and Sensibility, Scholars Redefine Jane Austen." *Chronicle of Higher Education,* August 17, 2001.

Monk, Samuel Holt. *The Sublime: A Study of Critical Theories in XVIII-Century England.* Ann Arbor: University of Michigan Press, 1960.

Montagu, Elizabeth. *An Essay on the Writings and Genius of Shakespear, Compared with the Greek and French Dramatic Poets, with Some Remarks upon the Misrepresentations of Mons. de Voltaire. To Which are Added, Three Dialogues of the Dead.* London, 1769.

Mooneyham, Laura. *Romance, Language, and Education in Jane Austen's Novels.* New York: St. Martin's Press, 1988.

Moore, Lisa L. *Dangerous Intimacies: Toward a Sapphic History of the British Novel.* Durham, N.C.: Duke University Press, 1998.

More, Hannah. *Essays on Various Subjects, Principally Designed for Young Ladies.* London, 1777.

_____. "Preface to the Tragedies (Observations on the Effect of Theatrical Representations with Respect to Religion and Morals)." In *The Works of Hannah More,* vol. 2, 1–27. London, 1803.

_____. *Strictures on the Modern System of Female Education.* In *The Works of Hannah More,* vol. 4. London, 1803.

Morgan, Susan. *In the Meantime: Character and Perception in Jane Austen's Fiction.* Chicago: University of Chicago Press, 1980.

Morrissey, Lee. *From the Temple to the Castle: An Architectural History of British Literature, 1660–1760.* Charlottesville: University Press of Virginia, 1999.

Mowl, Timothy. *Horace Walpole: The Great Outsider.* London: John Murray, 1996.

Mudrick, Marvin. *Jane Austen: Irony as Defense and Discovery.* Princeton, N.J.: Princeton University Press, 1952.

Mulford, Wendy. *This Narrow Place: Sylvia Townsend Warner and Valentine Ackland, Life, Letters and Politics, 1930–1951.* London: Pandora, 1988.

Mullan, John. *Sentiment and Sociability: The Language of Feeling in the Eighteenth Century.* Oxford and New York: Oxford University Press, 1988.

Murray, E. B. *Ann Radcliffe.* New York: Twayne, 1972.

Myles, Eileen. "On the Death of Robert Lowell." In *Maxfield Parrish: Early and New Poems,* 187. Santa Rosa, Calif.: Black Sparrow, 1995.

Napier, Elizabeth. *The Failure of Gothic: Problems of Disjunction in an Eighteenth-Century Literary Form.* Oxford and New York: Oxford University Press, 1987.

Necker, Suzanne [Curchod]. *Mélanges extraits des manuscrits de Mme. Necker.* 3 vols. Paris, 1798.

Nicholls, James C., ed. *Mme Riccoboni's Letters to David Hume, David Garrick, and Sir Robert Liston, 1764–1783.* In *Studies on Voltaire and the Eighteenth Century,* edited by Theodore Besterman, vol. 149. Oxford: Voltaire Foundation at the Taylor Institution, 1976.

Nicolson, Marjorie Hope. *Mountain Gloom and Mountain Glory: The Development of the Aesthetics of the Infinite.* Ithaca, N.Y.: Cornell University Press, 1959.

Nokes, David. *Jane Austen: A Life.* London: Fourth Estate, 1997.

O'Brien, Sharon. *Willa Cather: The Emerging Voice.* Oxford and New York: Oxford University Press, 1987.

Ostergard, Derek E., ed. *William Beckford, 1760–1844: An Eye for The Magnificent.* New Haven and London: Yale University Press, 2001.

Owen, Alex. *The Darkened Room: Women, Power, and Spiritualism in Late Victorian England.* Philadelphia: University of Pennsylvania Press, 1990.

Pevsner, Nikolaus. *The Englishness of English Art.* London: Architectural Press, 1956.

Piggott, Stuart. *Ruins in a Landscape: Essays in Antiquarianism.* Edinburgh: Edinburgh University Press, 1976.

Pinkerton, John. *A Dissertation on the Origin and Progress of the Scythians or Goths, Being an Introduction to the Ancient and Modern History of Europe.* London: John Nichols, 1787.

Pinney, Susanna, ed. *I'll Stand by You: Selected Letters of Sylvia Townsend Warner and Valentine Ackland: With a Narrative by Sylvia Townsend Warner.* London: Pimlico, 1998.

Polhemus, Robert M. *Comic Faith: The Great Tradition from Austen to Joyce.* Chicago: University of Chicago Press, 1980.

Poovey, Mary. "Ideology in *The Mysteries of Udolpho.*" *Criticism* 21 (1979): 307–30.

_____. *The Proper Lady and the Woman Writer: Ideology as Style in the Works of Mary Wollstonecraft, Mary Shelley, and Jane Austen.* Chicago: University of Chicago Press, 1984.

Porter, Cole. *Cole.* Edited by Robert Kimball, with a biographical essay by Brendan Gill. New York: Holt, Rinehart and Winston, 1971.

_____. *The Complete Lyrics of Cole Porter.* Edited by Robert Kimball, with a foreword by John Updike. New York: Knopf, 1983.

_____. *A Treasury of Cole Porter.* Edited by Lee Snider. New York: Chappell, 1972.

Porter, Roy. *Mind-Forg'd Manacles: A History of Madness in England from the Restoration to the Regency.* London: Athlone Press, 1987.

Praz, Mario. *The Romantic Agony.* Translated by Angus Davidson. London: Oxford University Press, 1954.

Prins, Yopie. *Victorian Sappho.* Princeton, N.J.: Princeton University Press, 1999.

Punter, David. *Gothic Pathologies: The Text, the Body, and the Law.* New York: St. Martin's Press, 1998.

_____. *The Literature of Terror: A History of Gothic Fiction from 1765 to the Present Day.* London: Longman, 1980.

_____, ed. *A Companion to the Gothic.* Oxford: Blackwell, 2000.

Radcliffe, Ann, *The Mysteries of Udolpho.* Edited by Bonamy Dobrée with an introduction by Terry Castle. Oxford and New York: Oxford University Press, 1998.

Railo, Eino. *The Haunted Castle: A Study of the Elements of English Romanticism.* London and New York: G. Routledge and Son, 1927.

Reeve, Clara. *The Progress of Romance and the History of Charoba, Queen of Egypt.* London, 1785. Rpt. New York: Facsimile Text Society, 1930.

Reynolds, Margaret, ed. *The Sappho Companion.* London: Chatto and Windus, 2000.

Reynolds, Myra. *The Learned Lady in England, 1650–1820.* Boston and New York: Houghton Mifflin, 1920.

Riccoboni, Marie-Jeanne [de Heurles de Laboras de Mezières]. "Correspondance de Laclos et de Madame Riccoboni au sujet des *Liaisons dangereuses*." In *Oeuvres complètes de Choderlos de Laclos,* edited by Maurice Allem, 710–22. Paris: Gallimard, 1951.

_____, ed. and trans. *Un Nouveau théâtre anglais.* Paris, 1768.

Richardson, Samuel. *Clarissa: or, The History of a Young Lady.* Edited by Angus Ross. Middlesex, Eng.: Penguin Books, 1985.

Richetti, John J. *The English Novel in History, 1700–1780.* London and New York: Routledge, 1999.

_____, ed. *The Cambridge Companion to the Eighteenth-Century Novel.* Cambridge and New York: Cambridge University Press, 1996.

Richter, David H. *The Progress of Romance: Literary Historiography and the Gothic Novel.* Columbus: Ohio State University Press, 1996.

Riva, Maria. *Marlene Dietrich.* New York: Knopf, 1993.

Rogers, Deborah D. *Ann Radcliffe: A Bio-Bibliography.* London and Westport, Conn.: Greenwood Press, 1996.

_____, ed. *The Critical Response to Ann Radcliffe.* London and Westport, Conn.: Greenwood Press, 1994.

Rogers, Katharine. *Feminism in Eighteenth-Century England.* Brighton: Harvester, 1982.

Sabor, Peter, ed. *Horace Walpole: The Critical Heritage.* London: Routledge and Kegan Paul, 1987.

Sackville-West, Vita. *The Letters of Vita Sackville-West to Virginia Woolf.* Edited by Louise DeSalvo and Mitchell A. Leaska. New York: William Morrow, 1985.

Sage, Victor. *Horror Fiction in the Protestant Tradition.* London: Macmillan, 1988.

_____, ed. *The Gothick Novel: A Casebook.* London: Macmillan, 1990.

Saintsbury, George. *The Peace of the Augustans: A Survey of Eighteenth-Century Literature as a Place of Rest and Refreshment.* London, 1916. Rpt. London: Oxford University Press, 1946.

Sappho. *Sappho—A Garland: The Poems and Fragments of Sappho.* Translated by Jim Powell. New York: Farrar, Straus and Giroux, 1993.

Schurman, Anna Maria van. *Opuscula hebraea, latina, graeca, gallica, prosaica et metrica.* Leiden, 1648.

Scott, Geoffrey. *The Architecture of Humanism: A Study in the History of Taste.* New York: Norton, 1974.

Scott, Sir Walter. *Lives of Eminent Novelists and Dramatists.* Rev. ed. London and New York: Frederick Warne, 1887.

_____. "Prefatory Memoir to Mrs. Ann Radcliffe." In *The Novels of Mrs. Ann Radcliffe.* London and Edinburgh: Ballantyne's Novelist's Library, 1824.

Sedgwick, Eve Kosofsky. "Across Gender, Across Sexuality: Willa Cather and Others." *South Atlantic Quarterly* 88 (1989): 53–72.

_____. *Between Men: Male Homosocial Desire in English Literature.* New York: Columbia University Press, 1985.

_____. *The Coherence of Gothic Conventions.* New York: Arno Press, 1980.

Seward, Thomas. "The Female Right to Literature." In *A Collection of Poems by Several Hands,* edited by Robert Dodsley, 6th ed., vol. 2, 294–300. London, 1758.

Sherman, Leona. *Ann Radcliffe and the Gothic Romance: A Psychoanalytic Approach.* New York: Arno Press, 1980.

Siskin, Clifford. *The Work of Writing: Literature and Social Change in Britain, 1700–1830.* Baltimore: Johns Hopkins University Press, 1998.

Smith, R. J. *The Gothic Bequest: Medieval Institutions in British Thought, 1688–1863.* Cambridge: Cambridge University Press, 1987.

Snider, Lee, ed. *A Treasury of Cole Porter.* New York: Chappell, 1972.

Snyder, Jane McIntosh. *Lesbian Desire in the Lyrics of Sappho.* New York: Columbia University Press, 1997.

Southam, Brian C., ed. *Jane Austen: The Critical Heritage.* 2 vols. London: Routledge and Kegan Paul, 1968.

Spacks, Patricia Meyer. *Desire and Truth: Functions of Plot in Eighteenth-Century English Novels.* Chicago: University of Chicago Press, 1990.

Spector, Robert Donald. *The English Gothic: A Bibliographic Guide to Writers from Horace Walpole to Mary Shelley.* Westport, Conn.: Greenwood Press, 1984.

Staël, Anne-Louise Germaine Necker, Madame de. *De l'Allemagne.* Edited by Comtesse Jean de Pange. 4 vols. Paris: Hachette, 1958–59.

_____. *Essai sur les fictions.* In *Oeuvres complètes de Mme. la baronne de Staël,* vol. 2, 173–216. Paris, 1820–21.

_____. *De la Littérature, considérée dans ses rapports avec les institutions sociales.* Edited by Paul Van Tieghem. 2 vols. Geneva: Droz, 1959.

_____. *Madame de Staël on Politics, Literature, and National Character.* Edited and translated by Morroe Berger. Garden City, N.Y.: Doubleday, 1964.

Stein, Gertrude. *A Stein Reader.* Edited by Ulla E. Dydo. Evanston, Ill.: Northwestern University Press, 1993.

Stephen, Sir Leslie. *English Literature and Society in the Eighteenth Century.* New York and London: G. P. Putnam's Sons, 1907.

Stoler, John A. *Ann Radcliffe: The Novel of Suspense and Terror.* New York: Garland, 1980.

Summers, Montague. *A Gothic Bibliography.* New York: Fortune Press, 1941.

_____. *The Gothic Quest: A History of the Gothic Novel.* London: Fortune Press, 1938.

Summerscale, Kate. *The Queen of Whale Cay: The Eccentric Story of "Joe" Carstairs, Fastest Woman on Water.* London: Fourth Estate, 1997.

Swift, Jonathan. *The Battle of the Books.* In *"A Tale of a Tub," "The Battle of the Books," and*

"The Mechanical Operation of the Spirit," edited by A. C. Guthkelch and D. Nichol Smith, 2d ed. Oxford: Clarendon Press, 1958.

[Talfourd, Sir Thomas Noon. From information supplied by William Radcliffe.] "Memoir of the Life and Writings of Mrs. Radcliffe." Prefixed to Gaston de Blondeville. London, 1826. Rpt. New York, 1972.

Tanner, Tony. Jane Austen. London: Macmillan, 1986.

Thomas, Keith. Religion and the Decline of Magic. New York: Charles Scribner's Sons, 1971.

Thurman, Judith. Secrets of the Flesh: A Life of Colette. New York: Knopf, 1999.

Todd, Janet. Feminist Literary History. Cambridge: Polity Press, 1988.

_____. Mary Wollstonecraft: A Revolutionary Life. London: Weidenfeld and Nicolson, 2000.

_____. The Sign of Angellica: Women, Writing, and Fiction, 1660–1800. London: Virago, 1989.

_____, ed. Dictionary of British and American Women Writers 1660–1800. Totowa, N.J.: Rowman and Littlefield, 1985.

_____, ed. A Wollstonecraft Anthology. Bloomington and London: Indiana University Press, 1977.

Todorov, Tzvetan. The Fantastic: A Structural Approach to a Literary Genre. Translated by Richard Howard. Ithaca, N.Y.: Cornell University Press, 1975.

Tompkins, J. M. S. The Popular Novel in England 1770–1800. London, 1932. Rpt. Lincoln: University of Nebraska Press, 1961.

_____. The Work of Mrs. Radcliffe and Its Influence on Later Writers. London, 1921. Rpt. New York: Garland, 1980.

Trumpener, Katie. Bardic Nationalism: The Romantic Novel and the British Empire. Princeton, N.J.: Princeton University Press, 1997.

Tucker, George Holbert. A Goodly Heritage: A History of Jane Austen's Family. Manchester: Carcanet Press, 1983.

"Unfortunately, It's Too Late to Get On Howard Stern." Esquire, January 1996, 60.

Vanita, Ruth. Sappho and the Virgin Mary: Same-Sex Love and the English Literary Imagination. New York: Columbia University Press, 1996.

Varma, Devendra P. The Gothic Flame. New York: Russell and Russell, 1966.

Vidler, Anthony. The Architectural Uncanny: Essays in the Modern Unhomely. Cambridge, Mass.: MIT Press, 1992.

Wahl, Elizabeth. Invisible Relations: Representations of Female Intimacy in the Age of Enlightenment. Stanford, Calif.: Stanford University Press, 1999.

Walpole, Horace. The Castle of Otranto. Edited by E. J. Clery. Oxford and New York: Oxford University Press, 1996.

Warner, Sylvia Townsend. The Diaries of Sylvia Townsend Warner. Edited by Claire Harman. London: Chatto and Windus, 1994.

_____. I'll Stand by You: Selected Letters of Sylvia Townsend Warner and Valentine Ackland: With a Narrative by Sylvia Townsend Warner. Edited by Susanna Pinney. London: Pimlico, 1998.

_____. The Letters of Sylvia Townsend Warner. Edited by William Maxwell. New York: Viking, 1982.

Warner, William Beatty. *Licensing Entertainment: The Elevation of Novel Reading in Britain, 1684–1750.* Berkeley: University of California Press, 1998.

Warton, Thomas. *The History of English Poetry from the Close of the Eleventh to the Commencement of the Eighteenth Century.* 2 vols. London: J. Dodsley, 1778.

Watt, Ian. *The Rise of the Novel.* Berkeley: University of California Press, 1957.

_____, ed. *Jane Austen: A Collection of Critical Essays.* Englewood Cliffs, N.J.: Prentice-Hall, 1963.

Weinbrot, Howard D. *Britannia's Issue: The Rise of British Literature from Dryden to Ossian.* Cambridge and New York: Cambridge University Press, 1993.

White, Edmund. *The Farewell Symphony.* New York: Random House, 1997.

Wollstonecraft, Mary. "On Poetry and Our Relish for the Beauties of Nature." In *A Wollstonecraft Anthology,* edited by Janet Todd, 170–75. Bloomington and London: Indiana University Press, 1977.

_____. *Vindication of the Rights of Woman.* Edited by Miriam Kramnick. Middlesex, Eng.: Penguin Books, 1975.

Woolf, Virginia. *The Diary of Virginia Woolf.* Edited by Anne Olivier Bell. 5 vols. San Diego and New York: Harcourt Brace Jovanovich, 1978.

_____. "Gothic Romance." In *The Essays of Virginia Woolf,* edited by Andrew McNeillie, vol. 3, 304–7. London: Hogarth Press, 1988. First published in *Times Literary Supplement,* May 5, 1921.

_____. "Phases of Fiction." In *The Collected Essays of Virginia Woolf,* edited by Leonard Woolf, vol. 2, 56–102. New York: Harcourt, Brace and World, 1967. First published in *The Bookman,* April–June 1929.

index